First World War

and Army of Occupation

War Diary

France, Belgium and Germany

15 DIVISION
44 Infantry Brigade
Gordon Highlanders
8/10th Battalion
30 April 1916 - 17 August 1918

WO95/1938/3

The Naval & Military Press Ltd
www.nmarchive.com
Published in association with The National Archives

Published by

The Naval & Military Press Ltd

Unit 10 Ridgewood Industrial Park,

Uckfield, East Sussex,

TN22 5QE England

Tel: +44 (0) 1825 749494

www.naval-military-press.com

www.nmarchive.com

This diary has been reprinted in facsimile from the original. Any imperfections are inevitably reproduced and the quality may fall short of modern type and cartographic standards.

Contents

Document type	Place/Title	Date From	Date To
Heading	WO95/1938 44 Inf Bde 15 Division 8/10 Btn Gordon Highlanders May 1916-Aug 1918		
Heading	15th Division 44th Infy Bde 8/10th Bn Gordon Hdrs 1916 May-Aug 1918		
Heading	WO95/1938 8/10 May 1916		
Heading	War Diary 8th/10th Service Battn The Gordon Highlanders Come 26 Bde 6.5.16 From 31.4.16. To 31.5.16 Vol 12		
War Diary		30/04/1916	09/05/1916
War Diary	Bethune	10/05/1916	15/05/1916
War Diary	Labourse	15/05/1916	19/05/1916
War Diary	Trenches	20/05/1916	22/05/1916
War Diary	Vermelles	23/05/1916	01/06/1916
Heading	War Diary Of 8th/10th Service Battn The Gordon Highlanders From 1.6.1916 To 30.6.1916. Vol 13		
Heading	War Diary. D.A.G Base. Herewith My War Diary For Period 1st June To 30th June, 1916		
War Diary	Vermelles	01/06/1916	04/06/1916
War Diary	Verquineul & Annequin	05/06/1916	05/06/1916
War Diary	Verquineul	06/06/1916	12/06/1916
War Diary	Hulluch	15/06/1916	27/06/1916
War Diary	Labourse	28/06/1916	30/06/1916
Heading	44th Infantry Brigade. Appendix "A"	29/06/1916	29/06/1916
War Diary	War Diary Of 8/10th Service Bn. The Gordon Highlanders Volume 15 July 1st 1916 To July 31st 1916 Vol 14		
War Diary	La Bourse	01/07/1916	05/07/1916
War Diary	Vermelles	06/07/1916	21/07/1916
War Diary	Noeux-Les-Mines	22/07/1916	22/07/1916
War Diary	Dieval	23/07/1916	25/07/1916
War Diary	Maizieres	26/07/1916	26/07/1916
War Diary	Barly	27/07/1916	27/07/1916
War Diary	Gazaincourt	28/07/1916	30/07/1916
War Diary	Naours	31/07/1916	31/07/1916
Heading	44th Brigade 15th Division. 8/10th Battalion Gordon Highlanders August 1916		
War Diary	Naours	01/08/1916	03/08/1916
War Diary	Pierregot.	04/08/1916	04/08/1916
War Diary	Behencourt	05/08/1916	07/08/1916
War Diary	Albert (10004 Do. E. Of)	08/08/1916	11/08/1916
War Diary	Albert	08/08/1916	11/08/1916
War Diary	Contalmaison	12/08/1916	31/08/1916
Heading	War Diary Of 8/10th Service Battn The Gordon Highlanders From 1st September 1916 To 30th September 1916 Volume 17		
War Diary	Albert (Bivouac)	01/09/1916	03/09/1916
War Diary	The Dingle In Contalmaison	04/09/1916	04/09/1916
War Diary	Quadrangle (X. 23. C)	05/09/1916	05/09/1916
War Diary	Quadrangle	06/09/1916	07/09/1916
War Diary	Trenches Bazentin le Petit	08/09/1916	08/09/1916

War Diary	Bazentin le Petit.	09/09/1916	11/09/1916
War Diary	Bivouac Albert.	12/09/1916	14/09/1916
War Diary	Contalmaison	15/09/1916	16/09/1916
War Diary	Trenches Martinpuich	17/09/1916	17/09/1916
War Diary	Trenches Contalmaison Sector	18/09/1916	18/09/1916
War Diary	Lavieville	19/09/1916	19/09/1916
War Diary	Franvillers.	20/09/1916	30/09/1916
Heading	War Diary Of 8/10th (Service) Battn The Gordon Highlanders From 1st October, 1916 To 31st October 1916 Volume 18		
War Diary	Franvillers.	01/10/1916	05/10/1916
War Diary	Becourt Wood	06/10/1916	06/10/1916
War Diary	Becourt	07/10/1916	07/10/1916
War Diary	Le Sars Trenches	08/10/1916	08/10/1916
War Diary	Le Sars	09/10/1916	10/10/1916
War Diary	Bazentin Le-Petit.	11/10/1916	11/10/1916
War Diary	Bazentin	12/10/1916	13/10/1916
War Diary	Bazentin-Le-Petit	13/10/1916	16/10/1916
War Diary	Balentin	17/10/1916	17/10/1916
War Diary	Crescent Alley (nr Martinpuich)	18/10/1916	18/10/1916
War Diary	Le Sars Front Trenches	19/10/1916	19/10/1916
War Diary	Le Sars	20/10/1916	21/10/1916
War Diary	Bazentin Le-Petit	22/10/1916	22/10/1916
War Diary	Bazentin	23/10/1916	31/10/1916
Heading	War Diary Of 8/10th Service Battalion, The Gordon Highlanders For Period November 1st 1916 To 30th November 1916 Volume 19		
War Diary	Le Sars	01/11/1916	02/11/1916
War Diary	Becourt	03/11/1916	05/11/1916
War Diary	Bresle	06/11/1916	30/11/1916
Heading	War Diary Of 8/10th Service Battn The Gordon Highrs. From 30.11.1916 To 31.12.1916 Vol 19		
War Diary	Bresle	30/11/1916	30/11/1916
War Diary	Albert	01/12/1916	07/12/1916
War Diary	Camp X 23	07/12/1916	15/12/1916
War Diary	Scots Redoubt South.	16/12/1916	16/12/1916
War Diary	South Redoubt	17/12/1916	18/12/1916
War Diary	Scots Redoubt Front Line	19/12/1916	19/12/1916
War Diary	Lesars	19/12/1916	21/12/1916
War Diary	Acid Drop Camp	22/12/1916	23/12/1916
War Diary	Villacamp	24/12/1916	26/12/1916
War Diary	Villacamp & Scots Redoubt South	27/12/1916	27/12/1916
War Diary	Scots Redoubt South	28/12/1916	30/12/1916
War Diary	Front Line	31/12/1916	31/12/1916
Heading	8/10th (S) Battn, The Gordon Highlanders January, 1917		
Heading	War Diary Of 8/10th Service Battn The Gordon Highlanders. From 1st January 1917 To 31st January 1917 Volume 21, Vol 20		
War Diary	Front Line	01/01/1917	04/01/1917
War Diary	Pioneer Camp	05/01/1917	06/01/1917
War Diary	Sevenelms	07/01/1917	08/01/1917
War Diary	Scots Redoubt (South)	09/01/1917	12/01/1917
War Diary	Acid Drop Camp (Contalmaison)	13/01/1917	13/01/1917
War Diary	Villa Camp	14/01/1917	15/01/1917
War Diary	Villa Camp (Contalmaison)	16/01/1917	16/01/1917

War Diary	In The Line	16/01/1917	20/01/1917
War Diary	Scots Redoubt (South)	21/01/1917	24/01/1917
War Diary	Pioneer Camp	24/01/1917	28/01/1917
War Diary	Maxwell Trench	29/01/1917	29/01/1917
War Diary	Front Line	29/01/1917	30/01/1917
War Diary	Front Line (Maxwell TR)	31/01/1917	31/01/1917
Heading	8/10th (S) Battn. The Gordon Highlanders February, 1917		
Heading	Summary Of Operations Appendix 29		
Heading	War Diary Of 8/10th Service Battn, The Gordon Highlanders From 1st February 1917 To 28th February 1917 Volume 22, Vol 21		
War Diary	Front Line (Max TR)	01/02/1917	01/02/1917
War Diary	'C' Camp Becourt.	02/02/1917	04/02/1917
War Diary	Contay	05/02/1917	13/02/1917
War Diary	Beauval	14/02/1917	14/02/1917
War Diary	Gezaincourt	15/02/1917	15/02/1917
War Diary	Reserve	16/02/1917	16/02/1917
War Diary	Gauchin	17/02/1917	17/02/1917
War Diary	Monts-En-Ternois	18/02/1917	22/02/1917
War Diary	Izel-Les-Hameau	23/02/1917	28/02/1917
Heading	War Diary Of 8/10th Service Battalion The Gordon Highlanders From 1st March 1917 To 31st March 1917 Volume 23, Vol 22		
War Diary	Izel-Les-Hameau	01/03/1917	10/03/1917
War Diary	Arras	11/03/1917	26/03/1917
War Diary	Habarcq	27/03/1917	30/03/1917
War Diary	Arras	31/03/1917	31/03/1917
Miscellaneous	Preliminary Instructions For Offensive Operations Appendix I		
Diagram etc	Appendix "B" Formations Position Of Moppers Up Etc.		
Miscellaneous	44th Infantry Brigade Appendix "B"		
Heading	War Diary Of 8/10th Service Battn, The Gordon Highlanders, For Period 1st April 1917 To 30th April 1917 Volume 24, Vol 23		
War Diary	Arras	02/04/1917	11/04/1917
War Diary	Arras Area	11/04/1917	12/04/1917
War Diary	Arras	12/04/1917	23/04/1917
War Diary	Arras Front.	23/04/1917	28/04/1917
War Diary	Arras	29/04/1917	30/04/1917
Operation(al) Order(s)	8/10th (Service) Battalion The Gordon Highlanders Operation Order No. 24 Appendix 1	03/04/1917	03/04/1917
Miscellaneous	Arrangements for Move. Issued in conjunction with O.C. No. 84. Appendix 1		
Operation(al) Order(s)	8/10th (Service) Battalion, The Gordon Highlanders Operation Order No. 90 Appendix 2	07/04/1917	07/04/1917
Operation(al) Order(s)	Operation Order No. 82 by Lieut Col. J.G. Thom. M.C. Comdg. 8/10 Bn Gordon Highrs.	05/04/1917	05/04/1917
Miscellaneous	8/10th Gordon Highrs Appendix 4	06/04/1917	06/04/1917
Operation(al) Order(s)	8/10th (Service) Battalion The Gordon Highlanders. Operation Order No. 93. Appendix 11	22/04/1917	22/04/1917
Miscellaneous	Headquarters, 44th Infantry Brigade.	01/04/1917	01/04/1917
Operation(al) Order(s)	8/10th (Service) Battalion The Gordon Highlanders. Operation Order No. 93	22/04/1917	22/04/1917

Heading	War Diary Of 8/10th Service Battalion The Gordon Highlanders From 1.5.1917 To 31.5.1917 Volume 25, Vol 24		
War Diary	Simencourt	01/05/1917	08/05/1917
War Diary	Grand Rullecourt	09/05/1917	21/05/1917
War Diary	Rebreuve	22/05/1917	22/05/1917
War Diary	Fillievres	23/05/1917	31/05/1917
Heading	War Diary. Of 8/10th (Service) Battn. The Gordon Highlanders. For Period From 1.6.1917 To 30.6.17 Volume 26, Vol 25		
War Diary	Fillievres	01/06/1917	21/06/1917
War Diary	Croiselles.	22/06/1917	22/06/1917
War Diary	Valhuon	23/06/1917	23/06/1917
War Diary	Ecquedecques	24/06/1917	25/06/1917
War Diary	Isebergue	26/06/1917	26/06/1917
War Diary	Toronto Camp	27/06/1917	30/06/1917
Heading	War Diary Of 8/10th (Service) Battn The Gordon Highlanders From 1st July 1917 To 31st July 1917 Volume 27, Vol 26		
War Diary	In Trenches	01/07/1917	05/07/1917
War Diary	Support Camp Near Ypres	05/07/1917	09/07/1917
War Diary	Toronto Camp	10/07/1917	10/07/1917
War Diary	Rubrouck	11/07/1917	21/07/1917
War Diary	Winnezeele	22/07/1917	22/07/1917
War Diary	Watou	23/07/1917	23/07/1917
War Diary	Bivouac Camp	24/07/1917	28/07/1917
War Diary	Front Line	29/07/1917	31/07/1917
Map	Map No. 1a, Appendix No. 1		
Heading	War Diary Appendix 1 1st July 1917		
Map	Frezenberg		
Heading	War Diary Appendix 1 1st July 1917		
Operation(al) Order(s)	Operation Order No. 106 App. No. 2	04/07/1917	04/07/1917
Miscellaneous	Arrangements for Relief		
Operation(al) Order(s)	Operation Order No. 107 App. No. 3	07/07/1917	07/07/1917
Operation(al) Order(s)	8/10th (Service) Battalion, The Gordon Highlanders. Operation Order No. 108. App. No. 4	09/07/1917	09/07/1917
Heading	8/10th Gordon Highlanders. August 1917		
Heading	War Diary Of 8/10th (Service) Battalion The Gordon Highlanders. For Period 1st August 1917 To 31st August 1917 Volume 28, Vol 27		
War Diary	Front Line	01/08/1917	03/08/1917
War Diary	Bivouac Camp	04/08/1917	04/08/1917
War Diary	Winnizeele	05/08/1917	18/08/1917
War Diary	Brandhoek Area No. 3 (1 Mile South of Poperinghe)	18/08/1917	19/08/1917
War Diary	Forward Camp	20/08/1917	20/08/1917
War Diary	In The Line	21/08/1917	30/08/1917
War Diary	Watou Area No. 2	30/08/1917	31/08/1917
Map	Frezenberg		
Operation(al) Order(s)	Operation Order No. 103 Appendix No. 2	21/08/1917	21/08/1917
Miscellaneous	8/10th (Service) Battalion, The Gordon Highlanders. Preliminary Instructions No 1. Ypres-August 1917	19/08/1917	19/08/1917
Miscellaneous	Addendum No. 1 To Preliminary Instructions No. 1	20/08/1917	20/08/1917
Miscellaneous	Addendum No. 2. To Preliminary Instructions No. 1	20/08/1917	20/08/1917
Map	Frezenberg		
Heading	Appendix No. 3 22nd August 1917		

Heading	War Diary Of 8/10th (Service) Battalion, The Gordon Highlanders From 1st September 1917 To 30th September 1917 Volume 29, Vol 28		
War Diary	Watou Area No. 2	01/09/1917	02/09/1917
War Diary	Caestre	02/09/1917	03/09/1917
War Diary	Montenescourt	04/09/1917	08/09/1917
War Diary	Rifle Camp	09/09/1917	14/09/1917
War Diary	Trenches	15/09/1917	16/09/1917
War Diary	In Trenches	17/09/1917	21/09/1917
War Diary	In Support (Stirling Camp)	22/09/1917	30/09/1917
Operation(al) Order(s)	8/10th (Service) Battalion, The Gordon Highlanders Operation Order No. 109. By Lieut Colonel C. Reid Appendix I	01/09/1917	01/09/1917
Miscellaneous	Appendix 2 Notices		
Operation(al) Order(s)	8/10th (Service) Battalion, The Gordon Highlanders. Operation Order No. 112 By Lieut-Colonel C. Reid, Comdg. Appendix 3	06/09/1917	06/09/1917
Miscellaneous			
Map	Left Sector, Appendix 4		
Heading	8/10th Gordon Highlanders October 1917		
Heading	War Diary Of 8/10th (Service) Battalion The Gordon Highlanders. For Period. 1st October 1917 To 31st October 1917 Volume 30, Vol 29		
War Diary	Stirling Camp	01/10/1917	01/10/1917
War Diary	Balmoral Camp	02/10/1917	09/10/1917
War Diary	Front Trenches	10/10/1917	10/10/1917
War Diary	Trenches	10/10/1917	17/10/1917
War Diary	Wilderness Camp	18/10/1917	25/10/1917
War Diary	Arras	26/10/1917	31/10/1917
Operation(al) Order(s)	8/10th (Service) Battalion, The Gordon Highlanders. Operation Order No. 115. By Lieut-Colonel Charles Reid, Comdg. Appendix 1	30/09/1917	30/09/1917
Operation(al) Order(s)	8/10th (Service) Battalion. The Gordon Highlanders. Operation Order No. 116 Appendix 2		
Map	43rd Inf. Bde. Map No. 1, Appendix 3		
Operation(al) Order(s)	Operation Order No. 117 Appendix 4		
Operation(al) Order(s)	8/10 Gordon Highrs. Operation Order No. 118 Appendix 5	13/10/1917	13/10/1917
Miscellaneous	A Form. Messages And Signals. Appendix 6		
Miscellaneous	A Form. Messages And Signals.		
Operation(al) Order(s)	8/10th (S) Bn. The Gordon Highlanders Operation Order No. 119 By Lieut-Colonel Charles Reid, Comdg. Appendix 7	16/10/1917	16/10/1917
Operation(al) Order(s)	8/10th (Service) Battalion, The Gordon Highlanders. Operation Order No. 120 By Major J.B. Wood, M.C., Comdg Appendix 8	20/10/1917	20/10/1917
Operation(al) Order(s)	8/10th (Service) Battalion. The Gordon Highlanders. Operation Order No. 121 By Major J.B. Wood, M.C Comdg. Appendix 9	24/10/1917	24/10/1917
Heading	War Diary Of 8/10th (Service) Bn, The Gordon Highlanders Period 1st November 1917 1st December 1917 Volume 31, Vol 30		
War Diary	Arras	01/11/1917	11/11/1917
War Diary	Near Fampoux	11/11/1917	17/11/1917
War Diary	Rifle Camp	18/11/1917	18/11/1917
War Diary	Arras	19/11/1917	26/11/1917

War Diary	Stirling Camp	27/11/1917	27/11/1917
War Diary	Arras	28/11/1917	01/12/1917
Heading	War Diary Of 8/10th (Service) Battalion The Gordon Highlanders For Period. 2nd December 1917 31st December 1917 Volume 32, Vol 31		
War Diary	Trenches	02/12/1917	17/12/1917
War Diary	Arras	18/12/1917	23/12/1917
War Diary	Trenches	23/12/1917	31/12/1917
Operation(al) Order(s)	8/10th (Service) Battalion, The Gordon Highlanders. Operation Order No. 139 By Lieut-Colonel D. Macleod, D.S.O. Comdg.	08/12/1917	08/12/1917
Operation(al) Order(s)	8/10th (Service) Battalion, The Gordon Highlanders. Operation Order No. 133 By Captain. J. B. Wood. M.C., Comdg.	12/12/1917	12/12/1917
Operation(al) Order(s)	8/10th (Service) Battalion, The Gordon Highlanders. Operation Order No. 134. By Major Charles Reid. Comdg.	16/12/1917	16/12/1917
Operation(al) Order(s)	8/10th (Service) Battalion, The Gordon Highlanders. Operation Order No. 135. By Major The Lord. Dudley Gordon D.S.O. Comdg.	22/12/1917	22/12/1917
Operation(al) Order(s)	8/10th (Service) Battalion. The Gordon Highlanders Operation Order No. 136 By Major The Lord Dudley Gordon. D.S.O., Comdg.	26/12/1917	26/12/1917
Heading	War-Diary Of 8/10th (Service) Battn., The Gordon Highlanders For Period 2nd January 1918 31st January 1918 Volume 33, Vol 32		
Operation(al) Order(s)	8/10th (Service) Battalion, The Gordon Highlanders. Operation Order No. 137. By Major The Lord Dudley Gordon. D.S.O., Comdg.	30/12/1917	30/12/1917
Heading	War Diary Of 8/10th (Service) Battalion, The Gordon Highlanders For Period 1st February, 1918-28th February 1918, Vol 33		
War Diary	Arras	01/02/1918	04/02/1918
War Diary	Trenches	05/02/1918	17/02/1918
War Diary	Bois De Boeufs Camp.	18/02/1918	22/02/1918
War Diary	Trenches	23/02/1918	28/02/1918
Heading	44th Brigade. 15th Division. 8/10th Battalion The Gordon Highlanders March 1918		
War Diary	Trenches	01/03/1918	07/03/1918
War Diary	Billets	09/03/1918	09/03/1918
War Diary	Trenches	12/03/1918	31/03/1918
Operation(al) Order(s)	8/10 Gordon Highrs Operation Order No. 153 By Major Charles Reid Comdg.	25/03/1918	25/03/1918
Operation(al) Order(s)	O.O. No. 154 By Major Reid Comdg 8/10th Gordon Highrs	28/03/1918	28/03/1918
Operation(al) Order(s)	8/10 Gordon Highrs Operation Order No. 155 By Major Charles Reid Comdg.	29/03/1918	29/03/1918
Miscellaneous	A Form. Messages And Signals.		
Miscellaneous	8/10th (Ser) Battalion, The Gordon Highlanders.	31/03/1918	31/03/1918
Miscellaneous	1. Narrative-21st-24th March 1918	21/03/1918	21/03/1918
Miscellaneous	A Form. Messages And Signals.		
Map	8/10 Gordon Highrs.		
Heading	15th Division. 44th Brigade. War Diary. 8/10th Battalion The Gordon Highlanders April 1918		

Heading	War Diary Of 8/10th (Service) Battalion, The Gordon Highlanders For Period 1st April 1918 27th April 1918 Volume 36, Vol 35		
War Diary	Trenches	03/04/1918	04/04/1918
War Diary	Arras	05/04/1918	08/04/1918
War Diary	Trenches	09/04/1918	14/04/1918
War Diary	Arras	15/04/1918	20/04/1918
War Diary	Trenches	21/04/1918	23/04/1918
Operation(al) Order(s)	8/10th Gordon Highrs. Operation Order No. 156 By Major Charles Reid.	30/04/1918	30/04/1918
Operation(al) Order(s)	8/10th Gordon Highrs. Operation Order No. 157 By Major Charles Reid.	04/04/1918	04/04/1918
Operation(al) Order(s)	8/10 Gordon Highrs Operation Order No. 160 By Major Charles Reid Comdg.	12/04/1918	12/04/1918
Operation(al) Order(s)	8/10 Gordon Highrs Operation Order No. 162 By Major Charles Reid Comdg.	17/04/1918	17/04/1918
Operation(al) Order(s)	The Gordon Highlanders. Operation Order No. 163. By Major Charles Reid. Comdg.	19/04/1918	19/04/1918
Heading	War Diary Of 8/10th (Service) Battalion, The Gordon Highlanders For Period From 1st May 1918 To 31st May 1918 Volume 37, Vol 36		
War Diary	Camblain-Chatelain	01/05/1918	03/05/1918
War Diary	Etrun Y huts. L. 2.c.5.6. Ref Map. 51.c.	04/05/1918	04/05/1918
War Diary	Wakefield Camp A. 28. C. 21 Ref Map 51.B. N.W.	06/05/1918	09/05/1918
War Diary	Roeux Sector	10/05/1918	10/05/1918
War Diary	Stirling Camp.	10/05/1918	17/05/1918
War Diary	Front Line.	17/05/1918	24/05/1918
War Diary	Wakefield Camp.	25/05/1918	31/05/1918
Miscellaneous	Appendix 1., O.O. 165a.	04/05/1918	04/05/1918
Operation(al) Order(s)	44th Highland Brigade Operation Order No. 254	03/05/1918	03/05/1918
Miscellaneous	Entraining at Pernes Station.		
Miscellaneous	44th Brigade G.41.-Warning Orders	01/05/1918	01/05/1918
Operation(al) Order(s)	The Gordon Highlanders. Operation Order No. 165 By Lieut-Colonel The Lord Dudley Gordon, D.S.O., Comdg. Appendix 2	06/05/1918	06/05/1918
Operation(al) Order(s)	The Gordon Highlanders. Operation Order No. 167. By Lieut-Colonel The Lord Dudley Gordon, D.S.O., Comdg. Appendix 3	03/05/1918	03/05/1918
Operation(al) Order(s)	44th Highland Brigade Operation Order No. 266 Appendix 4	09/05/1918	09/05/1918
Miscellaneous	Ration Supply To Right Section, Centre Sector, XVII Corps Front.	09/05/1918	09/05/1918
Operation(al) Order(s)	Administrative Instructions Issued In Conjunction With Operation Order No. 266	09/05/1918	09/05/1918
Operation(al) Order(s)	44th Highland Brigade Operation Order No. 267. Appendix 5	16/05/1918	16/05/1918
Operation(al) Order(s)	The Gordon Highlanders Operation Order No. 169 By Captain N.G. Pearson Comdg. Appendix 6	23/05/1918	23/05/1918
Operation(al) Order(s)	44th Highland Brigade Operation Order No. 268	25/05/1918	25/05/1918
Miscellaneous	Table Of Reliefs To Accompany 44th Brigade Operation Order No. 258		
Heading	Training Cadre 39th Division 118th Infy Bde 8-10th Bn Gordon Hdrs Jun-Aug 1918 Disbanded 17.8.18		
Heading	War Diary. Of For Period From 1st June 1918 To 30th June 1918 Volume 38, Vol 37		
War Diary	Trenches	01/06/1918	07/06/1918

War Diary	Gouves	09/06/1918	09/06/1918
Operation(al) Order(s)	The Gordon Highlanders. Operation Order No. 170. By Lieut-Colonel The Lord Dudley Gordon, D.S.O., Comdg.	31/05/1918	31/05/1918
Operation(al) Order(s)	8/10th (S) Bn The Gordon Highrs Operation Order No. 171. By. Lieut. Colonel The Lord Dudley Gordon, D.S.O. Comdg	06/06/1918	06/06/1918
War Diary	Barlin	09/06/1918	09/06/1918
War Diary	Nortkerque	11/06/1918	17/06/1918
War Diary	Landrethun Les Ardres	18/06/1918	21/06/1918
War Diary	Mentque	26/06/1918	26/06/1918
War Diary	Landrethun Les Ardres	30/06/1918	30/06/1918
Heading	War Diary Of 8/10th (Service) Battalion, The Gordon Highlanders. For Period 1st July 1918 To 31st July, 1918. Volume 39, Vol 32		
War Diary	Landrethun Les Ardres	02/07/1918	25/07/1918
War Diary	Zutkerque	26/07/1918	27/07/1918
War Diary	Watten	27/07/1918	31/07/1918
Operation(al) Order(s)	Battalion Order No. 1 By Lieut-Colonel The Lord Dudley Gordon, D.S.O., Comdg.	22/07/1918	22/07/1918
Miscellaneous	The Gordon Highlanders Battalion Orders By Lieut-Colonel The Lord Dudley Gordon, DSO., Comdg.	25/07/1918	25/07/1918
Miscellaneous	D.A.G., 3rd Echelon, G.H.Q.	20/08/1918	20/08/1918
War Diary	Penton Camp 27/F8 a 4.9	01/08/1918	17/08/1918

WO 95/1938

44 INF BDE

15 DIVISION

8/10 BTN GORDON HIGHLANDERS

May 1916 – Aug 1918

15TH DIVISION
44TH INFY BDE
8/ 10TH BN GORDON HDRS
~~JULY 1915~~ - AUG 1918
1916 MAY
DISBANDED
8 GORDONS FROM 9 DIV 26 BDE 6 AR 1916
amalgamated with 10 GORDONS FROM
from May 1916
44 BDE
DISBANDED 17 8 18

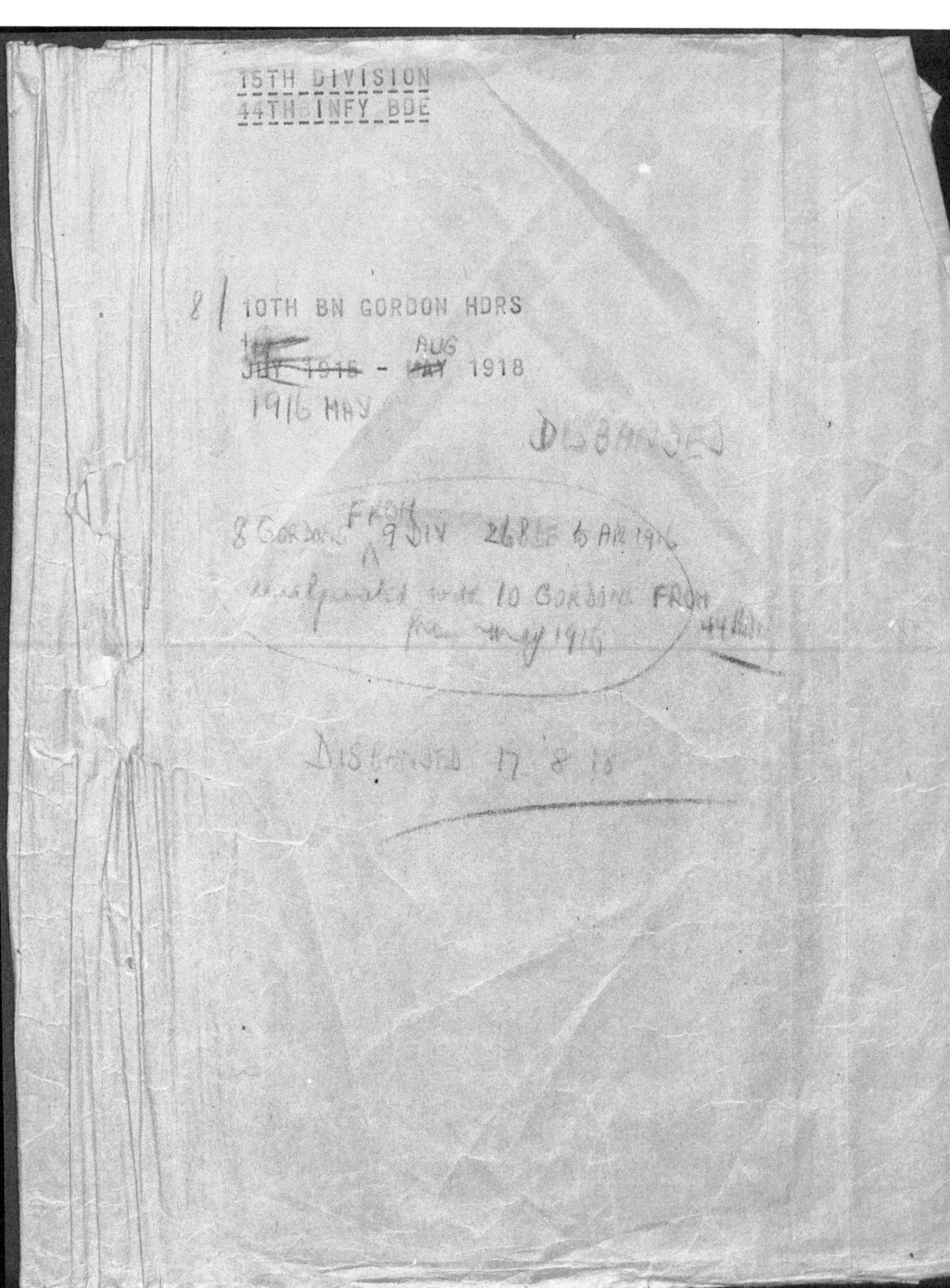

WO 95/1938

8/10
MAY 1916

44/15.

8th Gordons

Vol 12

~~IX~~ XV

CONFIDENTIAL

WAR DIARY

8th/10th (Service) Battn The Gordon Highlanders

Came from 26 Bde 6.5.16.

From 31/4/16 To 31/5/16.

Instructions regarding War Diaries and Intelligence Summaries are contained in F. S. Regs., Part II. and the Staff Manual respectively. Title pages will be prepared in manuscript.

WAR DIARY
or
INTELLIGENCE SUMMARY.
(Erase heading not required.)

119.

Army Form C. 2118.

Hour, Date, Place	Summary of Events and Information	Remarks and references to Appendices
April 30th	No events of importance. Weather still fine & hot, wind in same quarter.	CASUALTY C coy. S/1385 Pte F. LEE. Died of wounds.
May 1st	Three Platoons of South Africans spent night of May 1st/2nd in rest billets with us, they were attached 1 platoon to A B & C coys respectively. Weather still fine & hot & wind E. Inclined to be thundry.	
May 2nd	Testing of Grenadiers by 2/Lt CALLENDER, who went round to each farm in turn testing. We received definite orders that we were not to go into the Trenches tomorrow, which we ordinarily would have done. This indicates that the splitting up of the Battn & subsequent amalgamation with the 10th Battn, which has been impending for so long, is at last about to take place. The Commanding Officer inspected C coy in the Forenoon. The Turnout was Satisfactory	WCM
May 3rd	Parades were under company arrangements. Much work was done in cleaning up, scrubbing packs, and generally getting the men smartened up, clean coats and new kilts. Flashes being badly wanted by a good many. As a result of yesterdays examination of Grenadiers, 70 men passed out of 100 — a very satisfactory	

(73989) W4141—463. 400,000. 9/14. H.&J.Ltd. Forms/C. 2118/10.

Instructions regarding War Diaries and Intelligence Summaries are contained in F. S. Regs., Part II. and the Staff Manual respectively. Title pages will be prepared in manuscript.

WAR DIARY
or
INTELLIGENCE SUMMARY.
(Erase heading not required.)

Sheet 120.

Army Form C. 2118.

Hour, Date, Place	Summary of Events and Information	Remarks and references to Appendices
May 3rd	Result. Weather fine.	
May 4th	We received our orders for the move and hand over. We (the 8th Battn) are to proceed to join the 15th Division and amalgamate with the 10th Battn in the 44th Brigade. Our place in the 26th Brigade is to be taken by the 10th Argyll & Sutherland Highrs. In the 27th Brigade the place of the 10th Argyll & Sutherland Highrs is to be filled up by the 6th K.O.S. Borderers. The 28th Brigade will cease to exist, since the 10th & 11th H.L.I., having amalgamated, go to the 15th Division, the 9th Scottish Rifles go to the 27th Brigade vice the 6th Royal Scots Fusiliers who also go to the 15th Division for amalgamation. This will only leave two Scottish Brigades in the 9th Division (the 26th and 27th) the other brigade being the South African Brigade. The reasons for this breaking up of Scottish Battalions are not hard to find. In every engagement in this war, the Scottish regiments have taken a prominent part and have suffered casualties out of all proportion to the male population of Scotland, as compared with England and Ireland. In many parts of Scotland especially in the North, the male	W.E.M.

Instructions regarding War Diaries and Intelligence Summaries are contained in F. S. Regs., Part II. and the Staff Manual respectively. Title pages will be prepared in manuscript.

WAR DIARY
or
INTELLIGENCE SUMMARY.
(*Erase heading not required.*)

Sheet 121

Army Form C. 2118.

Hour, Date, Place	Summary of Events and Information	Remarks and references to Appendices
May 4th	population has been badly depleted, and is now quite exhausted. It is therefore most advisable to reduce the number of Scottish Battalions. C.O., 2nd in command, QrM & Adjt. dined at 26th Brigade H.Q.	
May 5th	We were excused all working parties in the afternoon, in order to get ready for the handing over and to enable the men to get cleaned up for the impending move. General FURSE the G.O.C. 9th Division dined with us at SOYER FARM. In the middle of dinner, a gas alarm went, some way to the South of ARMENTIERES, about BOIS GRENIER. Heavy firing was heard. Green S.O.S Rockets were seen, and Gas Horns, & Bells were rung, the alarm spreading north towards us as far as LE BIZET.	
May 6th	We handed over at 10.0 am. All Lewis Guns complete with Drums, S.A.A., and Two Limbers, Horses & Harness, were handed over to the South African Brigade. All other Equipment was handed over to the 6th K.O.S.B who also took over our billets. The Battn marched out of billets for	W.C.M.

(73989) W4141–463. 400,000. 9/14. H.&J.Ltd. Forms/C. 2118/10.

Instructions regarding War Diaries and Intelligence Summaries are contained in F. S. Regs., Part II. and the Staff Manual respectively. Title pages will be prepared in manuscript.

WAR DIARY
or
INTELLIGENCE SUMMARY.
(Erase heading not required.)

Sheet. 122.

Army Form C. 2118.

Hour, Date, Place	Summary of Events and Information	Remarks and references to Appendices
May 6th (continued)	CIMETIERE (STEENJE) a village about 3 miles from BAILLEUL at 4 0pm, passing our Transport Lines by Companies at 5 minutes intervals about 4.30 pm. General RITCHIE commanding the 26th Brigade and all the Brigade Staff were there to see us off. The Battn halted at the Junction of the ~~Lille~~ BAILLEUL – ARMENTIERES and PAPOT-ROMARIN roads for 1/4 of an Hour. We found more officers here to wish us good bye, and the Pipe Band of the BLACK WATCH, SEAFORTHS and CAMERONS. After we had crossed the level crossing over the BAILLEUL – ARMENTIERES RLY. GENERAL FORSE inspected the Battn as it marched past. We arrived in billets about 7.45pm rather later than we had expected. We found billets were very good and comfortable. Late this evening we received orders for entraining at STEENWERCK on the 7th at 4pm, also for our riding Horses to proceed by road to BETHUNE, and we received instructions that ~~our~~ Transport after taking our baggage to the station was to go to the Divl Train at LA CRECHE and in course of	W.Mc

(73989) W4141—463. 400,000. 9/14. H.&J.Ltd. Forms/C. 2118/10.

Instructions regarding War Diaries and Intelligence Summaries are contained in F. S. Regs., Part II. and the Staff Manual respectively. Title pages will be prepared in manuscript.

WAR DIARY
or
INTELLIGENCE SUMMARY.
(Erase heading not required.)

Sheet 123.

Army Form C. 2118.

Hour, Date, Place	Summary of Events and Information	Remarks and references to Appendices
May 6th (continued)	time proceed to the Base. This was a great blow as our Transport is undoubtedly the best in every way in the 9th Divn. The Commanding Officer dined at Divl H.Q.	
May 7th	We received word that GENERAL FURSE would inspect us at 1.40pm in Mass before we left for the Station. The Battn was drawn up in mass in a pasture field, and after the usual compliments were paid the General inspected the Battn and spoke to the Battn. His address in precis was as follows — He was very sorry to part with the Battn from his Division. He greatly admired the Battn and had at all times been proud of the bravery, soldierly behaviour, tone, and appearance of the Battn. He regretted the impending amalgamation, but thought it was for the best. He concluded in wishing all ranks the best of luck. After this address three cheers were given and the Battn marched off for the Station, arriving there at about 3.15pm. En route, a Guard of Honour from the 105th Coy A.S.C. turned out and the Divl Band played us into the Station. It was found that the 6th Royal Scots Fusiliers and	WCM

Instructions regarding War Diaries and Intelligence Summaries are contained in F. S. Regs., Part II. and the Staff Manual respectively. Title pages will be prepared in manuscript.

WAR DIARY
or
INTELLIGENCE SUMMARY.
(Erase heading not required.)

Sheet 124.

Army Form C. 2118.

Hour, Date, Place	Summary of Events and Information	Remarks and references to Appendices
	ourselves were to go in the same Train. The 6th R.S.F entrained	
May 7th	first, the Battn waiting outside the Station till their entrainment was	
	complete, we then entrained and all baggage etc was loaded and the	
	Train ready to start at 5pm. We had an uneventful journey and	
	arrived at BETHUNE station at 7.30pm. Here detrainment was	
	speedily effected, baggage loaded on Motor Lorries & ASC wagons	
	and we ~~arrived~~ marched up to billets. 1/2 Battn (A & B coys	
	and HQ) were billetted in the ECOLE MICHELET and 1/2 Battn	
	(C & D) in the Tobacco Factory, and all the Officers billetted in	
	the RUE DE LILLE close by.	
May 8th.	Early in the morning we received orders that GOC 15th Divn	
	(General McCRACKEN) would inspect us at 10.0 am. He	
	inspected C & D coys in Columns of platoons in the yard of the	
	Tobacco Factory, A & B coys in Line in the RUE MICHELET.	
	After the Inspection he was introduced to all the Officers of	
	the Battn. We received more orders with regard to the impending	
	amalgamation, and learnt that Colonel H.P. BURN DSO	
	our Commanding Officer was to command, and that in other	
	respects with the exception of 8th Battn HQ Staff	WCM

Instructions regarding War Diaries and Intelligence Summaries are contained in F.S. Regs., Part II. and the Staff Manual respectively. Title pages will be prepared in manuscript.

WAR DIARY
or
INTELLIGENCE SUMMARY.
(*Erase heading not required.*)

Sheet 125.

Army Form C. 2118.

Hour, Date, Place	Summary of Events and Information	Remarks and references to Appendices
	which would remain "in TOTO", the Battn would be formed out of an equal proportion of Officers, NCOs & men from the 8th and 10th Battalions. We were also told that the amalgamation would take place about May 10th when the 10th Battn came out of the Trenches to rest billets in BETHUNE.	
May 9th	Day was spent in cleaning up equipment etc. Wet day. Brigadier General BAIRD CMG. DSO, who recently commanded the 1st Battn visited us. We also saw Major General LANDON who formerly commanded the 9th Division when it first came out to FRANCE. May 9th is the anniversary of the arrival of the Battn in France. About 15 % of the NCOs and men who originally came out with the Battn are still serving with the Battn. Only 5 Officers namely MAJOR D. MACLEOD, DSO, CAPTAIN W G. MAXWELL, CAPTAIN A.M. WALLACE, CAPTAIN J. MARTIN CAPT & QMr W. DRUMMOND, who originally came out with the Battn are still here, and of these Major MACLEOD and CAPTAIN MAXWELL were wounded on Sept 25th and have since rejoined.	W.C.M.

(73989) W4141—463. 400,000. 9/14. H.&J.Ltd. Forms/C. 2118/10.

Instructions regarding War Diaries and Intelligence Summaries are contained in F. S. Regs., Part II. and the Staff Manual respectively. Title pages will be prepared in manuscript.

WAR DIARY
or
INTELLIGENCE SUMMARY.
(Erase heading not required.)

Sheet 125.

Army Form C. 2118.

Hour, Date, Place	Summary of Events and Information	Remarks and references to Appendices
May 10th Bethune	Battn went for Route March, through VERQUINEUL. Dress Drill order. Battn returned by 12.30 pm. Fine day. Received orders for the amalgamation of 8th & 10th Battns for the 11th. We received instructions that Lt Colonel H.P. Burn DSO was to command the amalgamated Battn. The other arrangements were, the whole of Battn Headquarters, Transport & QrMr & Orderly room staff of the 8th Battn would take over "in toto". The 8th Battn were to find Two Complete Coys with specialists Etc, and the 10th Battn Two Complete Coys. Our old A & B coys finding the new A coy, old C & D coys the new B coy, I & K coy 10th Battn the new C coy, M & L coys the new D coy. A & B coys were to be officered by 8th Battn Officers, C & D coys by 10th Battn Officers. It was decided that the surplus from each Battn should form an 11th Entrenching Battn under Lt Colonel W.W. McGregor DSO (Commanding Officer of the 10th Battn) with an Establishment of Two coys of 250 each. The remaining surplus were to be sent to the Tunnelling Companies and to the Base.	WCM

Instructions regarding War Diaries and Intelligence Summaries are contained in F. S. Regs., Part II. and the Staff Manual respectively. Title pages will be prepared in manuscript.

WAR DIARY
or
INTELLIGENCE SUMMARY.
(Erase heading not required.)

Sheet 126.

Army Form C. 2118.

Hour, Date, Place	Summary of Events and Information	Remarks and references to Appendices
May 11th	As arranged the Amalgamation Parade was held at 2.30 pm. Owing to limited space etc a good deal of confusion ensued but things were straightened out after a few hours time and the new 8/10th Battn came into existance. The Officers of the new Coys & Battn HQ are as follows.	

Battn HQ.	A	B	C	D
Lt Colonel HP Burn DSO	Captain J. Martin	Capt A.M Drummond	Captn J.G. Thom	Capt: F.J.C Moffatt
Major D. McLeod DSO	Captain A.P. Beith	Capt J. Lambie	Lieut J.D. Wood	Capt J.G. Paterson
Capt & Adjt W.G. Maxwell	Lieut D.W. McLeod	Lieut M.L. Gordon	Lieut C.G. Harper TO	Lieut L.G. Robertson
Lt & Qr W. Drummond	" E. McCallum	Lieut J. Lyme	Lieut A Inglis	2/Lt G.W. Jackson
2/Lt W.T.C. Birnie MGO.	2/Lt G.P. Geddes	2/Lieut A.C.S Buist	2/Lt A.N Bain	2/Lt R.M. Riddell
MO. Captain Lumley	2/Lt A.T.R. Walter	2/Lieut L. Gellatly	2/Lt A.F. Sprott	2/Lt R.A.M. Black.
	2/Lt C.R. Brooke (Train offr)	2/Lieut D.R McNaught	2/Lt A F Priday	
	2/Lt W.A. Glennie	2/Lieut R.O. Lunn	2/Lt J. Smith	

Of these Officers Captain Beith, Lieut Inglis are in Divl & Brigade Employ respectively. Nominal rolls were received in the Orderly room in a somewhat jumbled and inaccurate state causing considerable labour in correct compilation of Bn. nominal roll.

During course of afternoon we heard that the Germans had taken 600 yards of our front line on HOHENZOLLERN Sector. Brigade asked us if we would be ready to move as a fighting

WCM

(73989) W4141—463. 400,000. 9/14. H.&J.Ltd. Forms/C. 2118/10.

127

Army Form C. 2118.

Instructions regarding War Diaries and Intelligence Summaries are contained in F. S. Regs., Part II. and the Staff Manual respectively. Title pages will be prepared in manuscript.

WAR DIARY
or
INTELLIGENCE SUMMARY.
(Erase heading not required.)

Hour, Date, Place	Summary of Events and Information	Remarks and references to Appendices
May 11th. Bethune	Unit — a difficult question to ask a Battn which had only been formed 6 Hours!	
May 12th Bethune	Heard officially that Battn was to be known as the 8/10th Battn. Day was spent in organising the new Coys	
May 13th Bethune	The 11th Entrenching Battn under Lt Col W.W. McGregor DSO left BETHUNE for VERQUIN at 10.0 am. Our Pipers played them out.	
May 14th	We received sudden orders at 1pm to march and take up new billets at LABOURSE. We left BETHUNE at 4pm and marched via BEUVRY arriving at LABOURSE at 5.30pm. Coys soon got fixed up in billets. We had considerable difficulty with regard to Transport. Such things as Blankets, Officers valises and Mess kits take a lot of carrying and the Battn Transport cannot cope with it. We managed however to get two motor lorries, and all the stuff arrived safely at LABOURSE before dark.	W.C.M.
May 15th	Since our arrival in BETHUNE we have paid great attention to Gas precautions; apparently this Division is not quite so proficient	

Instructions regarding War Diaries and Intelligence Summaries are contained in F.S. Regs., Part II. and the Staff Manual respectively. Title pages will be prepared in manuscript.

WAR DIARY
or
INTELLIGENCE SUMMARY.
(Erase heading not required.)

1
128

Army Form C. 2118.

Hour, Date, Place	Summary of Events and Information	Remarks and references to Appendices
May 15th (LABOURSE Contd.)	in Gas Precautions as the 9th Bn. When we were in BETHUNE we heard rumour that Tower Respirators were not a success in the last GAS attack, we accordingly got hold of the Divl Gas Expert and asked him to Test one of those taken over from 10th Gordon Hghrs. He tried it in a gas Cloud and reported that it worked perfectly. We found working parties of 300 men. Some working on Village Line and 100 working in the front Trenches HOHENZOLLERN REDOUBT sector at night. Unfortunately the latter had several casualties (see margin) caused by Explosion of Enemy Trench Mortar Bomb. The Commanding Officer Lectured to Officers & platoon Sergts, and directed that the "Fighting Tens" or "Battle sections" in each Coy were to be thoroughly organised.	Casualties night 15/16th KILLED S/6619 L/Cpl C WALLS A Coy DIED of WOUNDS S/7971 Pte D. Grant – " WOUNDED S/4644 Pte F Stewart " S/9948 " M Millward " S/10578 " W. Marshall "
May 16th Labourse.	Parades under Coy arrangements. Divl Baths at LABOURSE were allotted to the Battn but owing to our strength and fact that only 4 hours were allotted (2pm – 6pm) only 3 Coys could Bathe. They reported arrangements & baths as being First Rate. The Organisation of Battn Snipers & Pioneers was completed and	WCM

(73989) W4141—463. 400,000. 9/14. H.&J.Ltd. Forms/C. 2118/10.

129

Army Form C. 2118.

WAR DIARY
or
INTELLIGENCE SUMMARY.
(*Erase heading not required.*)

Instructions regarding War Diaries and Intelligence Summaries are contained in F.S. Regs., Part II. and the Staff Manual respectively. Title pages will be prepared in manuscript.

Hour, Date, Place	Summary of Events and Information	Remarks and references to Appendices
May 16th (Contd)	following Establishment arrived at Bn Pioneers 1 Offr (2/Lt Brooke) 1 Sergt & 20 men, Battn Sniper 1 Officer (Lt Mc Gordon) 1 Sergt and sixteen men. Battn found working parties for 180 men mostly working on Village Line. D Coy did Gas Helmet Drill.	
May 17th Labourse	2/Lt C. HOGGE proceeded to base under authority 44th Bde. 2/Lt Elliot & 50 men proceeded to LAPUGNOY for attachment to 8th RLY Coy there. This leaves the Battn "on" strength. This strength does not, however, include Divl & Brigade Employ men who total up to some 50. We received orders that we would taken over centre section of HOHENZOLLERN SECTOR, on the 19th. This sector comprises Trenches recently taken from 6/7th RSF by the Germans and the Line is by no means safe & highly complicated. C.O. Adjt, 2 Coy Commanders (Captains THOM & MOFFAT) and Sniping Officer went up to inspect Trenches We found matters hardly as bad as they had been described, but noted four salient features which must be put in hand at once (a) WIRE, (b) Support Line to SACKVILLE STREET (c) a new Battn HQ (d) a new Battn Aid Post.	W.Mc

(73989) W4141—463. 400,000. 9/14. H.&J.Ltd. Forms/C. 2118/10.

Instructions regarding War Diaries and Intelligence Summaries are contained in F.S. Regs., Part II. and the Staff Manual respectively. Title pages will be prepared in manuscript.

WAR DIARY
or
INTELLIGENCE SUMMARY.
(Erase heading not required.)

Sheet ~~126~~ 130

Army Form C. 2118.

Hour, Date, Place	Summary of Events and Information	Remarks and references to Appendices
May 17th LABOURSE.	As regards (A) There is no wire & apparently no effort is being made by Battn in the line to put wire out. (B) The fact of the GERMANS taking the ANCHOR Trench to which Sackville Street was support Trench demands the immediate construction of new ST to SACKVILLE STREET. (C) The old Battn HQ was far too close up and was destroyed by Shell fire (D) The old Battn Aid post was far too close up and has also been destroyed. Found Captain L. Carr 92nd Highrs as Brigade Major of the 45th Brigade holding this sector. Heavy Bombardment of our Guns from 6.30 pm onwards Divl Band played in billets.	
May 18th LA BOURSE	Morning hazy - day fine & very warm - wind easterly (3 to 4 miles per hour). The Second in command 2 Company command-ers (Capts Drummond & Martin), & Battn M.G.O. visited trenches to be taken over by Battn tomorrow. Battn supplied working party of 2 officers and 100 men. Companies carried out small manoeuvres with "fighting tens" in forenoon and	WCW

(73989) W4141—463. 400,000. 9/14. H.&J.Ltd. Forms/C. 2118/10.

WAR DIARY

DATE + PLACE	SUMMARY OF EVENTS	REMARKS
May 18th (Contd)	in the afternoon a Muster Parade of the Battn. by Coys. was held in order to finally check strength and regtl. nos. etc. Pioneers commenced work on new Battn. Headquarters.	
May 19th	Weather fine - very warm - wind easterly. Battn relieved 6/7th R.S.F. during forenoon - the Coys. disposed as follows viz:- "C" Coy (right) and "D" Coy (left) Front line - "A" Coy in Support occupying part of GORDON ALLEY and T heads adjoining, - with "B" Coy in reserve in VILLAGE LINE. The relief was carried out in good order considering the circumstances, but the trenches were not in a satisfactory state in point of cleanliness. Situation normal during day, except that enemy sent over a few rifle grenades to our right front trench (SACKVILLE STREET) causing the casualties marginally noted (1). In the evening another casualty occurred caused by a rifle bullet, see margin (2). Night quiet and uneventful.	CASUALTIES. KILLED (1) 2nd LIEUT. A.N. BAIN, "C" Coy. PTE. BLAND. " WOUNDED (2) SERGT. LEASK "C" Coy.

W.G.Y.

SHEET 132.

WAR DIARY

DATE & PLACE	SUMMARY OF EVENTS	REMARKS
May 20th. (Trenches)	Weather fine - very warm - wind easterly (2 miles p.h.). Situation during day Normal. At night good work was done in digging new trench (to be known as DRUMMOND TRENCH) as support line to SACKVILLE STREET, and in putting out wire along the Battn. front. Men from "C" & "D" Coys. patrolled various parts of "No man's land" without mishap. The casualties mentioned in (1) occurred during the wiring and the other casualty (2) took place in RESERVE TRENCH near Orderly Room from a piece of anti-aircraft shell.	CASUALTIES WOUNDED (1) (2) SICK 2nd LIEUT. McNAUGHT.
May 21st. (Trenches.)	Weather continues fine & very warm - wind veering from East to South. Shortly after noon the enemy exploded a mine on the left of the Brigade front and caused several casualties to 7th Cameron Highrs. Otherwise situation during day Normal. Sergt. KEIR (Orderly Room) was wounded in the head by the explosion of a Mills hand grenade which was being abstracted from the ammunition pouch of a wounded man.	WCM

WAR DIARY

DATE + PLACE	SUMMARY OF EVENTS	REMARKS CASUALTIES
May 21st (contd.)	At night the work in hand was continued and satisfactory progress was made both with DRUMMOND TRENCH and the wiring. The wiring party sustained one casualty. "C" + "D" Coys had patrols out in front during the night. Situation normal.	
May 22nd (Trenches)	Weather still fine and warm - wind S.W. At 11.15 am we exploded a mine opposite Sap 8 KAISERIN TRENCH causing a crater immediately in front of the enemy line. Our artillery and trench mortars fired on the Hun trenches, and he retaliated rather vigorously on our supports without doing any damage. No attempt was made to occupy the crater. Remainder of day was normal. At night work was continued on DRUMMOND TRENCH and more wire was put out in front. Night was quiet and uneventful.	WCM

SHEET 134.

Army Form C. 2118.

Instructions regarding War Diaries and Intelligence Summaries are contained in F. S. Regs., Part II. and the Staff Manual respectively. Title pages will be prepared in manuscript.

WAR DIARY
or
INTELLIGENCE SUMMARY.
(Erase heading not required.)

Place	Date	Hour	Summary of Events and Information	Remarks and references to Appendices
VERMELLES.	May 23		Weather fine, wind S.E. by E. At 7.30 am Enemy exploded a mine opposite our extreme left of near our junction with the Cameron Highlanders. The mine caused us 7 casualties & caused the Camerons 35, but of the latter only 3 were killed. We occupied the near lip of the crater while the Germans occupied the further lip. There was no artillery fire on either side. At 8pm the Germans shelled Batt HQ with 4.2 howitzers. They sent over about 10 salvoes in a very short space of time. We had no casualties. At night we opened on ANCHOR TRENCH with Lewis Guns & rifle grenades, the 18-prs firing a few salvoes at the same time. The Germans gave us some trouble with a heavy minenwerfer between 8 & 9 pm. We asked for retaliation from the howitzers & got 4 rounds from them – all blind shells. More wire was put out along the Battalion front at night. There is now quite a fair entanglement all the way along. Very heavy shelling was heard in the South at dusk. This turned out to be a	WGM

SHEET 135.

Army Form C. 2118.

Instructions regarding War Diaries and Intelligence Summaries are contained in F. S. Regs., Part II. and the Staff Manual respectively. Title pages will be prepared in manuscript.

WAR DIARY
or
INTELLIGENCE SUMMARY.
(Erase heading not required.)

Place	Date	Hour	Summary of Events and Information	Remarks and references to Appendices
VERMELLES	May 23 (contd)		Counter attack launched by us to retake the VIMY RIDGE which we had lost the day before. The counter-attack failed.	
	May 24		The Germans were active with their large minnenwerfer from 7–8 am + again from 10–11 am. We turned on the 6-inch + 4.5 howitzers in retaliation. These fired some 30–40 rounds between them but few burst well. There were many half-bursts and blinds. A very large number of our howitzer shells are blind nowadays, the slight increase there has been in the quantity of the shells allowed being largely counter-balanced by their decrease in quality – this a very serious state of affairs. The German artillery was busy at intervals during the day. Our trench mortars – 2-inch + 4-inch – also fired some rounds. We blew 2 mines at THE HAIRPIN (Black Watch line) at 9 pm, + opened on the German with STOKES guns + rifle grenades on the mines exploding. Many cries + much shouting were heard in the German trenches.	W.C.

T.134. Wt. W708–776. 500000. 4/15. Sir J. C. & S.

SHEET 136

Army Form C. 2118.

Instructions regarding War Diaries and Intelligence Summaries are contained in F. S. Regs., Part II. and the Staff Manual respectively. Title pages will be prepared in manuscript.

WAR DIARY
or
INTELLIGENCE SUMMARY.
(Erase heading not required.)

Place	Date	Hour	Summary of Events and Information	Remarks and references to Appendices
VERMELLES.	May 25		A quiet day. We put in some good work in our trenches & further wire was put out in front by night. "A" & "B" Coys relieved "C" & "D" Coys in the front line commencing at 9 a.m. The heavy German minenwerfer was active at intervals through the night, POKER ST. & VIGO ST. being demolished in places. The Germans sent over a few 4.2 howitzer shells to which we replied with 18-pr.	
"	May 26		A quiet morning. The Germans fired about a dozen 4.2 howitzer shells into our trenches at 6 p.m. We replied with ~~20~~ 15 4.5 how" shells but of these 12 were "blind" while 2 others only partially exploded. The percentage of blinds amongst our heavy shells is assuming large proportions & is most disquieting. At 7.30 p.m. the Germans fired a mine in "No man's land" opposite the Battalion front. The mine caused some damage to our trenches & two men were buried in a sap but they were successfully dug out uninjured by a party under Lieut A.C.S. BUIST who did excellent work. Five minutes after the explosion	WJa

T.134. Wt. W708–776. 500000. 4/15. Sir J. C. & S.

SHEET 137.

Army Form C. 2118.

Instructions regarding War Diaries and Intelligence Summaries are contained in F. S. Regs., Part II. and the Staff Manual respectively. Title pages will be prepared in manuscript.

WAR DIARY
or
INTELLIGENCE SUMMARY.
(Erase heading not required.)

Place	Date	Hour	Summary of Events and Information	Remarks and references to Appendices
	1916.			
VERMELLES.	26 May		of the mine the Germans opened fire with minenwerfer, light heavy artillery, trench mortars + rifle grenades. They kept this fire up for 20 minutes or more but through good fortune we had no casualties. Our guns replied, the 6-inch howitzers sending over some 20 shells. Our 2-inch mortars also opened. At 8 pm all was quiet + the night working + wiring parties got to work. Excellent work was done by both these parties. The latter put out 85 knifenests in front of our trenches.	
"	27 May		An exceptionally quiet day. In the evening information was received that a deserter of the 9th Pioneer Battalion had surrendered at CALONNE + had stated that the Germans intended attacking LOOS while a subsidiary attack may be expected in this area. He further said that gas was installed along the whole of the fronts of the IV Corps + IX Reserve Corps. On receipt of this information 2 platoons were moved up into close support in DRUMMOND'S trench while all ranks were warned to be prepared for a gas attack. It	W.C.M.

T.134. Wt. W708–776. 500000. 4/15. Sir J. C. & S.

SHEET 138

Army Form C. 2118.

WAR DIARY
or
INTELLIGENCE SUMMARY.
(Erase heading not required.)

Instructions regarding War Diaries and Intelligence Summaries are contained in F. S. Regs., Part II. and the Staff Manual respectively. Title pages will be prepared in manuscript.

Place	Date	Hour	Summary of Events and Information	Remarks and references to Appendices
VERMELLES.	May 27 (contd)		was omitted to state that at 2.30 a.m. a mine was sprung by us near CUINCHY, about 1½ miles to the North of the Battalion trenches. The explosion of the mine was followed by much artillery fire & bombing. At night the usual working parties from the reserve	
"	~~May 28~~		coys were employed, some 230 men working on DRUMMOND'S TRENCH, this being our new support line. Wiring parties were also out & some 45 "knifeRests" were added to the entanglements in front of our trenches.	
"	May 28		Another exceptionally quiet day on the Battalion front. Our 2-inch mortars (60-lb bombs) sent over a dozen rounds in the morning while the 1½-inch mortars (10-lb bombs) sent over some 25 rounds during the day. Large working parties were again employed at night on DRUMMOND'S TRENCH while the usual wiring parties were engaged in front of the line. An aerial reconnaissance made during the afternoon & evening reported that the roads from DOUVRAIN to HAINES (opposite the Battalion front) were packed with ~~troops~~ transport, while South of that some 5000 troops were moving across the open. Our heavy guns at once engaged HAINES.	WCM

T.134. Wt. W708–776. 500000. 4/15. Sir J. C. & S.

Instructions regarding War Diaries and Intelligence Summaries are contained in F. S. Regs., Part II. and the Staff Manual respectively. Title pages will be prepared in manuscript.

WAR DIARY
or
INTELLIGENCE SUMMARY.
(*Erase heading not required.*)

SHEET 139

Army Form C. 2118.

Place	Date	Hour	Summary of Events and Information	Remarks and references to Appendices
(Contd) VERMELLES	May 28		It was also arranged that the 18-prs should fire salvoes at intervals during the night at cross-roads & other points behind the enemy's lines, while all available trench mortars kept up an intermittent fire during the night. The Bde M.G. Coy & Lewis Guns also kept up a steady rate of fire while rifle grenades were fired continuously. Altogether things were made most unpleasant for the Germans.	
F E VERMELLES	May 29th		There was a good deal of hostile artillery retaliation in the early morning. This was on account of 1/2 an hours very heavy Bombardment by our guns at 3.45 am. Throughout the morning the enemy put over some Heavy shells (5.9") in GORDON ALLEY and round Battn Headquarters. Luckily there were no casualties. The 2nd in command Major D MACLEOD DSO had a narrow escape from a shell in GORDON ALLEY and work was temporarily suspended at Battn Headquarters some of the most prominent members of the Battn Staff having to take refuge in a deep dug out near by. Another scare in the shape of information from the RFC stating that 12 Trains had been seen arriving at PROVIN 1200 yards E of HAISNES, also that assembly Trenches had been dug near HULLUCH. In	

T. 2134. Wt. W708-776. 500000. 4/15. Sir J. C. & S.

Instructions regarding War Diaries and Intelligence Summaries are contained in F. S. Regs., Part II. and the Staff Manual respectively. Title pages will be prepared in manuscript.

WAR DIARY
or
INTELLIGENCE SUMMARY.
(Erase heading not required.)

Army Form C. 2118.

Sheet 140

Place	Date	Hour	Summary of Events and Information	Remarks and references to Appendices
VERMELLES	29		Spite of all these alarming signs the demeanour of the Germans opposite us was quite normal – if anything quieter than usual. The Commanding Officer went on leave & handed over command to Major D. MACLEOD DSO.	
Ditto.	30th		A quiet morning as far as Enemy Artillery Fire was concerned. Our Heavies put in a good deal of shooting – a large number of these were blind. The Germans confined themselves mostly to shelling our Batteries. Meanwhile work in the sector is going on apace – DRUMMOND Trench is being improved & first class progress has been made a lot of work has been done on our Front Line particularly in SACKVILLE Street. A large party wired after dark in front of DRUMMOND Trench. The wire was put up in Gap & Triangle System and seems to be a most successful obstacle. 9th Black Watch Officers came up to see the Trenches and were shewn work in hand and details of Defence by the respective company commanders. All details for the Relief on the 31st were satisfactorily arranged and an exhaustive report shewing work on hand together with maps shewing, Garrison, Gas Precautions, SAA & Bomb Stores Lewis Gun positions, telephonic system Etc were handed over to the Officer Comdg 9th Black Watch.	WLr
"	31st		Fine morning. Enemy were quiet. Relief was completed by 10.30 am and	

T.134. Wt. W708–776. 500000. 4/15. Sir J. C. & S.

Instructions regarding War Diaries and Intelligence Summaries are contained in F. S. Regs., Part II. and the Staff Manual respectively. Title pages will be prepared in manuscript.

WAR DIARY
or
INTELLIGENCE SUMMARY.
(Erase heading not required.)

Sheet 141

Army Form C. 2118.

Place	Date	Hour	Summary of Events and Information	Remarks and references to Appendices
VERMELLES	31st		went off without a hitch of any kind. Our position in Brigade Support is also follows. Batt. HQ at Bart's Alley where Railway crosses Trench. A coy Lancashire Trench, B coy 1 platoon Junction Keep, 3 platoons Railway Reserve Trench, C coy Lancashire Trench D coy 1 platoon Junction Keep, 3 platoons Lancashire Trench. On the whole very comfortable quarters after 12 continuous days in the Front Line.	
			During our Tour in this sector which is by common consent to be about the worst place in the whole British front we had the following casualties — Killed 1 Officer 2/Lt AN BAIN, Other ranks 9, Other ranks wounded 31. The names are as follows —. KILLED - Other Ranks: S/1482 Sgt J. Dryburgh, S/4901 Sgt A McAllister, S/12093 Pte J. Bland, S/13232 Pte J Rankin, S/12844 Pte W. Campbell S/7422 Pte A. Hunter, S/8475 Pte T. Simpson, S/10686 Pte W. Milne, S/10573 Pte D. Graham	
			WOUNDED - Other Ranks - S/10433 Sgt A. Leask, S/1703 Sgt J. F. Keir, 9484 Sgt J. Innes, S/6546 Sgt D. Mitchell, S/1550 Sgt J. Cadger, S/4860 L/C. F. Riach, S/3880 L/C. J. Smith, S/10577 L/Cpl J. Davidson, S/13180 L/Cpl J Currier, S/5226 L/Cpl. T. Milne; S/9609 Pte R. Dow, S/9917 Pte W. Brown, S/5793 Pte C. Logan, S/6686 Pte H Walker, S/8772 Pte J. Whitelaw, S/13582 Pte F. Savage, S/10305 Pte R. Gordon, S/8393 Pte G. Forrest, S/11107 Pte Hoyle, S/6881 Pte W. Samuels	WCM

Instructions regarding War Diaries and Intelligence Summaries are contained in F. S. Regs., Part II. and the Staff Manual respectively. Title pages will be prepared in manuscript.

WAR DIARY
or
INTELLIGENCE SUMMARY.
(Erase heading not required.)

Sheet 142

Army Form C. 2118.

Place	Date	Hour	Summary of Events and Information	Remarks and references to Appendices
VERMELLA	31st May		S/4839 Pte. D. Swanson, S/13186 Pte J. Ivison, S/4949 Pte. Wm Gray, S/13404 Pte. Wm Kemp, S/8707 Pte. D. Brown, S/5192 Pte. C. Logan, S/12867 Pte. J. Todd, S/13486 Pte. W. Wade, S/12888 Pte. J. Smith S/13611 Pte. J. Veitch, 3/6626 Pte. A. Hunter.	

T.134. Wt. W708-776. 500000. 4/15. Sir J. C. & S.

Instructions regarding War Diaries and Intelligence Summaries are contained in F. S. Regs., Part II. and the Staff Manual respectively. Title pages will be prepared in manuscript.

WAR DIARY
or
INTELLIGENCE SUMMARY.
(*Erase heading not required.*)

Sheet 143.

Army Form C. 2118.

Place	Date	Hour	Summary of Events and Information	Remarks and references to Appendices
VERMELLE	31st		On arrival in Support Trenches we found that we have to supply daily permanent fatigue parties amounting to about 150 men. In addition to this were were told to provide a working party of 5 officers and 200 men to work from 9.30pm to 2.0am. The work was digging a new Trench 250 yards long (25 bays) a support line to SACKVILLE Street South of HULLUCH alley leading from Highland Trench to CROWN Trench. In spite of the fact of the men being naturally greatly fatigued from 12 days in the front Trenches, they worked with a will and dug down an average of 3'6" with an average depth of 4'6" a very creditable performance. We were unofficially informed that the Brigade and Division were delighted with the good work we had done this Tour. There is no doubt that this praise was well deserved.	WCen
VERMELLE	1st June		Fine day. We supplied a carrying party of 200 to carry up wiring material to the Black Watch. Otherwise there were no fatigues bar the permanent ones mentioned above. Heavy firing was heard in South. Obviously an intense German Bombardment. VIMY Ridge or LOOS probably the centre of this activity.	

T.134. Wt. W708–776. 500000. 4/15. Sir J. C. & S.

CONFIDENTIAL

WAR DIARY

OF

8th/10th (Service) Battn THE GORDON HIGHLANDERS

FROM 1-6-1916 TO 30-6-1916.

SUBJECT: WAR DIARY.

D. A. G.

BASE.

Herewith my WAR DIARY for period 1st June to 30th June, 1916.

Please acknowledge receipt.

H. P. Bully

Lt. Colonel,

Comdg 8/10th (Service) Battn

The Gordon Highrs

75/53.
4/7/16.

8/10 Gordons
Vol 13
June

Instructions regarding War Diaries and Intelligence Summaries are contained in F. S. Regs., Part II. and the Staff Manual respectively. Title pages will be prepared in manuscript.

WAR DIARY
or
INTELLIGENCE SUMMARY.
(Erase heading not required.)

Army Form C. 2118.

Sheet 144.

Place	Date	Hour	Summary of Events and Information	Remarks and references to Appendices
(Continued)			It afterwards transpired that the firing heard was an abortive effort on our part to carry out a Raid on a large scale assisted by mines. During the night 1/2nd June, a good deal of heavy firing an Trench mortaring was heard from direction of CUINCHY.	
VERMELLES	1st June		This day. No incident of note occurred. We supplied a large working party wiring &	
"	2nd June.		carrying on with the work started by us on the 31st on the new Support Line to SACKVILLE Street (SPURN Head). Good progress was made in spite of the heavy machine gun fire the working party were subjected to. The party worked from 9pm to 2 am and were under supervision of Captain Martin. The wiring was in Triangular System as done in front of DRUMMOND Trench.	
"	3rd June		No incidents of note during forenoon. In afternoon the Brigade on our Right was heavily shelled with 5.9" & 8" shells to such an extent that we received message from Brigade to be ready for eventualities. All was quiet by 8pm. We again found large working parties, for SPURN Head & improving and deepening of SAVILLE ROW. At about 7.30pm we received Wireless news of the Great Naval Battle off JUTLAND, which reads most disastrously for us. Preparations were made for the Relief on June 4th and we were informed that the 10th Scottish Rifles would relieve us and that we were to go into rest Headquarters & 2 Coys at VERQUINEUL with other Two Coys at ANNEQUIN — a most inconvenient arrangements in view of the fact that ANNEQUIN is at least 4 miles from VERQUINEUL.	HPK

T.134. Wt. W708–776. 500000. 4/15. Sir J. C. & S.

Instructions regarding War Diaries and Intelligence Summaries are contained in F. S. Regs., Part II. and the Staff Manual respectively. Title pages will be prepared in manuscript.

WAR DIARY
or
INTELLIGENCE SUMMARY.
(Erase heading not required.)

Army Form C. 2118.

Sheet 145.

Place	Date	Hour	Summary of Events and Information	Remarks and references to Appendices
VERMELLES	4th June.		Fine day as usual. Strong wind from the West. We were duly relieved at about 1pm and reached respective billets at 2.30pm, all arrangements going off without hitch of any kind. C&D Coys were at VERQUINEUL and A&B at ANNEQUIN under Detachment Command of CAPTAIN A.M. DRUMMOND. Billets at both these places leave much to be desired, and a good deal of trouble was experienced at VERQUINEUL in getting Officers' billets as we found a very large number of Departmental Officers billetted here, and in possession of the best billets.	
VERQUINEUL & ANNEQUIN	5th June.		Detail of working parties required during rest also a scale of parades during rest, were received from 44th Brigade. Working parties have now been changed three times greatly to inconvenience of Battns. We find only 140 men per diem, most of these go by Bus. Other work in billets during Rest comprises, Steady Drill, Assault Course, Gas Helmet Drill Rapid Loading, Lewis Gun Training Squads, Practice Bombing Squads, Sergt Sitters Class (16 NCOs & 1 officer). At the same time the following classes assembled under Brigade and Divisional arrangements, Engineering Class which 2/Lt Brooke & 8 NCO' attended, Gas Course which 2/Lt Milne & 3 NCOS attended, Bombing Course for Trained Bombers attended by 2/Lt Geddes and 16 other ranks, also Two Officers at Officers Training School 2/Lts JACKSON & Smith. The Commanding Officer & Adjutant visited ANNEQUIN during forenoon & inspected billets there.	HPR

T.134. Wt. W708-776. 500000. 4/15. Sir J. C. & S.

Instructions regarding War Diaries and Intelligence Summaries are contained in F. S. Regs., Part II. and the Staff Manual respectively. Title pages will be prepared in manuscript.

WAR DIARY
or
INTELLIGENCE SUMMARY. Sheet 146

(Erase heading not required.)

Army Form C. 2118.

Place	Date	Hour	Summary of Events and Information	Remarks and references to Appendices
VERGUINEUL	June 6th		A very wet day. Much inconvenience was caused by non arrival of buses for working parties; eventually parties went off though very late. The Battn was paid out today. Pipe Band played Retreat at ANNEQUIN. They played retreat in VERQUINEUL on the 5th. They are now a very smart & good Pipe Band.	
VERQUINEUL	June 7th		Inspection of Transport by Commanding Officer. Turnout of beasts and harness was very good although many animals still show signs of neglect in grooming and feeding, but there is even now a vast difference from the state they were taken over. Persistent rumours during forenoon of the Drowning of LORD KITCHENER were confirmed in the afternoon much to the consternation of all ranks. C&D Coys & HQrs Bathed at Div. Baths in afternoon	
	June 8th		Commanding Officer inspected in full marching order A. B & Headquarters. Turnout of A was decidedly bad, greatly contrasting with B Coy who were quite faultlessly turned out and reflected great credit in view of the fact that large working parties were found from this Coy on 7th. Headquarters inspection was also very satisfactory especially the Pipe Band. A&B Coys bathed at ANNEQUIN. There is a bath in the mine – unfortunately in a part which is shelled almost daily – but hot water can be obtained and about 200 men bathed in a day. No change of shirts or socks are provided, but we arrange to	

T.134. Wt. W708-776. 500000. 4/15. Sir J. C. & S.

H.P.B.

Instructions regarding War Diaries and Intelligence Summaries are contained in F. S. Regs., Part II. and the Staff Manual respectively. Title pages will be prepared in manuscript.

WAR DIARY
or
INTELLIGENCE SUMMARY.
(Erase heading not required.)

Army Form C. 2118.

Sheet 147.

Place	Date	Hour	Summary of Events and Information	Remarks and references to Appendices
VERQUINEUL	June 8th (Contd)		have these sent over under Battn arrangements. Message came in to the effect that unusual train activity from Lille towards LENS had been noticed. This message following on the numerous other messages we have received lately to the same effect, and in accordance with the statements of Deserters, all points to a German Offensive on a large scale being directed against the LOOS SALIENT.	
VERQUINEUL	June 9th		C.O inspected C & D coys in marching order at 2pm & 2.30pm respectively. C coys turn out was highly creditable though not so good as B coy but much better than A coy. This a very fine company – good NCOs etc. D coy's turnout was very bad and evidently no trouble had been taken to have a good turnout. Consequently this company was ordered to parade again on the 11th for another inspection. Weather fine though it is still fairly cold & showers of rain keep hanging about. A accident which might easily have proved fatal occurred in B coy today. Two men Ptes RAFFIN and HARLEY who were being instructed in LEWIS GUN by L/Cpl Macdonald were shot by a bullet from the Gun they were being instructed in. Apparently L/Cpl Macdonald was illustrating a fault with a live round and inadvertently let off the Gun. Both men were only very slightly wounded, but as stated above might easily have been killed owing to this L^ce^ Corpls carelessness, which is all the more	HPB

T2134. Wt. W708–776. 500000. 4/15. Sir J. C. & S.

Instructions regarding War Diaries and Intelligence Summaries are contained in F. S. Regs., Part II. and the Staff Manual respectively. Title pages will be prepared in manuscript.

WAR DIARY
or
INTELLIGENCE SUMMARY.
(Erase heading not required.)

Sheet 148

Army Form C. 2118.

Place	Date	Hour	Summary of Events and Information	Remarks and references to Appendices
VERQUINEUL	June 9th		Culpable in view of the fact that CAPTAIN LAMBIE had previously warned him not on any account to use live rounds.	
VERQUINEUL	June 10th		No incident of note during day.	
VERQUINEUL	June 11th		Commanding Officer inspected D Coy again. Result still unsatisfactory. CO & Adjt Company commanders visited Trenches in afternoon. We are to take over from 6th CAMERON Highlanders in left subsection, HULLUCH sector. We found Trenches in a most disgraceful condition. Clear evidence of gross idleness and inefficiency on the part of Battns who have recently occupied this subsection. The CAMERON Battn was very weak – averaging only 60 Rifles per Coy and taking this into consideration and the fact that we are still a strong battn we decided to hold Front Trenches with 2 coys (finding their own supports) instead of three, with one Coy in Support in OG 1. We received permission from the Brigade to have the other Coy in Reserve in OB I. Trenches were very wet after recent heavy rain. The Commanding Officer returned from leave at 7. pm.	
VERQUINEUL	June 12th		A Company of 11th Kings Own Royal Lancs Regt (Bantams) joined us at 9.30 am ~~One platoon was sent to each Company.~~ for 4 days instruction in the trenches. JRR	

T2134. Wt. W708–776. 500000. 4/15. Sir J. C. & S.

Instructions regarding War Diaries and Intelligence Summaries are contained in F. S. Regs., Part II. and the Staff Manual respectively. Title pages will be prepared in manuscript.

WAR DIARY
or
INTELLIGENCE SUMMARY.
(*Erase heading not required.*)

Sheet 149.

Army Form C. 2118.

Place	Date	Hour	Summary of Events and Information	Remarks and references to Appendices
VERQUINEUL.	June 12th		one platoon was allotted to each Coy & the men were further split up amongst our platoons. The Battn marched to the trenches at 11.15 am & relieved the 6th Cameron Highlanders, 45th Bde, in the left Sub-Section, HULLUCH Section. The relief was complete at 3.0 pm. The trenches were, as already stated, in a very poor state of repair & it was apparent that little or no work had been done on them for many weeks. The bombs were not collected in stores as should have been the case but were lying about everywhere. Many of them were rusty & unfit for use. Many rifles & much material of all kinds was left lying about. There was scarcely a signboard to show the names of the trenches in the whole line & it was impossible to find one's way about. Shortly after the relief the Germans sent over several large trench-mortar bombs (rumjars) but these did no damage. A mining officer reported that the Germans were working on six galleries coming towards our front line & that it was too late for our	HPB

T2134. Wt. W708—776. 500000. 4/15. Sir J. C. & S.

Instructions regarding War Diaries and Intelligence Summaries are contained in F. S. Regs., Part II. and the Staff Manual respectively. Title pages will be prepared in manuscript.

WAR DIARY
or
INTELLIGENCE SUMMARY.
(Erase heading not required.)

Sheet 150.

Army Form C. 2118.

Place	Date	Hour	Summary of Events and Information	Remarks and references to Appendices
VERQUINEUL	Jun 12th (contd)		miners to arrest their progress. Accordingly the garrison of the front trenches was reduced to a minimum, the left of the line to a distance of 300 yds. being held by 2 posts of 6 men each by day & 3 posts by night. At night the German sent over some aerial torpedoes & more heavy trench mortar bombs together with rifle grenades. No trench stores had been left behind by the Battn we relieved & the advanced R.E. dump was unable to provide more than a very limited quantity of wire, sandbags or pickets. There were scarcely any intrenching tools in the lines. Very wet & cold all day. No casualties.	
AULLUCH.	June 13th		Again very wet & cold & trenches flooded being nearly knee-deep in water in places. German were active with heavy trench mortars & aerial torpedoes between 9.30 & 10.30 am. We replied heavily with our 2-inch mortars (60-lbers) & STOKES guns (11 lbers). Finally the Germans sent over 3 salvoes of	JHPR

T2134. Wt. W708—776. 500000. 4/15. Sir J. C. & S.

Instructions regarding War Diaries and Intelligence Summaries are contained in F. S. Regs., Part II. and the Staff Manual respectively. Title pages will be prepared in manuscript.

WAR DIARY
or
INTELLIGENCE SUMMARY.
(Erase heading not required.)

Sheet 151.

Army Form C. 2118.

Place	Date	Hour	Summary of Events and Information	Remarks and references to Appendices
HULLUCH.	June 13th (contd)		'77 cent. & one salvo of 4.2 howitzers which ended the affair. The German mortars again became active at 12 noon & we again replied. Good work was done by us in the construction & repair of firesteps which was very necessary while a considerable amount of wire was put out in front at night. Work was commenced on a new battle Battalion H.Q. dugout ~~etc~~ & on a new defensive emplacement for the 2-inch trench mortars. The Brigadier visited the Battalion's trenches at 7.30 am & afterwards visited Battalion H.Q. At 5.0 pm it was reported that all telephone wires to the artillery covering the Battalion front were broken & a report was forwarded to Bde H.Q. to this effect. Not till 9 pm the following night was communication re-established with the artillery, & then only with one Battery. A quiet night except for a few salvoes of bombs which were thrown at one of our	HPR

T2134. Wt. W708—776. 500000. 4/15. Sir J. C. & S.

Instructions regarding War Diaries and Intelligence Summaries are contained in F. S. Regs., Part II. and the Staff Manual respectively. Title pages will be prepared in manuscript.

WAR DIARY
or
INTELLIGENCE SUMMARY.
(Erase heading not required.)

Sheet 152.

Army Form C. 2118.

Place	Date	Hour	Summary of Events and Information	Remarks and references to Appendices
HULLUCH.	June 13th (contd)		wiring parties:- Casualties NIL. Russians reported to have captured 114,000 prisoners in GALICIA.	
	June 14th		Again very wet & cold in the morning but it cleared up later. Some slight shelling by the Germans but only a little material damage done. At 7.0 pm the Germans fired a small mine in front of our trenches at SEAFORTH crater but did no damage beyond a little material damage to a sap-head – no casualties. At dusk a new BOYAU (communication trench) between the front line & QUARRY BAY was marked out & work was commenced on it with 64 men. It was dug to a depth of 3 feet throughout its length of about 120 yards. Two men were wounded by machine gun fire at the Batt. ration dump about a mile behind the front line. At night good progress was made with the wiring of the front, some 40 knife-rests & 40 coils of barbed wire being put out. A patrol discovered a large German wiring party which was later dispersed	

T2134. Wt. W708—776. 500000. 4/15. Sir J. C. & S.

Instructions regarding War Diaries and Intelligence Summaries are contained in F. S. Regs., Part II. and the Staff Manual respectively. Title pages will be prepared in manuscript.

WAR DIARY
or
INTELLIGENCE SUMMARY.
(Erase heading not required.)

Sheet 153.

Army Form C. 2118.

Place	Date	Hour	Summary of Events and Information	Remarks and references to Appendices
HULLUCH	June 14th (contd)		by Lewis Gun fire. Another German wiring party was reported to one of our Lewis Guns by some men of the Black Watch. The Gun opened on them & cries & groans were heard.	
"	June 15th		A fine day but still very cold. It is hoped that this wintry weather will destroy the German crops. The Germans bombed our Sap-heads in the morning but caused no casualties. This was brought about by our snipers who accounted for 2 Germans from one of these Sap-heads, & by a Serjeant (Sgt McCue) who accounted for 2 others. One of these Germans is believed to have been an officer. The day was then quiet till 6 pm when the Germans put some 50 6-inch howitzer shells into the vicinity of Battn H.Q. & the reserve line. No damage done although all shells burst with a terrific explosion. We replied to this bombardment with a few light shells from field-guns. At 8 pm we exploded a small mine between LOOKOUT ~~&~~ CRATER & BEN NEVIS. The mine contained 2000 lbs of explosive. On the mine going up our 18-prs	

Instructions regarding War Diaries and Intelligence Summaries are contained in F. S. Regs., Part II. and the Staff Manual respectively. Title pages will be prepared in manuscript.

WAR DIARY
or
INTELLIGENCE SUMMARY.
(Erase heading not required.)

Sheet 154.

Army Form C. 2118.

Place	Date	Hour	Summary of Events and Information	Remarks and references to Appendices
HULLUCH	June 15th (contd.)		Enfiladed the German front line with Shrapnel to catch any of the enemy who might be running away from the mine. Our snipers were also on the lookout for any Germans who, through curiosity, might look over the parapet. They got no opportunities however. A quiet night. Some good patrol work was done & one patrol narrowly missed capturing 2 Germans. This was unfortunate as a prisoner is badly wanted for identification purposes. A German wiring party was dispersed by Lewis gun fire. We had several men, including 5 of the 11th King's own Regt. who are attached to us for instruction, slightly wounded by German shells.	
"	June 16th		The coy of the 11th King's own Regt which had been attached to us left for rest billets & was replaced by a coy of the 13th East Surrey Regiment, one platoon of the latter being attached to each of our Coys. The German 6-inch howitzers put over about 20 rounds between 5 & 6 pm but those that fell in our area did no damage. "C" & "D" Coys relieved "A" & "B" Coys in the trenches. At 7 pm the	JPE

Instructions regarding War Diaries and Intelligence Summaries are contained in F. S. Regs., Part II. and the Staff Manual respectively. Title pages will be prepared in manuscript.

WAR DIARY
or
INTELLIGENCE SUMMARY.
(*Erase heading not required.*)

Sheet 155.

Army Form C. 2118.

Place	Date	Hour	Summary of Events and Information	Remarks and references to Appendices
	1916.			
HULLUCH.	June 16th (Contd.)		Germans exploded a mine just on the left of the Battalion front. Two men of the Scottish Rifles were wounded by the mine. Some slight shelling followed the explosion of the mine. Very good work was done by the Battalion in the trenches, especially as regards drainage. A gas wind was blowing in the afternoon & evening & the usual precautions against gas attack were taken. A telegram was received to the effect that the Russian captures in GALICIA had reached 2500 officers, 150,000 other ranks, 163 guns & 266 machine guns. A fine day but still cold. Several patrols went out at night to try & capture a German for identification purposes. Pte Moore, who volunteered for this duty although his Coy was not in the front line, was unfortunately killed on patrol, while his comrade, Pte Hunter, also a volunteer, was wounded. German machine guns rather more active than usual at night. Further wire was put out on the Battalion front.	
"	June 17th		Fine but cold. An East wind still blowing but it is rather too strong	HPB

T2134. Wt. W708—776. 500000. 4/15. Sir J. C. & S.

Instructions regarding War Diaries and Intelligence Summaries are contained in F. S. Regs., Part II. and the Staff Manual respectively. Title pages will be prepared in manuscript.

WAR DIARY
or
INTELLIGENCE SUMMARY.
(Erase heading not required.)

Sheet 156.

Army Form C. 2118.

Place	Date	Hour	Summary of Events and Information	Remarks and references to Appendices
HULLUCH	June 17th (contd)		for a successful hostile gas attack. It calmed down somewhat in the evening. We harried the German trenches all the morning with rifle grenades, some 60 of these being fired. Many direct hits were obtained. At 3 pm we exploded 2 mines in the HAIRPIN craters ¼ mile North of the Battn front. We had 5 Lewis Guns & all the Battn snipers in position to pick off any of the enemy whose curiosity might lead them to look over the parapet to see the result of the mine. Several heads appeared & each Lewis Gun fired a drum of ammunition. At 4 pm the Germans commenced to bombard our trenches heavily with minenwerfer, heavy trench mortars & rifle grenades. His field guns joined in later. In all he fired about 20 minenwerfer & 160 mortar bombs. We retaliated with 30 2-inch (60-lb) trench mortar bombs. We asked for retaliation by the howitzers but they did not fire. The 18-prs sent over some shells. At 5 pm all was quiet. We were fortunate in not having more casualties. Much good work was done in the trenches. At night very	HPR

T2134. Wt. W708—776. 500000. 4/15. Sir J. C. & S.

Instructions regarding War Diaries and Intelligence Summaries are contained in F. S. Regs., Part II. and the Staff Manual respectively. Title pages will be prepared in manuscript.

WAR DIARY
or
INTELLIGENCE SUMMARY.
(Erase heading not required.)

Army Form C. 2118.

Sheet - 157.

Place	Date	Hour	Summary of Events and Information	Remarks and references to Appendices
HULLUCH	17 June (contd)		large fatigue parties were found from the Battalion to carry up gas cylinders to the front trenches a little to the right of our front. All men were cautioned not on any account to talk of this or of any impending operation. Large fatigue parties were also found as usual for the R.E. & for the Tunnelling Coys. A quiet night.	
"	18 June.		A quiet morning till about 12 noon when the enemy bombarded our lines with minenwerfer & trench mortars together with aerial darts & rifle grenades. We called for retaliation from the howitzers & eventually got 10 shells of which 8 failed to explode. The 18-prs also sent over a few salvoes. The German mortars were active again in the afternoon. Our 2-inch mortars fired some 15 or 20 rounds during the day. Some very good work was put in by our Coys in the front line as regards the general upkeep & repair of trenches. At night we found large parties again to carry up gas cylinders to the trenches of the Batt on our right. (The Black Watch. 9th Batt.). The usual R.E. & mining fatigues were also found. The wind continued from the N.E. the	JHB

T2134. Wt. W708—776. 500000. 4/15. Sir J. C. & S.

Instructions regarding War Diaries and Intelligence Summaries are contained in F. S. Regs., Part II. and the Staff Manual respectively. Title pages will be prepared in manuscript.

WAR DIARY
or
INTELLIGENCE SUMMARY.
(*Erase heading not required.*)

Army Form C. 2118.

Sheet 158.

Place	Date	Hour	Summary of Events and Information	Remarks and references to Appendices
HULLUCH	18 June (contd.)		being favourable for a hostile gas attack. The usual precautions against gas were taken. A quiet night.	
"	19 June		Dull morning. Wind very light N.W. changing later to N.E. In the evening it was very favourable for a hostile gas attack. The German minenwerfer & mortars showed great activity all day, bombarding our trenches at 2 pm, 4 pm & 9 pm besides a few rounds in the morning. On each occasion the enemy fired rifle grenades as well as aerial darts. Our 2-inch mortars (60-lbers) retaliated vigorously, as did the STOKES guns, the former firing 61 rounds & the latter 59 rounds. We called for fire from our howitzers on two occasions but we only got 4 rounds all told & all of these were "blinds". The 18-prs sent over some shells. Excellent work was done in the trenches by "C" & "D" coys as regards the construction of parapets & traverses & the deepening of the trenches. A large party cleared CHAPEL ALLEY in the afternoon. At night 1 officer, 8 NCOs & 64 men carried gas cylinders up to the trenches of the Battalion on our right while other parties worked	

T2134. Wt. W708—776. 500000. 4/15. Sir J. C. & S.

Instructions regarding War Diaries and Intelligence Summaries are contained in F. S. Regs., Part II. and the Staff Manual respectively. Title pages will be prepared in manuscript.

WAR DIARY
or
INTELLIGENCE SUMMARY.
(Erase heading not required.)

Sheet 159.

Army Form C. 2118.

Place	Date	Hour	Summary of Events and Information	Remarks and references to Appendices
HULLUCH.	~~July~~ June 19th (contd)		under the R.E. & miners. At 2 pm the Germans sprang a small mine in the craters on our front. No damage was done to us & we suffered no casualties from the mine. None of our mine galleries were in any way damaged. At 7 pm we exploded a mine at the HAIRPIN CRATERS, ½ mile N. of our trenches. The explosion was followed by considerable trench mortar & rifle grenade fire on our part & the 18-prs joined in to catch any "runners".	
"	June ~~19th~~ 20th		A fine day. light W. wind. The Battalion was relieved in the trenches by the 8th Seaforth Highlanders, the relief being over by 12 noon. The Battalion moved into Bde support with H.Q. in CURLEY CRESCENT. "A" coy in O.B.5", "B" coy in O.B.4 & O.B.5, "C" coy in 10th Avenue & "D" coy in 10th Avenue & LONE TREE REDOUBT. At night very large working parties were found by the Battalion aggregating some 550 men. Of these 150 were told off to dig a new support trench between HAY ALLEY & SEVENTH AVENUE. A coy of the 11th K.O. Royal Lancaster Regt joined the Battalion for instructional purposes. They assisted to find the	

T2134. Wt. W708—776. 500000. 4/15. Sir J. C. & S.

Instructions regarding War Diaries and Intelligence Summaries are contained in F. S. Regs., Part II. and the Staff Manual respectively. Title pages will be prepared in manuscript.

WAR DIARY
or
INTELLIGENCE SUMMARY.
(Erase heading not required.)

Sheet 160 -

Army Form C. 2118.

Place	Date	Hour	Summary of Events and Information	Remarks and references to Appendices
HULLUCH.	~~July~~ June	20th (contd.)	fatigue parties required. At 10.30 pm a heavy bombardment was heard about 8 miles to the North. This lasted for about 45 minutes.	
"	~~July~~ June	21st	A fine day. Wind light W. The Battalion spent the day resting. At night some 550 men were again found for various fatigues, including 150 to dig the support trench commenced on the previous night. At 9pm we fired a fairly large mine at ANCHOR SAP, near the HOHENZOLLERN REDOUBT. Much trench-mortaring, bombing & artillery fire followed the explosion of the mine. During the afternoon Lieut. Colonel J.K. DICK CUNYNGHAME D.S.O. G.S.O.2 1st Corps, & Major L. CARR, D.S.O. Bde Major 45th Bde, 15th Div, both of the 2nd Gordon Hrs, visited Battn. H.Q. During the day another small mine had been sprung, this time by the enemy, in the sector we had just left. It resulted in 3 miners being killed & 2 wounded.	
"	~~July~~ June	22nd	A fine day. Wind light S.W. at first changing later to S.E. At 8.30 am a German aeroplane, a FOKKER, brought down one of our machines near	HPB

T2134. Wt. W708—776. 500000. 4/15. Sir J. C. & S.

Instructions regarding War Diaries and Intelligence Summaries are contained in F. S. Regs., Part II. and the Staff Manual respectively. Title pages will be prepared in manuscript.

WAR DIARY
or
INTELLIGENCE SUMMARY.
(Erase heading not required.)

Sheet 161

Army Form C. 2118.

Place	Date	Hour	Summary of Events and Information	Remarks and references to Appendices
HULLUCH	~~July~~ June 22nd (contd)		the HOHENZOLLERN REDOUBT after a fight in which the advantage of speed was all with the enemy. The usual artillery fire continued at intervals throughout the day – our 60-lbrs being active. At night the Battalion found the usual working & carrying parties, a total of over 500 men in all being employed. The attached Coy of 11th Kings Own Royal Lancaster Regt helped to find these. The Brigadier held a Conference of Commanding officers at Battalion H.Q. to arrange details of coming events.	
"	~~July~~ June 23rd		Battn still in Bde Support. Fine morning with light W. wind. Heavy thunderstorm in afternoon & rain at night. A quiet day. Secret orders received that the gas on the Bde front would be discharged at the first favourable opportunity from night of 24/25th June inclusive. Orders were also received for each discharge of gas to be followed by a strong patrol to deal with any of the enemy found gassed in their front trenches or dugouts. We were also notified that our 18-prs wd commence cutting the enemy's wire at intervals throughout the	JHPB

T2134. Wt. W708–776. 500000. 4/15. Sir J. C. & S.

Army Form C. 2118.

Instructions regarding War Diaries and Intelligence Summaries are contained in F. S. Regs., Part II. and the Staff Manual respectively. Title pages will be prepared in manuscript.

WAR DIARY
or
INTELLIGENCE SUMMARY.
(Erase heading not required.)

Sheet 162.

Place	Date	Hour	Summary of Events and Information	Remarks and references to Appendices
HULLUCH.	June 23rd (contd)		Divisional front at 3 pm on the following day. Much aeroplane activity again on our ~~front~~ side. No hostile machines seen. A Coy of 13th East Surrey Regt arrived to be attached to the Battalion for 3 days, vice the coy of 11th King's Own Royal Lancaster Regt (Bantams) which left for reserve billets.	
"	June 24th		The Battn relieved 9th Black Watch in Centre Sub-section, HULLUCH Section. Much rain & trenches full of mud & water. Trenches better than those recently experienced but much work is required on them. The absence of sign boards makes it very difficult to find ones way about. Bomb stores are required in suitable places near entrances to C.Ts & the lack of dug-outs must have been responsible for many un-necessary casualties. The line was held by "A" & "B" Coys with 2 ~~coys~~ platoons East Surreys attached. C & D Coys & 2 ~~c~~ platoons E. Surreys were in reserve. Battalion HQ in 9th Avenue. Our guns, chiefly 18-prs, kept up an intermittent fire on the hostile trenches & ground in rear all through the day & night. It was thought that if our artillery were heavier better results	JHPB

T2134. Wt. W708—776. 500000. 4/15. Sir J. C. & S.

Instructions regarding War Diaries and Intelligence Summaries are contained in F. S. Regs., Part II. and the Staff Manual respectively. Title pages will be prepared in manuscript.

WAR DIARY
or
INTELLIGENCE SUMMARY.
(Erase heading not required.)

Army Form C. 2118.

Sheet 163.

Place	Date	Hour	Summary of Events and Information	Remarks and references to Appendices
HULLUCH.	June 24th (contd)		would accrue. German artillery not very active although his 6-inch howitzers fired 12 or 15 rounds in the evening registering various points. Our 60-lbers were active most of the day. Orders were received re the operations of the next few days. If the wind remains favourable the gas on the Battalion front, in common with that all along the line, will be released at 1 am on 26th inst. From 1.0 am to 1.10 am only gas will be released, bursts of Machine Gun fire drowning the noise of the cylinders. From 1.10 am to 1.15 am Smoke Candles will be lit, the smoke & gas being mixed. From 1.15 am to 1.25 am smoke only will be sent over, this time from Smoke bombs. At 1.45 am a raiding party of 3 officers & 70 men will follow in the footsteps of the gas to kill any Germans who may be left alive in their trenches & to destroy or remove all weapons & material found. Wire cutters of various kinds were got together for use against the German wire & to cut a way out through our own. The 70 men selected for the raid were divided into 7 squads of 1 NCO & 10 men each. As regards	

T2134. Wt. W708—776. 500000. 4/15. Sir J. C. & S.

Instructions regarding War Diaries and Intelligence Summaries are contained in F. S. Regs., Part II. and the Staff Manual respectively. Title pages will be prepared in manuscript.

WAR DIARY
or
INTELLIGENCE SUMMARY.
(Erase heading not required.)

Army Form C. 2118.

Sheet 163.

Place	Date	Hour	Summary of Events and Information	Remarks and references to Appendices
HULLUCH.	June 24th (contd)		would accrue. German artillery not very active although his 6-inch howitzers fired 12 or 15 rounds in the evening registering various points. Our 60-lbers were active most of the day. Orders were received re the operations of the next few days. If the wind remains favourable the gas on the Battalion front, in common with that all along the line, will be released at 1 am on 26th inst. From 1.0 am to 1.10 am only gas will be released, bursts of Machine Gun fire drowning the noise of the cylinders. From 1.10 am to 1.15 am Smoke Candles will be lit, the smoke & gas being mixed. From 1.15 am to 1.25 am smoke only will be sent over, this time from smoke bombs. At 1.45 am a raiding party of 3 officers & 70 men will follow in the footsteps of the gas to kill any Germans who may be left alive in their trenches & to destroy or remove all weapons & material found. Wire cutters of various kinds were got together for use against the German wire & to cut a way out through our own. The 70 men selected for the raid were divided into 7 squads of 1 NCO & 10 men each. As regards	

T2134. Wt. W708—776. 500000. 4/15. Sir J. C. & S.

Instructions regarding War Diaries and Intelligence Summaries are contained in F. S. Regs., Part II. and the Staff Manual respectively. Title pages will be prepared in manuscript.

WAR DIARY
or
INTELLIGENCE SUMMARY.
(Erase heading not required.)

Sheet 162.

Army Form C. 2118.

Place	Date	Hour	Summary of Events and Information	Remarks and references to Appendices
HULLUCH.	June 23rd (contd)		Divisional front at 3 pm on the following day. Much aeroplane activity again on our ~~front~~ side. No hostile machines seen. A Coy of 13th East Surrey Regt arrived to be attached to the Battalion for 3 days, vice the Coy of 11th Kings' own Royal Lancaster Regt (Bantams) which left for reserve billets.	
"	June 24th		The Battn relieved 9th Black Watch in centre sub-section, HULLUCH section. Much rain & trenches full of mud & water. Trenches better than those recently experienced but much work is required on them. The absence of sign boards makes it very difficult to find ones way about. Bomb stores are required in suitable places near entrances to C.T.s & the lack of dug-outs must have been responsible for many un-necessary casualties. The line was held by "A" & "B" Coys with 2 ~~coys~~ platoons East Surreys attached. C & D Coys & 2 ~~a~~ platoons E. Surreys were in reserve. Battalion HQ in 9th Avenue. Our guns, chiefly 18-prs, kept up an intermittent fire on the hostile trenches & ground in rear all through the day & night. It was thought that if our artillery were heavier better results	HPB

T2134. Wt. W708—776. 500000. 4/15. Sir J. C. & S.

Instructions regarding War Diaries and Intelligence Summaries are contained in F. S. Regs., Part II. and the Staff Manual respectively. Title pages will be prepared in manuscript.

WAR DIARY
or
INTELLIGENCE SUMMARY.
(Erase heading not required.)

Sheet 164.

Army Form C. 2118.

Place	Date	Hour	Summary of Events and Information	Remarks and references to Appendices
HULLUCH	June 24th (contd)		artillery fire for the night operations it was arranged that from 1.0 am to 1.10 am no firing would take place. From 1.10 am to 1.20 am the fire would be intense. From 1.20 am to 1.40 am the fire would be slow. 1.40 am to 1.50 am, form barrage round raiding parties. It will thus be seen that no warning whatever will be given to the enemy of the gas attack. The gas is said to kill instantly. Wind light westerly.	
"	June 25th		a fine day. Wind again light westerly. Much aeroplane activity, two German machines making an intricate reconnaissance of our lines at a low altitude. Many of our machines about but none to drive off the Germans. Our 18-prs active all day. German guns quiet till about 9.30 pm when they turned a 5.9 in howitzer, a battery of 4.2 howitzers & some field guns onto the trenches of the 7th Cameron Highlanders on our immediate right. At 11.30 pm a wire was received in code to the effect that the gas would not be released this night, the wind not being altogether	

T2134. Wt. W708—776. 500000. 4/15. Sir J. C. & S.

Instructions regarding War Diaries and Intelligence Summaries are contained in F. S. Regs., Part II. and the Staff Manual respectively. Title pages will be prepared in manuscript.

WAR DIARY
or
INTELLIGENCE SUMMARY.
(*Erase heading not required.*)

Army Form C. 2118.

Sheet 165.

Place	Date	Hour	Summary of Events and Information	Remarks and references to Appendices
HULLUCH	June 25th (Contd)		favourable. German sent over a few aerial darts at 12 midnight.	
"	June 26th		Wet day. Wind westerly but changeable. Our 60-pdrs (5-inch guns) & 18-pdrs active. The 12-inch howitzers put over some rounds, their target being a supposed telephone exchange in St. ELIE. Shells burst fairly well. Our 60-lb mortars (2-inch) were active during the day & drew retaliation from the German mortars. DUDLEY TRENCH, DEVON LANE & H.L.I. trench were all damaged in places by mortar bombs. Some wire-cutting was done by the 60-lb mortars & 18-pdrs opposite our front prior to a raid which was carried out by the Black Watch (9th Battn) at night. This wire-cutting was not entirely successful. The gas-attack was again cancelled, this time at 11 pm, the wind not being favourable. Some good work was done in our trenches especially by the Battn pioneers who made considerable progress with a deep dugout they were constructing.	
"	June 27th (Contd)		At 3.15 am the 9th Black Watch carried out a raid on a salient in	

Instructions regarding War Diaries and Intelligence Summaries are contained in F. S. Regs., Part II. and the Staff Manual respectively. Title pages will be prepared in manuscript.

WAR DIARY
or
INTELLIGENCE SUMMARY.
(Erase heading not required.)

Army Form C. 2118.

Sheet 166.

Place	Date	Hour	Summary of Events and Information	Remarks and references to Appendices
HULLUCH	June 27th (contd)		the German line opposite our left front where hostile mine shafts were suspected. This raid was carried out by the Black Watch since they were the Battalion we relieved in the trenches & all arrangements for the raid had been made before we came in. At 3 am a bombardment of the German lines commenced by guns & trench mortars. Very few howitzers or heavy guns however took part, these having been withdrawn farther South. The bombardment was not confined to our front but was kept up throughout the Divisional area. At 3.15 am the Black Watch attacked but from the first they were held up by the German wire. Eventually they withdrew having bombed the German trenches. They suffered 15 casualties, all wounded, but only two seriously. It is probable that the German suffered more than this since our bombardment was fairly heavy & the STOKES Guns alone on the Brigade front fired 583 bombs. The 2-inch mortars were also very active. The German artillery was notably silent - this a most unusual phenomenon. Possibly they were saving up their	

T2134. Wt. W708—776. 500000. 4/15. Sir J. C. & S.

Instructions regarding War Diaries and Intelligence Summaries are contained in F. S. Regs., Part II. and the Staff Manual respectively. Title pages will be prepared in manuscript.

WAR DIARY
or
INTELLIGENCE SUMMARY.
(Erase heading not required.)

Sheet 167.

Army Form C. 2118.

Place	Date	Hour	Summary of Events and Information	Remarks and references to Appendices
HULLUCH	June 27th (cont.)		ammunition for larger operations which they may be suspecting on our part. Intermittent artillery fire during the day. The German guns still very quiet however. Wind light Westerly & up to 10 pm it seemed most suitable for the twice postponed gas attack. A message in code was received from Brigade H.Q. to the effect that the gas would probably be released at 1 am. All preparations were made by the Special Coy of Royal Engineers in charge of the cylinders & by the Battalion as regards the discharge of smoke which was to accompany the gas. The wind continued to be favourable for the gas attack although it calmed down somewhat as the night went on. However at 1 am the gas was released & at 1.10 am smoke was mixed with it, the smoke continuing till 1.25 am to conceal the fact that the gas had stopped & generally to confuse & mislead the enemy. A full account of the raid will be found in Appendix "A". After the raid No. S/9229 Pte DANIEL MARSHALL & No. 3/6641 L/Cpl DOUGLAS HOOPS distinguished themselves by carrying in several wounded men	Appendix

Instructions regarding War Diaries and Intelligence Summaries are contained in F. S. Regs., Part II. and the Staff Manual respectively. Title pages will be prepared in manuscript.

WAR DIARY
or
INTELLIGENCE SUMMARY.
(Erase heading not required.)

Army Form C. 2118.

Sheet 168.

Place	Date	Hour	Summary of Events and Information	Remarks and references to Appendices
HULLUCH	June 27th (contd)		under fire. At the same time as our raid took place raids were carried out by the 8th Seaforth Highlanders on our left & the 7th Cameron Highlanders on our right. The former took place under cover of smoke only, & the latter was preceded by gas & smoke. Both raids failed. It will thus be seen that all the raids undertaken by the Battalions of 44th Bde failed in their object, none of the troops engaged entering the hostile trenches. In each case the fact that the hostile wire had not been previously cut was the cause of failure. In the case of this Battalion it had been pointed out that there was little likelihood of the men being able to get through the wire as it was very strong & high, but the answer received was that there was no artillery available to cut it, nor were there any heavy trench mortars to be had for the purpose. The failure can only be attributed to the lack of artillery preparation without which it has been proved over & over again that the infantry cannot negotiate strongly prepared positions. Among those lost in the raid	

JHPB

T.131. Wt. W708–776. 500000. 4/15. Sir J. C. & S.

Instructions regarding War Diaries and Intelligence Summaries are contained in F. S. Regs., Part II. and the Staff Manual respectively. Title pages will be prepared in manuscript.

WAR DIARY
or
INTELLIGENCE SUMMARY.
(Erase heading not required.)

Army Form C. 2118.

Sheet 169.

Place	Date	Hour	Summary of Events and Information	Remarks and references to Appendices
HULLUCH	June 27th (contd)		were Ptes CAMERON + JEFFREY, two of the most gallant soldiers in the Battalion, both of whom were killed. Pte BOYD was wounded for the 4th time in this campaign, fortunately only slightly.	
LABOURSE	June 28th		This day the Battalion was relieved in the trenches by the 12th Highland Light Infantry 46th Brigade. The relief commenced at 12.30 pm + was finished at 4 pm. The Battalion marched by platoons to LA BOURSE where we took over billets from the 7/8th King's Own Scottish Borderers. A fine day + all ranks very glad to have a quiet night after 16 days in the trenches.	
	June 29th		Germans put a few 5.9-inch shells + a few 4.2 shells into billets one of these unfortunately wounding Captain M. L. GORDON the Battalion Sniping Officer who was lying ill in bed. He had a most lucky escape from being killed as his room was completely wrecked. One of our 12-inch howitzers which is situated in LA BOURSE, fired a few rounds. In the afternoon about 600 men had baths at the Divisional bath rooms in LA BOURSE.	

HPB

Instructions regarding War Diaries and Intelligence Summaries are contained in F. S. Regs., Part II. and the Staff Manual respectively. Title pages will be prepared in manuscript.

WAR DIARY
or
INTELLIGENCE SUMMARY.
(Erase heading not required.)

Sheet 170.

Army Form C. 2118.

Place	Date	Hour	Summary of Events and Information	Remarks and references to Appendices
LABOURSE.	June 30th		Parades & inspections were carried out by companies. 150 men proceeded by motor-bus to the trench area as working parties. News was received that the Russians had captured 221 more officers & 10185 men & many guns in the BUKOVINA, thus increasing their captures in this neighbourhood to some 205,000 men. It was also reported that Sir ROGER CASEMENT had been condemned to death for high treason. This gave general satisfaction.	
"	~~July~~			

T.134. Wt. W708–776. 500000. 4/15. Sir J. C. & S.

Appendix "A".

44th Infantry Brigade.

Report on Raid carried out by 8/10th Battn The Gordon Highlanders, on night of 27/28th June 1916, in Centre Sub-section, Hulluch Section.

Time Table:

1.0 am.	Gas released on a front of about 300 yards between Boyaux 77 and 79.
1.10 am.	Artillery Bombardment commenced.
1.10 - 1.15 am	Smoke Candles ignited.
1.15 am.	Gas turned off.
1.15 am - 1.25 am.	Smoke Bombs ignited.
1.45 am.	Raiding party went out.

Raiding party consisted of 2 Officers and 60 men, divided into 2 groups of 1 Officer and 30 men each. Each group was further sub-divided into three squads of 10 men each.

Right Group. Most of the men of this group succeeded in reaching the German wire, whilst Sergt. PAXTON and L/c FINDLATER actually reached the German parapet. Lce Cpl FINDLATER was killed here. The men of this group between them threw some 30 or 40 bombs into the German Trench. They were fired on after theyhad proceeded about half way across "No man's Land" by 3 Machine Guns and a few Riflemen.

The Riflemen and 1 of the Machine Guns were in front, the remaining Machine Guns were on either flank. Sergt PAXTON saw three Germans in the Trench. They all bolted after throwing a few bombs. Lieut. McCALLUM, who commanded this group was Wounded on his way across "No man's Land".

Most of the Casualties were caused by a M.G. at about H.13a 1½.6½ which fired along the German wire. Several Bombs were thrown at this M.G. but it could not be silenced. Near the M.G. three Germans were firing rifles and about three throwing bombs. No dead Germans were seen in the trench by Sergt. PAXTON, nor could he see if the Germans were wearing Gas Helmets.

Three N.C.Os tried to cut the German wire with the shears which were issued for the purpose. The wire was about ⅛" thick and simply slipped out of the shears. The shears were found to be quite useless.

The German wire entanglements were about 3 feet high and 8 to 10 yards through.

Left Group.

This group was under the Command of 2nd Lieut BUIST.

At 1.45am he led the first squad over the parapet. When he reached a point about 30 yards out he noticed that he had only one sergeant (Sergt. MORTON) and three men with him. He stopped and sent a man back to see what had become of the remainder. This man did not return. 2/Lieut. BUIST then went back himself. He also failed to return. Sergt. MORTON then went back and found Lieut. BUIST and nearly all the squad Gassed.

The second squad went over the parapet and found the first squad gassed as stated. They therefore decided that it was of no good to go on in face of the gas, so they, with the assistance of the third squad, brought in the gassed men. Of the first squad of 10 men, 7 were gassed. This group had come under Machine Gun and Rifle Fire from the moment they left our trenches.

NOTES. 1. Throughout the Gas Attack the Germans kept up some sniping, though not till our men went over the parapet did this become at all heavy. They also reserved the fire of their M.Gs till our men went out. They sent up occasional flares from the front throughout the smoke and gas attacks.

2. The Gas cloud, and likewise the smoke, drifted slightlyS.E., but both Gas and Smoke undoubtedly went over part of the front attacked, if not all.

3. The Gas was clearly visible. It was practically noiseless on leaving the cylinders.

4. The wind was very light - about 3 miles per hour. It is suggested that this wind was scarcely strong enough to carry the gas through the long grass. The Officers in charge of the Smoke arrangements are of the opinion that the smoke never reached the German trenches, the wind being insufficient to carry it forward.

5. The Smoke Candles were very good. The Smoke Bombs were also satisfactory, but not as good as the candles. The flare of the latter, however, undoubtedly showed up the men as they advanced.

6. On our front the Germans sounded no gas gongs and put up no red lights, although many redlights were put up by them on our right where another gas attack took place.

7. The German Artillery opened fire at 1.11am, one minute after ours. They had five or six field guns and one 4.2 Howitzer firing on our trenches, mostly on the Support Line till the Smoke Bombs were thrown when they opened on the front line. One 5.9 Howitzer fired on the Reserve Lines. No doubt their Artillery fire would have been more intense had the whole line not been involved.

8. A bugle was used to recall the raiding party to our trenches at a fixed time. This arrangement worked well.

9. Our casualties amounted to:-

Officers. 1 Wounded, 1 Gassed.

Men. 5 Killed, 8 Wounded, 7 Gassed.

I should like to place on record myappreciation of the good conduct of Lieut. HIEMENS and the N.C.Os and men of the Gas Coy, which was working on my front. Lieut. HIEMENS gave all possible assistance in dealing with the men who were gassed, while his men even offered to take the places of my sentries on the fire-step after having finished their task, in spite of the hostile shell fire to which the trenches were subjected.

I am submitting a special report re the conduct of Sergt CRIGHTLY.

H. P. Bale

29/6/16.

Lt. Colonel,
Comdg. 8/10th Bn. The Gordon Highlanders.

15 July

44/15

8/10 Gordons

Vol 14

CONFIDENTIAL

WAR DIARY

OF

8/10th (Service) Bn The Gordon Highlanders

VOLUME 15.

July 1st 1916 to July 31st 1916.

[illegible] Major

Comdg 8/10th Bn. The Gordon Highlanders.

Instructions regarding War Diaries and Intelligence Summaries are contained in F. S. Regs., Part II. and the Staff Manual respectively. Title pages will be prepared in manuscript.

WAR DIARY or INTELLIGENCE SUMMARY.

(Erase heading not required.)

Army Form C. 2118.

Sheet 171.

Place	Date	Hour	Summary of Events and Information	Remarks and references to Appendices
LA BOURSE.	July 1st		Battalion in rest billets. A very unfortunate bombing accident occurred resulting in the death of 2 Lieut R.M. Riddel & in the wounding of 20 men. 2 Lieut Riddle was explaining the use of a No. 1 General Service grenade when it exploded in his hands. ~~In the~~ In 2 Lieut Riddle the Battalion has lost a valuable & gallant officer who had seen much service this war having been present at the actions of NEUVE CHAPELLE, FESTUBERT & LOOS besides being 19½ months in the trenches. His funeral took place in the afternoon to the cemetery at SAILLY LA BOURSE. The pipers & drummers, all available officers & a large party from his Company attended the funeral. This day news was received that the British 3rd & 4th armies had advanced on the SOMME on a front of 17 miles to an average depth of 1 kilometre, while the French had made a similar advance further to the South. There was considerable artillery fire during the day & again at night. 150 men proceeded to the trench area on fatigue.	

T.134. Wt. W708-776. 500000. 4/15. Sir J. C. & S.

Instructions regarding War Diaries and Intelligence Summaries are contained in F. S. Regs., Part II. and the Staff Manual respectively. Title pages will be prepared in manuscript.

WAR DIARY
or
INTELLIGENCE SUMMARY.
(Erase heading not required.)

Army Form C. 2118.

Sheet 172

Place	Date	Hour	Summary of Events and Information	Remarks and references to Appendices
LA BOURSE	July 2nd		At 12.30 am a very heavy bombardment took place near the town of LOOS. Distant artillery fire was heard in the South, this being the main attack of the British on the SOMME. The Battalion provided 250 men to work in the trenches. These were taken as far as PHILOSOPHE in motor buses. At 6pm the Germans shelled our captive balloon at LA BOURSE causing the occupant, a sailor, to make a hurried descent in a parachute. At 10pm heavy firing was heard & many red & some green lights were seen in the LOOS Salient, this being another gas attack on our part, the red lights being the signal put up by the German infantry to inform their gunners that a gas attack is taking place. It is believed that the green lights are put up by them to denote that in certain places the line is intact & all is well. We heard today that the Russians had taken other 12000 prisoners, the French 4500 & the British 3500.	
"	July 3rd		It was ascertained that no gas attack had taken place the night before, but that we had released smoke from our trenches, the Germans evidently	

Instructions regarding War Diaries and Intelligence Summaries are contained in F. S. Regs., Part II. and the Staff Manual respectively. Title pages will be prepared in manuscript.

WAR DIARY
or
INTELLIGENCE SUMMARY.
(Erase heading not required.)

Army Form C. 2118.

Sheet 173.

Place	Date	Hour	Summary of Events and Information	Remarks and references to Appendices
LA BOURSE	July 3rd (contd)		thinking it was gas judging by the number of red lights they put up. A very fine day & hot sunshine. The Battalion found 250 men for work in the trench area, the majority being employed in removing spoil from dugouts which are under construction in various parts of the line. In the evening a concert was held under the auspices of the Rev. H.K. CORNISH, the chaplain to the Battalion.	
"	July 4th		News was received that the number of prisoners taken by the French on the Somme had risen to 8000 besides 7 batteries including 3 heavy batteries. The British prisoners amount to 5000 besides some guns. Brig General A.W.F. Baird, CMG, DSO, (late 92nd Highrs) Commanding 100th Brigade, 33rd Division, came to lunch at the H.Q. mess. Much rain in the afternoon.	
"	July 5th		Battalion remained in billets. Preparations were made for proceeding to the trenches on the following day.	
VERMELLES	July 6th		Battalion relieved 11th Argyll & Sutherland Highlanders, 45th Brigade, in the centre sub-section of the HOHENZOLLERN Section. The Battalion had held these trenches on a previous occasion, viz from May 19th – 31st. We	

T2134. Wt. W708–776. 500000. 4/15. Sir J. C. & S.

Instructions regarding War Diaries and Intelligence Summaries are contained in F. S. Regs., Part II. and the Staff Manual respectively. Title pages will be prepared in manuscript.

WAR DIARY
or
INTELLIGENCE SUMMARY.
(Erase heading not required.)

Sheet 174.

Army Form C. 2118.

Place	Date	Hour	Summary of Events and Information	Remarks and references to Appendices
VERMELLES	July 6th (contd)		now found these trenches in a most dilapidated state & far worse in every respect than they were when we last handed them over. It was obvious that no real work has been put into them at all. Damage by shell fire has not been repaired & no attempt has been made to keep the trenches dry or even clean. One dugout has been used as a refuse pit for rubbish of all kinds. The bombs has been neglected as has the bomb stores. In two places it was found that boxes full of bombs were being used as stepping stones in the wet parts of the line, while tins of solution for VERMOREL sprayers were being used in another place for a like purpose. There was less wire in front of the trenches than there was 5 weeks ago, no attempt having been made to repair damage done to the wire by the enemy's artillery & mortars. It is quite clear that, without permanent occupation of the line by two Battalions relieving one another alternately, no continuous work will ever be put into the trenches & the present state of chaos will continue. The day	

T2134. Wt. W708—776. 500000. 4/15. Sir J. C. & S.

Instructions regarding War Diaries and Intelligence Summaries are contained in F. S. Regs., Part II. and the Staff Manual respectively. Title pages will be prepared in manuscript.

WAR DIARY
or
INTELLIGENCE SUMMARY.
(Erase heading not required.)

Sheet 175.

Army Form C. 2118.

Place	Date	Hour	Summary of Events and Information	Remarks and references to Appendices
VERMELLES	July 6th (contd)		passed quietly except for a few shells fired from the enemy's field guns at VIGO STREET. Our 60-prs & 18-prs sent over some shells in the evening. The Germans sent some gas shells into VERMELLES at dusk. We did some useful work in the trenches, & put out some wire at night. There was a good deal of rain during the day. Information received that the number of prisoners taken on the SOMME has reached the following figures. British 6000. French 9500. While one French Army Corps alone has captured 60 guns.	
"	July 7th		at 6 am Germans exploded a small mine opposite KAISERIN TRENCH. One of our men was killed by falling debris & some saps were partially blocked, otherwise no damage done. During the day our STOKES guns fired at intervals. The Germans retaliated with heavy mortars & aerial darts. Our aeroplanes active. They used heavy rifle & machine-gun fire. The field guns on both sides were active during the day & our 60-lbrs sent over some shells. Much good work was done by the Battalion in the	

T. 134. Wt. W708–776. 500000. 4/15. Sir J. C. & S.

Instructions regarding War Diaries and Intelligence Summaries are contained in F. S. Regs., Part II. and the Staff Manual respectively. Title pages will be prepared in manuscript.

WAR DIARY
or
INTELLIGENCE SUMMARY.
(Erase heading not required.)

Sheet 176.

Army Form C. 2118.

Place	Date	Hour	Summary of Events and Information	Remarks and references to Appendices
VERMELLES.	July 7th (Contd)		firing line & support trenches & 50 coils of "concertina" barbed wire were put out in front of the line. The Germans showed considerable nervousness at night, keeping up a continuous fire with rifles & machine guns. The wind being light westerly it is more than probable that they suspected another gas attack by us. We fired many "drums" from the LEWIS guns during the night.	
"	July 8th		a quiet day. Distant artillery heard in the South, this being the battle on the SOMME. Germans put a few 5·9 shells into GORDON ALLEY in the morning, one shell wounding 4 men. He also put some mortar bombs into VIGO ST. & DRUMMOND TRENCH during the morning. Between 7 & 8 pm 12 or 13 of our aeroplanes were hovering over the HOHENZOLLERN REDOUBT. NO German aeroplanes in sight at this time though two had been over earlier. Our 18-pr fired a few rounds during the day & the 60-lbrs were active again at night. Much good work was again done in the trenches, parapets, traverses, parados & fire-steps being built up & repaired, while 3 new bomb stores were built. At 9.45 pm the Germans opened a heavy	

T2134. Wt. W708-776. 500000. 4/15. Sir J. C. & S.

Instructions regarding War Diaries and Intelligence Summaries are contained in F. S. Regs., Part II. and the Staff Manual respectively. Title pages will be prepared in manuscript.

WAR DIARY
or
INTELLIGENCE SUMMARY.
(Erase heading not required.)

Sheet 177.

Army Form C. 2118.

Place	Date	Hour	Summary of Events and Information	Remarks and references to Appendices
VERMELLES	July 8th (contd)		bombardment on the trenches of the Bde on our right. (40th Bde) At 9.50 pm the S.O.S. signal was seen to go up from a point to the South of the HAIRPIN group of craters. Our artillery opened a heavy fire on the front in question. At night some 50 barbed wire concertinas & several coils of French wire were put out in front of our trenches. Information was received that during the past 2 days the Russians have captured 22,000 prisoners & 45 guns.	
"	July 9th		A very quiet day on our front. The usual exchanges of field guns & trench mortars took place. More good work was done in the trenches, particularly by "C" Coy under Captain J.G. THOM. The Battalion pioneers continued working on some dugouts they had commenced in DRUMMOND'S TRENCH. The 18-prs claimed to have secured a direct hit on a light field gun which the Germans had brought up to their front trench opposite POKER STREET. This gun had been firing point-blank at our front line. The 18-prs fired salvoes at intervals during the night to prevent removal of the gun. Lieut. Colonel J.S. DREW, 2/7 Middlesex Regiment, arrived to be	

T.134. Wt. W708-776. 500000. 4/15. Sir J. C. & S.

Instructions regarding War Diaries and Intelligence Summaries are contained in F. S. Regs., Part II. and the Staff Manual respectively. Title pages will be prepared in manuscript.

WAR DIARY
or
INTELLIGENCE SUMMARY.
(Erase heading not required.)

Army Form C. 2118.

Sheet 178.

Place	Date	Hour	Summary of Events and Information	Remarks and references to Appendices
VERMELLES	July 9th (contd)		attached to the Battalion. 2 Lieuts ELLIOTT, ADAM, SUTHERLAND + KEMP joined the Battalion for duty.	
"	July 10th		Another quiet day. Work proceeded as usual on the trenches which are now assuming quite a reasonable appearance. Lack of timber prevents work being continued on the deep dugouts which are so necessary to provide bomb-proof cover for the men. Preparations were made to fire a large number of rifle grenades at night to create a diversion on our front while a raid is made by the 8th Seaforth Highlanders on our left. Various points in the enemy's line were registered with rifle grenades during the day. Some type-written documents which has been issued by 1st Corps for the purpose, were fired with "blind" rifle grenades into the German trenches. These documents containing a summary of recent events on the Russian, French + British fronts. At 11.30 pm the raid of the 8th Seaforth Highlanders took place. The raiding party, which consisted of two companies, went over the parapet shortly before this hour + on a mine exploding at 11.30 pm they rushed the German trench which they entered. At 11.30 pm also our	

T.134. Wt. W708—776. 500000. 4/15. Sir J. C. & S.

Instructions regarding War Diaries and Intelligence Summaries are contained in F. S. Regs., Part II. and the Staff Manual respectively. Title pages will be prepared in manuscript.

WAR DIARY
or
INTELLIGENCE SUMMARY.
(Erase heading not required.)

Army Form C. 2118.

Sheet 179.

Place	Date	Hour	Summary of Events and Information	Remarks and references to Appendices
VERMELLES	July 10th (Contd)		artillery opened fire along the entire Brigade front while trench mortars + rifle grenade throwers ~~also~~ also joined in the bombardment. On the Battalion front we sent over 139 rifle grenades. The German guns + trench mortars soon became very active, heavily bombarding our front, support + communication trenches. We, however, had no casualties as all men except sentries had been withdrawn into dugouts in anticipation of trouble. It is estimated that the Germans fired some 400 shells into the Battalion's trenches. Considerable material damage was done but all this can be repaired. The battle lasted till 12.15 am when all was quiet. The Seaforth Highlanders took one prisoner, a Bavarian officer. They claim to have killed many Germans. Their losses were 7 killed and about 50 wounded. During the action a STOKES Gun which was in the Battalion area (VIGO ST.) was blown up by a trench mortar bomb. Fortunately it had finished firing + the team had been withdrawn.	
"	July 11th		A quiet day. The German mortars sent over some bombs at 10 am + again	

T.134. Wt. W708-776. 500000. 4/15. Sir J. C. & S.

Instructions regarding War Diaries and Intelligence Summaries are contained in F. S. Regs., Part II. and the Staff Manual respectively. Title pages will be prepared in manuscript.

WAR DIARY *or* INTELLIGENCE SUMMARY.

(Erase heading not required.)

Sheet 180.

Army Form C. 2118.

Place	Date	Hour	Summary of Events and Information	Remarks and references to Appendices
VERMELLES.	July 11th (contd.)		at dusk. Our guns gave the German front line 2 minutes bombardment at 1 pm + 2 minutes more at 6 pm. The trench mortars joined in + we sent over about 40 rifle grenades on each occasion. Again much good work was done throughout the trench area + work on the new deep dugouts proceeded, some timber having been received from O.C. 74th Coy R.E. At 9 pm the German mortars again became active but our 2-inch mortars quietened them. Some bombing took place at the HOHENZOLLERN craters at 1.45 am. Hostile machine guns were active throughout the night + interfered with our wiring parties + caused us 3 casualties. Our snipers smashed 2 German periscopes. We sent over further news of the allied offensive to the German trenches by means of blind rifle grenades.	
"	July 12th		Hostile artillery active all the morning shelling our front + support lines. The trenches were knocked about a good deal but we had no casualties. Some bombing had taken place at the craters at 1.45 am. The behaviour of the Germans opposite us has somewhat changed, indicating a relief. Possibly the II Bavarian Corps which was opposite us has gone to the SOMME or	

Instructions regarding War Diaries and Intelligence Summaries are contained in F. S. Regs., Part II. and the Staff Manual respectively. Title pages will be prepared in manuscript.

WAR DIARY
or
INTELLIGENCE SUMMARY.
(Erase heading not required.)

Sheet 181.

Army Form C. 2118.

Place	Date	Hour	Summary of Events and Information	Remarks and references to Appendices
VERMELLES	July 12th		to VERDUN. An attempt is being made to capture a prisoner to secure an identification. The new Battalion opposite us is inclined to show itself & several of them have been seen scanning our lines with field glasses. We sent them over the usual extract from the press on a blind rifle grenade. We also sent them over 70 or 80 live rifle grenades. In this latter shoot the 2-inch & STOKES mortars joined in. The Germans retaliated with minenwerfer. We silenced them with 5 salvoes from the 18-prs & a few rounds from the 4'5 howitzers. At 2'30 pm & again at 4'30 pm the artillery carried out 2 minutes bombardment of the hostile trenches, mortars & rifle grenades joining in. At night our Lewis Guns fired 10 drums into the neighbourhood of a new German trench tramway. Our snipers claimed one hit. More good work was done on the trenches & at night some wire was put out in front. In the morning the Corps Commander, Lieut. General CAVANAGH, presented the following medals to N.C.O. & men of the Battalion:—	

Instructions regarding War Diaries and Intelligence Summaries are contained in F. S. Regs., Part II. and the Staff Manual respectively. Title pages will be prepared in manuscript.

WAR DIARY
or
INTELLIGENCE SUMMARY.
(*Erase heading not required.*)

Sheet 182.

Army Form C. 2118.

Place	Date	Hour	Summary of Events and Information	Remarks and references to Appendices
VERMELLES.	July 12th (Contd)		No. S/1748 Sergt J. MORRICE. — Distinguished Conduct Medal.	
			" S/4358 " J. KERR. — " " "	
			" S/8460 " W. MASSON. — " " "	
			" S/10306 L/cpl F. SKELTON — " " "	
			" S/5249 Pte T. ALLAN — " " "	
			" S/1673 Sergt R. PAXTON — Military Medal.	
			" S/12201 L/cpl A. ROSS — " "	
			" 3/6441 " D. HOOPS — " "	
			The presentation took place in the field outside CHATEAU DES PRÉS. near SAILLY LA BOURSE.	
			Information was received that No. S/9229 Pte D. MARSHALL had been granted the Distinguished Conduct Medal for gallantry in the raid carried out by the Battalion on the morning of 12th June.	

2353 Wt. W2544/1454 700,000 5/15 D. D. & L. A.D.S.S./Forms/C. 2118.

Instructions regarding War Diaries and Intelligence Summaries are contained in F. S. Regs., Part II. and the Staff Manual respectively. Title pages will be prepared in manuscript.

WAR DIARY
or
INTELLIGENCE SUMMARY.
(Erase heading not required.)

Army Form C. 2118.

Sheet 183.

Place	Date	Hour	Summary of Events and Information	Remarks and references to Appendices
VERMELLES.	July 13th		Germans shelled our trenches fairly heavily between 8 a.m. & 10 a.m. – It was thought that they were registering new Batteries. Remainder of day quiet. Enemy has been firing more "blind" shells than usual which is encouraging. We bombarded his lines with STOKES Gun & rifle grenades. Little reply from him. During the day a great deal of work was again done on the trenches while at night 50 barbed wire "concertinas" were put out. The wire on this front is now fairly satisfactory. Our snipers got 3 Germans. There is no doubt that a relief has taken place opposite us, the new comers being careless about exposing themselves & over-curious as to their surroundings. They have new uniforms, some light grey & some dark grey. At 3 p.m. we exploded a mine in the HAIRAN CRATERS on the right flank of the Battalion. At 7 p.m. the German exploded a mine near the same place, while at 8.30 p.m. he exploded another further to the North.	
"	July 14th		Germans very quiet. We annoyed them with the STOKES Gun, & rifle grenades from the battery in PARK STREET. Our 2-inch mortars also fired. Our snipers shot 3 Germans & destroyed 5 periscopes. In the morning "A" & "B" coys relieved "C" & "D" coys in the front line. At night the Germans shelled our Battalion "dump" with four salvoes of 4.2 howitzers, all shells were however "blind". This most encouraging & very unusual	

2353 Wt. W2544/1454 700,000 5/15 D. D. & L. A.D.S.S./Forms/C. 2118.

Instructions regarding War Diaries and Intelligence Summaries are contained in F. S. Regs., Part II. and the Staff Manual respectively. Title pages will be prepared in manuscript.

WAR DIARY
or
INTELLIGENCE SUMMARY.
(Erase heading not required.)

Sheet 134.

Army Form C. 2118.

Place	Date	Hour	Summary of Events and Information	Remarks and references to Appendices
VERMELLES.	July 14th (Contd.)		A telegram was received to the effect that Lieut Colonel H.P. Burn, D.S.O. has been appointed to the command of the 152nd Brigade, 51st Division. He accordingly handed over command of the Battalion to Major D. MacLeod D.S.O.	
VERMELLES	July 15th.		Our Trench Mortars and Rifle grenades were very active during the whole day. Our Artillery also heavily shelled the enemy's trenches. A relief has evidently taken place opposite this Battn. The new troops are exceedingly curious of their surroundings and exposed themselves to our snipers who accounted for a good number of them. A relief of Artillery has also taken place as his guns - of all calibres - have been registering on all our trenches, doing a good deal of damage.	[initials]
VERMELLES	July	16th.	Our Artillery very heavily bombarded the enemy's front and support trenches, assisted by our Trench Mortars and Rifle grenades. Considerable damage was done to the German Lines. At night the enemy were very alert and put up many lights. A Patrol from "B" Company went out at midnight from Sap 8A ~~north~~ to try and capture a prisoner, but they found the German wire very strong everywhere and impossible to get through. They discovered the body of an Officer just outside the German wire and brought back a silver Cigarette Case which	

Instructions regarding War Diaries and Intelligence Summaries are contained in F. S. Regs., Part II. and the Staff Manual respectively. Title pages will be prepared in manuscript.

WAR DIARY
or
INTELLIGENCE SUMMARY.
(Erase heading not required.)

Sheet 185

Army Form C. 2118.

Place	Date	Hour	Summary of Events and Information	Remarks and references to Appendices
VERMELLES	July (Contd)	16th	was sent to Brigade Hd Qrs; no documents were found on the body.	
VERMELLES	July	17th	The day was very misty for Artillery operations, both sides were very quiet during the day, but the enemy commenced a very heavy bombardment of CROWN TRENCH held by the 7th Cameron Highlanders on our right, about 8.30pm; we received orders to stand by, but the enemy's Infantry did not attack and the situation became quiet again.	
VERMELLES	July	18th	The Battalion was relieved in the front-Line by the 9th Black Watch, and came back into Brigade Reserve in LANCASHIRE TRENCH. Our Artillery carried out a heavy bombardment of the enemys front and Support Lines, Trench Mortars, and Machine Guns emplacements, doing great damage, the bombardment went on from 12 noon until 3.30 p.m. The enemy again subjected Crown Trench to a heavy bombardment in the evening but no attack followed. C.S.M. Angus MacLean A. Company was awarded the Military Cross for distinguished service at the battle of Loos.	[initials]
VERMELLES	July	19th	Our Artillery again bombarded the enemys Lines, carrying out the same programme as yesterday, doing considerable damage, especially the fire of our 9.2 which destroyed the enemys front Line opposite Kaiserin	

Sheet 186

Instructions regarding War Diaries and Intelligence Summaries are contained in F. S. Regs., Part II. and the Staff Manual respectively. Title pages will be prepared in manuscript.

WAR DIARY
or
INTELLIGENCE SUMMARY.
(Erase heading not required.)

Army Form C. 2118.

Place	Date	Hour	Summary of Events and Information	Remarks and references to Appendices
VERMELLES	July (Contd.)	19th	Trench. Owing to casualties suffered by the 7th Cameron Highlanders last night "C" Company moved up to O.B.4. in support of them.	
"	"	20th	Perfectly quiet day.	
"	"	21st	Another very quiet day. The French on the Somme captured 3.000 prisoners 3 Guns and 30 Machine Guns.	
NOEUX-les-MINES	"	22nd	The Battalion was relieved at 4 p.m. by the 1st Royal Irish Rifles, 25th Brigade, and marched to billets in Noeux-les-Mines, the billets were very good. Captain Bethell and Lt Ingles joined from the Divisional School.	[initials]
DIEVAL	"	23rd	Battalion paraded at 8 A.M. and marched via BRUAY – DIVION to DIEVAL, a march of 14 miles, the day was warm and the roads dusty, but the men marched well very few falling out. The Battalion marched past the Divisional Commander at a point on the road one mile beyond	

2353 Wt. W2544/1454 700,000 5/15 D. D. & L. A.D.S.S./Forms/C. 2118.

Instructions regarding War Diaries and Intelligence Summaries are contained in F. S. Regs., Part II. and the Staff Manual respectively. Title pages will be prepared in manuscript.

WAR DIARY
or
INTELLIGENCE SUMMARY.
(Erase heading not required.)

Sheet 187

Army Form C. 2118.

Place	Date	Hour	Summary of Events and Information	Remarks and references to Appendices
DIÉVAL	July (Contd.)	23rd	BRUAY. The General expressed his satisfaction at the fitness and general bearing of the men, the Battalion arrived in billets a 2 pm.	
DIEVAL	"	24th	The Battalion rested and devoted the day to general cleaning and fitting Equipment. The deficiencies of Kit and Equipment were completed.	
"	"	25th	This day spent in company training in special formations suitable for the offensive on the SOMME in which we expect to take part soon. The 9th Division marched through on their return from the SOMME, our pipers played each Battalion in turn through the village.	
MAIZIERES	July	26th	The Battalion paraded at 7.30 A.M. and marched to MAIZIERES - about 8 miles - arriving there at 11 A.M. the men marched well and we got good billets.	
BARLY	"	27th	The Battalion paraded at 7.15 A.M. and marched to BARLY - 12 miles - this was a most trying march, the day being very hot and the roads very dusty, about 20 men fell out suffering from sore feet; of the other 3 Battalions in the Brigade over 100 each fell out; the Battalion marched past the Divisional General at the end of 11 miles, although tired they marched in splendid order and the General again expressed his	

2353 Wt. W2544/1454 700,000 5/15 D. D. & L. A.D.S.S./Forms/C. 2118.

Instructions regarding War Diaries and Intelligence Summaries are contained in F. S. Regs., Part II. and the Staff Manual respectively. Title pages will be prepared in manuscript.

WAR DIARY
or
INTELLIGENCE SUMMARY.
(*Erase heading not required.*)

Sheet 188

Army Form C. 2118.

Place	Date	Hour	Summary of Events and Information	Remarks and references to Appendices
BARLY	July (Contd)	27th	Satisfaction with the Battalion.	
GAYAINCOURT	"	28th	The Battalion marched at 7 A.M on a short march of 6 miles and got to new billets by 9.30 A.M. The men are in good billets but the Officers are very poor. In the afternoon all were able to bath in a clear stream.	
"	"	29th	This day was devoted to training in special formations for the SOMME offensive and a short march in the evening.	
"	"	30th	Companies went out on a short route march early in the morning and the Battalion attended Divine service at 11 A.M there is no afternoon parades as we march at 4 A.M tomorrow morning.	
NAOURS	"	31st	The Battalion paraded at 4.50 A.M and marched 10 miles to NAOURS, the men marched very well without anyone falling out, the whole Brigade (44th Brigade) found good billets here. the afternoon was devoted to lectures on the lessons gathered from the SOMME offensive. The day was very hot.	[initials]

44th Brigade.

15th Division.

8/10th BATTALION

GORDON HIGHLANDERS

AUGUST 1 9 1 6

Instructions regarding War Diaries and Intelligence Summaries are contained in F. S. Regs., Part II. and the Staff Manual respectively. Title pages will be prepared in manuscript.

WAR DIARY or INTELLIGENCE SUMMARY.

(Erase heading not required.)

Army Form C. 2118.

Sheet 189

Place	Date	Hour	Summary of Events and Information	Remarks and references to Appendices
NAOURS.	1st	Augt.	The day was devoted to training under Coy: arrangements from 9.30 A.m to 12 noon, ~~that~~ all went out ~~for~~ running before breakfast and for a short route march in the evening.	
"	2nd	"	Training as yesterday, nothing of importance to record, the weather is very hot.	
"	3rd	"	Work, and weather, was the same as yesterday.	
PIERREGOT.	4th	"	The Battn paraded at 4.30 AM and marched 6 miles to new billets here, the men marched well, no one falling out; the men are in good billets, but there are very few for the officers. The 9th Gordons being in billets here for the night afforded a pleasant meeting for old Comrades of both Battalions after many months of separation. Major C.J.C.G. Cumine joined from sick leave.	
BENENCOURT	5th	"	The Battn paraded at 7.10 AM and marched 6 miles to new billets, no one fell out on the march, the roads were very dusty & the day was very hot; the Battn went past the Brigadier (Genl Marshall) at the end of the march in splendid order & as fresh as when they started, the efforts made to get the men fit since we left the trenches on 22nd July brought about most satisfactory results, the men's feet are now in good condition and the Battn can undertake real hard work.	

Instructions regarding War Diaries and Intelligence Summaries are contained in F. S. Regs., Part II. and the Staff Manual respectively. Title pages will be prepared in manuscript.

WAR DIARY
or
INTELLIGENCE SUMMARY.
(Erase heading not required.)

Sheet 190

Army Form C. 2118.

Place	Date	Hour	Summary of Events and Information	Remarks and references to Appendices
BEHENCOURT	5th (Contd)	Augt	The afternoon was devoted to training in special formations for the SOMME offensive and training Reserve of Lewis gunners. The day was very hot.	
"	6th	"	In the morning the Coys went out for a run before breakfast as usual, and the forenoon and afternoon was devoted to training in special formations (combined) with Lewis guns + trench mortars. Coys went out for a short route march in the evening. The men are getting very fit after their long tour of inactivity in the trenches.	
"	7th	"	Went out for the usual run before breakfast; but as we got orders to move to the battle front on the SOMME tomorrow, the remainder of the day was given up to washing in order to march in clean underclothing + have a clean change with them. After tea the Commanding Officer address the whole Battn and explained the nature of the work + the part the Battn is to take in the SOMME offensive. The whole Battn seem to be delighted at the opportunity of "at last" taking part in the operations.	
ALBERT (1,000 yds E. of)	8th	"	The Battn paraded at 12.30 Am and marched 16½ miles to the Old British Line 1,000 yards East of ALBERT on the SOMME battle front and took up position in Divisional reserve at 7.15 A.m. The men marched well, there were none	

T2134. Wt. W708–776. 500000. 4/15. Sir J. C. & S.

Instructions regarding War Diaries and Intelligence Summaries are contained in F. S. Regs., Part II. and the Staff Manual respectively. Title pages will be prepared in manuscript.

WAR DIARY
or
INTELLIGENCE SUMMARY.
(Erase heading not required.)

Sheet 191

Army Form C. 2118.

Place	Date	Hour	Summary of Events and Information	Remarks and references to Appendices
ALBERT	8th Augt (Contd.)		were sick or unable to undertake the march, and none fell out during the march. Only 20 Officers allowed in the operations with the Battn., Lieut. Col. D. Macleod D.S.O, Commanding, Lt & Adjt. D.W. McLeod, Capt. J. Lambie, and 2nd Lt. G.P. Geddes are the Battn. Hd Qrs officers. A. Coy - Capt. J. Martin, 2nd Lts Cornford, K.M.K Duff, W.J.G. Binnie. B. Coy - Capt. A.M. Drummond, Lt. W. McCall, 2nd Lts A. Browning, O.C.F. ELLIOT. C. Coy - Capt. J.G. Thom, 2nd Lts A.F. Sprott, A.K Priday, J. Smith. D. Coy - Capt. F.J.C Moffet; Lt. L.G. Robertson, 2nd Lts H.L. Knowles, and A.D Sutherland. The following were left in reserve for reinforcements, Major G.J.G.G. Clemine, 2nd in Comd. A. Coy. 2nd Lts C.R. Brooke, J.E. Adam, C.P. Brower, B. Coy - 2nd Lts J.A. Plummer, W.S. Kemp, and Lt. J. Lynn. C. Coy. Capt. A.P. Bethell, Lt. J.B. Wood, 2nd Lts P. Booth, and G. Mutch. D. Coy. Capt. N.G. Pearson, 2nd Lts J. Robertson, W.A. Johnstone, and R.A.M Black. At 9.15 pm our Artillery opened a heavy bombardment, lasting 1½ hour, of the enemy's position round MOUQUET FARM in support of an attack by the Australians, who captured it and took 170 prisoners. Our Guns fired a good deal throughout the night.	

T2134. Wt. W708—776. 500000. 4/15. Sir J. C. & S.

Instructions regarding War Diaries and Intelligence Summaries are contained in F. S. Regs., Part II. and the Staff Manual respectively. Title pages will be prepared in manuscript.

WAR DIARY or INTELLIGENCE SUMMARY.

(Erase heading not required.)

Sheet 192

Army Form C. 2118.

Place	Date	Hour	Summary of Events and Information	Remarks and references to Appendices
ALBERT	9th	Augt	Nothing of importance to record, the day being a normal day in Divisional Reserve: the weather is still very hot.	
ALBERT	10th	Augt	After an intense bombardment lasting from 12 midnight till 12.15 a.m the Division on our left attacked and gained a considerable portion of ground. Seventy prisoners were taken and from the new position it is possible to enfilade the German trenches further North. From 4 p.m till 8 p.m the enemy bombarded the whole of Sausage Valley, East of BECOURT. WOOD and did considerable damage; otherwise the day was quiet. The day was dull with some rain, Later in the evening the enemy continued to shell our lines and registered several hits on our trenches. Three men were buried in a dug-out, but fortunately none of them were seriously injured. We retaliated by bombarding the enemy's front with guns of all calibre from 10 p.m till 10.15 p.m.	
"	11th	Augt	This was a quiet day throughout. About 7.80 pm the enemy heavily bombarded our Batteries in the Sausage Valley. Throughout the night our Artillery maintained a barrage along the whole front without much in retaliation from the enemy.	
CONTALMAISON	12th	"	The Battn moved up in the evening to SCOTT's Redoubt and Peak's WOOD in Support of the 45th Brigade. At 10.32 pm after an intense bombardment for ½ an hour the 45th and 46th Brigades attacked the SWITCH TRENCH. On the left the 45th were	

Instructions regarding War Diaries and Intelligence Summaries are contained in F. S. Regs., Part II. and the Staff Manual respectively. Title pages will be prepared in manuscript.

WAR DIARY
or
INTELLIGENCE SUMMARY.
(Erase heading not required.)

Army Form C. 2118.

Sheet 193

Place	Date	Hour	Summary of Events and Information	Remarks and references to Appendices
CONTALMAISON (Contd)	12th Augt		successful, but on the right the attacking Battn of the 46th had to retire owing heavy Machine Gun fire.	
"	13th	"	A quiet day, nothing of importance to report: At 10 p.m the Division on our left (Australians) assaulted and captured 500 yds. of the enemy's trenches South of POZIERES.	
"	14th	"	The Battn relieved the 6/7 Royal Scots Fusiliers, and 6th Cameron Highlanders in the firing Line opposite the SWITCH TRENCH covering MARTINPUICH. The relief was complete at 8.30 A.m. The trenches were mere ditches having been heavily bombarded by our own artillery in capturing them and, badly damaged since by the enemy's heavy guns.) Snipers were very active and proved very difficult to locate, as they had taken up excellent positions in shell holes in front of our line. Shortly after taking over the trenches one of our sentries observed a man signalling from a shell hole about 80 yards in front of Gloster sap. Sergt Meines at once went out and discovered the man to be a wounded Royal Scots Fusilier who had been there for two days, and although subjected to most annoying fire from Snipers Sergt Meines brought the man in to our	

T2134. Wt. W708—776. 500000. 4/15. Sir J. C. & S.

Instructions regarding War Diaries and Intelligence Summaries are contained in F. S. Regs., Part II. and the Staff Manual respectively. Title pages will be prepared in manuscript.

WAR DIARY or INTELLIGENCE SUMMARY.

(*Erase heading not required.*)

Sheet 194

Army Form C. 2118.

Place	Date	Hour	Summary of Events and Information	Remarks and references to Appendices
CONTALMAISON (Contd)	14th Augt		trenches. (Sergt Mims who took a leading part in destroying the enemy's snipers was unfortunately killed later in the day) The wounded Royal Scots Fusilier (Pte McGlasson) informed us that Corpl Harrison of his Battn was also lying in a shell hole badly wounded in front of our position, Corpls Hedley, ~~and~~ Sutherland, and Pte Graham succeeding in finding him, but owing to the serious nature of his wounds & snipers activity he could not be removed during the day, but he was given food & water & Pte Grahame dressed his wounds. At night although our trenches were subjected to active sniping and considerable shell fire Pte Grahame & Lce Corpl. Mackay went out ~~and~~ brought Corpl Harrison in, being then delirious they experienced great difficulties in bringing him in. The Highland Light Infantry on our right captured a portion of the SWITCH trench by bombing parties about 10 A.M. but as they were not supported they failed to hold it. Our Lewis Guns co-operated and accounted for 30 of the enemy as they retired over the open, a bombing party of A.Coy advanced into the North end of the SWITCH to cut the enemy's retreat, they found the trench deserted but full of dead bodies, (Germans)	[initials]

T2134. Wt. W708—776. 500000. 4/15. Sir J. C. & S.

Instructions regarding War Diaries and Intelligence Summaries are contained in F. S. Regs., Part II. and the Staff Manual respectively. Title pages will be prepared in manuscript.

WAR DIARY
or
INTELLIGENCE SUMMARY.
(*Erase heading not required.*)

Army Form C. 2118.

Sheet 195

Place	Date	Hour	Summary of Events and Information	Remarks and references to Appendices
CONTALMAISON (Contd.)	14th	Augt	They brought back a German Machine Gun in perfect order which, as we captured plenty of German Ammunition, was in action against the enemy within 12 hours. Two Wounded Germans came in from Shell holes in front of our line and surrendered. Our trenches were subjected to considerable shelling by enemy's heavy guns throughout the night. In the Evening the Australians on our left attacked, the Centre succeeded but both flanks were held up by machine Gun fire, and eventually the whole line withdrew carrying with them 11 prisoners and one Machine Gun they Captured.	
"	15th	"	The day was comparatively quiet, thanks to our splendid snipers who destroyed or drove off the enemy's annoying snipers. An attack arranged to Capture the SWITCH trench in front of our right flank was not carried out as during the night the enemy's heavy barrage on our support trenches put the Stoke's Guns, who were to support the attack, out of action. This was a great disappointment to the Battn as our tour of 48 hours in the front line did not permit of another attack being arranged, as it took considerable time to replace Stoke Guns, destroyed ammunition and Casualties in the teams.	

T2134. Wt. W708—776. 500000. 4/15. Sir J. C. & S.

Instructions regarding War Diaries and Intelligence Summaries are contained in F. S. Regs., Part II. and the Staff Manual respectively. Title pages will be prepared in manuscript.

WAR DIARY or INTELLIGENCE SUMMARY.

(*Erase heading not required.*)

Sheet 196

Army Form C. 2118.

Place	Date	Hour	Summary of Events and Information	Remarks and references to Appendices
CONTALMAISON	16th	Augt	The Battn was relieved early in the morning by the 9th Black Watch, and came back into Brigade reserve in SCOTS Redoubt.	
"	17th	"	Considerable artillery activity on both sides during the day. At 8.55 A.m. the 7th Cameron Highlanders attacked and captured the SWITCH TRENCH in our Brigade front, the enemy attacked along the trench from South against the Cameron's right flank by bombing parties, but they were repulsed by 2 Coy's of the 8th Seaforths who delivered a Counter attack. Three Platoons of the Battn were ordered up in support. The enemy heavily shelled our trenches all day and throughout the night, the Brigade suffered heavy Casualties, probably through too many troops being employed in this attack.	
"	18th	"	The 1st Division, on our right attacked in the afternoon assisted by smoke screen prepared by our Division. One man was killed and 7 wounded this morning by the explosion of an old German shell. The 1st Division succeeded in establishing themselves in the German trench N.W. of High Wood. At 6pm the Australians & 48th Division, on our left attacked & captured Mouquet Farm.	

T2134. Wt. W708—776. 500000. 4/15. Sir J. C. & S.

Instructions regarding War Diaries and Intelligence Summaries are contained in F. S. Regs., Part II. and the Staff Manual respectively. Title pages will be prepared in manuscript.

WAR DIARY
or
INTELLIGENCE SUMMARY.
(Erase heading not required.)

Sheet 197

Army Form C. 2118.

Place	Date	Hour	Summary of Events and Information	Remarks and references to Appendices
CONTALMAISON	19th Aug		The Battn moved forward and relieved the 9th Black Watch & took up position in Support. The enemy's artillery were not active during the day.	
"	20th	"	The Battn relieved the 8th Seaforth Highrs in the front line early in the morning. Enemy's artillery was very active throughout the day & night our trenches were badly damaged blown in many places. Lt Sprott was buried twice & had to be sent to the Ambulance suffering from shell shock. Capt Moffat was wounded ~~~~ by shrapnel. A Patrol brought in a German Machine Gun which is added to the Brigade battery.	
"	21st	"	This was a quiet day, but between 1 and 3 Am the enemy bombarded Battn H.Qrs with several hundreds of Gas shells, helmets had to be worn only 2 men were slightly effected through a Gas shell blowing in their dugout. 2nd Lt Duff joined the Trench Motor and 2nd Lt Brook replaced him in A Coy.	
"	22nd	"	The Battn was relieved by the 7th Camerons, and moved back to SCOTS Redoubt. During the last 24 hours in the firing line there was no Casualties throughout the Battn. This was due to holding the line as ~~~~ out-posts instead of the usual solid fashion.	

T2134. Wt. W708—776. 500000. 4/15. Sir J. C. & S.

Instructions regarding War Diaries and Intelligence Summaries are contained in F. S. Regs., Part II. and the Staff Manual respectively. Title pages will be prepared in manuscript.

WAR DIARY
or
INTELLIGENCE SUMMARY.
(Erase heading not required.)

Sheet 198

Army Form C. 2118.

Place	Date	Hour	Summary of Events and Information	Remarks and references to Appendices
CONTALMAISON	23rd Aug		Another quiet day. A Draft of sixty men joined. A french aeroplane was brought down near our trenches, the ~~pilot~~ Pilot escaped unhurt.	
"	24th	"	The Battn relieved the 8th Seaforths early in the morning, C & D Coys in Peake Wood and A & B Coys in Contalmaison. At 3.45 pm our Guns heavily bombarded the INTERMEDIATE LINE opposite the 45th Brigade and 1st Division. At 5.45 pm the 6th Camerons and 1st Division attacked, the former succeeded but the latter failed and had to retire. About 11 pm several 5.9 Shells fell at Battn Hd Qrs.	
"	25th	"	During the morning the enemy's Aeroplanes were very active, considerable amount of fighting ensued, over our lines, between them and our ~~machines~~ battle-planes, the enemy had to retire but no machines were brought down. 2nd Lt Mulch joined to replace 2nd Lt Smith admitted to Hospital.	
"	26th	"	The Battn relieved the 8th Seaforths in Support. The Australians, on our left, attacked ~~last~~ late at night and made good progress. One of our Aeroplanes had to suddenly land behind our Support trench, owing to engine trouble, the pilot was killed and the observer was seriously hurt. Large parties worked on the front Line at night; Highland Trench was wired, and Shetland & Gloster	

T2134. Wt. W708—776. 500000. 4/15. Sir J. C. & S.

Instructions regarding War Diaries and Intelligence Summaries are contained in F. S. Regs., Part II. and the Staff Manual respectively. Title pages will be prepared in manuscript.

WAR DIARY
or
INTELLIGENCE SUMMARY.
(Erase heading not required.)

Sheet 199

Army Form C. 2118.

Place	Date	Hour	Summary of Events and Information	Remarks and references to Appendices
			ALLEY were completed to the firing line	
CONTALMAISON	27th	Augt	The enemy heavily shelled our Support Line from 12 M.N. to 2 A.M without inflicting any casualties.	
"	28th	"	The Battn relieved the 8th Seaforths in the firing Line. The trenches were badly damaged by the enemy's heavy guns. Between 7.30 & 8.30 pm the enemy heavily shelled Gordon Alley and Highland Trench with 5.9s doing considerable damage.	
"	29th	"	The enemys artillery was very active all day. Highland trench was heavily shelled in the evening and during the night.	
"	30	"	The Battn was relieved by the 26th Northumberland Fusiliers, the relief was complete by 8 A.M and the Battn marched back to bivouacs beyond ALBERT. It has been raining heavily for 24 hours and the men were soaking wet, the Camping Ground was in a very bad state and there was only 16 tents for the whole Battn, however an application to the C.R.E. resulted in getting shelters for the whole Battn and an appeal to the Brigadier produced an issue of Rum which the men required badly and much appreciated. The 45th & 46th Bdes Captured the INTERMEDIATE Line with 4 officers & 142 other ranks	

T2134. Wt. W708—776. 500000. 4/15. Sir J. C. & S.

Instructions regarding War Diaries and Intelligence Summaries are contained in F. S. Regs., Part II. and the Staff Manual respectively. Title pages will be prepared in manuscript.

WAR DIARY
or
INTELLIGENCE SUMMARY.
(Erase heading not required.)

Sheet 200

Army Form C. 2118.

Place	Date	Hour	Summary of Events and Information	Remarks and references to Appendices
CONTALMAISON	31st Aug.		An ordinary day in Camp nothing of importance to report.	

T2134. Wt. W708—776. 500000. 4/15. Sir J. C. & S.

16.

CONFIDENTIAL VOL ~~15~~

44/15

WAR DIARY

OF

8/10th (Service) Batt.n The Gordon Highlanders

From 1st September, 1916 To 30th September, 1916

VOLUME 17.

[signature] Lt. Colonel.
Comdg 8/10th Bn The Gordon Highlanders.

WAR DIARY
or
~~INTELLIGENCE SUMMARY~~.
(Erase heading not required.)

Instructions regarding War Diaries and Intelligence Summaries are contained in F. S. Regs., Part II. and the Staff Manual respectively. Title pages will be prepared in manuscript.

SHEET 302

Army Form C. 2118.

Place	Date	Hour	Summary of Events and Information	Remarks and references to Appendices
ALBERT. (Bivouac)	1.IX.16.		Fine day. Camp straightened up, small Canteen installed, tents and bivouacs rearranged and general atmosphere made comfortable and cheerful. Capt. Pearson + 2/Lt BOOTH reported from Reinforcement camp for duty with the Battⁿ. A draft of 60 arrived in the afternoon, including several men of the old Battalion. Machine-gun (Lewis) classes were started for officers, with intention of making every officer an efficient gunner. Day otherwise uneventful.	44th I.B. BM102 issued, announcing 1st Div. Offensive
ALBERT. (Bivouac).	2.IX.16		Another good day. Bathing parade for the Battⁿ, town baths at ALBERT having been placed at our disposal. All recently joined drafts were inspected by the Commanding Officer. About 30% of them are men of previous service wounded earlier in the Campaign. These look a very good lot. The others who have only about 4 months service are evidently in the army on compulsion and require much attention to make them efficient. Day without incident of note.	
Ditto.	3.IX.16.		Fine in forenoon, with rain later. All new drafts were inspected by the Brigadier. A good turn-out. Orders received to move into forward position of Divisional Reserve. Heavy bombardment by our artillery + big attack launched at noon. 1st Division used large Flammenwerfer + cleared High Wood easily. They took over 80 prisoners, but German counter-attack caused them to withdraw to original position. The Australians on our left were successful + gained objective.	RWR

Instructions regarding War Diaries and Intelligence Summaries are contained in F. S. Regs., Part II. and the Staff Manual respectively. Title pages will be prepared in manuscript.

WAR DIARY
or
INTELLIGENCE SUMMARY.
(Erase heading not required.)

SHEET. 303

Army Form C. 2118.

Place	Date	Hour	Summary of Events and Information	Remarks and references to Appendices
	3.IX.16		2nd + 5th Coys also attacked, but made no progress and were unable to reach the German line. On our right, a successful attack was made on Guillemont + Guinchy, which are now in our hands, and our line consolidated about 1000 yds. beyond them. The French also attacked and took part of the village of 'Clery.' The counter-attack on the 1st Division was executed by the Bavarians, who are fresh to this sector and excellent troops.	
The DINGLE. nr. CONTALMAISON.	4.IX.16.		Moved from Bivouac at ALBERT at 5.0 am. and took up position in Reserve Trenches in the DINGLE. The morning was cold and wet and the move uncomfortable. We relieved the 5th CAMERONS in the DINGLE, and took over their dug-outs and trenches in a very dirty condition. Continued to rain all day. Nothing of importance occurred.	
QUADRANGLE. (X.23.c)	5.IX.16		Relieved 7/8th K.O.S.B's in QUADRANGLE about 12 noon. The Batt. took over from 3 Coys. K.O.S.B's, and as these were very weak, the accomodation for our 4 full Coys was quite inadequate. Rain continued to fall and the men had no shelter. On enquiry at Brigade as to what further accomodation there might be in the area we were told we must "dig for it." This, to say the least of it, is unsatisfactory. About 10.0 pm peculiar sweet smell in the air, unlike any of the gases previously encountered. As the wind was fairly high however it passed over quickly. No effects were visible. News arrived today of a further French success, with the capture of 5,700 prisoners. Lieut McColl returned from T.M. Course, full of enthusiasm for new 'Heavy' T.M.	DWV

T2134. Wt. W708—776. 500000. 4/15. Sir J. C. & S.

Instructions regarding War Diaries and Intelligence Summaries are contained in F. S. Regs., Part II. and the Staff Manual respectively. Title pages will be prepared in manuscript.

WAR DIARY
or
INTELLIGENCE SUMMARY.

(*Erase heading not required.*)

SHEET 302.

Army Form C. 2118.

Place	Date	Hour	Summary of Events and Information	Remarks and references to Appendices
E. 7. QUADRANGLE.	6.IX.16		Weather good. Much work done by Batt. on this area, and nearly all the men now have shelters. New orderly Room and 2 new Coy. H.Q. finished. Usual daily activity of our artillery continued during the day, chiefly confined to 6" guns. Three enemy aeroplanes came over during the day. Two in the forenoon beat a hasty retreat pursued by our machines; the third in the afternoon was unmolested & made a good reconnaissance of this area, before withdrawing on account of our anti-aircraft fire. About 8.30 pm. a heavy bombardment commenced on our right. The French are apparently again attacking. No incident of importance occurred.	
QUADRANGLE	7.IX.16.		Quiet day. Preparations being made for move into front system tomorrow morning. Two platoons went up to-night as working parties and take over right front at dawn. Enemy aeroplanes very active during forenoon. Much air fighting but no visible results. The 9.2" Battery just behind Batt. H.Q. did some counter-battery shooting during the forenoon. "O.K." received back twice from observing aeroplanes. Usual artillery activity during the Day. No mail has been received for last 2 days, so that we have NO news of progress of Russians & Rumanians. The French have again been active and further artillery bombardment is still going on on their front.	5/14116 Pte T. Muir wounded.
TRENCHES BAZENTIN LE PETIT.	8.IX.16		We relieved the 24th Northumberland Fusiliers in the front line trenches early this morning	

Dun

T2134. Wt. W708—776. 500000. 4/15. Sir J. C. & S.

Instructions regarding War Diaries and Intelligence Summaries are contained in F. S. Regs., Part II. and the Staff Manual respectively. Title pages will be prepared in manuscript.

WAR DIARY
or
INTELLIGENCE SUMMARY.
(Erase heading not required.)

SHEET 305

Army Form C. 2118.

Place	Date	Hour	Summary of Events and Information	Remarks and references to Appendices
BAZENTIN le PETIT	9.IX.16.		The relief was carried out in darkness and was without incident save for 2 German aeroplanes which came over our lines flying very low while relief was in progress. The day was fairly quiet, but our casualties were relatively heavy. SWANSEA Trench is accurately registered and practically every shell is a direct hit. Some of our own 18-pdr guns are also firing short and we had 3 casualties (1 killed) from them. About 7 p.m. the 1st Division on our right and about 2 Coys of the 9th Black Watch attacked the western end of High Wood and a small trench extending along the road from the N.W. corner of the Wood. The attack was quite successful and the captured area is still being held. No details are yet to hand as to enemy casualties or prisoners. New "jumping-off" trenches are being dug in front of our line. ~~Last~~ During the night 8/9 Sept. we dug one about 350 yards long from JUTLAND Alley extension to SOMME Extension + road CUTTING in S.2.b. The digging party was evidently seen going out as enemy opened rapid fire and put up red-rockets. These latter brought heavy artillery fire on our trenches. The working party reported our own M.G's firing "indirect" to be causing them casualties. The new trench dug-in is now garrisoned by 30 men + 2 Lewis-guns.	Casualties: Off. K. W. M; O.R. 5. 15. 1.
Do.	10.IX.16		Quiet day. Battn was unlucky and received many more direct hits than usual. Casualties fairly large	K. W. M; O.R. - 14 -
Do.	11.IX.16.		2 front line Coys were relieved by 6th E Yorks, and the Battn then relieved the 26th Northd Fusiliers. New + more troops are being crowded into the line and accomodation is becoming scarce. 2 Coys moved into GOURLAY Trench at 7.0 a.m., were again moved to KOYLI Trench + REDOUBT about 5.0 p.m. + finally had to vacate the redoubt at about 8.0 p.m. Accomodation	Drw.

2353 Wt. W2544/1454 700,000 5/15 D. D. & L. A.D.S.S./Forms/C. 2118.

Instructions regarding War Diaries and Intelligence Summaries are contained in F. S. Regs., Part II. and the Staff Manual respectively. Title pages will be prepared in manuscript.

WAR DIARY
or
INTELLIGENCE SUMMARY.
(Erase heading not required.)

Army Form C. 2118.

SHEET 306.

Place	Date	Hour	Summary of Events and Information	Remarks and references to Appendices
BAZENTIN le PETIT.	11.9.16.		was found around Batt H.Q. for some of the men, and the officers of 1 Coy were accomodated in B. H.Q. for the night. Altogether a very trying day, where men from front trenches had no place to stay in.	11th K. W. M 3. 11. –
BIVOUAC. ALBERT.	12.9.16.		The Battn was relieved by the 7th Cameron High in the early morning, and proceeded to Bivouac about ¾ of a mile E. of ALBERT. Relief without incident, save for a flight of 5 German aeroplanes over the trenches while relief was in progress. Battn got back into Bivouac about 10.30 am. A small canteen was installed in camp, washing tubs were provided and the men had a thorough clean up. Enemy shot some heavy shells into ALBERT during the afternoon.	
Bivouac ALBERT.	13.9.16.		A quiet day in camp. Baths were allotted but only 2 Coys could bathe, as water-supply ran out. Coys organised + fully re-fitted for going back into line	
Do.	14.9.16.		Fine day during early part. Operation orders for the attack tomorrow have been issued. About 8.0 pm. the Battn moved into forward area as "A" Battn of 44th Bde which is in Reserve. At 10.30 pm. Battn was settled in new locality with H.Q. in the CUTTING, CONTALMAISON. Extra guns are being brought up into forward positions, and the "Tanks" have moved up to front line area. Germans are reported to have attacked Canadian Division on our left, and to have entered the front line. This has not been confirmed	
CONTALMAISON	15.9.16		Splendid morning: slightly hazy, but sun coming out. At 6.0 am. intense Bombardment along the whole enemy front and the attack has been launched. Canadians, 15th Div, 50th Division and whole of 4th Army to the right are attacking. The tanks are reported as having worked excellently and done great execution. One is however broken down + reported as "Smoking.	Dow.

2353 Wt. W2544/1454 700,000 5/15 D. D. & L. A.D.S.S./Forms/C. 2118.

Army Form C. 2118.

Instructions regarding War Diaries and Intelligence Summaries are contained in F. S. Regs., Part II. and the Staff Manual respectively. Title pages will be prepared in manuscript.

WAR DIARY
or
INTELLIGENCE SUMMARY.
(Erase heading not required.)

SHEET 307

Place	Date	Hour	Summary of Events and Information	Remarks and references to Appendices
CONTALMAISON.	15.9.16.	6.45am.	Attack is going well. Whole of 1st objective of 15th Div. has been gained. At first advance the enemy retired to his trenches in MARTINPUICH. Heavy casualties taken by our M.G.s + Artillery.	
		7.30am	Over 100 prisoners have already passed down, nearly all Bavarians.	
		8.30am	Whole objective of Division has been taken. No news from the Left Div. (CANADIAN). We have established a signal station in MARTINPUICH, and are consolidating second objective.	
		9.30am	Over 200 prisoners have now passed down, and difficulty is being experienced in clearing them. 2nd Canadian Divn. have captured whole objective and are pushing on towards COURCELETTE. Three German officers, Battn. Comdr., Adjutant + F.O.O. were brought to Battn. H.Q. They appeared very little depressed and are convinced that things are going all right for them, still.	
		2.0pm	Canadian attack on second objective postponed. 50th Div have occupied PRUE TRENCH well ahead on the right and 15th Division has been ordered to advance further in order to join up with their left flank. Attack began at 3.0pm + at 5.0pm. 45th + 46th Bdes. were reported as having reached objective and digging in.	
			Battn. moved at 4.0pm. into Corps line and Pearl Alley.	
			Further report on attack of 50th Div. on the right state they have reached FLERS, and a line between GINCHY and les BOEUFS.	
		9.45pm	2nd Canadian Division have captured COURCELETTE.	
		10.10pm	Total number of prisoners taken by 3rd Corps for today 35 officers + 1200 other Ranks.	[initials]

2353 Wt. W2544/1454 700,000 5/15 D. D. & L. A.D.S.S./Forms/C. 2118.

Army Form C. 2118.

Instructions regarding War Diaries and Intelligence Summaries are contained in F. S. Regs., Part II. and the Staff Manual respectively. Title pages will be prepared in manuscript.

WAR DIARY
or
INTELLIGENCE SUMMARY.
(Erase heading not required.)

SHEET ~~307~~ 308.

Place	Date	Hour	Summary of Events and Information	Remarks and references to Appendices
CONTAL-MAISON.	16.9.16		Enemy reported to have made a feeble counter-attack on right (45th) Bde. This was easily repulsed.	
		9.30 am	Heavy hostile barrage on COURCELETTE and MARTINPUICH for about 2 hours. At the end of this period the barrage ceased without any infantry attack developing. Word received that Battn is temporarily attached to 46th Bde. We moved into trenches about 5.30 pm. Shelled during relief.	
Trenches MARTINPUICH.	17.9.16.		Battn is now holding GUNPIT ROAD + Part of MARTINPUICH Village. Gunpit Road is an old German position, ~~exactly~~ accurately registered and heavily shelled. The village of MARTINPUICH is a heap of ruins, containing much German stores, shelled regularly + constantly by enemy's 8" shells, desolate and dangerous. The enemy is however over 500 yards away, and has been well-beaten.	
		3.0 pm.	Report had been received that an artillery officer had reconnoitred the German trench in front, and had found it unwired + void of enemy. We were ordered in conjunction with 10/11 HLI. on our right to send out a reconnoitring patrol and afterwards to man the trench. The patrols from this Battn + from HLI set out at 4.30 pm. and found that the reconnaissance previously reported was entirely inaccurate. They were fired on by rifles + M.G's, found the trench wired and well garrisoned + had to retire. In addition their appearance caused the enemy to expect an attack. He put a very heavy barrage on our trenches for nearly 3 hours and caused many casualties. Inaccurate reports rendered by passenger-visitors to the front line are not worthy of forming the basis of offensive operations, and our men have suffered accordingly. The whole of this day during which we have been attached to 46th Bde. has been unpleasant. All orders were rushed, enquiries were numberless, arrangements were bad and the general result of the day depressing. Tonight we return to 44th Bde.!	D.W.M.

Army Form C. 2118.

Instructions regarding War Diaries and Intelligence Summaries are contained in F. S. Regs., Part II. and the Staff Manual respectively. Title pages will be prepared in manuscript.

WAR DIARY
or
INTELLIGENCE SUMMARY.
(Erase heading not required.)

Sheet ~~308~~ 309.

Place	Date	Hour	Summary of Events and Information	Remarks and references to Appendices
Trenches. Contalmaison Sector.	18.XI.16.		The Battn was relieved in the front trenches by the 9th Black Watch, about 7.0 pm on the 17th. The relief was held up by shelling and two platoons were unable to get out till 7.0 am today. A wet day and the trenches are in very bad condition. We have moved into Lancs Trench + Bacon Trench as Brigade Reserve. It rained persistently all day and the men have no shelter.	
		5.0pm	The 23rd Division has begun to relieve the 15th Div. in the line which moves tonight into Corps Reserve. The 11th West Riding Regt is taking over from this Battn. Relief under wretched conditions otherwise without incident. We moved into camp at E.5.b. near ALBERT and got finally settled about 8.30 pm. Tent accomodation is good, but the ground is very wet and muddy.	
~~ALBERT~~. LAVIEVILLE.	19.XI.16.		Moved at 10.0 am today from ALBERT to camp at LAVIEVILLE, taking over from 45th I. Bde. Still wet and the march though short is exhausting, for the men have as yet had no opportunity of drying or cleaning themselves since leaving the front line. Arrived in camp about 2.0 pm. The tents were situated in a very wet and muddy locality, so we have shifted the entire camp on to a dry hill. Day uneventful.	D.W.M.
FRANVILLERS.	20.XI.16		Left camp at LAVIEVILLE at 10.0 am today + marched to FRANVILLERS. The weather is still bad but the constant rain of the last few days shows signs of breaking up.	

T2134. Wt. W708—776. 500000. 4/15. Sir J. C. & S.

Instructions regarding War Diaries and Intelligence Summaries are contained in F. S. Regs., Part II. and the Staff Manual respectively. Title pages will be prepared in manuscript.

WAR DIARY
or
INTELLIGENCE SUMMARY.
(Erase heading not required.)

Sheet 310.

Army Form C. 2118.

Place	Date	Hour	Summary of Events and Information	Remarks and references to Appendices
FRANVILLERS.	20.IX.16.		Arrived at Franvillers about 2.0 pm. A small French village full of troops and Transport but we have been allotted Billets which give first opportunity of good rest and of cleaning up. Day uneventful.	
FRANVILLERS.	21.IX.16.		The entire day today is being devoted to cleaning up, kit inspections, making up deficiencies and generally overhauling. The weather has cleared up and though chilly is now dry. A programme of training is being prepared with a ~~few~~ view to getting the men into condition again, and probably equipping them for further offensive on this front. Rev. H.K. CORNISH who has been missing for 2 or 3 days has been officially reported missing to Brigade today. Baths were allotted us today.	
FRANVILLERS.	22.IX.16.		Training on the new scheme has been begun and is now well under way. Hours of work - 9.0 am - 12 noon + 2 pm - 3.0 pm, with a half-hour's physical training from 7.0 - 7.30 am. daily. All the officers from Reinforcement Camp have rejoined so that there are now 32 Officers in the 4 Coys, apart from H.Q.^s Rev. H.K. Cornish is now reported as having been admitted to No 3 General Hospital suffering from head-wounds received near ALBERT. A shell burst on the road killed 3 horses, and several men and wounded the 'padre'! Everyone is pleasantly	Dwr.

Instructions regarding War Diaries and Intelligence Summaries are contained in F. S. Regs., Part II. and the Staff Manual respectively. Title pages will be prepared in manuscript.

WAR DIARY
or
INTELLIGENCE SUMMARY.
(Erase heading not required.)

Sheet 311.

Army Form C. 2118.

Place	Date	Hour	Summary of Events and Information	Remarks and references to Appendices
	22.IX.16		relieved at discovering him again. Leave to AMIENS is now granted and advantage is being taken of it as far as possible. This is a boon to men from a 6 weeks trip in SOMME-land. (pleasantly)	
FRANVILLERS.	23.IX.16		Training in Rest Billets still going on. Days uneventful.	
"	24.IX.16 to 28.IX.16		Four quiet days, with a prolonged spell of good weather. Training is being continued and the men looking very fit again. Heavy fighting has been going on all along the SOMME front. We have now advanced our line considerably beyond the line we left, have completely captured Courcelette, Flers, Gueudecourt, MORVAL & Les Boeufs and have penetrated the Le Sars line in the region of our right flank. THIEPVAL is also taken and our line consolidated well beyond. Rumour today reports that Thiepval has been re-attacked and taken by the enemy but there is no official news of this. Very heavy fighting is however in progress at	
	28th	10.0pm	the present moment but we have no news as to its object or locality. Inoculation carried out on men of A Coy not inoculated within last 12 months.	
Do.	29th Sept.		A wet day which put a stop to outdoor training most of the day given up to lectures. Brigade Sports have been notified and preliminary preparations made.	[illegible]

T2134. Wt. W708—776. 500000. 4/15. Sir J. C. & S.

Instructions regarding War Diaries and Intelligence Summaries are contained in F. S. Regs., Part II. and the Staff Manual respectively. Title pages will be prepared in manuscript.

WAR DIARY
or
INTELLIGENCE SUMMARY.
(Erase heading not required.)

Sheet 312.

Army Form C. 2118.

Place	Date	Hour	Summary of Events and Information	Remarks and references to Appendices
FRANVILLERS.	30.11.16.		Rain in morning but bright + sunny later. A quiet day with no ~~events~~ movements to relate. A 'Sports' meeting was held at HQ with a view to organising Battn Sports. A good programme was made out and general enthusiasm evident. First two officers for '3 days leave to Paris' left today.	[signature]

T2134. Wt. W708—776. 500000. 4/15. Sir J. C. & S.

Vol 17

CONFIDENTIAL

WAR DIARY

OF

8/10th (Ser.) Battn The Gordon Highlanders.

From 1st October, 1916 To 31st October, 1916.

VOLUME 18.

G. J. Cumming
Major for Lt. Col.
Comdg 8/10th Bn The Gordon Highlanders

Instructions regarding War Diaries and Intelligence Summaries are contained in F. S. Regs., Part II. and the Staff Manual respectively. Title pages will be prepared in manuscript.

WAR DIARY
or
INTELLIGENCE SUMMARY.
(*Erase heading not required.*)

SHEET 313.

Army Form C. 2118.

Place	Date	Hour	Summary of Events and Information	Remarks and references to Appendices
FRANVILLERS	1.X.16.		A quiet Sunday: Church parade well attended. Mr Bone (Black + White artist) visited the Battn + made various sketches, including one of the Battn at Divine Service.	
"	2.X.16.		Rained unceasingly throughout the day. Battn Sports which had been arranged for the afternoon had to be postponed	
"	3.X.16.		Rain continued. The 2nd part of Battn Sports which had been arranged for today was badly interfered with. Tug-of-war, jumping + running were however got through with under very bad conditions	DWL
"	4.X.16.		Brigade Sports were to have been held today. All arrangements were made field laid out + programmes published. Late last night however Battn got sudden orders to move up to forward area. Complete preparations were made and Battn almost ready to move off, when movement was cancelled. Dancing competition was held in the mess after dinner: Reel, sword dance and Highland fling. The events were well contested and a pleasant evening spent. A good attendance from the Coy was present in the mess, which is in a French café and holds quite a number of men.	
"	5.X.16.		~~Battn~~ 44th Bde today practised an attack over training area here. This was	

T2134. Wt. W708—776. 500000. 4/15. Sir J. C. & S.

Instructions regarding War Diaries and Intelligence Summaries are contained in F. S. Regs., Part II. and the Staff Manual respectively. Title pages will be prepared in manuscript.

WAR DIARY or INTELLIGENCE SUMMARY.

(Erase heading not required.)

Sheet 314.

Army Form C. 2118.

Place	Date	Hour	Summary of Events and Information	Remarks and references to Appendices
			over ground representing as near as possible an actual attack to be made by the Brigade shortly. Gordons + Black Watch attacked together in front line, with Camerons in Support + Seaforths in Reserve. Divisional + Brigade commanders were present. The first attempt was unsuccessful, as the programme had been too elaborately arranged, and long halts occurred under fire while Strong points + M.G. Emplacements were being dealt with. The second attempt was more successful. The whole attack was carried out without stop and final objective gained under an hour. The Batt^n is now under orders to move to forward area to-morrow, to take up position in the line shortly afterwards.	[signature]
BECOURT WOOD	6.X.16		Batt^n moved to BECOURT today leaving FRANVILLERS at 1.30 pm. It rained again practically all day, and no provision of shelters was made in BECOURT WOOD. The Batt^n arrived wet and tired and had to bivouac amongst the mud + tree-stumps. Some tents and shelters finally arrived about 10.0 pm by which time most of the men had gone to sleep and were careless as to provision of shelters or otherwise. Fortunately the night cleared up + no very great hardship was involved.	
BECOURT	7.X.16		A fair day. Arrangements were made as far as possible for equipping Batt^n for the line	

Instructions regarding War Diaries and Intelligence Summaries are contained in F. S. Regs., Part II. and the Staff Manual respectively. Title pages will be prepared in manuscript.

WAR DIARY
or
INTELLIGENCE SUMMARY.
(Erase heading not required.)

Sheet 315.

Army Form C. 2118.

Place	Date	Hour	Summary of Events and Information	Remarks and references to Appendices
Becourt.	7.X.16.		Day otherwise uneventful	
Le SARS Trenches	8.X.16.		Orders to move came with a rush at 11.0 a.m. ordering Battalion to proceed to the line at 5.0 p.m. Surplus officers were despatched to ALBERT, equipping finally completed and Battn moved off at hour ordered. Just before moving off word was received that Ptes Gentleman & Moreland (2 Headquarters runners) had been awarded the D.C.M. for gallantry.	
			We took over from the 12th D.L.I. (Lt Col. Macgregor who formerly commanded the 10th Gordons). This Battn had been in almost unceasing action for 48 hours, was badly depleted (150 men left) and the position is uncertain. The guides sent to lead in our Battn had little knowledge of the route. All lost themselves and relief was finally complete at 3.0 a.m. Even then positions had to be taken up at random, and daylight had to be awaited for final sorting out. The 47th Div (22nd London Regt) on our Right did a small attack during relief, and our lines were heavily shelled. The sole communication trench up to front line was almost obliterated and relief had to go over the open.	
Le SARS.	9.X.16.		A good day. The position we have taken up has now become clear and is unique in site. The attack on the right had failed. Our left flank has gone beyond Le SARS and we now form a flank along the E. edge of the village, back to the old German front line	

T2134. Wt. W708—776. 500000. 4/15. Sir J. C. & S.

Instructions regarding War Diaries and Intelligence Summaries are contained in F. S. Regs., Part II. and the Staff Manual respectively. Title pages will be prepared in manuscript.

WAR DIARY or INTELLIGENCE SUMMARY.

(Erase heading not required.)

Army Form C. 2118.

Sheet 316

Place	Date	Hour	Summary of Events and Information	Remarks and references to Appendices
Le Sars	9.x.16		part of which we hold and part of which is untenable. Our line forms almost 2 sides of a square, with 2 isolated platoons in a road-cutting on the right flank. We are unable to ascertain the whereabouts of the advanced posts of the 47th Div. and can get no information from them. The trenches are in a horrible state of filth. There is no latrine accomodation and dead bodies (British and German) are everywhere. Troops have been so busy fighting that no burying has been possible and the sight is gruesome. We are on the downward slope of the ridge & can see WARLENCOURT & BAPAUME further up on the other slope. We hope soon to be in possession of these. Meanwhile we are living practically in the open, for there is almost no trench accomodation. A patrol went out this afternoon to try to locate the enemy. They came on an unsuspected post and had an Officer and a Sergeant wounded. Apart from this we have as yet practically no knowledge of where the enemy is. Tonight we are digging a new assembly trench and trying to straighten up the position prior to advancing. The night is bright moonlight and work is difficult. Men are everywhere overcrowded and during a severe shelling from 6 pm. - 7 pm we have had a good many casualties. Enemy shelling has been constant & heavy throughout the day and we have had about 30 casualties, about 5 being killed.	RMcG

Instructions regarding War Diaries and Intelligence Summaries are contained in F. S. Regs., Part II. and the Staff Manual respectively. Title pages will be prepared in manuscript.

WAR DIARY or INTELLIGENCE SUMMARY.

(Erase heading not required.)

Sheet 317

Army Form C. 2118.

Place	Date	Hour	Summary of Events and Information	Remarks and references to Appendices
Le SARS.	10.X.16.		Good weather. We have somewhat straightened out the congestion and things are more comfortable. The enemy has shelled the position steadily throughout the day, luckily without causing any great damage. The enemy has a very commanding position, on the side of a high ridge rising up towards BAPAUME. Considerable movement can be seen all along and behind the front line. Our artillery is doing good work amongst them but the position looks very strong and will require much dash in the taking. The Londoners (22nd) on our right are quite done up & their position is for the moment uncertain. We have dug new assembly trenches & connected up with the Black Watch round the N. end of Le SARS.	[illegible]
"		10.0 pm	Our relief is being unduly held up owing to the 7th Camerons waiting for their rations before coming up. Rations can easily be got even in front line trenches but they are unwilling to move up.	
night	10/11.		Relief going on. The 7th Camerons are relieving both Battns in the line, and have evidently changed their arrangements after operation orders had been issued, and without informing us. Result is that guides have got mixed up and we finally leave the trenches in pitch dark at 3.30 a.m. The Battn goes back to BAZENTIN & trenches in front.	

T2134. Wt. W708—776. 500000. 4/15. Sir J. C. & S.

Instructions regarding War Diaries and Intelligence Summaries are contained in F. S. Regs., Part II. and the Staff Manual respectively. Title pages will be prepared in manuscript.

WAR DIARY
or
INTELLIGENCE SUMMARY.
(Erase heading not required.)

Sheet 38.

Army Form C. 2118.

Place	Date	Hour	Summary of Events and Information	Remarks and references to Appendices
BAZENTIN-le-Petit.	11·X·16.		Everybody got lost during relief and the whole Battn wandered in separate parties all over the country until daylight when they finally sorted out and arrived in the proper area, about 6·30 a.m. The remainder of the day was spent in resting. Every man is very tired and glad to get a short distance away from the heavy shelling in order to get some sleep. Nothing else of importance to record.	
BAZENTIN.	12·X·16.		The 9th Division came into the line on the right of our sector last night. Today at 2·5 p.m. they attacked the German line with the BUTTE-de-WARLENCOURT on their left flank as objective. The main intention is to straighten out the line, prior to further assault. There is little news of the progress of affairs. The S.A. Bde & the 26th Bde. went over side by side and were met by a terrific M.G. fire previously unparalleled. The German present position is excellent for this and all the valleys & approaches are swept by their guns. Later news reports the objective gained, but with very heavy losses to the two Brigades carrying out the assault. Wounded have been coming down all afternoon and throughout the night 12/13th and from them the only news obtainable is culled. Evidently a weak counter-attack was made but with NO success.	[signature]

T2134. Wt. W708—776. 500000. 4/15. Sir J. C. & S.

Instructions regarding War Diaries and Intelligence Summaries are contained in F. S. Regs., Part II. and the Staff Manual respectively. Title pages will be prepared in manuscript.

WAR DIARY
or
INTELLIGENCE SUMMARY.
(Erase heading not required.)

Army Form C. 2118.

Sheet 319.

Place	Date	Hour	Summary of Events and Information	Remarks and references to Appendices
			A fine morning but cold. Winter weather has finally settled in. There is still no	
BAZENTIN.	13.X.16		official news of yesterday, but though successful the task evidently proved more difficult than was anticipated. Today we are refitting and finally reorganising and go back into line tomorrow, probably at night. Our casualties since going into trenches last time have amounted to about 60 (all ranks)	[illegible]

T2134. Wt. W708—776. 500000. 4/15. Sir J. C. & S.

Instructions regarding War Diaries and Intelligence Summaries are contained in F. S. Regs., Part II. and the Staff Manual respectively. Title pages will be prepared in manuscript.

WAR DIARY
or
INTELLIGENCE SUMMARY.
(Erase heading not required.)

SHEET/320

Army Form C. 2118.

Place	Date	Hour	Summary of Events and Information	Remarks and references to Appendices
BAZENTIN le-petit	13.X.16.		Operations carried out by 9th Div are now reported as having failed, chiefly on account of lack of previous artillery preparation and underestimating the enemy. Big preparations are now to be made prior to next advance.	
			Capt J. G. THOM left to attend training School for commanding Officers at ALDERSHOT.	
			A large digging party (300 men) were out for the greater part of the night digging new trenches in the front system.	
BAZENTIN le-petit.	14.X.16		very cold, with a touch of frost. We have cleared the bombs out of this old German store, have erected partitions and made the place fairly comfortable. Good winter accomodation can be had here if the place is put into a state of repair. The proposed move of the Batt: to the trenches has been cancelled and the 44th Bde has been relieved in the front line by the 46th. A party of 300 men continued the work on new trenches in LE SARS. 2/Lt O. C. F. ELLIOTT was killed while officer in charge of a section of this party. He was buried the following day in BECOURT Cemetery. Pipe band attended and officers party.	
BAZENTIN-le-petit.	15.X.16.		Digging fatigue is becoming permanent. Party of 200 men again out digging trenches in LE SARS front system. The nights are very dark and good work almost impracticable. Cold weather continues and men are suffering from lack of accomodation and shelter.	[initials]

T2134. Wt. W708—776. 500000. 4/15. Sir J. C. & S.

Instructions regarding War Diaries and Intelligence Summaries are contained in F. S. Regs., Part II. and the Staff Manual respectively. Title pages will be prepared in manuscript.

WAR DIARY
or
INTELLIGENCE SUMMARY.
(Erase heading not required.)

SHEET 321.

Army Form C. 2118.

Place	Date	Hour	Summary of Events and Information	Remarks and references to Appendices
BAZENTIN-le-petit	15.X.16		Enemy aeroplanes have been unusually active today, and hostile balloons have put in an appearance. Our anti-aircraft guns however give his aeroplanes little chance and balloons decend precipitately as soon as our machines put in an appearance. Some heavy barrages were put on the sector immediately to our left during the night 15/16th. The Canadians are still slightly short of their objective and are evidently going to have trouble in getting it.	[signature]
Ditto	16.X.16		Uneventful. Today we have had an issue of rum and an issue of coke, signs of approaching winter. Officers have been brought up from Reinforcement Camp to relieve some of those who have been continually in the line. Maj. G. T. G. C. Cumine D.S.O. (2nd in Comd) has come up to relieve the C.O. for a day or two. C.O. adjutant and several company officers have gone to ALBERT to rest. Enemy aerial activity again above normal, and several of their planes flew well in rear of our lines. There is a rather marked improvement in this branch of enemy's service of late.	
BAZENTIN	17.X.16		Weather broken. Heavy rain throughout the night still continues and the prospect for trenches is dreary. Warning order has today been received for probable move into Support area tomorrow	

T2134. Wt. W708—776. 500000. 4/15. Sir J. C. & S.

Instructions regarding War Diaries and Intelligence Summaries are contained in F. S. Regs., Part II. and the Staff Manual respectively. Title pages will be prepared in manuscript.

WAR DIARY
or
INTELLIGENCE SUMMARY.
(Erase heading not required.)

SHEET 322.

Army Form C. 2118.

Place	Date	Hour	Summary of Events and Information	Remarks and references to Appendices
CRESCENT Alley (Nr MARTINPUICH)	18.X.16		Rain continues and the whole country side is awash. The Battn moved up into CRESCENT Alley (Support Trenches) at dusk today, relieving the 10th Sco. Rifles. Trenches are in a frightful state, Battn HQ is the stairway of an unfinished dug-out, and there is neither room nor shelter for anybody. The night is exceedingly dark and nothing can be done till daylight tomorrow	
LE SARS (front trenches)	19.X.16		The Battn moved into the front line at dusk today and relieved the 12th H.L.I. Several further showers during the day made the trenches almost impassable, and the relief which began at about 6.0 pm. was not complete until about 4.0 am. Mud in the trenches was fully 2 feet deep, and 3 feet in many places. Men stuck in the mud all along the line and had to be dug out time and again. Luckily enemy shelling on communication trenches was very slight or our casualties would surely have been heavy. Several men were left stuck thigh deep in the mud and were only extricated in daylight the following morning. Parties got lost, stuck or stranded all over the area, rations could not be got past Battn HQrs and the whole relief was the most hopeless one yet encountered. In future we have decided to relieve over the open, and take chance of shelling preferably to being buried in mud.	[illegible]

T2134. Wt. W708—776. 500000. 4/15. Sir J. C. & S.

Instructions regarding War Diaries and Intelligence Summaries are contained in F. S. Regs., Part II. and the Staff Manual respectively. Title pages will be prepared in manuscript.

WAR DIARY
or
INTELLIGENCE SUMMARY.
(Erase heading not required.)

SHEET 323.

Army Form C. 2118.

Place	Date	Hour	Summary of Events and Information	Remarks and references to Appendices
Le Sars	30.x.16		weather has cleared somewhat, but the trenches are still bad. The Coys. have however got properly settled with fairly good dug-outs in each case for Coy H.Q. The position on the right is still uncertain, and the exact location of the enemy indefinite. Our artillery shell the BUTTE de WARLENCOURT incessantly. The enemy is known to hold the trenches in this vicinity fairly strongly and the BUTTE itself appears to be well set up with machine-guns. The general trench system in our sector has been somewhat straightened out, the line made more definite and posts established well out in front. During the day enemy artillery activity has been normal. Battn H.Q. which is near a trench junction, appears to be a well marked spot and gets considerable attention. In this sector men wander about in the open everywhere even in front of the front line. Today parties from the Div. on our right can be seen wandering about almost on the crest 200 yards in front of their position, and a patrol from our trenches in broad daylight walked across our front, and out beyond the BUTTE on the right. Our ceaseless artillery bombardment apparently has deprived enemy infantry of all its powers of observation. The weather has now appearances of keeping fine.	DMcG

T2134. Wt. W708—776. 500000. 4/15. Sir J. C. & S.

Instructions regarding War Diaries and Intelligence Summaries are contained in F. S. Regs., Part II. and the Staff Manual respectively. Title pages will be prepared in manuscript.

WAR DIARY
or
INTELLIGENCE SUMMARY.
(*Erase heading not required.*)

SHEET 32a.

Army Form C. 2118.

Place	Date	Hour	Summary of Events and Information	Remarks and references to Appendices
LE SARS.	21.x.16		Night uneventful, except for bitter cold in H.Q. dug-out. There is no accomodation for one to stretch one's legs, and the cold at night is very severe. Today we have established two observation posts, from which we hope to obtain good information as to Enemy's position & movement. His most frequented traffic routes are shelled continually by our artillery and we hope to discover his lines of communication in ~~the~~ immediate rear of his front trenches.	
			Batt.n was relieved by the 7th CAMERONS, relief being complete about 1.0 a.m. The Camerons came up across the open almost to the front line, and this expedited the relief considerably. It is the only possible way with trenches in their present condition.	[signature]
BAZENTIN le-petit.	22.x.16		We are back in reserve in our old position. ~~The~~ Batt.n H.Q. has been considerably improved by the Seaforths. We have now 2 rooms, both fairly large and fairly comfortable. The other end of the dug out has been reclaimed by the R.A.M.C. and is now being used by them as H.Q. Mess.	
BAZENTIN	23.x.16 to 29.x.16		Batt.n has been in reserve position all the time. The "attack" has been postponed 3 times during this period on account of bad weather, and the Batt.n which is being	

T2134. Wt. W708—776. 500000. 4/15. Sir J. C. & S.

Instructions regarding War Diaries and Intelligence Summaries are contained in F. S. Regs., Part II. and the Staff Manual respectively. Title pages will be prepared in manuscript.

WAR DIARY
or
INTELLIGENCE SUMMARY.
(Erase heading not required.)

Army Form C. 2118.

SHEET 375.

Place	Date	Hour	Summary of Events and Information	Remarks and references to Appendices
23rd to 29th Cont.d			saved for this attack is having a favourable time. Conditions in rear are appalling. Owing to prolonged bad weather communication is becoming almost impossible; roads are 2 feet deep in mud, traffic blocks occur everywhere, and with darkness as an added drawback, only the most determined work enables the thing to go on at all. Difficulties in getting up rations, material and ammunition are almost insuperable, entirely due to the fact that while the advance was forging ahead and the weather good, little attention was paid to getting good communication trenches dug, roads remade, and supply lines well established. We have now been on the eve of moving into assembly position three times and each time have had it cancelled just in time to prevent our moving.	DMcG
BAZENTIN	30.X.16.		Again today we were to have gone into the front line and again the move has been cancelled on account of rain. A regular downpour came on during the afternoon and the whole area is again feet deep in mud. The move is accordingly postponed to await further orders and presumably better weather, which is unlikely except for perhaps a short period during the rest of winter.	
			A German prisoner taken tonight by the 10th Sco. Rifles passed through here	

T2134. Wt. W708–776. 500000. 4/15. Sir J. C. & S.

Army Form C. 2118.

Instructions regarding War Diaries and Intelligence Summaries are contained in F. S. Regs., Part II. and the Staff Manual respectively. Title pages will be prepared in manuscript.

WAR DIARY
or
INTELLIGENCE SUMMARY.
(Erase heading not required.)

SHEET 326

Place	Date	Hour	Summary of Events and Information	Remarks and references to Appendices
	30.x.16.	(Cont'd)	on his way to the cage. Several Germans have of late been coming into our lines, all very anxious to get out of the stress of continual battle. The effect of our continual artillery fire is beginning to tell heavily on them.	D.W.G.
BAZENTINE	31 x 16		A quiet day. Battalion moved to front line trenches 5.30 pm.	

T2134. Wt. W708—776. 500000. 4/15. Sir J. C. & S.

CONFIDENTIAL

Vol ~~17~~ 18

WAR DIARY

OF

8/10th (Service) Battalion, The Gordon Highlanders

FOR PERIOD

November 1st 1916 TO 30th November, 1916

VOLUME 19.

G. J. Cumming Major

Comdg 8/10th (Ser) Battn, The Gordon Highlrs.

Instructions regarding War Diaries and Intelligence Summaries are contained in F. S. Regs., Part II. and the Staff Manual respectively. Title pages will be prepared in manuscript.

WAR DIARY
or
INTELLIGENCE SUMMARY.
(Erase heading not required.)

Army Form C. 2118.

Sheet 327.

Place	Date	Hour	Summary of Events and Information	Remarks and references to Appendices
Le Sars.	1st Nov		Morning very dull but dry. There was very little shelling until later in the day. Observation Posts established. The trenches were very wet & muddy but great progress was made during the night clearing the mud & water from SCOTLAND TRENCH. LE SARS N. & S. Enemy shelled around entrance to Bn HQrs at intervals during the day. R.S.M. had doorway of his dugout blown in. Heavy shelling with big shells on our left. A Message was sent off by carrier pigeon. 2Lt. A.D SUTHERLAND slightly wounded by shell fire. Enemy began a heavy shoot on our front line trenches & those of the Div. on our right. No attack was made. EAUCOURT L'ABBAYE was continuously shelled by heavies. Our artillery retaliated & enemy soon stopped. 2Lt T. Cornford was slightly wounded.	JL
Le Sars	2nd		During early morning there was a very thick mist. During night 1/2 enemy shelled intermittently our front line system & also communications. He obtained 4 direct hits on Trench beside HQrs. Some rain fell during forenoon but the afternoon was fine. The Battn was relieved by the 8th WORCESTER. Relief was completed by 9.30 PM	

T2134. Wt. W708—776. 500000. 4/15. Sir J. C. & S.

Instructions regarding War Diaries and Intelligence Summaries are contained in F. S. Regs., Part II. and the Staff Manual respectively. Title pages will be prepared in manuscript.

WAR DIARY

or

~~INTELLIGENCE~~ ~~SUMMARY~~. Sheet 328

(Erase heading not required.)

Army Form C. 2118.

Place	Date	Hour	Summary of Events and Information	Remarks and references to Appendices
	2-11-16		The Battn arrived in Billets of Huts & Tents – at BECOURT.	[initials]
BECOURT	3-11-16		Mud is very bad here. The men are staying in tents with no floor boards & the officers in huts. Weather is fine & dry. 2Lt. PIPE joined the Battn from the 4th Battn. Cleaning up is proceeding.	
BECOURT	4-11-16		Battn still at BECOURT. No word of leaving yet. Heavy rain during the night & morning is very dull. The officers from the reinforcement camp rejoined Battn today. The men had a bath at the BECOURT bath house.	
BECOURT.	5-11-16		Nothing of importance has happened. Everyone trying to kill time & wishing they would get a move on somewhere. At last orders are received to effect ~~that~~ Battn will proceed to BRESLE on 6th.	
BRESLE	6-11-16		The morning is fine & all are ready to go. The Battn marched to billets at BRESLE. We are in Tents again. The camp is this time on the slope of a hill & is very dry. The Tents have floorboards & things are pretty comfortable. Everyone is busy cleaning up	

T2134. Wt. W708–776. 500000. 4/15. Sir J. C. & S.

Instructions regarding War Diaries and Intelligence Summaries are contained in F. S. Regs., Part II. and the Staff Manual respectively. Title pages will be prepared in manuscript.

WAR DIARY
or
~~INTELLIGENCE~~ SUMMARY. Sheet 329

(*Erase heading not required.*)

Army Form C. 2118.

Place	Date	Hour	~~Summary of Events and Information~~	Remarks and references to Appendices
BRESLE	7-11-16		The day was spent cleaning & kit inspections. Weather is very bad.	[illegible]
"	8-11-16		Company training is being carried on. Specialists etc are also	
"	9-11-16		being trained. Nothing ~~important~~ has taken place	
"	10-11-16		It is now settled we are to remain here during our whole rest period.	
			Rifle Range completed & range practice can now be started	
"	11-11-16		The massed bands of the Brigade played Retreat.	
"	12-11-16		The Divisional Band played in LEICESTER SQUARE. No parades.	
"	13-11-16		A working party of 300 men & 12 officers went to BECOURT to build huts	
			there. This has broken up our training programme badly.	
	14-11-16		Brigade sports are announced for the 19th. Battn has short-	
			men for them were sent down from the fatigue party.	
	15-11-16		Very little training can be gone over on account of the small	
	to 19-11-16		number of men left. The G.O.C III Corps addressed the Brigade	
	20-11-16.		on the afternoon of the 19th. Paris leave can now be applied for	
			The Brigade sports were held on the 20th but the Battn did not do	
			very well as it was badly handicapped by the working party being away.	

T2134. Wt. W708—776. 500000. 4/15. Sir J. C. & S.

Instructions regarding War Diaries and Intelligence Summaries are contained in F. S. Regs., Part II. and the Staff Manual respectively. Title pages will be prepared in manuscript.

WAR DIARY
or
~~INTELLIGENCE~~ SUMMARY.
(Erase heading not required.)

Sheet 330

Army Form C. 2118.

Place	Date	Hour	Summary of Events and ~~Information~~	Remarks and references to Appendices
BRESLE.	20-10-16 to 31-10-16		The working party returned on the evening of the 19th. The usual training was carried on during the whole of this period. ~~[illegible]~~ Major General F.W.N. McCRACKEN C.B. D.S.O. inspected the Battn at work on the 27th. Movement orders received. Battn to move up to ALBERT on the 1st Nov. A Race meeting was held on afternoon of the 29th & there were five races. Regimental Officers flat Race. Pack Pony race ridden by Subaltern Officers. Mule race ridden by drivers, & the Highland Plate & Martinpuich Plate. Also a Clydesdale Scramble. The Battn did very well in each one. Chief event of the day. The Martinpuich Plate - was won by the Officer Commanding 44th Brigade, Brig. General Marshall.	[initials]

T2134. Wt. W708—776. 500000. 4/15. Sir J. C. & S.

Vol 19

CONFIDENTIAL

WAR DIARY

OF

8/10th (Service) Battn, The Gordon Highrs.

FROM 30. 11. 1916 TO 31. 12. 1916.

VOLUME ~~20~~

[illegible]

Lt. Major
Comdg.
8/10th (Ser) Bn The Gordon Highlanders.

Instructions regarding War Diaries and Intelligence Summaries are contained in F. S. Regs., Part II. and the Staff Manual respectively. Title pages will be prepared in manuscript.

WAR DIARY
or
INTELLIGENCE SUMMARY. Sheet 331
(Erase heading not required.)

Army Form C. 2118.

Place	Date	Hour	Summary of Events and Information	Remarks and references to Appendices
BRESLE	30-11-16		St Andrews Day. The Officers of the Battn held a dinner in the camp, the PLAT du JOUR being the 'Haggis'. The King's health was drunk & speeches were made. As the Battn was moving early next morning we were forced to close very early in the evening. The meeting ending very quietly.	
ALBERT	1-12-16		The Battn marched to Billets in Albert this morning. Morning dull & frosty. The day was spent putting billets in order ~~&~~ cleaning up the place	[initials]
"	2-12-16		The day was spend cleaning up billets which were not too clean. Most of them were very cold & a few wet. A fatigue party of 200 men were employed by the Town Major cleaning roads.	
"	3-12-16		The Battn was duty battn for the Bde. This consisted in supplying all sorts of Working & Fatigue parties. These were engaged chiefly in road cleaning the streets being very dirty	
		4-5.	In the evening the Bosche got angry & shelled the town very steadily for fully an hour. No particular spot was strafed but shells were dropped indiscriminately all over the town. Very little damage was done.	

T2134. Wt. W708–776. 500000. 4/15. Sir J. C. & S.

Instructions regarding War Diaries and Intelligence Summaries are contained in F. S. Regs., Part II. and the Staff Manual respectively. Title pages will be prepared in manuscript.

WAR DIARY
or
~~INTELLIGENCE~~ SUMMARY.
(Erase heading not required.)

Army Form C. 2118.

Sheet 332

Place	Date	Hour	Summary of Events and Information	Remarks and references to Appendices
ALBERT.	3-12-16.		The evening passed off with no repetition of the shelling.	
ALBERT	4-12-16.		The usual training took place during the forenoon. The coys went to Baths in the afternoon. The Commanding Officer returned from Leave. Enemy shelled town intermittently during the evening, but none came unpleasantly close to our billets.	
ALBERT	5-12-16		The weather was very dull & cold. The Battn went for a Route March through BOUZINCOURT. & MILLANCOURT. We encountered a heavy rainstorm on route but it was fine when we finished. No parade in afternoon.	[initials]
~~ALBERT~~	~~6-12-16~~		~~The weather still dull & cold~~, 2Lt. Lee & 2Lt Kendal joined the Battn from Home.	
ALBERT	6-12-16		The weather still dull & cold. The Battn received orders to move up to camp S.W. of MAMETZ WOOD, on the 7-12-16.	
ALBERT.	7-12-16		Very dull morning & cold. The Battn moved up to camp S.W. of MAMETZ WOOD & relieved the 11 A & S.H. arriving about 3PM. The Battn is in tents but these luckily have floor boards.	
Camp X23 Central.	7-12-16.		2Lt. Smith & Capt the Rev Bourchier proceeded on leave to the United Kingdom.	

T2134. Wt. W708—776. 500000. 4/15. Sir J. C. & S.

Instructions regarding War Diaries and Intelligence Summaries are contained in F. S. Regs., Part II. and the Staff Manual respectively. Title pages will be prepared in manuscript.

WAR DIARY
or
~~INTELLIGENCE SUMMARY.~~ Sheet 333.
(Erase heading not required.)

Army Form C. 2118.

Place	Date	Hour	Summary of Events and Information	Remarks and references to Appendices
Camp X.23 Central	8-12-16		The day was very wet, Rain fell practically all the time. The Battn had big working parties from each coy, working on roads etc. These started off at 6 AM & returned at 3.30 PM. There is nothing of any importance to note. 2 Lt. A.C.S. BUIST is awarded the Military Cross. Sergt A Mathews is awarded the D.C.M.	[initials]
Camp X.23 Central	9-12-16		The day was again very wet, rain falling heavily all day. The usual working parties were out all day. Capt E.S. Bell left for a Lewis Gun course at Le Touquet. Rain still falling at night. Headquarters mess was improved	
—do—	10-12-16		The day was very wet, much rain fell during the whole time. The usual working parties were out from 7 AM. until 4 P.M. working on roads.	
—do—	11-12-16		A fine morning with a little frost developing later in the day to rain which fell steadily from about 4 PM onwards. The usual working parties were out. 2 Lt Mackay & 2Lt Fischer returned from three days leave to Paris. During the forenoon aircraft were very busy over our camp	

T2134. Wt. W708—776. 500000. 4/15. Sir J. C. & S.

Instructions regarding War Diaries and Intelligence Summaries are contained in F. S. Regs., Part II. and the Staff Manual respectively. Title pages will be prepared in manuscript.

WAR DIARY
or
~~INTELLIGENCE~~ ~~SUMMARY~~. Sheet 334.
(Erase heading not required.)

Army Form C. 2118.

Place	Date	Hour	Summary of Events and Information	Remarks and references to Appendices
Camp X.23 (cont)	11-12-16.		No German planes were seen. 2 Lt. T. Forster joined Battn from the 3rd. Bn.	JL
— do —	12-12-16.		A very wet morning with a heavy fall of snow, this however did not lie & was followed by heavy rains. The usual working parties were away from the Battn. 2Lt A.K. Priday made Acting Capt.	
— do —	13-12-16.		The morning was dry but very dull. No rain fell during the day but towards evening there were slight showers. The usual working parties were away from the Battn. working on roads. Several shells fell fairly near the area but were all duds.	
— do —	14-12-16		The morning was very dull but dry. During the forenoon the weather became more threatening & soon after 12 noon heavy showers of rain fell. The usual working parties were away from the Battn during the day. Act. Capt A.K. Priday went off on leave to the United Kingdom.	
— do —	15-12-16		The morning was very wet. The usual working parties were away. Orders were received to move over to Huts in Scots Redoubt South	

T2134. Wt. W708—776. 500000. 4/15. Sir J. C. & S.

Instructions regarding War Diaries and Intelligence Summaries are contained in F. S. Regs., Part II. and the Staff Manual respectively. Title pages will be prepared in manuscript.

WAR DIARY
or
INTELLIGENCE SUMMARY.
(Erase heading not required.)

Sheet 335

Army Form C. 2118.

Place	Date	Hour	Summary of Events and Information	Remarks and references to Appendices
Camp X.23 (Contd) + Scots Redoubt South.	16-12-16		The morning was dry + dull, developing later in the day into frost and snow. The Battn moved over into Huts at Scots Redoubt South. A draft of 145 joined the Battn from the Base. Working parties only worked until 12 midday this day.	JL
Scots Redoubt.	17-12-16		The weather was very cold but no rain. Men were engaged in inspections + cleaning up camp. Lt. Logan, 2Lt. Stewart + 2Lt Hay joined Battn from home Depot. 2Lt Kemp returned from Leave + 2Lt Dull rejoined from C.C.S.	
Scots Redoubt.	18-12-16		The weather is still very dull + cold. Orders were received for moving into Line on the 19th. During the evening frost set in + the mud soon froze hard enough to walk over. There was a C.O's conference at Brigade office. 2Lt. Geddes returned from Leave + rejoined Battn from Brigade employ.	
SCOTS REDOUBT (S) + Front Line	19-12-16		A hard frost was experienced during the night of the 18th/19. + still held fast during the day. Just before the Battn moved snow began to fall. The Battn moved into front line on the North + West of LE SARS.	

T2134. Wt. W708—776. 500000. 4/15. Sir J. C. & S.

Instructions regarding War Diaries and Intelligence Summaries are contained in F. S. Regs., Part II. and the Staff Manual respectively. Title pages will be prepared in manuscript.

WAR DIARY
or
INTELLIGENCE SUMMARY.
(Erase heading not required.)

Sheet 336

Army Form C. 2118.

Place	Date	Hour	Summary of Events and Information	Remarks and references to Appendices
LE SARS	19-12-16		The Battn relieved the 11th A & S H. with two companies in front & two in support.	
LE SARS	20-12-16		The weather is still very frosty, the mud being frozen hard enough to walk over. There was very little shelling on the part of the enemy but our guns kept up the usual barrages. We got into touch with the 51st Div on our left and found exactly where their nearest post to us was. There is a small gap of about 200 yards between that post & ours. A system of patrols was instituted between the two companies. Warning order of relief was received.	JL
LE SARS	21-12-16		During the night of the 20th/21st thaw set in & by daylight all signs of frost had disappeared. The enemy shelled the BAPAUME ROAD at the point where it enters LE SARS with 5·9 H.E. During the afternoon O.G.I & 26th AVENUE were heavily shelled, 'C' coys headquarter dug out was damaged & 'A' coy had several men buried. The Battn was relieved by two Battns 8th SEAFORTH HIGHRS & 7th CAMERON HIGHRS, one company from each in the line.	

T2134. Wt. W708—776. 500000. 4/15. Sir J. C. & S.

Instructions regarding War Diaries and Intelligence Summaries are contained in F. S. Regs., Part II. and the Staff Manual respectively. Title pages will be prepared in manuscript.

WAR DIARY
or
INTELLIGENCE SUMMARY.
(Erase heading not required.)

Sheet 337.

Army Form C. 2118.

Place	Date	Hour	Summary of Events and Information	Remarks and references to Appendices
LE SARS	21-12-16		On relief the Battn moved into Huts at ACID DROP CAMP near CONTALMAISON. Hot soup was ready for the men when they came in, also dry socks.	
ACID DROP CAMP	22-12-16		The weather was very wet. The day was spent in cleaning & drying. Deficiencies were taken. Operation Orders received again changing previous dispositions.	JL
—do—	23-12-16.		During the forenoon a terrific gale sprang up & blew a number of tents down. This continued until late in the afternoon. The Battn moved up to VILLA CAMP near CONTALMAISON VILLA. This camp was found to be very wet & muddy. The tents had been knocked about by the gale.	
VILLA CAMP	24-12-16		During the night 23/24 a shell fell near one of the tents & wounded one man. Parties were busy all day clearing up the camp & making roadways. 2Lt ROBERTSON joined the Battn from the 42nd Training Battn. Working parties were away from the Battn in the evening.	
VILLA CAMP	25-12-16.		Christmas Day but no holiday. The working parties were away as usual [in the]	

T2134. Wt. W708—776. 500000. 4/15. Sir J. C. & S.

Instructions regarding War Diaries and Intelligence Summaries are contained in F. S. Regs., Part II. and the Staff Manual respectively. Title pages will be prepared in manuscript.

WAR DIARY
or
INTELLIGENCE SUMMARY.
(Erase heading not required.)

Sheet 338.

Army Form C. 2118.

Place	Date	Hour	Summary of Events and Information	Remarks and references to Appendices
VILLA CAMP	25-12-16		in the evening. Showers of rain fell at intervals during the day. Our artillery carried out several short Bombardments of the enemy's rear areas. The Commdg Officer and 2nd in Command dined with the 9th (Pioneer) Gordon Highrs.	[initials]
VILLA CAMP	26-12-16		The weather is still very dull. Heavy showers of rain fell at intervals during the day. Operation orders received referring to Brigade relief & Battn was ordered to proceed to SCOTS REDOUBT. SOUTH. The working parties were away from the Battn in the evening, digging & carrying.	
VILLA CAMP & SCOTS REDOUBT SOUTH.	27-12-16		An excellent morning with a bright sun. The Battn moved into Div. Reserve at SCOTS REDOUBT SOUTH being relieved in VILLA CAMP by 10/11 H.L.I.	
SCOTS REDOUBT SOUTH	28-12-16		Inspections of all kinds were carried out. A fatigue party of 300 men were carrying Duck Boards from Mametz Wood to Contalmaison. Battn attended bath. There was a hard frost during the night but a thaw set in during the day. A little rain fell during the afternoon	
— do	29-12-16		The weather was as usual very wet. We were Duty Battn. this day.	

T2134. Wt. W708–776. 500000. 4/15. Sir J. C. & S.

Instructions regarding War Diaries and Intelligence Summaries are contained in F. S. Regs., Part II. and the Staff Manual respectively. Title pages will be prepared in manuscript.

WAR DIARY
or
INTELLIGENCE SUMMARY. Sheet 339

(Erase heading not required.)

Army Form C. 2118.

Place	Date	Hour	Summary of Events and Information	Remarks and references to Appendices
SCOTS REDOUBTS.	29-12-16		Lt-Col MacLeod went down sick & Major Cumine took over command of the Battn	JL
— do —	30-12-16		Operation Orders received regarding the move into the line. Company Commanders visited new area. The Battn had a day clear of all fatigues. All preparations made for move up.	
Front Line	31-12-16		The Battn moved into the line Right Sector Right Subsection. Blankets etc were stored in PIONEER CAMP. Capt Bell went down sick. We relieved the 11th A & SH in the line. Relief was completed by 9PM.	

T2134. Wt. W708—776. 500000. 4/15. Sir J. C. & S.

8/10th (S.) Batt'n,
The Gordon Highlanders

January, 1917

17th Bn Australians.

T2134. Wt. W708—776. 500000. 4/15. Sir J. C. & S.

44 Bde – 15 Div –

CONFIDENTIAL.

Vol 20

WAR DIARY

OF

8/10th (Service) Battn., The Gordon Highlanders.

From 1st January, 1917. To 31st January, 1917.

(VOLUME 21.)

Instructions regarding War Diaries and Intelligence Summaries are contained in F. S. Regs., Part II. and the Staff Manual respectively. Title pages will be prepared in manuscript.

WAR DIARY
or
INTELLIGENCE SUMMARY.
(Erase heading not required.)

Sheet 340.

Army Form C. 2118.

Place	Date	Hour	Summary of Events and Information	Remarks and references to Appendices
FRONT. LINE	1-1-17.		The new year came in very quietly. The enemy's artillery were very quiet during the night. An Observation Post was established at M.25b.3.6. This was rebuilt and a loophole put in, with headcover. The weather was very dull & towards afternoon, got very misty. During the day the enemy's artillery put a few shells around Battn. Hdqrs. but did no damage. Our Snipers claimed seven hits, & stretcher bearers were seen carrying these away.	
FRONT. LINE	2-1-17.		During the night of the 1/2 patrols were sent out with the object of capturing a Hun but failed as our barrage prevented them from entering the enemy trenches & no patrols were encountered. Wiring was carried on along our front. Battn Hd Qrs received attention during the day from 4·2" & a few 77 mm. The Battn carried out an internal relief 'A' & 'C' coys being relieved in the line by 'B' & 'D' coys respectively. Our Artillery carried out a strafe on LOUPART. WOOD. during the afternoon & did a very good shoot. Lt. J. B. WOOD rejoined the Battn from a course in the duties of a Staff Captain. 2Lt RAM BLACK & Lt Mutch rejoined from the Base. During the relief we had two men wounded.	

T2134. Wt. W708—776. 500000. 4/15. Sir J. C. & S.

204

Instructions regarding War Diaries and Intelligence Summaries are contained in F. S. Regs., Part II. and the Staff Manual respectively. Title pages will be prepared in manuscript.

WAR DIARY
or
INTELLIGENCE SUMMARY.
(Erase heading not required.)

Sheet 341.

Army Form C. 2118.

Place	Date	Hour	Summary of Events and Information	Remarks and references to Appendices
FRONT LINE	3-1-17		The morning was very cloudy & misty. Enemys artillery was very quiet during the forenoon. In the afternoon the weather cleared a bit and enemys artillery shelled the back areas intermittently. Operation Orders were received regarding relief in the line.	
FRONT LINE	4-1-17		The morning was very misty & quiet. In the afternoon the weather cleared & enemy then shelled various points fairly heavily – Especially round Battn Headquarters. Major Cumine D.S.O went off to a Senior Officers course at Aldershot. Lt D.D. McLeod, the adjutant, went to Heilly to be interviewed before proceeding to the R.F.C. Capt N.G. Pearson assumed command of the Battn & Lt J.B. Wood became acting-adjutant. The Battn was relieved in the line by the 9th Black Watch & proceeded into reserve at PIONEER CAMP.	
PIONEER CAMP.	5-1-17		The day was spent in inspections & cleaning up every man receiving a clean change. The camp consisted of Nissen Huts. Acting Capt J Martin was gazetted Temp. Capt dating from May 12th	

T2134. Wt. W708–776. 500000. 4/15. Sir J. C. & S.

Instructions regarding War Diaries and Intelligence Summaries are contained in F. S. Regs., Part II. and the Staff Manual respectively. Title pages will be prepared in manuscript.

WAR DIARY
or
INTELLIGENCE SUMMARY.
(Erase heading not required.)

Sheet 342

Army Form C. 2118.

Place	Date	Hour	Summary of Events and Information	Remarks and references to Appendices
PIONEER CAMP.	5-1-17.		Lt D. W. McLeod & Lt. Harper proceeded on leave to U.K. 2/Lt C. McGregor reported to Battn from base. 2/Lt RA. M. Black, 2/Lt Birnie & Lt G. Mutch rejoined the Battn.	
— do —	6-1-17		Rain fell very heavily during the night of the 5/6. The Battn relieved the 7th Cameron Highrs in the support position in RRUE. TRENCH. STARFISH. LINE & SEVEN ELMS, Battn Hd. Qrs being at SEVEN ELMS. The relief was reported complete at 6.30 PM.	
SEVEN. ELMS.	7-1-17.		The Battn had several working parties out, no casualties. The day was very cold & damp. The enemy's artillery shelled Battn head quarters for a short time. No damage was done. During the evening there was considerable shelling of Martinpuich & road to Eaucourt l'Abbaye. We had working parties & carrying parties, working on MAXWELL SUPPORT & carrying up revetting material. The ration party was caught by hostile shelling & suffered 4 casualties all wounded. In the evening rain fell very heavily & continued to do so during the night.	JL

206

T2134. Wt. W708–776. 500000. 4/15. Sir J. C. & S.

Instructions regarding War Diaries and Intelligence Summaries are contained in F. S. Regs., Part II. and the Staff Manual respectively. Title pages will be prepared in manuscript.

WAR DIARY
or
~~INTELLIGENCE SUMMARY.~~ Sht 348.
(Erase heading not required.)

Army Form C. 2118.

Place	Date	Hour	Summary of Events and Information	Remarks and references to Appendices
SEVEN ELMS.	8-1-17.		The weather was excellent with bright sunshine. Our aircraft were very busy & large numbers of them hovered over the enemy lines for a long time. No enemy's machines were seen & very few 'archies' were fired at them. The Battn was relieved by the 10/11 H.L.I. & went back to SCOTS REDOUBT SOUTH, into Divisional Reserve. The relief was completed by 9-30 PM, no casualties. The enemy's artillery was very quiet during the whole relief.	JF
SCOTS REDOUBT. (South)			The day was very wet. Some snow fell during the night.	
	9-1-17.		Major J G Thom rejoined after 2 months absence at a Senior Officers course at Aldershot, and took over command of the battalion.	
	10-1-17.		While 44th Brigade was in divisional reserve (Jan 9th–12th) each battalion supplied all the fatigues on one day leaving the others comparatively free for inspections etc. 8/10 GORDONS were duty battalion on the 10th and nearly all the men were out on working parties.	JGP
			During the period Jan 1st–8th there were only 6 cases of trench feet in the 44th Brigade.	207

T2134. Wt. W708–776. 500000. 4/15. Sir J. C. & S.

Army Form C. 2118.

Instructions regarding War Diaries and Intelligence Summaries are contained in F. S. Regs., Part II. and the Staff Manual respectively. Title pages will be prepared in manuscript.

WAR DIARY
or
~~INTELLIGENCE SUMMARY.~~
(Erase heading not required.)

Sheet 344.

Place	Date	Hour	Summary of Events and Information	Remarks and references to Appendices
SCOTS REDOUBT SOUTH.	12-1-17		The 44th Brigade relieved the 45th in the left section of divisional front. 9th BLACK WATCH and 8th SEAFORTHS in the line, 7th CAMERONS in support at VILLA CAMP, 8/10 GORDONS in reserve at ACID DROP CAMP (CONTALMAISON). In the line the 51st Division was on our left, the 46th Brigade on our right, and beyond them the 50th Division. 15th Division frontage M.17.d.1.8 to M.15.a.5.6. Right section M.17.d.1.8 to M.16.b.1.7. Left section M.16.b.1.7. to M.15.a.5.6. Each section divided into right and left sectors at M.16.d.7.8 and M.15.b.7.8 respectively.	[illegible]
Acid Drop Camp (CONTALMAISON)	13.1.17		Fall of snow during forenoon. Although not on duty on this date large fatigue parties supplied in the evening.	[illegible]
VILLA CAMP	14.1.17		Moved into support relieving 7th Camerons. Hd. Qrs and 3 Coys (A.B.&C) at VILLA CAMP and "D" Coy in R36c (Gunpit Road area)	
	15.1.17		A few shells landed in Camp - no casualties. H.Qrs suffered slightly from "mud drops" from one shell which landed close by.	20 Y

T2134. Wt. W708-776. 500000. 4/15. Sir J. C. & S.

Instructions regarding War Diaries and Intelligence Summaries are contained in F. S. Regs., Part II. and the Staff Manual respectively. Title pages will be prepared in manuscript.

WAR DIARY
or
~~INTELLIGENCE SUMMARY~~. Sheet 345.
(*Erase heading not required.*)

Army Form C. 2118.

Place	Date	Hour	Summary of Events and Information	Remarks and references to Appendices
VILLA CAMP (CONTALMAISON)	16.1.17		Hard frost during night, consequently water pipes frozen in the morning – "delay action" in shaving water taking place. The Btn moved into the line – left sub-section left sector, relieving the 8th Seaforths – Right Front B Coy – Scotland Trench (right), HEALTH TRENCH and SCOTLAND SUPPORT; Centre Front – "C" Coy. – SCOTLAND TRENCH (left), CABLE TRENCH, CHALK TRENCH; Left Front – 'A' Coy – O.G.1, O.G.2, and Advanced Posts on Left of CABLE TRENCH; Reserve – 'D' Coy – Junction of 70th and 26th Avenue; Battn H. Qrs – 26th Avenue M.21d 3.1; Bde. H Qrs M.32a 2½.2½. Guides were met at Bde H.Qrs at 5.15 p.m. and proceeded via CHALK PIT WALK.	Events
In the Line	"		A fine quiet night helped the relief greatly and by 8 p.m. relief was completed. At No. 2 Post a wounded Prisoner – a Cpl of the II Guards Reserve Regt had been taken in by the Seaforths and handed over to us & afterwards passed through our Aid Post. Work was commenced on Posts, fire steps & revetting. Shelters were erected in SCOTLAND SUPPORT also	209

Instructions regarding War Diaries and Intelligence Summaries are contained in F. S. Regs., Part II. and the Staff Manual respectively. Title pages will be prepared in manuscript.

WAR DIARY ~~or INTELLIGENCE SUMMARY~~.

(Erase heading not required.)

Sheet 346

Army Form C. 2118.

Place	Date	Hour	Summary of Events and Information	Remarks and references to Appendices
In the Line (Contd)	16.1.17		also digging Post No 13 in Reserve Line. During night 16/17 snow began to fall heavily and this along with the darkness made work impossible, wiring &c had therefore to be discontinued.	
"	17.1.17		Morning - 6.30 am - snow 2/3" deep. Still snowing. Considerable work done during night. Enemy exceedingly quiet. Patrols went out but saw no signs of the enemy. Quiet night.	
"	18.1.17		During night improving Posts &c continued and large quantity of wire put out. A relief of about 20 strong was seen leaving trench at M9 C12 and our sniper in Fr Post claimed seven hits. Five apparently were killed as the enemy stretcher bearers, wearing a white flag, came out of the same trench and carried two away. Our Lewis Guns which opened fire on the same party may have caused some of the casualties. Front Battn Hd Qrs between 5 and 9 pm got shelled with 4.2's but no damage was done. About M15 A79 the enemy opened M.G. fire on one of our Patrols. An attempt to dislodge our Patrol from the CHALK PIT by aerial darts	[illegible] 2/0

Instructions regarding War Diaries and Intelligence Summaries are contained in F. S. Regs., Part II. and the Staff Manual respectively. Title pages will be prepared in manuscript.

Army Form C. 2118.

WAR DIARY
or
~~INTELLIGENCE SUMMARY~~. Sheet 347.
(Erase heading not required.)

Place	Date	Hour	Summary of Events and Information	Remarks and references to Appendices
In the Line	18.1.17 (CONTD)		fired from direction of M9 d 1.5. Another Patrol which went out from "B" Post reached within 50 yds of the enemy wire which appeared to be weak. About 10 am still being worried with aerial darts and got our artillery to retaliate. During the day area left Coy H.Q. was shelled with 4.2s. About 3 pm. the area of the SHELTER was shelled with 5.9s. Five shots burst just beside C. Coy H.Q. but fortunately only one man was wounded. Luckily the SHELTER is close to the bank & a direct hit is rather a difficult job. What a "bag" if one did get on the mark - being a combined H.Q. with the Coy of Camerons on our right - officers, servants, signallers, C.S.M.'s &. Tracks in the snow showed up very clearly & these were shelled during the day. A Patrol left No 3 Post to establish touch with the 2nd Div (Oxfords) advanced Post at about M 15 c 0.5. ~~An Officer~~ & 2 NCOs were brought back to show them our post. Our Snipers in 7. Post (M 15 a 1.9) claim two hits near M 9 c central. - Lewis Gun in G Post (M 15 2½ 6) claim 5 hits	

T2134. Wt. W708—776. 500000. 4/15. Sir J. C. & S.

Instructions regarding War Diaries and Intelligence Summaries are contained in F. S. Regs., Part II. and the Staff Manual respectively. Title pages will be prepared in manuscript.

WAR DIARY
or
~~INTELLIGENCE SUMMARY.~~ Sheet. 348.

(*Erase heading not required.*)

Army Form C. 2118.

Place	Date	Hour	Summary of Events and Information	Remarks and references to Appendices
In the line	18/1/17 (contd)		at about the same spot.	
			"D" Coy relieved "C" Coy (less one Platoon). - Two prisoners came in on our right (Cameron area). They stated they were out on Patrol but from the appearance of one of their rifles with breech cover on it didn't look as if they were out for business but for the one - giving themselves up. Still snowing slightly.	[initials]
"	19/1/17		Dull misty morning - very quiet. The Brigade rang us up in the morning and told us the General was highly pleased with the wire put out during the night. Owing to the snow tracks from Bn. H.Q to all Coy. H.Qs & Posts were easily spotted when the mist cleared and along the tracks quite a few direct hits with 4.2s were got. Around Bn. H.Q was shelled during the afternoon. Aerial Darts were also fired from direction of M9d15. After our bombardment in the evening the firing of aerial Darts ceased.	
"	20/1/17		Very quiet night. About 3 pm 5.9s were fired on CHALK TRENCH, HEALTH TRENCH and SCOTLAND TRENCH. HEALTH TRENCH was	[initials]

T2134. Wt. W708—776. 500000. 4/15. Sir J. C. & S.

Instructions regarding War Diaries and Intelligence Summaries are contained in F. S. Regs., Part II. and the Staff Manual respectively. Title pages will be prepared in manuscript.

WAR DIARY ~~or~~ ~~INTELLIGENCE SUMMARY~~. Sheet 349

(*Erase heading not required.*)

Army Form C. 2118.

Place	Date	Hour	Summary of Events and Information	Remarks and references to Appendices
In the Line	20/1/17		suffered rather badly. Two Lewis Gunners were killed and a few buried. This was rather unfortunate as it was within a few hours of relief and in fact nearing the end of a very fine tour in the trenches. The two men killed (a L/Cpl & man) were very 'old hands'.	
			The Brigade relief took place in the evening. We were relieved by the 7/8 K.O.S.B. The night was rather fine and before scheduled time the K.O.S.B had passed the Guides point & had therefore to pick up our Guides further along CHALK PIT WALK. This being the 3rd time the 7/8th K.O.S.B. were in this Sector made the relief ever so easier - result being a first class relief. This finished our four days in the line - a fine spell, in which the Battn done a great amount of work. 'A' Coy H.Q. was left in a much better condition than when we entered - a vile dug out it was and during our tour in about 800 sandbags of rubbish was taken out also half a pig was dug up. A report by our M.O. with suggestions as to improving sanitation in this dug out was	

Instructions regarding War Diaries and Intelligence Summaries are contained in F. S. Regs., Part II. and the Staff Manual respectively. Title pages will be prepared in manuscript.

WAR DIARY ~~or~~ ~~INTELLIGENCE SUMMARY.~~ Sheet 350.

(Erase heading not required.)

Army Form C. 2118.

Place	Date	Hour	Summary of Events and Information	Remarks and references to Appendices
In the Line	20/1/17		sent to Brigade. A great amount of work was done enlarging Battn. H.Q. The result was very noticeable and the incoming Battn. found a much more comfortable dug out than when we entered. The Battn moved back to SCOTS REDOUBT (South) and although slippery trench boards hindered the "speed limit," all landed safely in Camp by 11 am, and found a fire burning in every hut – a splendid scheme by ~~our~~ the Quartermaster.	[illegible]
SCOTS REDOUBT (South).	21/1/17		Keen frost & the cold intense resulting in a sleepless night for the most of us. A medical inspection of the Battn took place in the ~~afternoon~~ forenoon. The health of the men generally was very good. The afternoon was spent in cleaning up.	
"	22/1/17		Frost still very keen. Bath being allotted to our Battn bathing parade by Coys carried out. A Conference in the afternoon of all Coy Commanders by the CO took place re proposed raid by us on the BUTTE DE WALENCOURT and QUARRY on the night of 29/30th.	74

Army Form C. 2118.

Instructions regarding War Diaries and Intelligence Summaries are contained in F. S. Regs., Part II. and the Staff Manual respectively. Title pages will be prepared in manuscript.

WAR DIARY
or
~~INTELLIGENCE SUMMARY~~. Sheet 351

(Erase heading not required.)

Place	Date	Hour	Summary of Events and Information	Remarks and references to Appendices
SCOTS REDOUBT (SOUTH)	23/1/17		Still freezing. Being "Duty Battn" on this date large working parties supplied by us.	
"	24/1/17		Splendid morning - very cold and keen frost. In the afternoon we moved to PIONEER CAMP and relieved the 13th Royal Scots. In the evening the CO had a conference with Coy Commanders as to Raid & general matters.	
PIONEER CAMP "	25/1/17		Keen frost and although bright sunshine the cold is very severe and very much felt. During the afternoon we practiced the forthcoming stunt - raiding the BUTTE & QUARRY. After dark another rehearsal took place.	[signature]
"	26/1/17		Still very keen frost - high wind & very very cold. Conference by the CO. in the evening re Raid.	
"	27/1/17		Very fine morning - bright sunshine - high wind & severe cold - still freezing hard. Although the 27th (KAISER'S BIRTHDAY) & celebration by the enemy looked forward to - disappointment set in - very quiet day. On the	21

T2134. Wt. W708—776. 500000. 4/15. Sir J. C. & S.

Army Form C. 2118.

Instructions regarding War Diaries and Intelligence Summaries are contained in F. S. Regs., Part II. and the Staff Manual respectively. Title pages will be prepared in manuscript.

WAR DIARY
~~or~~
~~INTELLIGENCE SUMMARY.~~ Sheet 352.
(*Erase heading not required.*)

Place	Date	Hour	Summary of Events and Information	Remarks and references to Appendices
PIONEER CAMP	27/1/17 (Contd)		night. However our troops celebrated the event by raiding enemy trenches, capturing 6 officers & 200 men and a short length of trench. Owing to snow still on the ground white garments are being made and helmets painted white all in preparation for the raid.	[initials]
PIONEER CAMP	28-1-17		The night was very cold, hard frost continues. The morning was fine. Battn prepared to move up into the line in the evening. Companies moved off by platoons at 4.45 PM & relief of 9th BLACK WATCH was completed by 8.30 PM. We sustained no casualties but Germans spotted the relief & swept ground with machine gun fire. A fairly heavy barage was placed on tracks near MARTINPUICH.	[initials]
MAXWELL TRENCH	29-1-17		The weather is still very frosty. During the night of 28/29 preparations were carried on for the raid on night of 29/30th. Tapes, marking starting points, were laid down. Enemy's artillery was fairly quiet during the night. In the morning several enemy planes came over our lines but were turned by our anti-air-craft guns & pursued by fighting planes.	316

T2134. Wt. W708—776. 500000. 4/15. Sir J. C. & S.

Instructions regarding War Diaries and Intelligence Summaries are contained in F. S. Regs., Part II. and the Staff Manual respectively. Title pages will be prepared in manuscript.

WAR DIARY
or
~~INTELLIGENCE SUMMARY~~. Sheet 353.

(Erase heading not required.)

Army Form C. 2118.

Place	Date	Hour	Summary of Events and Information	Remarks and references to Appendices
Front Line	29-1-17		The afternoon passed off quietly & enemy's artillery fire was normal. The preparation for the raid was absolutely ready & nothing remained to be done [Special ~~description~~ account below]. The night was very still & frosty sounds could be heard a long way off	
— do —	30-1-17		On the night of the 29th/30th a raid was carried out by 'B' & 'D' coys on the BUTTE DE WARLENCOURT and the QUARRY (M17a0.7). At 12 midnight the two assaulting companies, clad in white smocks & with whitened Steel Helmets moved up into position along tapes which were laid the night previously by Capt MARTIN & Capt PRIDAY. Lt Mutch was in command of B coy with 2Lt Kemp, 2Lt Walker & 2Lt Hofford, Lt. Kenyon was in command of D coy with 2Lt. Knowles & 2Lt Forster. Some difficulty was experienced in getting the men into place but this was accomplished safely by 1.30 AM. The German wire was all cut by our artillery & gaps were made ~~by~~ in our own. During all this time there was practically no shelling by either side. Prompt to a second at Zero. 1.45 AM. our artillery of all calibres placed an intense barrage	

Instructions regarding War Diaries and Intelligence Summaries are contained in F. S. Regs., Part II. and the Staff Manual respectively. Title pages will be prepared in manuscript.

WAR DIARY or INTELLIGENCE SUMMARY. Sheet 354.

(Erase heading not required.)

Army Form C. 2118.

Place	Date	Hour	Summary of Events and Information	Remarks and references to Appendices
(contd)	30-1-17		barrage on enemy trench in front of BUTTE – Stokes guns, Medium T.M. and M.G's assisted. Immediately this started the assaulting waves (2) commenced to cross No Mans Land at Zero +1 minute the barrage lifted at the rate of 50 yds per minute. Practically no opposition was offered to our advance with exception of the left flank which was held up for a short time by a M.G. on left of Quarry. The waves moved steadily forward & reached the BUTTE after 10 minutes. The ground was in a very bad condition & full of enormous craters. B Coy's objective was the BUTTE & Dugout in it. The right of B Coy encountered a German post held by six men who immediately surrendered. They then entered BUTTE TRENCH & discovered a Deep dugout & a trench mortar emplacement with the gun in position. This was destroyed and dugout bombed. The left & centre of B Coy saw no trench before reaching the BUTTE. Here they discovered several dugouts. The occupants were called upon to surrender. Those in the first refused so several Mills were thrown in one or [two]	

T2134. Wt. W708–776. 500000. 4/15. Sir J. C. & S.

Army Form C. 2118.

Instructions regarding War Diaries and Intelligence Summaries are contained in F. S. Regs., Part II. and the Staff Manual respectively. Title pages will be prepared in manuscript.

WAR DIARY or INTELLIGENCE SUMMARY.

(Erase heading not required.)

Sheet 355.

Place	Date	Hour	Summary of Events and Information	Remarks and references to Appendices
Contd.	30-1-17		two 'P' Bombs & a Stokes bomb were thrown in, wrecking the dugout & setting it on fire. One prisoner was got out of the second which was then treated similar to no. one. In the third 12 prisoners were captured & it also was wrecked.	
			Dicy's objective was the Quarry. This was reached after a short time, owing to the activities of a M.G. on the left edge. This gun was knocked out & then the advance continued to the Quarry. Here many Germans were discovered & killed. One dugout in right hand corner was successfully bombed. Six prisoners were reported to have been captured but they never reached adv. Battn. Hdqrs.	
			The whole raid was a great success. In all 17 prisoners passed through our hands. According to all reports many casualties were inflicted on the enemy. It is calculated that these amount to about 50 or 60 all told. Our casualties were slight amounting at the very outside to 16 or 17. There were three [officers]	

219

Instructions regarding War Diaries and Intelligence Summaries are contained in F. S. Regs., Part II. and the Staff Manual respectively. Title pages will be prepared in manuscript.

WAR DIARY
or
INTELLIGENCE SUMMARY.
(Erase heading not required.)

Sheet 356

Army Form C. 2118.

Place	Date	Hour	Summary of Events and Information	Remarks and references to Appendices
contd	30-1-17.		officer casualties, two, 2/Lt Forster & 2Lt Walker slightly wounded & 2Lt Knowles missing believed killed. The enemy did not put up a fight at all. No barrage was placed on our lines & no S.O.S signals were seen. It is thought ~~that~~ owing to the quietness that they were absolutely deceived as to our intentions & no thought of an attack occurred to them. On the admission of one of the prisoners who spoke a little English, it came as a complete surprise. The following message was received from the Division AAA The GOC congratulates you & your brigade on the operation so successfully carried out by E.T. Brigadier General Marshall adds. I wish to thank all ranks for the trouble taken in preparing for the raid & gallantry displayed in the execution. About 3.15 AM, ~~the~~ the dugouts on the BUTTE were blazing merrily at this hour an explosion occurred there & flames rose about 30 feet in the air, Bombs & S.A.A were also heard exploding. At 10 AM this morning the BUTTE was still smoking.	

T2134. Wt. W708—776. 500000. 4/15. Sir J. C. & S.

Army Form C. 2118.

Instructions regarding War Diaries and Intelligence Summaries are contained in F. S. Regs., Part II. and the Staff Manual respectively. Title pages will be prepared in manuscript.

WAR DIARY
or
~~INTELLIGENCE~~ SUMMARY. Sheet 357.

(Erase heading not required.)

Place	Date	Hour	Summary of Events and Information	Remarks and references to Appendices
FRONT LINE	30-1-17.		The Following message was received from the Corps. AAA General Pulteney congratulates Brigadier & Battn on last nights raid AAA The weather is still very frosty. In the evening snow again began to fall & continued to do so during the night 30th-31st.	[initials]
		7. PM.	The BUTTE was still smoking yesterday evening (30th).	
FRONT LINE (MAXWELL TR).	31-1-17.		A very clear morning, with hard frost. About 10 AM snow began to fall very lightly. Enemys artillery during the night 30th-31st searched the Ravine very thoroughly at intervals. Battn Hdqrs also received close attention. Scarcely any work was possible on account of the frozen state of the ground. Battn Hqrs again shelled 10.30 AM	
		10.30 AM	The relieving Battn of Australians sent up Coy Commdrs to look over new line.	
			The day passed quietly except for intermittent shelling of Valley & Bn Hdqrs. Operation Orders issued for relief in line on night of 1st/2nd by 17th Bn Australians.	

221
LB

T2134. Wt. W708—776. 500000. 4/15. Sir J. C. & S.

8/10th (S.) Batt'n,
The Gordon Highlanders

February, 1917

Appendix 29

Summary of Operations

Vol 21

CONFIDENTIAL.

WAR DIARY

OF.

8/10th (Service) Battn, The Gordon Highlanders

From 1st February, 1917. To 28th February 1917.

VOLUME 22.

Army Form C. 2118.

Instructions regarding War Diaries and Intelligence Summaries are contained in F. S. Regs., Part II. and the Staff Manual respectively. Title pages will be prepared in manuscript.

WAR DIARY
or
~~INTELLIGENCE SUMMARY.~~ Sheet 858
(Erase heading not required.)

Place	Date	Hour	Summary of Events and Information	Remarks and references to Appendices
FRONT LINE (MAX. TR)	1-2-17		During the night of 31st/1st our artillery was very active on tracks & points behind German lines as enemy relief was suspected. Snow fell at intervals during the night. Hard Frost still prevails. During the day there was a slight thaw, but this did not last any time. The weather is still bright but cold. The Battn was relieved in the line by the 17th Bn Australians. Guides met incoming Battn at CONTALMAISON at 6.15PM. and relief was complete by 10.30 PM. Some difficulty was experienced in relieving posts as Germans kept up a steady fire with M.G's. The Battn then marched back to BECOURT CAMP & occupied the HUTS in 'C' CAMP	J.D.
'C' CAMP BECOURT.	2-2-17		The weather is still frosty & very bright. The day was spent in cleaning up & resting.	UGP
— do —	4-2-17		The 44th Inf. Brigade moved to CONTAY for training; 9th BLACK WATCH and 8th SEAFORTHS at BRESLE. Billets at CONTAY were good. This was the first time the battalion had been in billets, with the exception of a few days at ALBERT in December, since October 4th.	UGP

223

Instructions regarding War Diaries and Intelligence Summaries are contained in F. S. Regs., Part II. and the Staff Manual respectively. Title pages will be prepared in manuscript.

WAR DIARY
or
~~INTELLIGENCE SUMMARY.~~
(Erase heading not required.)

Sheet 359

Army Form C. 2118.

Place	Date	Hour	Summary of Events and Information	Remarks and references to Appendices
	Feb. 1917.			
CONTAY	5th		Strength of battalion with the battalion 22 officers, 545 other ranks.	
	5-13		Training was done under difficult conditions. Keen frost continued. Bathing was impossible owing to bursting of pipes. Some alterations were made in company organisation by a G.H.Q. order. Platoons are to consist of 2 sections rifles, 1 section bombers, 1 Lewis Gun section. Platoons are not to fall below a strength of 28, and, if necessary, are to be amalgamated to effect this. A G.H.Q. pamphlet on recreational training was carried out. Training to be done in the afternoon and to consist of Football, Boxing, Cross-country running, and Bayonet training. The general idea was to have a varied interest and to enable the greatest possible number of men to take part. At CONTAY no football could be played owing to the hardness of the ground. The ordinary military training was carried out in the mornings. There was one route march and one day on the range.	WJR

T2134. Wt. W708—776. 500000. 4/15. Sir J. C. & S.

Instructions regarding War Diaries and Intelligence Summaries are contained in F. S. Regs., Part II. and the Staff Manual respectively. Title pages will be prepared in manuscript.

WAR DIARY or ~~INTELLIGENCE SUMMARY~~. Sheet 360.

(Erase heading not required.)

Army Form C. 2118.

Place	Date	Hour	Summary of Events and Information	Remarks and references to Appendices
	1917 Feb.			
BEAUVAL	14.		The battalion moved to excellent billets in BEAUVAL, a march of about 11 miles. This was part of the move of the 15th (SCOTTISH) division North to the ARRAS region. For the purposes of move and billeting the following were attached to the 44th Inf. Bde; — 91st Field Coy R.E., 47th Field Ambulance, and No 2 Coy Divisional Train. A draft of 100 men arrived.	Map LENS 11. 1/100,000. UGP
GEZAINCOURT	15.		Move to GEZAINCOURT. Fair billets.	UGP
REBREUVE	16.		Move to REBREUVE. Very good billets; abundance of straw. Battalion strength 31 officers, 733 other ranks. 6 new officers joined since the battalion came out of the line.	UGP
GAUCHIN.	17.		Move to GAUCHIN near ST POL. A very scattered village. Billeting was very difficult and billets not very good.	UGP
MONTS-EN-TERNOIS.	18.		After 4 days marching north the 44th Inf. Bde. turned S.E. and moved to BUNEVILLE area. The battalion moved to MONTS-EN-TERNOIS. Men's billets good for 3 companies. Officers billets bad. The frost came to an end and thaw precautions were ordered. The result of	UGP

T2134. Wt. W708–776. 500000. 4/15. Sir J. C. & S.

Instructions regarding War Diaries and Intelligence Summaries are contained in F. S. Regs., Part II. and the Staff Manual respectively. Title pages will be prepared in manuscript.

WAR DIARY
or
~~INTELLIGENCE SUMMARY~~. Sheet 361

(Erase heading not required.)

Army Form C. 2118.

Place	Date	Hour	Summary of Events and Information	Remarks and references to Appendices
MONTS-EN-TERNOIS	18.		this was that surplus stores left at CONTAY could not be fetched immediately.	Ref.
	19.		Training was continued, special attention being paid to attack on strong posts by platoons with their new organisation of a Lewis Gun section. Cooperation of Lewis Guns and rifle bombers in dealing with a strong point is to be practised daily.	LENS 11. 1/100,000. UGP
	21.		A warning order was received for a move eastwards on the 23rd.	UGP
	22.	8.30 a.m.	C company marched off at 8.30 a.m. as part of a 12-day working party to be provided by the 46th Inf Bde at AUXI-LE-CHATEAU. The whole party was 600 working strength, of which the battalion were to provide 100, and the 7th CAMERONS 500.	UGP
		11a.m.	A demonstration was given by D company of an attack on a strong point by 2 platoons.	UGP
IZEL-LES-HAMEAU.	23.	1 P.M.	The battalion moved with trench mortar battery to IZEL-LES-HAMEAU. Brigade H.Q., 9th BLACK WATCH, 8th SEAFORTHS moved to AMBRINES. A draft of 121 other ranks arrived, mainly CAMERONS. Strength of battalion 40 officers, 860 other ranks.	UGP

T2134. Wt. W708—776. 500000. 4/15. Sir J. C. & S.

Instructions regarding War Diaries and Intelligence Summaries are contained in F. S. Regs., Part II. and the Staff Manual respectively. Title pages will be prepared in manuscript.

WAR DIARY
or
~~INTELLIGENCE SUMMARY.~~
(Erase heading not required.)

Army Form C. 2118.

Sheet 362.

Place	Date	Hour	Summary of Events and Information	Remarks and references to Appendices
IZEL-LES-HAMEAU	Jn. 24–28		Training ~~[illegible]~~ continued. Special attention being paid to "the attack", also considerable practice in firing Mills No. 23 Rifle Grenade. Each Coy (A B C D) had a day at the Range also the Lewis Gun Class. Signalling & Lewis Gun Classes form part of our training programme. These Classes meet daily – L.G. Course extending over a period of seven days. The new Box Respirators have been issued to the Battn. This Respirator is a great improvement on the old P.H. Gas Helmet.	[illegible]

T2134. Wt. W708–776. 500000. 4/15. Sir J. C. & S.

CONFIDENTIAL

Vol 22

WAR DIARY

OF

8/10th (Service) Battalion The Gordon Highlanders

From. 1st March 1917 To 31st March 1917.

VOLUME 23.

Instructions regarding War Diaries and Intelligence Summaries are contained in F. S. Regs., Part II. and the Staff Manual respectively. Title pages will be prepared in manuscript.

WAR DIARY
~~or~~
~~INTELLIGENCE~~ SUMMARY. Sheet 363.

(Erase heading not required.)

Army Form C. 2118.

Place	Date	Hour	Summary of Events and Information	Remarks and references to Appendices
IZEL-LES-HAMEAU	1/3/17		The Battn carried out their programme of work - 'D' Coy had the use of the range, the other three Coys doing Physical Drill, bayonet fighting and Gas Drill with new Box respirators. Lewis Gun & Signalling Classes met. During the afternoon inter Platoon Football matches took place.	
"	2/3/17		Battn marched to the training area at LIGNEREUIL and practised attack over ground laid out representing enemy's trenches. - Inter Platoon Football matches during the afternoon.	
"	3/3/17		Divine Services in the forenoon - Football in the afternoon.	
"	4/3		During the morning the Coys practised the attack at the training area. In the afternoon the Battn Football team played the 8th Seaforth resulting in a win for us.	
"	5/3/17		2nd Lt. [illegible] appointed Adj. to Battn with effect from 11th Feb 1917 vice Lt D.W. M[illegible] to R.F.C.	
"	6/3/17		The "Attack" was again practised at LIGNEREUIL. Owing to [illegible] inspection in the afternoon by the C. in chief an early start had to be made. At midday the attack ended and we settled down to have lunch, - time did not permit of going back to billets. After covering the ground which	[illegible]

A5834 Wt. W4973/M687 750,000 8/16 D. D. & L. Ltd. Forms/C.2118/13.

Instructions regarding War Diaries and Intelligence Summaries are contained in F. S. Regs., Part II, and the Staff Manual respectively. Title pages will be prepared in manuscript.

WAR DIARY

~~or~~

~~INTELLIGENCE SUMMARY.~~

(*Erase heading not required.*)

Army Form C. 2118.

Sheet-364.

Place	Date	Hour	Summary of Events and Information	Remarks and references to Appendices
IZEL-LES-HAMEAU	6/3/17 (Contd)		owing to the snow & rain, was in rather a bad state, we certainly needed a brush up before the Inspection. The polishing room started and before marching off we were once more pretty free of mud. We marched to the Inspection ground at AMBRINES ~~and~~ got into position. After a wait of about an hour the G.O.C. in chief arrived and within half an hour the inspection was over and we marched back to billets after a long and hard day. Later in the day ~~the Gene~~ a message was received expressing the G.O.C.'s satisfaction with the inspection and the smart appearance of all on parade.	[illegible]
"	7/3/17		The Battn marched to training area and practised the Attack. The Battn Football team played the 45th Field Ambulance team, which resulted in a win for us. Temp Maj J.G. Thom M.C. to be acting Lt Col. whilst Commanding a Battalion (Extract from London Gazette supplement March 3rd 1917).	
"	8/3/17		Practising the Attack on training area. Football during afternoon	

A5834 Wt. W4973/M687 750,000 8/16 D. D. & L. Ltd. Forms/C.2118/13.

Instructions regarding War Diaries and Intelligence Summaries are contained in F. S. Regs., Part II. and the Staff Manual respectively. Title pages will be prepared in manuscript.

WAR DIARY

~~or~~

~~INTELLIGENCE SUMMARY.~~

(Erase heading not required.)

Sheet 365.

Army Form C. 2118.

Place	Date	Hour	Summary of Events and Information	Remarks and references to Appendices
IZEL-LES-HAMEAU	9/3/17		Competition for best turned out and smartest Platoon. Great keenness over the competition. The R.S.M. acting as judge, the forenoon was fully taken up showing Platoons for the final. At 1.30 the decision was declared viz:- "A" Coy No 2 Platoon, "B" Coy No 6 Platoon, "D" Coy No 14 Platoon ("C" Coy still on permanent working party). The "Final" took place in the afternoon, Capt Drummond acting as judge, gave his decision as follows:- 1st No 2 Platoon "A" Coy; No 6 "B" Coy and No 14 "D" Coy equal. The prize for the winning Platoon took the form of a silver Kilt pin to each man in the Platoon, also Platoon Officer. Battn Sports were fixed for the date but owing to the cold severe weather it was impossible to carry same out; with the exception of Piping & Dancing all other events were cancelled.	

A5834 Wt. W4973/M687 750,000 8/16 D. D. & L. Ltd. Forms/C.2118/13.

Instructions regarding War Diaries and Intelligence Summaries are contained in F. S. Regs., Part II. and the Staff Manual respectively. Title pages will be prepared in manuscript.

WAR DIARY
or
~~INTELLIGENCE SUMMARY.~~ Sheet 366.

(*Erase heading not required.*)

Army Form C. 2118.

Place	Date	Hour	Summary of Events and Information	Remarks and references to Appendices
IZEL-LES-HAMEAU	10/3/17		Part of forenoon spent in Gas drill with new respirators. at 2.30 pm the Battalion marched to Billets in ARRAS via HERMAVILLE, St POL-ARRAS ROAD, BAUDIMONT GATE. We arrived in ARRAS about 7 pm after a long march two men only falling out. The new billets chiefly consisted of cellars.	
ARRAS.	11/3/17		Relief of 45th I.B. by 44th I.B. We relieved the 6th Cameron Hldrs in the right sub-sector. "C" Coy relieved the front line Coy. 3 Platoons of "D" Coy in support with one Platoon in billets in ARRAS. "A" & "B" Coys in Reserve in billets in ARRAS. Hd Qrs billeted in ARRAS. Daylight relief and reported complete by 12 noon. The trenches were in a bad state & little seemed to have been done in the way of improving same. Considering the months of "remaining" in this section with every facility of making first class trenches it was very disappointing to find them in such a bad state.	

Trench strength 28 officers, 704 other ranks.

A5834 Wt. W4973/M687 750,000 8/16 D. D. & L. Ltd. Forms/C.2118/13

Army Form C. 2118.

Instructions regarding War Diaries and Intelligence Summaries are contained in F. S. Regs., Part II. and the Staff Manual respectively. Title pages will be prepared in manuscript.

WAR DIARY
or
~~INTELLIGENCE~~ SUMMARY.

(Erase heading not required.)

Sheet 367.

Place	Date 1917.	Hour	Summary of Events and Information	Remarks and references to Appendices
ARRAS.	March. 12.	A.M.	Some shelling on the Eastern side of the town. One platoon of 7th CAMERONS lost 20 killed and wounded while on the way to relieve one of our platoons in the cemetery. Frontage held by battalion was from sap 66 (about G.24.C.5.6.) on the left to 5 yards south of sap 62 (about G.30.a.7.8.) on the right. The brigade held with 2 battalions in front (each with 1 company in front line) and 2 battalions in ARRAS, one of which had to garrison the cemetery in G.29.b. with 2 platoons.	N.B. Right subsection. I.3 Sector. VI Corps.
		4 P.M.	There was very heavy shelling on support line for 20 minutes between 4 and 5 P.M. No casualties in the battalion, but considerable damage to trenches.	UGP
	13.	5.30 P.M.	Heavy enemy bombardment with field guns, 4.2's, 5.9's on support and reserve lines. Trenches damaged, but only 1 casualty. A coy relieved C coy in the front line; B relieved D in support. After dark 2nd Lt HOTCHKISS, who had been in a shell hole ~~[illegible]~~ near the enemy wire since 2 A.M., came safely in and reported the enemy front line to be held very lightly, if at all, through the day, but that he heard troops coming up to occupy it at dark.	UGP
	14.		Some enemy shelling in the afternoon.	
	15.	7 AM –12 noon.	9th BLACK WATCH and 8/10 GORDONS relieved by SEAFORTHS and CAMERONS. Moved back to cellars on East side of the GRANDE PLACE.	UGP

A5834 Wt. W4973/M687 750,000 8/16 D. D. & L. Ltd. Forms/C.2118/13.

Instructions regarding War Diaries and Intelligence Summaries are contained in F. S. Regs., Part II. and the Staff Manual respectively. Title pages will be prepared in manuscript.

WAR DIARY
or
~~INTELLIGENCE SUMMARY.~~
(Erase heading not required.)

Army Form C. 2118.

Sheet 368.

Place	Date	Hour	Summary of Events and Information	Remarks and references to Appendices
ARRAS.	16–19.		Battalion in support. Large working parties supplied mainly for digging new trenches near the front line.	Ref. LENS 11 1/100,000. KGT
	19.		The 44th Inf Bde was relieved by the 46th and moved back to huts in HAXBARCQ. 9th BLACK WATCH and 8/10 GORDONS were left in ARRAS to provide working parties of 450 to 500 men per day working 8 hours. Two companies employed on protecting cellars on West side of GRANDE PLACE with bricks; two worked in the sewers under the New Zealand tunneling company.	KGT
			Battalion casualties for the 8 days in front and support; — wounded 1 officer, 18 O.R.; killed 4 O.R.	
	20.		Battalion strength 22 officers 742 other ranks.	
		11.30 AM.	Order came through that VI Corps was to be ready to attack at 24 hours notice.	
		Noon.	Report arrived that troops opposite corps on our right had evacuated 2nd, 3rd and 4th lines.	KGT
	22.	A.M.	Preliminary instructions for offensive operations were issued.	V. Appendix I.
	26.	8 P.M.	The battalion was relieved in ARRAS by 8th SEAFORTHS and moved into billets at HABARCQ.	
			A reinforcement of 2 officers and 112 other ranks arrived.	KGT
			Battalion strength 23 officers, 810 other ranks excluding transport.	

Instructions regarding War Diaries and Intelligence Summaries are contained in F. S. Regs., Part II. and the Staff Manual respectively. Title pages will be prepared in manuscript.

WAR DIARY
or
~~INTELLIGENCE SUMMARY~~.

(Erase heading not required.)

Sheet 369.

Army Form C. 2118.

Place	Date 1917.	Hour	Summary of Events and Information	Remarks and references to Appendices
HABARCQ.	March 27.	3.30 P.M.	D company sent to AVESNES-LE-COMTE to provide a working party of 125 other ranks for cutting wood at BLAVINCOURT.	Ref. LENS 11. 1/100,000.
	28.	4 P.M.	Brig. General Marshall addressed company commanders on the general plan of the British offensive and on the different objectives of the 44th Inf. Bde.	UGP.
	29.	a.m.	Training was carried on by companies, particular attention being paid to organization of the rifle bombers.	
	30.	3 P.M.	The G.O.C. VI Corps inspected the battalion and presented one D.C.M. and three M.M.'s.	
ARRAS.	31.	5 P.M.	The battalion left HABARCQ and moved up to billets in ARRAS.	UGP.

A5834 Wt. W4973/M687 750,000 8/16 D. D. & L. Ltd. Forms/C.2118/13.

Appendix I WAR DIARY

PRELIMINARY INSTRUCTIONS FOR OFFENSIVE OPERATIONS.

Reference Sheets,
ARRAS, 51b N.W.3,
& 15 Div. Maps 3 & 3A.

SECRET.

---

1. The 15th Division is to attack the German Line between the following boundaries :-

(a) On south - The Road (inclusive) which runs from G.29c 45.85 through Cemetery to Support Line, and thence to Front Line just South of Sap 63 (G.30c 65.80) it then continues to German Sap W.22 (G.30b 15.75) and due East through H.25c 3.8., H.26c 3.6. to H.28d 1.1.

(b) On North. River SCARPE.

35th Infantry Brigade will be on our Right.

2. The 44th Infantry Brigade will attack the Right Section, and 45th Infantry Brigade the Left Section of the Divisional Sector.

46th Infantry Brigade will be in Reserve.

3. The First Objective is H.25c 3.8. through FREIS WOOD Northwards.

The Second Objective is the line through H.26c 3.6., H.20c 5.0., and H.13d 8.3.

The Third Objective is the Enemy Defences in H.28 and Northwards to the River.

44th and 45th Infantry Brigades will capture the 1st and 2nd Objectives; the 46th Infantry Brigade will capture the 3rd Objective

4. The Assaulting Battalions of the 44th Infantry Brigade will be:-

8/10th Bn., The Gordon Highlanders on the Right,

9th Black Watch on the Left.

The dividing line between battalions will be Sap 64 inclusive to 8/10th Gordon Highlanders and thence in an Easterly direction through G.24d 4.3. to H.20c 3.4½.

7th Bn. Cameron Highlanders will be in Support,

8th Bn. Seaforth Highlanders will be in Reserve.

5. The Battalion will be disposed as follows on the day of the Assault:-

A.Company on the Right } Dividing Line to be
B.Company on the Left } Point G.24c 7.1.
D.Company in Support
C.Company in Reserve
Bn.H.Qrs. G.23d 5½.3, in Dugout No 1 on Railway Embankment.

6. Method of Attack

(1) At Zero hour, all the waves of the Assaulting and Support Battalions, together with the Vickers, Trench Mortars & carrying parties will advance from their forming up trenches. The object to be aimed at is to cross "No man's Land" with as little delay as possible. On reaching the German Line, the waves will correct their intervals to 50 yards between waves. The two leading Coys of each Battalion will push on to the line of the first objective. Third and Fourth Companies will occupy areas as shewn in Appendix "C".

7th Camerons will occupy the first and second lines of the enemy's defences.

(2) When the leading Battalions advance to attack the second objective, the 7th Cameron Highlanders will move forward in support.

(3) The advance from the first objective to the second objective will begin at approximately Zero plus 1 hour and 40 minutes.

During the halt at the first objective the leading Battalions will be re-organized for the fresh advance. This re-organization must not interfere with the maintainence of steady fire on the enemy's position in front.

(4) On gaining first and second objectives, covering parties and patrols will be sent out at once. The duty of the former is to secure the tactical features in the immediate vicinity of the objectives; the duty of the latter is to maintain touch with the enemy (as far as our barrage permits) and with units on either flank.

Cont'd

6. Method of Attack. (Cont'd).

(4). (a) On reaching the first objective, after the patrols have been sent out, the troops will be reorganized into the formation in which the advance to the second objective will be made. This reorganization must be carried out as expeditiously as possible, and the fact that the enemy may make a local counter attack before the commencement of the advance to the 2nd objective must not be lost sight of.

(b). On reaching the second objective a further reorganization will be necessary, and consolidation of the position reached must be started at once. Commanders on the spot must bear in mind that the object of the consolidation is to enable us to break up a counter attack by the enemy, and that the enemy trench which has been captured, may not be the best position to occupy.

The front position must be strongly held, but a sufficient force must also be disposed in a support Line.

It is imperative also that the flanks of the position taken up are sufficiently protected, and the establishing of communication with the troops on either flank is also of the first importance.

(5) Battalion Headquarters will not move forward until after the capture of the first objective.

(6) Clearing of the trenches will be done by the waves which occupy them. But these waves will be preceded by small "Mopping Up" parties whose duty it is to prevent the egress of the enemy from his dug-outs till the arrival of the main body. Each of these parties will consist of 2 Bombing Squads from each of the Support and Reserve Coys. On reaching the trench which they are to mop up, one bombing squad will proceed to the left and one to the right to ensure that touch is kept with both flanks.

The position of these "mopping up" parties is shewn in Appendix "B".

7. Artillery, Machine Gun and Trench Mortar preparations, will be notified later.

8. DUMPS.

44th Brigade Dumps will be numbered:-

A.R. A - Brigade Dump at G.29c 7.8

A.R. B.1 - At G.29b 8½.8½.

A.R. B.2 - At G.23d 8½.3½.

A.R. C. - At G.30c 5.9½.

A.R. D. - At G.24d 7.5.

A.R. E. - At H.19d 6.7.

For contents of these stores see Appendix "E".

9. Signalling arrangements to be notified later.

Medical arrangements to be notified later.

Arrangements re Prisoners to be notified later.

(Signed) G.P.Geddes,

Lieut. and Adjutant.

Copies to O.C. Coys.
2nd in Command.
L.G.O.
44th Brigade
R.S.M.
Signals.
War Diary.
File.
3 Spare.

Appendix "B"

Formations: Position of Moppers Up Etc.

Attack on First Objective

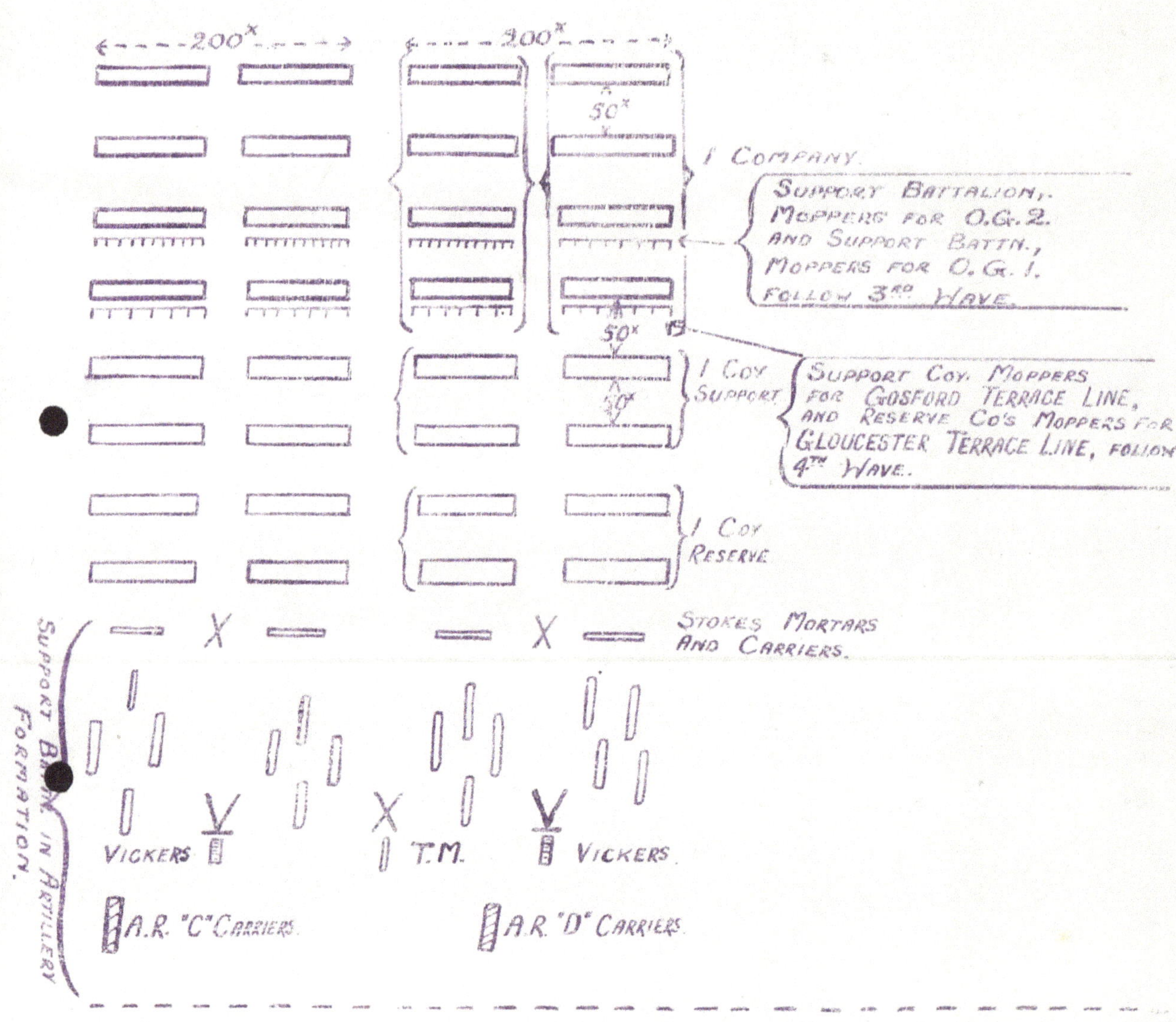

Detailed Formation of a Platoon

Inner Flank	Riflemen		Bombing Squad	Outer Flank
	10x		10x	
	Riflemen including rifle bombers of platoon		Lewis Gun	

CONTINUATION OF APPENDIX "B"

2. ATTACK ON SECOND OBJECTIVE

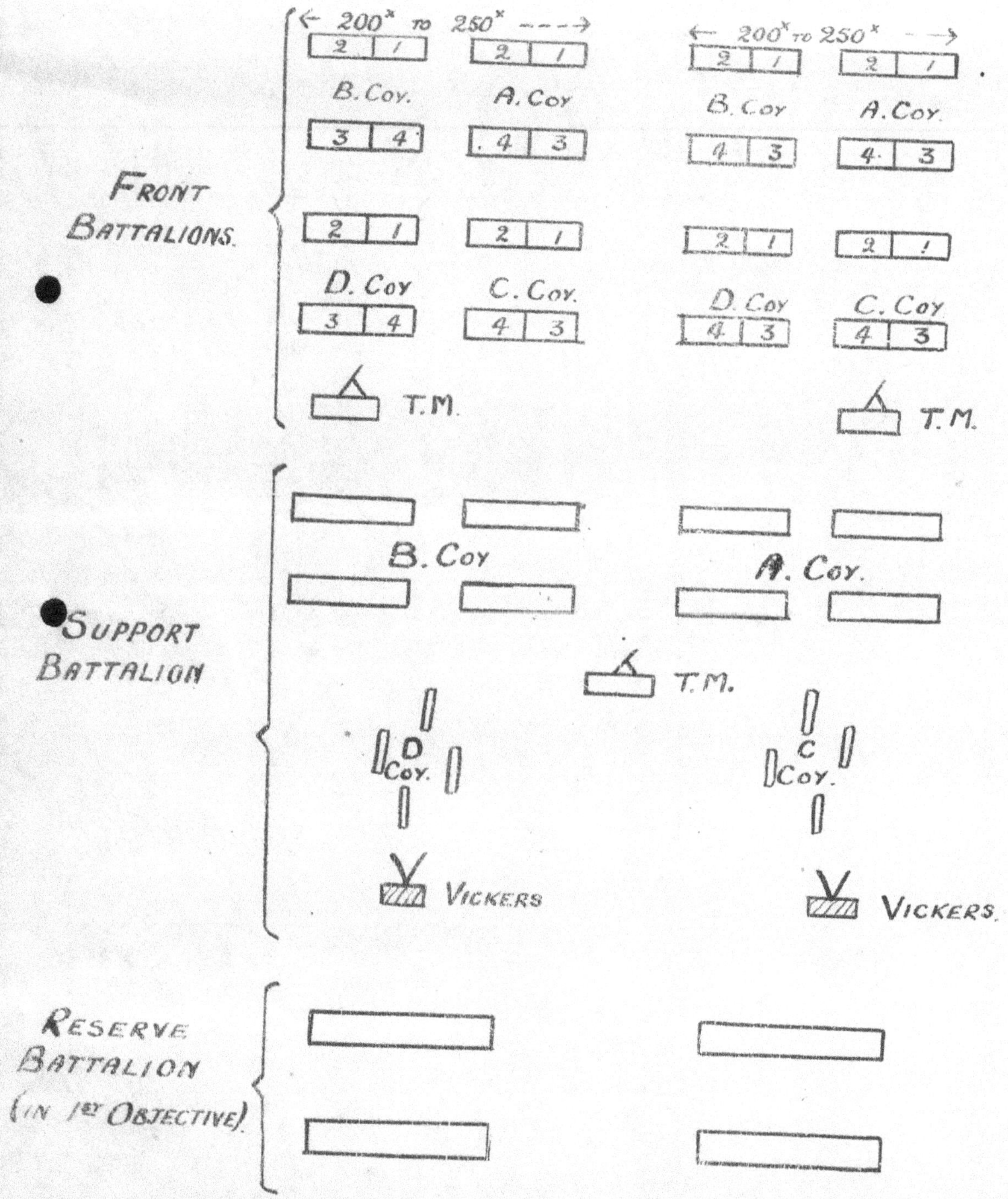

FRONT BATTALIONS.

← 200x TO 250x ---→

2	1		2	1
B. COY.			A. COY	
3	4		4	3
2	1		2	1
D. COY			C. COY.	
3	4		4	3

T.M.

← 200x TO 250x →

2	1		2	1
B. COY			A. COY.	
4	3		4	3
2	1		2	1
D. COY			C. COY	
4	3		4	3

T.M.

SUPPORT BATTALION

B. COY

A. COY.

T.M.

D COY.

C COY.

VICKERS

VICKERS.

RESERVE BATTALION (IN 1ST OBJECTIVE)

44th Infantry Brigade.

APPENDIX "E".

LIST OF STORES TO BE CARRIED FORWARD TO DUMPS.

STORES.	(1) To be held at Dumps before ZERO				(2) To be carried forward to 4R.D 1st journey by platoons of 4R.C and 4R.D.	(3) To be carried forward to 4R.E. within four hours after taking 2nd objective and this establishment to be maintained.
	4R.A.	4R. B1	4R. B2	4R.C		
Stokes shells rounds	3610	NIL	140	150	26	544
S.A.A. boxes	445	380	15	20	10	73
Mills No.5	224	500	40	20	20	182
Mills No.23	34[illegible]	334	30	40	13	70
P. Bombs, rounds	450	200				100
Stokes prepared for dugouts rounds	200	40				
Very Lights 1" white, rounds	4000	2000				300
Very Lights 1" red rounds	2000	1000				300
Very Lights 1" green rounds	2000	1000				300
Flares	4000	2000				400
Signal lights with artillery (not rockets)	2000	1000				
Smoke rifle grenades	600	300				
Revolver ammunition, boxes	[illegible]	4				
Shovels	100	NIL				
Picks	50	NIL				
Wire cutters long	44	24				
-do- Rifle	100	100				
-do- Nipper	120	80				

LIST OF STORES TO BE CARRIED FORWARD TO DUMPS.

	To be held at Dumps before Zero.				To be carried forward to ARD 1st journey by platoons of ARC & ARD.	To be carried forward to ARE within four hou[rs] after taking [illegible] objectives & th[e] establishment [illegible] be maintained.
	AR A	AR B1	AR B2	AR C		
Grenade carriers	300	400				
Hedgers gloves pairs	40	40				
water 2 gall. Tins	NIL	50				
Sandbags for carrying Stokes	250	250	100	150		
Very Lights 1½" boxes						3
Rockets red						3 doz.
Rockets green						3 doz.

8/10 Gordon Highlanders

April 1917

44/15

CONFIDENTIAL Vol 23

WAR DIARY

OF

8/10th (Service) Batt, The Gordon Highlanders.

FOR PERIOD

1st April 1917 to 30th April 1917.

VOLUME 24

Army Form C. 2118.

Instructions regarding War Diaries and Intelligence Summaries are contained in F. S. Regs., Part II. and the Staff Manual respectively. Title pages will be prepared in manuscript.

WAR DIARY
or
~~INTELLIGENCE SUMMARY.~~
(Erase heading not required.)

Sheet 370.

Place	Date 1917.	Hour	Summary of Events and Information	Remarks and references to Appendices
	April.			[initials]
ARRAS.	2.	P.M.	Operation orders were received by the battalion for move into battle positions on the night of the 3rd.	
	3.	2.P.M.	Operation orders were issued for the move.	Appendix 1.
		7 P.M.	The battalion moved into battle positions relieving the 7th Camerons and was disposed as follows:- One platoon of "B" Coy in front line, remainder of "B" Coy in Cemetery defences, and the other three Companies in cellars in Eastern streets of ARRAS. The relief was accomplished quietly and without casualties. Officers + men surplus to attacking strength went back to Duisans and FREVENT	Appendix 2
	4th		Preliminary bombardment began at 6 AM	
	4/6th		The battalion was constantly employed on the construction of assembly trenches + other preparations for attack. Our artillery was employed cutting enemy's wire opposite our front, + their work frequently drew artillery retaliation. Our patrols were active at night reconnoitring the enemy's wire, but owing to bright moonlight it was found impossible to observe the wire as closely as could have been desired.	

T2134. Wt. W708—776. 500000. 4/15. Sir J. C. & S.

Instructions regarding War Diaries and Intelligence Summaries are contained in F. S. Regs., Part II. and the Staff Manual respectively. Title pages will be prepared in manuscript.

WAR DIARY *or* INTELLIGENCE SUMMARY.

(Erase heading not required.)

Army Form C. 2118.

Sheet 371

Place	Date	Hour	Summary of Events and Information	Remarks and references to Appendices
Arras	April 7th	6pm	Orders were received for the Battalion to raid the trenches opposite our front for the purpose of obtaining identifications. "D" Coy was selected to carry out the raid. They were able to form up without being seen, & 3 platoons rushed to the enemy wire before coming under fire. It was then found that the wire had not been cut, & although the party remained out for 25 minutes only one NCO reached the enemy trench. The company was obliged to return without a prisoner. Casualties killed 1 OR. Wounded 1 Officer 7 ORs. A congratulatory message was received from the Brigadier General praising the gallantry & determination shown by our men in attempting to force their way through exceptionally thick & strong wire entanglements.	Appendix 3 / Appendix 4
	8th	9am	Although the raid failed in its main object, it proved of immense value as heavy trench mortars were detailed to assist in cutting the wire & their firing ~~today~~ appeared accurate & destructive.	
		2pm	The bombardment of our artillery intensified, & caused heavy retaliation on Cemetery Defences. This ceased about 5pm apparently as a result of Counter Battery work by our guns.	

T2134. Wt. W708—776. 500000. 4/15. Sir J. C. & S.

Army Form C. 2118.

Instructions regarding War Diaries and Intelligence Summaries are contained in F. S. Regs., Part II. and the Staff Manual respectively. Title pages will be prepared in manuscript.

WAR DIARY
or
INTELLIGENCE SUMMARY.
(Erase heading not required.)

Sheet 372.

Place	Date	Hour	Summary of Events and Information	Remarks and references to Appendices
ARRAS.	9th	2.30AM	At this hour the battalion began to move forward to assembly trenches for the attack. The battalion was reported in position at 4.30 am – one hour before Zero –, no casualties having occurred, & the enemy's suspicions apparently not having been aroused. Position of battalion as follows:– "A" Coy under Captain John Martin M.C. on right front "B" Coy " Captain W McCall on left front "D" Coy " 2 Lt B. Burnett in support "C" Coy " Lt P. Booth in reserve Strength:– Officers 20 ORs 702 At 5.30 am – Zero – our barrage opened with a thunder of sound & our support & reserve companies moved out of their trenches. At Zero plus 2 minutes in accordance with plan, the front companies climbed from their trenches & moved forward. The movement was made in perfect order, a tendency on the part of the men to follow our barrage too closely being the only point calling for officers' control	JG

T2134. Wt. W708–776. 500000. 4/15. Sir J. C. & S.

Instructions regarding War Diaries and Intelligence Summaries are contained in F. S. Regs., Part II. and the Staff Manual respectively. Title pages will be prepared in manuscript.

WAR DIARY
or
INTELLIGENCE SUMMARY.
(*Erase heading not required.*)

Army Form C. 2118.

Sheet 373

Place	Date	Hour	Summary of Events and Information	Remarks and references to Appendices
ARRAS	9th	5.30am	The enemy S.O.S. signal was put up about 30 seconds after Zero, and a field gun barrage was put down on our front line & communication trenches about 3 minutes later, causing a few casualties to "C" Coy before they got over our front line. At Zero plus 4 minutes our barrage lifted on to the enemy support line, and the two front Coys dashed into the enemy first line before opposition was possible. From this point until the taking of the 1st objective – 500 yards behind German front line – the front Companies moved forward behind our barrage with perfect steadiness & splendid courage. News of its capture was telephoned to Battn Hdqrs 7½ minutes after it was timed to be taken. Headquarters were advanced to the front line, & remained with the leading Companies throughout subsequent operations. A halt of 1 hour 40 minutes at this point allowed reorganisation. There was little shelling the enemy being engaged in withdrawing his guns	JB
		7.50am	At this point the battalion advanced to the second objective in the altered formation laid down. This objective represented a further advance of 1000 yards; A & B Companies remained in the front line of attack	

T2134. Wt. W708–776. 500000. 4/15. Sir J. C. & S.

Instructions regarding War Diaries and Intelligence Summaries are contained in F. S. Regs., Part II. and the Staff Manual respectively. Title pages will be prepared in manuscript.

WAR DIARY
or
INTELLIGENCE SUMMARY.
(Erase heading not required.)

Army Form C. 2118.

Sheet 374

Place	Date	Hour	Summary of Events and Information	Remarks and references to Appendices
Arras	9th	7.50 AM	Before the attack had advanced 150 yards it was held up by machine gun fire from RAILWAY TRIANGLE and a redoubt on our right. This redoubt was outside our area but Captain Martin seeing that the Division on our right were swinging away from the redoubt, instead of attacking it, at once organised two parties to storm it. With 2 Lt A.C. HAY he led these parties and captured the redoubt, both officers unfortunately being killed in doing so. Their effort coupled with the arrival of a tank, which advanced against Railway Triangle enabled the battalion to move forward & take the second objective. We reorganised & consolidated and at 12.10 pm the 46th Brigade advanced through our lines to attack the Division's third objective. They were successful and the 37th Division in turn pushed past them with MONCHY as its objective. The 9th Division on our left took all their objectives, but the 12th on our right failed to take their third objective which should have brought them into line with the 46th Brigade on our front. The battalion spent the night of the 9th in the trench system which had formed their second objective. Snow fell heavily & this with an intensely cold wind made conditions very trying.	JS

T2134. Wt. W708—776. 500000. 4/15. Sir J. C. & S.

Instructions regarding War Diaries and Intelligence Summaries are contained in F. S. Regs., Part II. and the Staff Manual respectively. Title pages will be prepared in manuscript.

WAR DIARY
or
INTELLIGENCE SUMMARY.
(Erase heading not required.)

Army Form C. 2118.

Sheet 375

Place	Date	Hour	Summary of Events and Information	Remarks and references to Appendices
ARRAS	April 10th		The morning of the 10th was still very cold. The battalion was refitting & completing establishment of ammunition when orders were received for us to proceed into the Western end of the village of FEUCHY and be prepared to move in a Southern direction in support of a renewed attack by the 12th & 3rd Divisions on their original third objectives. Passable billets in the battered houses of FEUCHY were found, and a little rest obtained.	Vo Appendix 5
	11th	1.30 AM	The battalion was ordered to move into position of attack in support of 45th & 46th Brigades, who were rendering assistance to the 12th Division in an attack on MONCHY. Our position was 2/300 yards in advance of our Divisions original third objective with our left resting on the railway.	Vo Appendix 6
		5 AM	The division attacked & we moved forward along with the 7th Cameron Highlanders. Both battalions only managed to advance about 200 yards when very heavy machine gun fire from MONCHY and from the wood on our left across the River Scarpe was opened. As we had no artillery support, progress was impossible, & both battalions dug in in shell holes	

T2134. Wt. W708—776. 500000. 4/15. Sir J. C. & S.

Instructions regarding War Diaries and Intelligence Summaries are contained in F. S. Regs., Part II. and the Staff Manual respectively. Title pages will be prepared in manuscript.

WAR DIARY
or
INTELLIGENCE SUMMARY.
(Erase heading not required.)

Sheet 376.

Army Form C. 2118.

Place	Date	Hour	Summary of Events and Information	Remarks and references to Appendices
Arras area	11th	3/pm	Orders were received to renew the attack on MONCHY, and favourably [?] a snow storm we were able to make progress for about 600 yards. Lt. Col. J. G. THOM then ordered a halt as both our flanks were in the air and the troops on our right appeared to be swinging off to the South. This position was held until operation orders were received, stating the battalion was being relieved by 6th Dorsets. To facilitate relief we withdrew about 300 yards to a position bringing us into line with the troops on our right and the relief was completed at 2 AM on the 12th.	[initials] Appendix 7
	12th	2 am	The battalion moved back to the trenches occupied on the night of the 9th. The night was again very cold & more snow fell.	[initials]
		11.30 am	We returned to billets in ARRAS, the battalion being played in by the pipebands of the 9th Gordon Highlanders and our own pipeband. Good billets were available and hot food & much needed rest obtained. Congratulatory messages to the Divisional Commander were received from the G.O.C. in C., the Army Commander, and the Corps Commander speaking in the highest terms of the work of officers & men.	Appendix 8

T2134. Wt. W708—776. 500000. 4/15. Sir J. C. & S.

Instructions regarding War Diaries and Intelligence Summaries are contained in F. S. Regs., Part II. and the Staff Manual respectively. Title pages will be prepared in manuscript.

WAR DIARY
or
INTELLIGENCE SUMMARY.
(Erase heading not required.)

Army Form C. 2118.

Sheet 377

Place	Date	Hour	Summary of Events and Information	Remarks and references to Appendices
Arras	April 12th		Our casualties in the three days fighting were:—	JG
			Officers killed 4 Wounded 4	
			O.Rs. killed 47 Wounded 162 missing 36	
			In the afternoon Major W M K MARSHALL joined the battalion.	
	13th		The work of refitting & re-equipping the Battalion occupied all day. Baths were obtained for the majority of the men. Our Pipe Band played retreat in the PLACE DE LA CROIX, being the first band to do so in ARRAS. Major G.J. CUMINE, D.S.O. rejoined the battalion from a Senior Officers Course in England.	JG
	14th		A little training was done, & re-equipping continued.	JG
	15th		LT. COL. D. MACLEOD, D.S.O. rejoined the battalion from sick leave. Training continued.	JG
	16th		LT. COL. D. MACLEOD, D.S.O. took over command of the Battalion from acting LT. COL. J.G. THOM. M.C. A good deal of training was done. Lewis Gun classes formed and started. Weather wet and unfavourable for much out door training.	JG

T2134. Wt. W708—776. 500000. 4/15. Sir J. C. & S.

Instructions regarding War Diaries and Intelligence Summaries are contained in F. S. Regs., Part II. and the Staff Manual respectively. Title pages will be prepared in manuscript.

WAR DIARY
or
INTELLIGENCE SUMMARY.
(*Erase heading not required.*)

Army Form C. 2118.

Sheet 378

Place	Date	Hour	Summary of Events and Information	Remarks and references to Appendices
ARRAS	APRIL 17th		Training continued. Re-equipment completed.	
	18th	7.30 pm	The Battalion took over the Brigade Sector for 48 hours relieving the 1st Inniskilling Fusiliers and the 1st Kings Own Scottish Borderers. The line to be held was consolidated, & the construction of attack trenches carried on. The period was uneventful although enemy shelling was frequent and heavy.	
	2~~1~~0st	10.30 pm	The battalion was relieved by the 8th Seaforth Highlanders & 7th Cameron Highlanders during the night of the 21st/22ND marched back to billets in ARRAS.	
	~~22nd~~		At 5.30 pm on the afternoon of the 21st the massed Pipe Bands of five Battalions of the Regiment the 1st 5th 6th 9th and 8/10th played Retreat in the GRANDE PLACE. The Corps Commander Lt. General J.A.L. HALDANE C.B. D.S.O, and many other officers were present, and a very large crowd assembled. The parade which is probably unique in the history of the regiment gave great pleasure to all and was highly praised by the Corps Commander.	

A5834 Wt. W4973/M687 750,000 8/16 D. D. & L. Ltd. Forms/C.2118/13

Army Form C. 2118.

Instructions regarding War Diaries and Intelligence Summaries are contained in F. S. Regs., Part II. and the Staff Manual respectively. Title pages will be prepared in manuscript.

WAR DIARY
or
INTELLIGENCE SUMMARY.
(Erase heading not required.)

Sheet 379

Place	Date	Hour	Summary of Events and Information	Remarks and references to Appendices
ARRAS	APRIL 22nd		Brigade Operation Order No. 159 received in continuation of Brigade Instruction No 1 of 18th April	Appendix 9
			Battalion Operation Order No 93 issued for the attack on 23rd in which the battalion is in reserve to the 44th Brigade.	Appendix 10 Appendix 11
		8.0 PM	The Battalion marched to BROWN LINE of attack on 9th April in the sector opposite + West of village of GUEMAPPE + was in position at 3 am	
	23rd	4.45am	The attack commenced at 4 45 am one Company being employed in carrying forward ammunition, while the other three Companies remained in positions at disposal of Brigade. The assaulting battalions of the Brigade could not reach their objective and at 12 noon	
		12 noon	two Companies were ordered forward in support to remain in the jumping off trenches of the Front Battalions.	
			Very heavy fighting went on during the day	
		6pm	At 6 pm the 46th Brigade continued the attack and the whole battalion moved forward to "A" and "B" trenches in support.	

Instructions regarding War Diaries and Intelligence Summaries are contained in F. S. Regs., Part II. and the Staff Manual respectively. Title pages will be prepared in manuscript.

WAR DIARY
or
INTELLIGENCE SUMMARY.
(*Erase heading not required.*)

Army Form C. 2118.

Sheet 380.

Place	Date	Hour	Summary of Events and Information	Remarks and references to Appendices
ARRAS FRONT.	23rd	6pm	The three assaulting battalions withdrew to N 15 a b + c (Reference Map 51 B. S.W. 2) for the night to reorganise, and the battalion was attached to the 46th Brigade from the night of 23rd inst	JO
	24th		At 4 pm the 46th Brigade again attacked the BLUE LINE the battalion being in support to the 10th Scottish Rifles, who were the Right Front Battalion and the 6th Cameron Highlanders were in support to the Left Front Battalion. Two Companies carried on the work of consolidation in shell holes, about 100 yards behind the Scottish Rifles, and two Companies remained another 150 yards in rear in SHOVEL TRENCH	Appendix 12 JO
			This attack failed to capture CAVALRY FARM, which formed part of the BLUE LINE, and at 7.50 pm orders were received from the 46th Brigade for the Battalion to attack the Farm from the North as soon as it was dark under cover of Stokes and machine gun barrage fire.	Appendix 13

Army Form C. 2118.

WAR DIARY
or
INTELLIGENCE SUMMARY.
(*Erase heading not required.*)

Instructions regarding War Diaries and Intelligence Summaries are contained in F. S. Regs., Part II. and the Staff Manual respectively. Title pages will be prepared in manuscript.

Sheet 381

Place	Date	Hour	Summary of Events and Information	Remarks and references to Appendices
ARRAS FRONT	APRIL 24th	7.50 PM.	Three Companies were detailed to carry out the attack, but as they were scattered in shell holes and as there was a heavy enemy barrage all night preparations were not complete until 3 AM	
	25th	3.20 AM.	At 3.20 am the Companies lined up 50 yards from the Farm, but before they could advance they were detected by the enemy who at once put down a very heavy barrage, which disorganised and eventually broke up the attack, and the Companies were forced to return to their trenches. The remainder of the night was spent in consolidating the ground held.	JO
			A congratulatory message from the Commander in Chief was addressed to the Division, and a similar message was addressed to all units of the Brigade by General MARSHALL.	Appendix 14
			The 46th Brigade was relieved by the 44th & 45th Brigades and the battalion, which was still attached to the 46th Brigade withdrew to reserve trenches just west of GUEMAPPE.	

Instructions regarding War Diaries and Intelligence Summaries are contained in F. S. Regs., Part II. and the Staff Manual respectively. Title pages will be prepared in manuscript.

WAR DIARY
or
INTELLIGENCE SUMMARY.
(*Erase heading not required.*)

Sheet 382

Army Form C. 2118.

Place	Date	Hour	Summary of Events and Information	Remarks and references to Appendices
ARRAS FRONT	APRIL 26th		Lt. Col. MACLEOD was slightly wounded in the leg on the night of the 25th + Major CUMINE came up on the morning of the 26th to take over command of the Battalion. The battalion rested during the day on 26th.	JB
		10.30pm	The 44th + 45th Brigades were ordered to attack CAVALRY FARM and the remainder of the BLUE LINE. The attack commenced at 10.30 pm, our battalion being in reserve. Two companies were employed in carrying up Stokes ammunition and at Zero hour occupied the jumping off trenches vacated by the 9th Black Watch, who were the Right Front Battalion. The third Company remained in SHOVEL TRENCH and the fourth Company in "A" trench, close to Battalion Headquarters. The attack advanced our line slightly, but failed to capture CAVALRY FARM.	Appendix #7 15
	27th.		The day of the 27th was quieter and after dark the Battalion relieved the 9th Black Watch on the Right Front of the Brigade Sub Sector from O.14.c 2½ to O.14.a 2 0, three Companies in front and one in support	Appendix 16 JB

A5834 Wt. W4973/M687 730,000 8/16 D. D. & L. Ltd. Forms/C.2118/13.

Army Form C. 2118.

Instructions regarding War Diaries and Intelligence Summaries are contained in F. S. Regs., Part II. and the Staff Manual respectively. Title pages will be prepared in manuscript.

WAR DIARY
or
INTELLIGENCE SUMMARY.
(*Erase heading not required.*)

Sheet 383.

Place	Date	Hour	Summary of Events and Information	Remarks and references to Appendices
ARRAS FRONT	28th.		The day of the 28th. was quiet, except for intermittent shelling and at night the battalion was relieved by the 3rd London Regiment, & returned to billets in ARRAS. During the day Major CUMINE was wounded in the leg, and was evacuated.	Appendix 17 [illegible]
			Total casualties from 23rd. were Officers:— Killed 4. Wounded 6 Gassed 1 ORs Killed 11 Wounded 131	
ARRAS	29th.	3.30pm	The battalion moved West to SIMENCOURT. The weather was very warm & marching was difficult to tired men, but the battalion made the move very well. The mens billets were NISSEN Huts.	[illegible]
	30th.		Warm weather continued. The battalion rested and cleaned up.	[illegible]

A5834 Wt. W4973/M687 750,000 8/16 D. D. & L. Ltd. Forms/C.2118/13.

Appendix 1.

Copy No WAR DIARY

SECRET. 8/10th (Service) Battalion The Gordon Highlanders

OPERATION ORDER No. 84.

By

Lieut. Colonel J.G.Thom, M.C., Commanding.

3rd April 1917

1. The Battalion will relieve the 7th Cameron Highlanders in the line to-night, 3rd April, taking over accommodation as detailed in Appendix "H" to "Preliminary Instructions". One Platoon of C.Company will be in the Front Line.
The Dividing Line between the 9th Black Watch and 8/10th Gordon Highlanders will be Sap 64, inclusive the 9th Black Watch.
Relief to be complete by 9.30pm.

2. The Battalion will move off in the following order:-

A.Coy at 7.0pm.
C.Coy at 7.15pm.
H.Qrs at 7.30pm.
D.Coy at 7.45pm.
B.Coy at 8.0pm.

2 Guides from 7th Cameron Highlrs will meet C.Coy's Front Line Platoon at H.Qrs, 7th Cameron Highlrs at 7.45pm.

Each Company except Headquarters, will first of all proceed to Brigade Headquarters (16 RUE GOGLIPAS), draw tools there from the Staff Captain (66% shovels & 34% picks), and then proceed to their positions via RUE DES AUGUSTINES, RUE DOINCRE, GRANDE PLACE, RUE ST. MICHAEL.

All movement to be by Platoons in single file at 75 yards interval.

3. Relief complete to be reported at once to Battalion H.Qrs (Dugout No 6).

(Signed) G.P.Geddes,
Lieut. and Adjutant.

Copies 1 - 4 All Coys.
5 R.S.M.
6 L.G.O.
7 7th Cameron Highlrs.
8 War Diary.
9 File.

Appendix 1

ARRANGEMENTS FOR MOVE.

Issued in conjunction with O.O. No. 84.

1. Blankets, securely rolled and clearly labelled in bundles of ten, will be dumped outside Company billets by 6.30 p.m.
O.C. Coys and R.S.M. will each detail a party of 1 N.C.O. and 6 men (from those returning to DUISSANS) to carry the blankets to BRIGADE store (No. 40 Billet, GRANDE PLACE). R.S.M. will detail a guard of 2 men to remain at the store.

2. Officers' valises and spare Mess kits will be returned to Transport to-night. Each Coy and Bn. H.Q. will detail one servant to meet the G.S. Wagon at Bn. H.Q. (46 RUE ST. MAURICE). The wagon will go round & collect all valises.
Mess Cart will collect the spare Mess kits.

3. (a) The 200 men detailed to return to DUISSANS to-night will parade in the RUE AUX OURS under Captain A.K. FRIDAY at 8.0 p.m. They will march to DUISSANS by platoons at 75 yards interval.

(b) The blankets of this party will be dumped at the junction of Brigade Square and the RUE AUX OURS by 7.30 p.m..
Captain FRIDAY will detail a party of 1 N.C.O. and 4 men to load the blankets on the limbers.

4. Rations for Z plus 1 day will be drawn by Companies this afternoon from No. 87 Billet, GRANDE PLACE. Ration parties will be there as follows :-

H.Qrs. .... 4.15 p.m.
A Coy ...... 4.30 p.m.
B " ...... 4.45 p.m.
C " ...... 5. 0 p.m.
D " ...... 5.15 p.m.

O.C. Coys must impress upon all ranks that these rations are for consumption on Z plus 1 day, and must on no account be consumed before then.

5. Arrangements for drawing MILLS' No. 23's will be notified later.

(signed) G.P. Geddes,
Lieut & Adjutant.

Copies 1 - 4 O.C. A, B, C, D Coys.
5 R.S.M.
6 L.G.O.
7. Quartermaster.
8. Transport Officer
9. War Diary
10. File.

Appendix 2

SECRET. Copy No...

8/10th (Service) Battalion, The Gordon Highlanders.

O P E R A T I O N   O R D E R   No. 90.

By

Lieut-Colonel J.G. Thom, M.C., Comdg.

7th April 1917

1. To the South of ARRAS, the enemy has fallen back to the HINDENBURG LINE.
About four enemy battalions hold the line from TILLOY to the River SCARPE.
On the front of the 15th Division is the 51st Infantry Regiment, 11th Division.

2. The VI Corps are to attack at ZERO hour on "Z" day.
The VII Corps are attacking on our right, and the XVII Corps on the left.
The attack is to be simultaneous along the whole front.
The 12th Division will be on the right and the 9th Division on the left. The 37th Division are in VI Corps reserve.
Dividing line between the 12th and 15th Divisions -
G.30.b.2.8 - H.25.b.6.8 - H.26.a.6.6 - H.28.c.8.2 - H.35.a.5.8

3. (1) The 15th Division will attack at ZERO hour, "Z" day, with the 44th Inf.Bde. on the Right, the 45th Inf.Bde. on the left, 46th Inf.Bde. in reserve.

(2) The 44th Inf.Bde. will attack with the 8/10th Gordon Highrs. on the right, 9th Black Watch on the left, 7th Cameron Highrs.in support and 8th Seaforth Highrs. in Reserve.
Dividing line between the 8/10th Gordon Highrs. and 9th Black Watch -
Sap 64 (inclusive to 8/10th Gordon Highrs.) and thence in an easterly direction through G.24.d.4.3 to H.20.c.3.4½.

4. The 8/10th Gordon Highlanders will be disposed as follows on the day of the ASSAULT:-

A Coy	on the right,	in Assembly Trenches	1 & 2.
B "	" " left,	" " "	" " "
D "	in support,	" " "	3.
C "	in Reserve,	" " "	4.

Bn.H.Qrs. - G.23.d.5½.3, in Dug-out No.6 on Railway Embankment.

Dividing Line between A & B Coys to be G.24.c.7.0.

5. (1) The attack will be carried out in stages :-

A. Attack on BLACK Line (H.25.a.2.8 - FRED'S WOOD - H.13.c.1.1)

B. Attack on BLUE Line (H.26.a.7.8 - H.20.a.6.2 - H.13.d.7.3)

C. Attack on BROWN Line (Enemy trenches North of H.28.c.8.2) and Northern slopes of ORANGE HILL.

(2) The BLACK and BLUE Lines will be captured by the 44th and 45th Inf.Bdes.

(3) During the attack on the BLACK and BLUE Lines, the 46th Inf.Bde. will move forward from Sewers and Cellars into a position of assembly in the German front line system.
The Brigade will be prepared to support the attack of the leading Brigades under Divisional Orders.

5. (4). At Zero plus 6 hours 40 minutes the 46th Infantry Brigade will advance through the Blue Line to attack the Brown Line.

After the capture of the Brown Line, posts will be established on the Northern slopes of ORANGE HILL.

The 44th and 45th Infantry Brigades will be prepared to support the Attack of the 46th Brigade on receipt of orders from Division.

6. ARTILLERY.

(1). The Divisional Artillery Group attacking under the orders of the Divisional Commander consists of the 15th and 33rd Divisional Artilleries. "H" and "I" Groups, VI Corps Heavy Artillery are supporting the Attack.

(2). The preliminary bombardment will continue for four days.

(3). After the capture of the Blue Line, the Divisional Artillery will move to Advanced positions for the attack on the Brown Line.

(4). 112th L.T.M.Battery will co-operate with 4 Stokes Guns.

From Zero – Zero + 4 minutes they will direct an intense bombardment on the following points:-

G.30b 1.8., G.30b 1½.9½., G.24d 2.1.

Dug-out No 2 (Front Line N. of Sap 62) is placed at their disposal after Zero plus 4 minutes.

7. The 44th Infantry Brigade will deliver the Assault in accordance with Preliminary Instructions which have been issued.

At Zero hour the four leading waves will get out of their trenches, but will not advance until Zero plus 4 minutes.

The remaining waves of the Assaulting Battalions will advance from their trenches at Zero hour, but will not pass through the first four waves should they reach them before they too advance.

8. At Zero plus 2 hours 20 minutes, the Assaulting and Support Battalions will advance against the BLUE line.

9. Zero day and hour, and arrangements for synchronizing watches will be issued later.

10. Instructions have been issued regarding :-

(1) Method of Attack.
(2) Carrying Parties and Dumps.
(3) Communications.
(4) Consolidation of Positions.
(5) Tanks and Artillery Barrage, (with 3 plans).
(6) Prisoners.
(7) Medical.
(8) Stragglers.

11. Any previous instructions at variance with this order are cancelled.

Copies to 1 – 4 O.C.Coys.
5 L.G.O.
6 44th Bde.
7 War Diary.
8 File.

(signed) G.P.Geddes,
Lieut. and Adjutant.

Appendix 3

SECRET

Operation Order No. 82
by
Lieut. Col. J. G. Thom, M.C.
Comdg
8/10 Bn. Gordon Hghrs

5th April 1917

1. The battalion will carry out a raid on the enemys trenches on the night of the 5/6th April.
Area to be raided -: G 30. b. 1½, 8 — 3½, 8 — 3, 9½ — 1½, 9½.

2. Raiding party will be provided by "D" Coy.

3. Object of the raid -: To capture prisoners and to obtain Identifications

4. Move to Assembly Trenches -:
D Coy. will rendezvous at C Coy. H. Qrs. (Dugout No. 3 G. 29. b. 8, 8½) at 1.30 a.m.
Guides (1 per platoon) will be provided by O.C. "C" Coy. to lead the raiding party into position. Platoons will move at 100 yards intervals.
Nos 1, 2 + 3 platoons will be lead into No. 1 Assembly Trench 35 minutes before Zero. No. 1 platoon will move out of No. 1 Assembly Trench and line up beyond our own wire, then No. 2 platoon will line up 20 yards behind No. 1 platoon, + No. 3 platoon 20 yard behind No. 2. No. 4 platoon will then mov into No. 1 Assembly Trench and will not mov forward until ordered to do so by O.C. "D" Coy. All movement into positions of assembly must be carried out with the utmost stealth

4 (Contd)

How far beyond our own wire No 1 Platoon will line up will depend entirely on how light it is at the time, and O.C. "D" Coy. will decide this point and give the necessary instructions.

Assembly Trench No 1 will be reconnoitred before dusk today by 2 Officers + 1 N.C.O from each platoon of "D" Coy.

5 Before moving to the position of Assembly all rifles will be loaded and bayonets fixed and dulled. No papers or maps will be carried by the raiders, and all identification marks will be removed by the men.

Every man will be warned that, should he fall into the hands of the enemy, he must on no account give any information except his name and Regiment.

6 Trench Mortar and Artillery Fire -:

(1) ~~Up to~~ Zero the artillery activity will be normal.

(2) At Zero:-

a Two Stokes guns will fire 15 rounds rapid each at Point G.30 b.1.8 and up to Sap W.22. They will subsequently maintain a steady rate of fire on front line S. of that point.

b A barrage will be put by 18 pounders on the German front line along the whole Divisional Front for one minute.

C. At Zero + 1 minute the barrage will lift on to the German Support line. Whenever the barrage lifts, Nos 1, 2 + 3 platoons will rush the German front line.

d a box barrage will be put round the

(3) At Zero + 4 minutes the barrage on Support line will lift sufficiently to permit the assaulting troops to enter the Support line.

(4) At Zero + 20 minutes, raiders must be clear of the Support line

(5) At Zero + 25 minutes, raiders must be clear of the German front line.

(6) At Zero + 30 minutes, artillery will resume its normal programme.

7. O.C 'C' Coy will be responsible that our wire is sufficiently cut to enable the raiding party to get through it. He will also detail guides to lead Nos 1, 2 + 3 platoons through the wire.

O.C C Coy will reinforce the front line with one other Lewis Gun. The Lewis Guns in the line during the raid will sweep the enemy's parapet on either side of the front to be raided. He will also be responsible for the placing + direction of the guns.

8. On returning the raiding party will reform in Assembly Trench No. 1 and in old front line, and will proceed via IMAGE STREET to their present positions.

9. Prisoners will be kept in the dugout near the junction of IMAGE ST + Front line till all is quiet, and will then be brought down via IMAGE ST to Battn. H.Qrs which will be in dugout No 3 during the Raid

10. Arrangements for synchronising watches will be notified later.

11. Zero hour to be notified later.

Copies 1-4: O.C Coys
5: L.G.O.
6: 44 Bde.
7: 9th B.W.
8: War Diary

G.P. Geddes
Lieut. + Adjutant
8th [illegible]

BM/561.

8/10th Gordon Highrs. Appendix 4

I wish to express to all ranks who took part in the raid last night my high appreciation of their behaviour.

The task they were called on to perform was not only difficult but was of the greatest importance to the Division and the Corps. The information required could not have been obtained in any other way. I congratulate you and thank you for your devotion to duty and self sacrifice which have undoubtedly done much to reduce the chance of serious casualties at a later date.

F J Marshall Brig Genl
Cong 44th Infy Bde.

6/4/17.

Appendix 11

Copy No 13

SECRET.

8/10th (service) Battalion The Gordon Highlanders.

OPERATION ORDER No.93.

Ref. Map.
Sheet 51b S.W.2.
VIS-EN-ARTOIS.

By

Lieut. Colonel E. Macleod, D.S.O., Commanding.

22nd April 1917.

1. The Third and First Armies will continue their attack and advance simultaneously along the whole front on the 23rd April 1917.

2. The 15th Division will attack at Zero hour on 23rd instant :-

44th Inf. Bde (H.Q. N.16b 1.8.) on the Right.
45th Inf. Bde (H.Q. N.10d 3.7.) on the Left.
46th Inf. Bde (H.Q. N.31 Central) in Reserve.

3. The 150th Brigade will attack on the Right of the 15th Division.

4. The boundaries of the Division are :-

(a) On the North. - Through N.12b 5.0. - 0.7 Central - 0.8.Central - 0.9a 0.0. - 0.9a 6.2. - 0.9b 8.7.

(b) On the South. - River COJEUL.

(c) Inter Brigade Boundary runs from N.18a 1.8 - 0.14a 9.5. 0.15b 2.4.

The Buildings and Enclosures in 0.14a inclusive to 44th Inf. Bde

5. OBJECTIVES.
First :- BLUE LINE.
Bridge at 0.20a 3.9½ up spur through 0.14 Central - 0.8c - to small wood in 0.8b 1.2. (exclusive).

Second :- RED LINE.
North West Corner of wood 0.21b 3½.0. - ST.ROHART FACTORY inclusive - up spur through 15 Central to Road (inclusive) about 0.9b 5.6.

6. Dispositions of Brigade at ZERO.

8th Seaforth Highlanders on the Right,
7th Cameron Highlanders on the Left,
9th Black Watch in support,
8/10th Gordon Highlanders in Reserve in OLD BROWN LINE (H.Q. N.16b 1.8).

All to be in position one hour before ZERO.

7. Attack.
8th Seaforth Highlanders will make a self-contained attack on the Village of GUEMAPPE. Tanks will co-operate in this Attack.
7th Cameron Highlanders and 9th Black Watch will capture and consolidate the BLUE LINE, and at ZERO plus 7 hours will continue the advance and will capture and consolidate the RED LINE.
8/10th Gordon Highlanders will move on orders from Brigade. the Battalion will furnish the following parties:-

7. (continued).

PARTY NUMBER (1). - "B" Company.
2 Officers and 60 Other Ranks to report to A.R. "A" Dump (N.16d 2.2)
This party will carry to A.R. "B" Dump (N.18a 6.3) until relieved
by Pack Animals. One Officer and 30 men will then move to A.R. "C"
Dump about O.14c 4.8. and be prepared to carry to A.R. "D" Dump about
O.15c 5.8. when the RED LINE is captured.
One Officer and 30 O.R. will remain at A.R. "A" Dump to load
pack animals and replace casualties.

PARTY NUMBER (11) - "B" Company.
1 Officer and 30 O.R. to report to A.R. "B" Dump. This party
will carry to A.R. "C" Dump as soon as the BLUE LINE is captured.
When A.R. "B" is emptied this party will carry from A.R. "C" Dump
to A.R. "D" Dump.

PARTY NUMBER (111) - "A" Company.
1 Officer and 30 O.R. to report to 91st R.E. Dump (N.22b 7.6).

O.C. Companies will be notified later the time at which these
parties will report.

PARTY NUMBER (1V) - "A" Company.
One Officer and 30 O.R. will construct a "Strong Point"
about O.14a 1.1. under supervision of the 74th Field Coy R.E. on
receipt of instructions from Brigade H.Q.
Two Lewis Guns will accompany this platoon which will form a
garrison of the strong point.
Party will report to 74th Field Coy R.E. at an hour to be notified
later.

PARTY NUMBER (V) - "A" Company.
A.Company will detail escorts for Tanks to remove wounded from
in front. Numbers and detailed instructions to be notified later.

PARTY NUMBER (V1) - "A" Company.
A.Company will man the Brigade Straggler Posts which will be
established as follows:-
(a) At N.16c 9.1. where BROWN LINE crosses the TILLOY WANCOURT Rd.
(b) At N.16b 2.8. where Infantry Track crosses BROWN LINE.
(c) At N.10d 0.7. where communication trench runs back from BROWN LINE towards TELEGRAPH HILL.

Each Post will consist of 1 reliable N.C.O. and 3 men.
Written orders will be issued to each N.C.O.

8. Stragglers Collecting Post and Prisoners of War Cage are at
N.10a 2.3. between BROWN LINE and AIRY CORNER.

9. Fighting Kit and Stores to be carried.
As for Ist Phase on 9th April, except that no Stokes Bombs or
"P" Bombs will be carried.

10. MEDICAL ARRANGEMENTS.
(1). 46th Field Ambulance have an Advanced Dressing Station near
N.9 Central for evacuation of wounded.
(2). The Divisional Main Dressing Station at ECOLE NORMAL will
will remain open.
(3). Walking Wounded. The route will be CAMBRAI ROAD through
ARRAS to the BASTION. O.C. 46th Field Ambulance will place a post
on the CAMBRAI ROAD with a Blue Flag and orders to stop returning
lorries for loading any walking wounded.

SECRET.

Headquarters,

44th Infantry Brigade.

Reference your B.M. 28 of 30th April 1917.
Herewith the narrative of the part taken by the Battalion in the recent operations:-

(1). On the night of the 18/19th, the Battalion took over the front line of Brigade Sector, relieving the 1st Inniskilling Fusiliers and 1st K.O.S.Bs, and the work of consolidation and digging of assembly trenches was carried on during the next two days.

(2). On the night of the 21/22nd the Battalion was relieved by the 8th Seaforth Highlanders and 7th Cameron Highlanders, and marched back to billets in ARRAS.

(3) On the night of the 22nd/23rd the battalion marched in and took up position in the BROWN LINE at 3.0am in Brigade Reserve.
On the 23rd the attack began at 4.45am. One Company was employed in carrying from A.R."A" to A.R."B" Dumps, and the remaining 3 Companies were held at the disposal of the Brigade.
At 12 noon, 2 Companies moved up to A.&.B. Assembly Trenches to support the 9th Black Watch and 7th Camerons, who had been held up.
At 6.0pm the 46th Brigade continued the attack. At 11pm the whole Battalion, which was now attached to the 46th Brigade occupied A.&.B. trenches in support.

(4). At 4.0pm 24th inst, the 46th Brigade again attacked, the objective being the BLUE LINE.
The Battalion was in close support to the right assaulting battalion.
The failure to capture CAVALRY FARM on our left flank prevented the right from reaching the BLUE LINE owing to being subjected to heavy machine gun fire from the FARM.
Two companies consolidated by connecting shell holes close behind the Scottish Rifles, the right front battalion and 2 Companies held SHOVEL TRENCH.
At 7.50pm the Battalion received orders from the 46th Bde to attack CAVALRY FARM from the North under cover of Stokes and Machine Gun fire as soon as it was dark. Captain Priday with 3 Companies was ordered to carry out the attack. 2/Lieut. A.W.Boyce was sent to deliver these orders, with instructions to assist Capt. Priday, and should that Officer become a casualty, to take command, as the arrangements had been thoroughly explained to him in person in addition to the orders issued.
As the Battalion was on the extreme right of the line and as it had got mixed up a good deal in the attack, the task of collecting the necessary force in the dark and marching them beyond our left to the North of the FARM, (subjected to annoying fire throughout) proved extremely difficult, consequently the arrangements were not complete until 3.0am. When the Companies lined up for the attack, about 50 yards from the FARM, the enemy commenced an intense barrage which compelled the attack to be abandoned.

(5). The night of the 25th was spent in consolidation of the ground occupied.

(6). At 11.0pm, 25th, the 46th Brigade was relieved by the 44th and 45th Brigades and the Battalion withdrew to the Reserve trenches west of GUEMAPPE, rejoining the 44th Brigade.

On the 26th inst. at 10.30pm when the 44th and 45th Brigades attacked CAVALRY FARM and remainder of BLUE LINE, the Battalion was in Reserve. Two Companies were employed in carrying up stokes ammunition, and at Zero hour occupied the jumping off trenches vacated by 9th Black Watch. The 3rd Company remained in SHOVEL TRENCH, and the 4th Company in "A" Trench near Battalion Headquarters.

(7). The day of the 27th was quiet, and at night the Battalion relieved 9th Black Watch on the Right of Brigade subsector from O.14c 2½.0 to O.14a 2.0. with 3 companies in front line and posts, and 1 company in support line.

(8). On night of the 28/29th, the Battalion was relieved by the 3rd London Regiment and returned to Billets in ARRAS.

The tasks allotted to this Battalion in the recent operations did not afford an opportunity to use Rifle Grenades, Trench Mortars or Vickers Guns, except the latter, which were employed to cover consolidation work.

Nothing in particular was noticeable which might prove a useful lesson for future operations.

1/5/17.

Lieut. Colonel,

Comdg. 8/10th Bn., The Gordon Highlanders.

11. COMMUNICATIONS.

1. Brigade Headquarters - N.16b 1.8.

Forward Brigade Station. -

(a) At ZERO - N.17d 1.2.
(b) After capture of first Objective about O.14a 2.3.
(c) After capture of second objective about O.15a 8.4.

2. (a) Communication between Battalion Headquarters and Brigade.

(1) Before moving up after capture of first objective, direct to Brigade.

(2) After moving up to first objective - via Brigade forward station.

(b) Communication between Companies and Battalion Headquarters

(1) Prior to move of Battalion Headquarters - via Brigade forward station.

(2) After move of Battalion Headquarters, - direct to Battalion Headquarters.

12. "ZERO HOUR" and hour for synchronising watches will be notified later.

Copies 1 - 4 All Coys,
5 Quartermaster,
6 Transport Officer,
7 Second in Command,
8 L.G.O.,
9 44th Infantry Brigade,
10 Medical Officer.
11 R.S.M.
12 Signals,
13 War Diary,
14 File.

(Signed) G.P.Geddes,
Lieut. and Adjutant.

SECRET. Copy No 14.

8/10th (service) Battalion The Gordon Highlanders.

OPERATION ORDER No.93.

By

Ref. Map.
Sheet 51b S.W.2.
VIS-EN-ARTOIS.

Lieut. Colonel E.Macleod, D.S.O., Commanding.

22nd April 1917.

1. The Third and First Armies will continue their attack and advance simultaneously along the whole front on the 23rd April 1917.

2. The 15th Division will attack at Zero hour on 23rd instant :-

44th Inf. Bde (H.Q. N.16b 1.8.) on the Right.
45th Inf. Bde (H.Q. N.10d 3.7.) on the Left.
46th Inf. Bde (H.Q. N.31 Central) in Reserve.

3. The 150th Brigade will attack on the Right of the 15th Division.

4. The boundaries of the Division are :-

(a). On the North. - Through N.12b 5.0. - 0.7 Central - 0.8.Central - 0.9a 0.0. - 0.9a 6.2. - 0.9b 8.7.

(b) On the south. - River COJEUL.

(c) Inter Brigade Boundary runs from N.18a 1.8 - 0.14a 9.5. 0.15b 2.4.

The Buildings and Enclosures in 0.14a inclusive to 44th Inf. Bde

5. OBJECTIVES.
First :- BLUE LINE.
Bridge at 0.20a 3.9½ up spur through 0.14 Central - 0.8c - to small wood in 0.8b 1.2. (exclusive).

Second :- RED LINE.
North West Corner of wood 0.21b 3½.0. - ST.ROHART FACTORY inclusive - up spur through 15 Central to Road (inclusive) about 0.9b 5.6.

6. Dispositions of Brigade at ZERO.

8th Seaforth Highlanders on the Right,
7th Cameron Highlanders on the Left,
9th Black Watch in support,
8/10th Gordon Highlanders in Reserve in OLD BROWN LINE (H.Q. N.16b 1.8).

All to be in position one hour before ZERO.

7. Attack.
8th Seaforth Highlanders will make a self-contained attack on the Village of GUEMAPPE. Tanks will co-operate in this Attack.
7th Cameron Highlanders and 9th Black Watch will capture and consolidate the BLUE LINE, and at ZERO plus 7 hours will continue the advance and will capture and consolidate the RED LINE.
8/10th Gordon Highlanders will move on orders from Brigade. the Battalion will furnish the following Parties:-

7 (Continued).

PARTY NUMBER (1). - "B" Company.
2 Officers and 60 Other Ranks to report to A.R. "A" Dump (N.16d 2.2)
This party will carry to A.R. "B" Dump (N.18a 6.3) until relieved by Pack Animals. One Officer and 30 men will then move to A.R. "C" Dump about O.14c 4.8. and be prepared to carry to A.R. "D" Dump about O.15c 5.8. when the RED LINE is captured.
One Officer and 30 O.R. will remain at A.R. "A" Dump to load pack animals and replace casualties.

PARTY NUMBER (11) - "B" Company.
1 Officer and 30 O.R. to report to A.R. "B" Dump. This party will carry to A.R. "C" Dump as soon as the BLUE LINE is captured.
When A.R. "B" is emptied this party will carry from A.R. "C" Dump to A.R. "D" Dump.

PARTY NUMBER (111) - "A" Company.
1 Officer and 30 O.R. to report to 91st R.E. Dump (N.22b 7.6).

O.C. Companies will be notified later the time at which these parties will report.

PARTY NUMBER (1V) - "A" Company.
One Officer and 30 O.R. will construct a "Strong Point" about O.14a 1.1. under supervision of the 74th Field Coy R.E. on receipt of instructions from Brigade H.Q.
Two Lewis Guns will accompany this platoon which will form a garrison of the strong point.
Party will report to 74th Field Coy R.E. at an hour to be notified later.

PARTY NUMBER (V) - "A" Company.
A.Company will detail escorts for Tanks to remove wounded from in front. Numbers and detailed instructions to be notified later.

PARTY NUMBER (V1) - "A" Company.
A.Company will man the Brigade Straggler Posts which will be established as follows:-
(a) At N.16c 9.1. where BROWN LINE crosses the TILLOY WANCOURT Rd
(b) At N.16b 2.8. where Infantry Track crosses BROWN LINE.
(c) At N.10d 0.7. where communication trench runs back from BROWN LINE towards TELEGRAPH HILL.

Each Post will consist of 1 reliable N.C.O. and 3 men.
Written orders will be issued to each N.C.O.

8. Stragglers Collecting Post and Prisoners of War Cage are at N.10a 2.2. between BROWN LINE and AIRY CORNER.

9. Fighting Kit and Stores to be carried.
As for 1st Phase on 9th April, except that no Stokes Bombs or "P" Bombs will be carried.

10. MEDICAL ARRANGEMENTS.
(1). 46th Field Ambulance have an Advanced Dressing Station near N.9 Central for evacuation of wounded.
(2). The Divisional Main Dressing Station at ECOLE NORMAL will will remain open.
(3). Walking Wounded. The route will be CAMBRAI ROAD through ARRAS to the BASTION. O.C. 46th Field Ambulance will place a post on the CAMBRAI ROAD with a Blue Flag and orders to stop returning lorries for loading any walking wounded.

11. <u>COMMUNICATIONS.</u>

1. Brigade Headquarters. - N.16b 1.8.

Forward Brigade Station. -

(a) At ZERO - N.17d 1.2.
(b) After capture of first Objective about O.14a 2.3.
(c) After capture of second objective about O.15a 8.4.

2. (a) <u>Communication between Battalion Headquarters and Brigade.</u>

(1) Before moving up after capture of first objective, direct to Brigade.

(2) After moving up to first objective - via Brigade forward station.

(b) <u>Communication between Companies and Battalion Headquarters</u>

(1) Prior to move of Battalion Headquarters - via Brigade forward station.

(2) After move of Battalion Headquarters, - direct to Battalion Headquarters.

12. "ZERO HOUR" and hour for synchronising watches will be notified later.

Copies 1 - 4 All Coys,
5 Quartermaster,
6 Transport Officer,
7 Second in Command,
8 L.G.O.,
9 44th Infantry Brigade,
10 Medical Officer.
11 R.S.M.
12 Signals,
13 War Diary,
14 File.

(Signed) G.P.Geddes,
Lieut. and Adjutant.

CONFIDENTIAL.

Vol 24

WAR DIARY

OF

8/10th (Service) Battalion The Gordon Highlanders

From 1.5.1917 To 31.5.1917

VOLUME 25.

WAR DIARY
or
INTELLIGENCE SUMMARY.
(*Erase heading not required.*)

Army Form C. 2118.

Sheet 384.

Instructions regarding War Diaries and Intelligence Summaries are contained in F. S. Regs., Part II. and the Staff Manual respectively. Title pages will be prepared in manuscript.

Place	Date	Hour	Summary of Events and Information	Remarks and references to Appendices
SIMENCOURT	1-5-17		The battalion commenced training in REST BILLETS, which includes:- Company training, and classes for Officers, N.C.O.s and men in Lewis Gun, also for Bombing and Rifle Grenades, Signallers, Stretcher Bearers, and instruction in wire entanglements.	
			Draft of 195 men arrived – majority of whom were invalided men rejoining – on a whole the draft was excellent.	
			The following were awarded the MILITARY MEDAL 3873 C.S.M. R THOMPSON. – 10961 Sergeant J. HINES. – 1833 Sergeant J. LINDSAY. – 6678 Sergeant H. LEITH – 5650 Sergeant J. TOLLERTON. – 6705 Corporal C. BAILLIE. – 7084 Corporal A. NEILSON – 5285 Corporal H. McNIVEN – 7070 Corporal R. PEASTON – 4384 Lce Corp J. COOK – 5548 Lce Corpl J. DAVIDSON – 7557 private A.H. WILSON 3250. private J. ORR – 13337 private G. KELLY – 5963 private A. SIMM. –	

T2134. Wt. W708–776. 506000. 4/15. Sir J. C. & S.

Instructions regarding War Diaries and Intelligence Summaries are contained in F. S. Regs., Part II. and the Staff Manual respectively. Title pages will be prepared in manuscript.

WAR DIARY
or
INTELLIGENCE SUMMARY.
(Erase heading not required.)

Army Form C. 2118.

Sheet 385.

Place	Date	Hour	Summary of Events and Information	Remarks and references to Appendices
SIMENCOURT	1.5.17		The ribbon for these medals were presented on parade by Lt. Genl. J.A. HALDANE, C.B., D.S.O. – The Corps Commander. The weather during the day was hot.	
"	2nd		Training continued in fine weather.	
"	3rd		Uneventful day – Training continued.	
"	4th		Training continued	
"	5th		Training continued. S/7919 A/C.S.M. M.A. MACKINNON awarded the MILITARY MEDAL.	
"	6th		Divine Service. The weather remained fine	
"	7th		Training continues. 22 OTHER RANKS rejoined the battalion.	
"	8th		The battalion marched, during heavy rain, a distance of 7 miles to new billets in GRAND RULLECOURT. The billets were good.	
GRAND RULLECOURT	9th		Training continued. – The following awards were	

T2134. Wt. W708–776. 500000. 4/15. Sir J. C. & S.

Instructions regarding War Diaries and Intelligence Summaries are contained in F. S. Regs., Part II. and the Staff Manual respectively. Title pages will be prepared in manuscript.

WAR DIARY
or
INTELLIGENCE SUMMARY.
(*Erase heading not required.*)

Sheet 386.

Army Form C. 2118.

Place	Date	Hour	Summary of Events and Information	Remarks and references to Appendices
GRAND RULLECOURT	9th		notified : MILITARY CROSS	
			Captain W. McCALL – 2/Lt. J. W. T. LEITH	
			BAR TO DISTINGUISHED CONDUCT MEDAL	
			S/10577. private J. MORELAND.	
			DISTINGUISHED CONDUCT MEDAL	
			S/4936. Sergeant J. DUNCAN	
			S/5242. private R. TAYLOR. –	
			Lieutenant D. MACFARLANE joined battalion.	[initials]
"	10th		Training continued	
"	11th		Training continued. – The following officers joined battalion	
			2/Lt. C. D. MACFARLANE – 2/Lt. J. H. C. GRIERSON.	
"	12th		Training continued. Weather still continues to be fine.	[initials]
"	13th		Divine Service.	
"	14th		Training continued	
"	15th		The Brigade parades for Tactical exercise. MAJOR	
			J. G. THOM, M.C. awarded the Distinguished Service Order.	

T2134. Wt. W708—776. 500000. 4/15. Sir J. C. & S.

WAR DIARY
or
INTELLIGENCE SUMMARY.
(*Erase heading not required.*)

Sheet 387.

Army Form C. 2118.

Instructions regarding War Diaries and Intelligence Summaries are contained in F. S. Regs., Part II. and the Staff Manual respectively. Title pages will be prepared in manuscript.

Place	Date	Hour	Summary of Events and Information	Remarks and references to Appendices
GRAND RULLECOURT	16th		The day was occupied in taking part in Brigade Field Firing.	[initials]
"	17th		The Battalion carried out musketry training.	
"	18th		The day was taken up by Brigade Tactical scheme.	[initials]
"	19th		Ordinary battalion training continued. Captain W.A. DYKE.- 2/Lt. H FYVIE.- 2/Lt. A.J.E. CAREY.- 2/Lt. A. WILSON 2/Lt. R.S RAITT joined from home. S/13859 L/Cpl. L. KINNAIRD.- S/10399 Private D. BUCHANAN were awarded the MILITARY MEDAL.	
"	20th		Battalion attended Divine Service.	[initials]
"	21st		The battalion marched to new billets at REBREUVE 7 miles. The billets were good. The men marched well and showed a marked improvement in fitness.	[initials]
REBREUVE	22nd		The battalion marched 9 miles to FILLIEVRES to fresh training area, where all ranks settled	

Instructions regarding War Diaries and Intelligence Summaries are contained in F. S. Regs., Part II. and the Staff Manual respectively. Title pages will be prepared in manuscript.

WAR DIARY
or
INTELLIGENCE SUMMARY.
(Erase heading not required.)

Army Form C. 2118.

Sheet - 388.

Place	Date	Hour	Summary of Events and Information	Remarks and references to Appendices
REBREUVE	22nd		comfortably in new billets.	[initials]
FILLIEVRES	23rd		Training resumed - Musketry being made a speciallity	[initials]
"	24th - 29th		Trained continued in fine weather. The undermentioned were Mentioned in Despatches (London Gazette dated 25. 5. 17.) :- MAJOR J. G. THOM, D.S.O, M.C. - 2/Lt. A.K. PRIDAY. - 3/7182 C.S.M. - D. ROSS (Since Died of Wounds). - S/9423 Sergt. C. Spence. - 5405 Sgt. A. GARNETT. - 5712 Cpl. T. SINCLAIR. - 7459 private J. KELLY.	[initials]
"	30th		The day was taken up with Brigade tactical scheme.	
"	31st		Ordinary battalion training continued. The weather is very hot	[initials]

T2134. Wt. W708—776. 506000. 4/15. Sir J. C. & S.

CONFIDENTIAL

Vol 25

WAR DIARY.

OF

8/10th (Service) Batt^n, The Gordon Highlanders.

For Period

From 1.6.1917. To 30.6.17.

VOLUME. 26.

Instructions regarding War Diaries and Intelligence Summaries are contained in F. S. Regs., Part II. and the Staff Manual respectively. Title pages will be prepared in manuscript.

WAR DIARY
or
INTELLIGENCE SUMMARY.
(*Erase heading not required.*)

Sheet 389.

Army Form C. 2118.

Place	Date	Hour	Summary of Events and Information	Remarks and references to Appendices
FILLIVERES	1-6-17		Battalion training continued – Weather fine.	
			Hon Lieutenant & Quartermaster J. MUNRO joined the Battalion on first appointment (from 9th Bn. Black Watch)	JB
"	2-6-17		Battalion training continued.	JB
"	3-6-17		Battalion paraded for Divine Service. 2/Lieutenant A MORRISON joined from the United Kingdom.	
			Captain N A DYKE left battalion to join the Labour Corps	JB
"	4-6-17		Battalion training continued. Nothing of importance to record	JB
"	5-6-17		Battalion paraded at 10 am for inspection by the G.O.C. 15th (Scottish) Division. – After minutely inspecting the whole battalion en mass, the G.O.C. saw B Compy at Musketry on the range; A Compy on outpost; C Compy in the attack, and D Compy at company drill, and expressed himself as highly	

Instructions regarding War Diaries and Intelligence Summaries are contained in F. S. Regs., Part II. and the Staff Manual respectively. Title pages will be prepared in manuscript.

WAR DIARY
or
INTELLIGENCE SUMMARY.
(Erase heading not required.)

Sheet 390.

Army Form C. 2118.

Place	Date	Hour	Summary of Events and Information	Remarks and references to Appendices
FILLIEVRES	5.6.17		satisfied with the general turnout of the battalion, and the way in which all carried out the various tasks allotted to them.	J.b.
"	6.6.17		In consideration of the high appreciation gained by the Battalion yesterday – The Commanding Officer ordered today to be observed as a holiday.	J.b.
"	7.6.17		Lieutenant N. N. FISCHER and 2/Lieut A.C. Sharp joined last night	
			Battalion took part in Brigade Tactical Scheme	J.b.
"	8.6.17		Battalion training in the morning; and Brigade Field Firing Test in the afternoon.	
			Captain N. DRUMMOND is awarded the MILITARY CROSS.	
			S/1799 R.Q.M.S. – R. MILNE awarded the Meritorious Service Medal.	
			Hon Lieut & Quartermaster J. MUNRO is awarded the D.C.M. (for services as R.Q.M.S. 9th Bn. Black Watch)	J.b.

Instructions regarding War Diaries and Intelligence Summaries are contained in F. S. Regs., Part II. and the Staff Manual respectively. Title pages will be prepared in manuscript.

WAR DIARY
or
INTELLIGENCE SUMMARY.
(*Erase heading not required.*)

Army Form C. 2118.

Sheet 371.

Place	Date	Hour	Summary of Events and Information	Remarks and references to Appendices
FILLIEVRES	9.6.17		Ordinary Battalion training continued.	[illegible]
"	10.6.17		The Battalion paraded for Divine Service. Draft of 19 OTHER RANKS joined battalion.	[illegible]
"	11.6.17		Battalion training continued. 37 OTHER RANKS joined battalion this day. Parties from the battalion have been supplied to French Farmers to assist them on their land. The Divisional Pierrot troupe entertained the battalion this evening	[illegible]
"	12.6.17		Battalion training continued. The Divisional Band played during the evening	[illegible]
"	13.6.17		Battalion training continued. The Divisional Cinema entertained the battalion in the evening.	[illegible]
"	14.6.17		The battalion carried out a tactical scheme with two TANKS attached. The weather still continues to be fine.	[illegible]

Instructions regarding War Diaries and Intelligence Summaries are contained in F. S. Regs., Part II. and the Staff Manual respectively. Title pages will be prepared in manuscript.

WAR DIARY
or
INTELLIGENCE SUMMARY.
(*Erase heading not required.*)

Sheet 392.

Army Form C. 2118.

Place	Date	Hour	Summary of Events and Information	Remarks and references to Appendices
FILLIEVRES	15.6.17		Battalion training continued. The day was very hot. A draft of 26 OTHER RANKS joined the battalion from home. The children of FILLIEVRES were entertained by the Officers of the 8th Bn Seaforth Highrs & 8/10th Bn Gordon Highlrs in the afternoon in appreciation of kindness & friendliness shewn to the troops during our stay. The children were highly delighted and expressed their gratitude in an address read out by one of the girls.	
"	16.6.17		Battalion training continued.	[initials]
"	17.6.17		Divine Service. – Major General Sir Frederick McCracken on leaving the Division to Command the 13th Corps saw the battalion on parade to thank them for their services and wish them farewell.	[initials]
"	18.6.17		Battalion training continued	[initials]
	19.6.17		Brigade tactical scheme.	[initials]

T2134. Wt. W708–776. 500000. 4/15. Sir J. C. & S.

Instructions regarding War Diaries and Intelligence Summaries are contained in F. S. Regs., Part II. and the Staff Manual respectively. Title pages will be prepared in manuscript.

WAR DIARY
or
INTELLIGENCE SUMMARY.
(Erase heading not required.)

Army Form C. 2118.

Sheet 393.

Place	Date	Hour	Summary of Events and Information	Remarks and references to Appendices
FILLIVERS.	20.6.17		Orders received to move North, into Belgium. The day was taken up with the necessary preparations for the move.	JB
	21.6.7		Battalion paraded 3.50 am and marched 7 miles to CROISELLES. The men marched well and arrived in Billets quite fresh showing the excellent result of the hard training the Battalion has undergone. – While of a detachment of 116 OTHER RANKS of the 46th Infantry Brigade attached to the battalion no less than 60 fell out during the march. The weather was fine during the morning but rain fell during the remainder of the day	JB
CROISELLES	22.6.7		The battalion paraded at 3.30 am and marched 9 miles to good billets in VALHUON. Heavy rain fell during most of the march. The men marched well and no one fell out. The detachment of the 46th Brigade	

T2134. Wt. W708–776. 506000. 4/15. Sir J. C. & S.

Instructions regarding War Diaries and Intelligence Summaries are contained in F. S. Regs., Part II. and the Staff Manual respectively. Title pages will be prepared in manuscript.

WAR DIARY
or
INTELLIGENCE SUMMARY.
(Erase heading not required.)

Sheet 394 Army Form C. 2118.

Place	Date	Hour	Summary of Events and Information	Remarks and references to Appendices
			improved considerably only 36 of whom fell out	
VALHUON	23.6.17		Battalion paraded at 8.50 AM and marched 12 miles to ECQUEDECQUES. The weather was fine and the men marched well, no one fell out. Our billets were very comfortable.	[initials]
ECQUEDECQUES	24.6.17		Divine Service. The Brigade rested during the day.	[initials]
~~Valhuon~~ "	25.6.17		Battalion paraded at 7.30 AM and marched 10 miles to billets at ISEBERGUE. The village was bombed by enemy aeroplanes in the early hours of the morning, 2 civilians were wounded no other damage done.	[initials]
ISEBERGUE	26.6.17		The battalion paraded at 2.30 AM and marched 13 miles to good billets in BREADE. The roads were not good, but the men marched well	[initials]

T2134. Wt. W708—776. 506000. 4/15. Sir J. C. & S.

Instructions regarding War Diaries and Intelligence Summaries are contained in F. S. Regs., Part II. and the Staff Manual respectively. Title pages will be prepared in manuscript.

WAR DIARY
or
INTELLIGENCE SUMMARY.
(Erase heading not required.)

Sheet 395

Army Form C. 2118.

Place	Date	Hour	Summary of Events and Information	Remarks and references to Appendices
TORONTO CAMP	27/6/17.		The battalion paraded at 4.15 AM, & marched 1 1/2 miles to ~~[illegible]~~ a camp two miles South West of VLAMERTINGHE. The battalion camped in the open, as the tents & huts to be occupied were not vacated by the 7/8th K.O.S.Bs until 9 pm. The day was fine.	JG
"	28/6/17		The battalion made final preparations for moving up into the line.	JG
"	29/6/17		The battalion less 10 officers and OR's paraded at 9.20 pm & moved up to a forward camp 1 mile west of YPRES preparatory to taking over in the front line on the night of the 30th June / 1st July. The surplus officers & men remained in Camp. A draft of 17 ORs arrived.	JG
	30/6/17		The day was quiet, there being no shelling of the forward Camp. Heavy rain fell. At 10.30 pm the battalion moved up to the front line between the MENIN Road, and the YPRES-ROULERS Railway, occupying half this front with the Black Watch on our left. The relief was effected quietly	JG

Vol 26

44/15

CONFIDENTIAL.

WAR DIARY

OF

8/10th (Serv.) Battn. THE GORDON HIGHLANDERS

FROM 1st JULY 1917. TO 31st JULY 1917.

(VOLUME 27.)

Instructions regarding War Diaries and Intelligence Summaries are contained in F. S. Regs., Part II. and the Staff Manual respectively. Title pages will be prepared in manuscript.

WAR DIARY ~~or~~ ~~INTELLIGENCE SUMMARY.~~

(Erase heading not required.)

Sheet 396

Army Form C. 2118.

Place	Date	Hour	Summary of Events and Information	Remarks and references to Appendices
In Trenches	1917 July 1		From 1.15 a.m. on the night of the 30th June/1st July a raid was made on the enemy by a battalion of the Division on our left. In retaliation the Enemy shelled the whole of the Corps Front. A number of shells fell in the Battalion area, but we had no casualties. The remainder of the day was quiet.	
			Lieutenant H. B. FINDLAY joined the Battalion from MACHINE GUN CORPS.	
"	2		Nothing of importance took place during the day. Between 6pm & 7pm enemy machines flew low over our trenches & opened machine gun fire. They were driven off by the fire of our Lewis guns before they caused any casualties. During the night gaps were cut in our wire to enable the 8th Seaforths to carry out a raid from this front on the night of the 7th/8th inst.	
			A fighting patrol from A Coy reconnoitred Crater No 5 between our lines and the enemy's. The enemy were understood to be holding this position, but no traces were found, & the patrol returned safely to our trenches	APP. 1 15th Div MAP No. 1A

T2134. Wt. W708—776. 500000. 4/15. Sir J. C. & S.

Instructions regarding War Diaries and Intelligence Summaries are contained in F. S. Regs., Part II. and the Staff Manual respectively. Title pages will be prepared in manuscript.

WAR DIARY

~~or~~

~~INTELLIGENCE SUMMARY.~~

(*Erase heading not required.*)

Sheet 397

Army Form C. 2118.

Place	Date	Hour	Summary of Events and Information	Remarks and references to Appendices
	1917 July			
In trenches	2nd		From 10 pm. to 12 pm all heavy batteries on the Corps Front heavily bombarded known enemy batteries.	J.S.
"	3rd		Last nights bombardment although silencing the enemy's gun fire at the time drew much retaliation from the enemy from midnight to 3 AM, the enemy apparently fearing attack. A good deal of damage was done to our trenches, but we had no casualties. The remainder of the day was quiet.	J.S.
"	4th		At 5.30 am. enemy field guns attempted to cut the wire on the battalion front with field-gun fire in co-operation with aeroplanes. The day was otherwise quiet except for some shelling of our reserve trenches between 10 am. & noon. The battalion, less "B" Company was relieved after dark by the 8th Seaforths & moved back to a support Camp one mile west of YPRES. The relief was effected quietly and without casualties	APP. No 2 J.S.
"	5th		"B" Coy were relieved at night by the remaining Coy of 8th Seaforths	J.S.

T2134. Wt. W708—776. 506000. 4/15. Sir J. C. & S.

Instructions regarding War Diaries and Intelligence Summaries are contained in F. S. Regs., Part II. and the Staff Manual respectively. Title pages will be prepared in manuscript.

WAR DIARY

or

~~INTELLIGENCE SUMMARY.~~

(*Erase heading not required.*)

Sheet 398

Army Form C. 2118.

Place	Date	Hour	Summary of Events and Information	Remarks and references to Appendices
SUPPORT CAMP near YPRES	1917 July	5th to 8th.	The battalion remained in Camp in support for four days and provided working parties for the Corps Heavy Artillery & 91st Field Coy R.E. The Camp was not shelled during the four days & our total casualties since moving up on the 30th June/1st July amounted to Died of Wounds: 1. O.R. Wounded: 4 ORs.	[initials]
"	8th		Captain J.B. WOOD, M.C. proceeded to the Senior Officers Course at ALDERSHOT.	[initials]
"	9th		On the night of the 8/9th the battalion moved back to TORONTO CAMP being relieved by the 11th Argyle & Sutherlands. During the day on the 9th the battalion cleaned up and rested.	APP. No. 3. [initials]
TORONTO CAMP	10th		The battalion marched to POPERINGHE and entrained for ANNEKE, marching therefrom to the RUBROUCK Training Area. Billets were very good but widely scattered.	APP No. 4. [initials]
RUBROUCK	11th		A battalion training programme was carried out. 2 LT E A SUCKLING joined the battalion.	[initials]
"	12th		The battalion was engaged in an attack scheme in cooperation with tanks.	[initials]

Instructions regarding War Diaries and Intelligence Summaries are contained in F. S. Regs., Part II. and the Staff Manual respectively. Title pages will be prepared in manuscript.

WAR DIARY
or
~~INTELLIGENCE SUMMARY.~~
(Erase heading not required.)

Sheet 399

Army Form C. 2118.

Place	Date	Hour	Summary of Events and Information	Remarks and references to Appendices
	1917 July			
RUBROUCK	13th		The forenoon was occupied by a Brigade Tactical Scheme on the RUBROUCK Training Area in very bad weather.	
			Lt. Col. D. MACLEOD DSO assumed command of the 19th Corps Reinforcement Depot at MERKEHAM, Major J.G. THOM, DSO. MC taking over command of the battalion	JG
	14th		The battalion in conjunction with the remainder of the Brigade practised the attack over trenches representing those to be attacked in forthcoming operations.	JG
			A draft of 36 ORs joined the battalion	JG
"	15th		Divine service was held.	
			2 LT R.N.P. FINDLAY + 2 LT. A LAING joined the battalion; 2 LT J.P. WALKER rejoined having recovered from wounds received in JANUARY	JG
"	16th		A Brigade Tactical Scheme was practised on the LEDERZEELE Training Area	JG
"	17th		Battalion training was carried out under Company arrangements	JG
"	18th		Inspections + training occupied the day. Nothing important to record	JG

T2134. Wt. W708—776. 500000. 4/15. Sir J. C. & S.

Instructions regarding War Diaries and Intelligence Summaries are contained in F. S. Regs., Part II. and the Staff Manual respectively. Title pages will be prepared in manuscript.

WAR DIARY
~~or~~
~~INTELLIGENCE SUMMARY.~~
(*Erase heading not required.*)

Sheet 400

Army Form C. 2118.

Place	Date	Hour	Summary of Events and Information	Remarks and references to Appendices
	1917 JULY			
RUBROUCK	19th		A Brigade attack scheme was practised on the LEDERZEELE trench Training Area	JB
"	20th		A certain amount of training was done and the remainder of the day occupied in preparations for tomorrow's move back to the line	JB
"	21st		The battalion marched to WINNEZEELE AREA starting at daybreak. Although the day was hot, & the roads bad, the men marched the 12 miles very well. Officers & men were in tents for the night	JB
WINNEZEELE	22nd		The battalion marched to WATOU Area No 2 – 7 miles – & was again billeted in tents. Divine service was held in the evening	JB
WATOU	23rd		The battalion marched to TORONTO CAMP & were billeted in the huts & tents occupied on the 10th of the month, when the battalion came out of trenches	
		9pm	The battalion less officers & men who were being left out of action marched to a bivouac Camp situated about one mile south of VLAMERTINGHE, taking over from the 7th Camerons who moved into the line	JB

T2134. Wt. W708—776. 500000. 4/15. Sir J. C. & S.

Instructions regarding War Diaries and Intelligence Summaries are contained in F. S. Regs., Part II. and the Staff Manual respectively. Title pages will be prepared in manuscript.

WAR DIARY

~~or INTELLIGENCE SUMMARY.~~

(*Erase heading not required.*)

Sheet 401

Army Form C. 2118.

Place	Date	Hour	Summary of Events and Information	Remarks and references to Appendices
BIVOUAC CAMP	1917 JULY 24		Captain C. Reid, previously of 4th Battalion of the Regiment joined the battalion from a Senior Officers Course of Instruction at ALDERSHOT, and assumed the duties of Second in Command. LIEUT. FISCHER left the battalion & proceeded to ENGLAND to take a Commission in the INDIAN Army. A draft of 27 O.R.s joined the Battalion.	[illegible]
	25th		From the 24th to the 27th the battalion remained in Camp and provided working and carrying parties for the forward areas. The period passed without incident.	[illegible]
	28th		The battalion marched up & took over the front line from the 7th Cameron Highlanders at 9 pm occupying the front from which the 44th Brigade will attack. Although two hours previous to our relief the Camerons had raided the German trenches and taken over 50 prisoners, the battalion was able to carry out the relief without suffering a single casualty although hostile shelling was met with.	[illegible]

T2134. Wt. W708—776. 500000. 4/15. Sir J. C. & S.

Sheet 402.

Army Form C. 2118.

Instructions regarding War Diaries and Intelligence Summaries are contained in F. S. Regs., Part II. and the Staff Manual respectively. Title pages will be prepared in manuscript.

WAR DIARY

~~or~~

~~INTELLIGENCE SUMMARY.~~

(*Erase heading not required.*)

Place	Date	Hour	Summary of Events and Information	Remarks and references to Appendices
FRONT LINE	1917 July 29		The battalion occupied the whole of the Brigade front of 700 yards in the Front Line with the right on the YPRES – ROULERS Railway. Strength. 20 Officers 507 ORs. The day was quiet in the line, as orders had been received that no movement was to be made during daylight, nor any activity to take place.	
"	30th		The battalion moved into battle positions after dark, closing to the right & allowing the Black Watch to divide the Brigade front with us. The move was accomplished without arousing the enemy's suspicions and the night passed uneventfully.	
"	31st		At Zero 3.50 am the battalion attacked with "C" Company – Captain Moffat – & "D" Coy – 2 Lt GARDINER – leading, "B" Coy – Lieut KEMP – in support & "A" Coy – Captain Lynn – in reserve. On our left were the 9th Black Watch in formation similar to ours and beyond them on the left were two attacking battalions of the 46th Brigade the 45th Brigade were in Divisional support, and on the battalion's right south of the Railway the 8th Division were attacking.	APPENDIX No. 5. APPENDIX No. 6

T2134. Wt. W708–776. 500000. 4/15. Sir J. C. & S.

Sheet 403

Army Form C. 2118.

Instructions regarding War Diaries and Intelligence Summaries are contained in F. S. Regs., Part II. and the Staff Manual respectively. Title pages will be prepared in manuscript.

WAR DIARY
or
INTELLIGENCE SUMMARY.
(Erase heading not required.)

Place	Date	Hour	Summary of Events and Information	Remarks and references to Appendices
FRONT LINE	1917 July 31	3.50 AM	The battalion advanced steadily behind the barrage & all companies got clear of the enemy's barrage on our front line which was not put down for 4 minutes. It was still dark, & difficulty was experienced in finding the right and left of the battalion front during the advance, more especially as the enemy ground had been so cut up by shell fire as to be almost unrecognisable even as to trenches and buildings. Shortly after 4 am however there was sufficient light to enable the battalion to see the line of the railway, and no more difficulty as to direction was experienced. It was early apparent that the enemy intended to make a stubborn fight for his positions, & even before we reached the BLUE LINE the leading companies not only came under machine gun fire but several hand to hand fights took place in one of which 2 Lt GRIERSON killed one of the enemy with the bayonet, but was himself killed soon afterwards by a shell. After severe fighting especially in and around WILDE WOOD the Blue Line was	

Instructions regarding War Diaries and Intelligence Summaries are contained in F. S. Regs., Part II. and the Staff Manual respectively. Title pages will be prepared in manuscript.

WAR DIARY
or
INTELLIGENCE SUMMARY.
(Erase heading not required.)

Sheet 404

Army Form C. 2118.

Place	Date	Hour	Summary of Events and Information	Remarks and references to Appendices
FRONT LINE	1917 July 31		captured at 4.25 am, casualties up to that time having been slight. At 5.5 am the advance was resumed and at 5.55 am the leading Companies reached the Black line, which was the Battalions final objective. This second advance was marked by keen fighting and many machine gun emplacements were rushed, the battalion advancing resolutely and steadily. A halt of 4 hours at this point was made to allow the artillery time to get forward the field guns and the battalion worked energetically consolidating the captured position. At 10.10 am the 45th Brigade advanced through the Divisional front, their objective being the Green Line. After advancing through our front about 400 yards the 11th Argylls were held up owing to the inability of the 8th Division on our right to get further than the Black Line. The Argylls were obliged to dig in and the battalion lent them assistance with overhead Lewis Gun fire. We also smashed an attempt to mass by the enemy for an attack on the 8th Division by directing enfilade fire on them with our Lewis Guns	

A5834 Wt. W4973/M687 750,000 8/16 D. D. & L. Ltd. Forms/C.2118/13

Instructions regarding War Diaries and Intelligence Summaries are contained in F. S. Regs., Part II. and the Staff Manual respectively. Title pages will be prepared in manuscript.

WAR DIARY ~~or~~ ~~INTELLIGENCE SUMMARY.~~

(Erase heading not required.)

Sheet 405

Army Form C. 2118.

Place	Date	Hour	Summary of Events and Information	Remarks and references to Appendices
FRONT LINE	1917 July 31		Throughout the day the 8th Division were unable to advance and as it was impossible for the 45th Brigade to go forward until they did, the position on our front remained unchanged. At 11-30 pm we relieved the 11th ARGYLES in the position they were occupying, 400 yards in front of the Black Line, as they had suffered heavy casualties from shell and machine gun fire. Very heavy rain had fallen continuously since 7 pm & the ground became very soft, and conditions trying. The conditions however enabled us to relieve the ARGYLES without enemy activity. The days casualties for the battalion were Officers 2 killed 10 wounded ORs (approximately) 25 killed 125 wounded. Lt Col THOM, MC DSO was wounded by shell fire about 7.30 AM when moving up to establish a forward Headquarters. 2 Lt GRIERSON was killed by a shell, after distinguishing himself in hand to hand fighting in which he bayonetted at least one of the enemy. 2 Lt A D SPARK was killed by machine gun fire at the first objective.	

A5834 Wt. W4973/M687 750,000 8/16 D. D. & L. Ltd. Forms/C.2118/13.

Appendix No 1

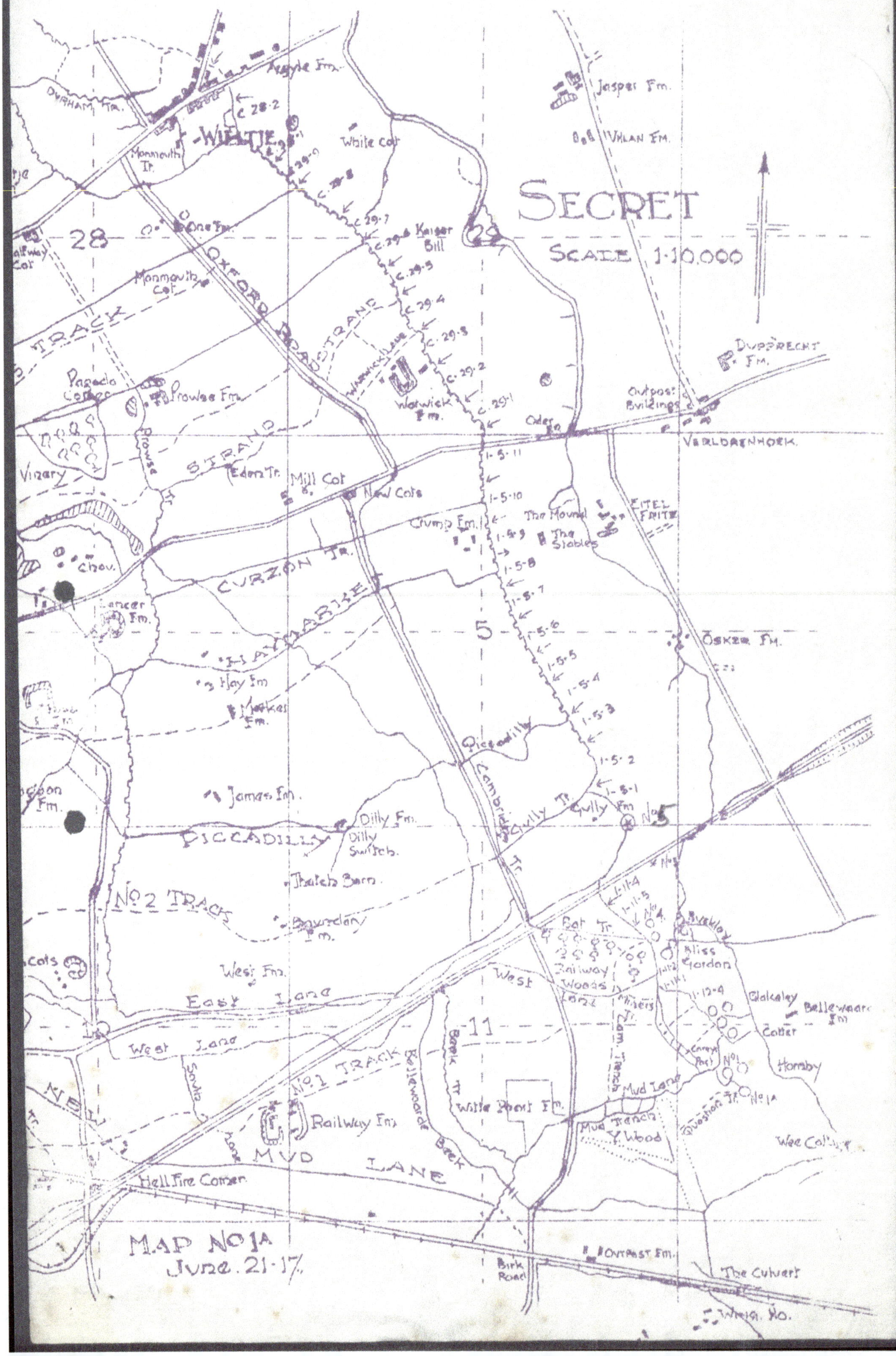

SECRET

SCALE 1:10,000

Argyle Fm.
Jasper Fm.
Uhlan Fm.
Durham Tr.
Wieltje
Monmouth Tr.
White Cot
C.28.2
C.29.7
C.29.6 Kaiser Bill
C.29.5
C.29.4
C.29.3
C.29.2
C.29.1
28
Oxford Road
Monmouth Cot
Track
Strand
Warwick Lane
Warwick Fm.
Pagoda Cottage
Prowse Fm.
Vinery
Prowse Tr.
Eden Tr.
Mill Cot
New Cots
Oder Ho.
Outpost Buildings
Dupprecht Fm.
Verldrenhoek
I.5.11
I.5.10
I.5.9
I.5.8
I.5.7
I.5.6
I.5.5
I.5.4
I.5.3
I.5.2
I.5.1
Crump Fm.
The Mound
The Stables
Eitel Fritz
Chou.
Curzon Tr.
Haymarket
Lancer Fm.
5
Osker Fm.
Hay Fm.
Mackes Fm.
Piccadilly
James Fm.
Cambridge Tr.
Gully Tr.
Gully Fm.
No 5
Dilly Fm.
Dilly Switch.
Piccadilly
Thatch Barn
No 2 Tracks
Bowden Fm.
Bat Tr.
No 4
I.11.4
I.11.5
Bliss
Gordon
Railway Woods
West Lane
West Fm.
East Lane
Miners Tr.
Com. Trench
I.12.4
Blakeley
Bellewaarde Fm
Cotter
11
West Lane
Hornby
No 1
No 1A
Carey's Post
No 1 Track
Bellewaarde Beek
Beek Tr.
Mud Lane
Mud Trench
Y Wood
Question Tr.
Wee Cottage
Railway Fm.
White Point Fm.
Mud Lane
Hell Fire Corner
New Tr.
Outpost Fm.
Birk Road
The Culvert

MAP NO 1A
June. 21·17

WAR DIARY

APPENDIX

1

1st July 1917

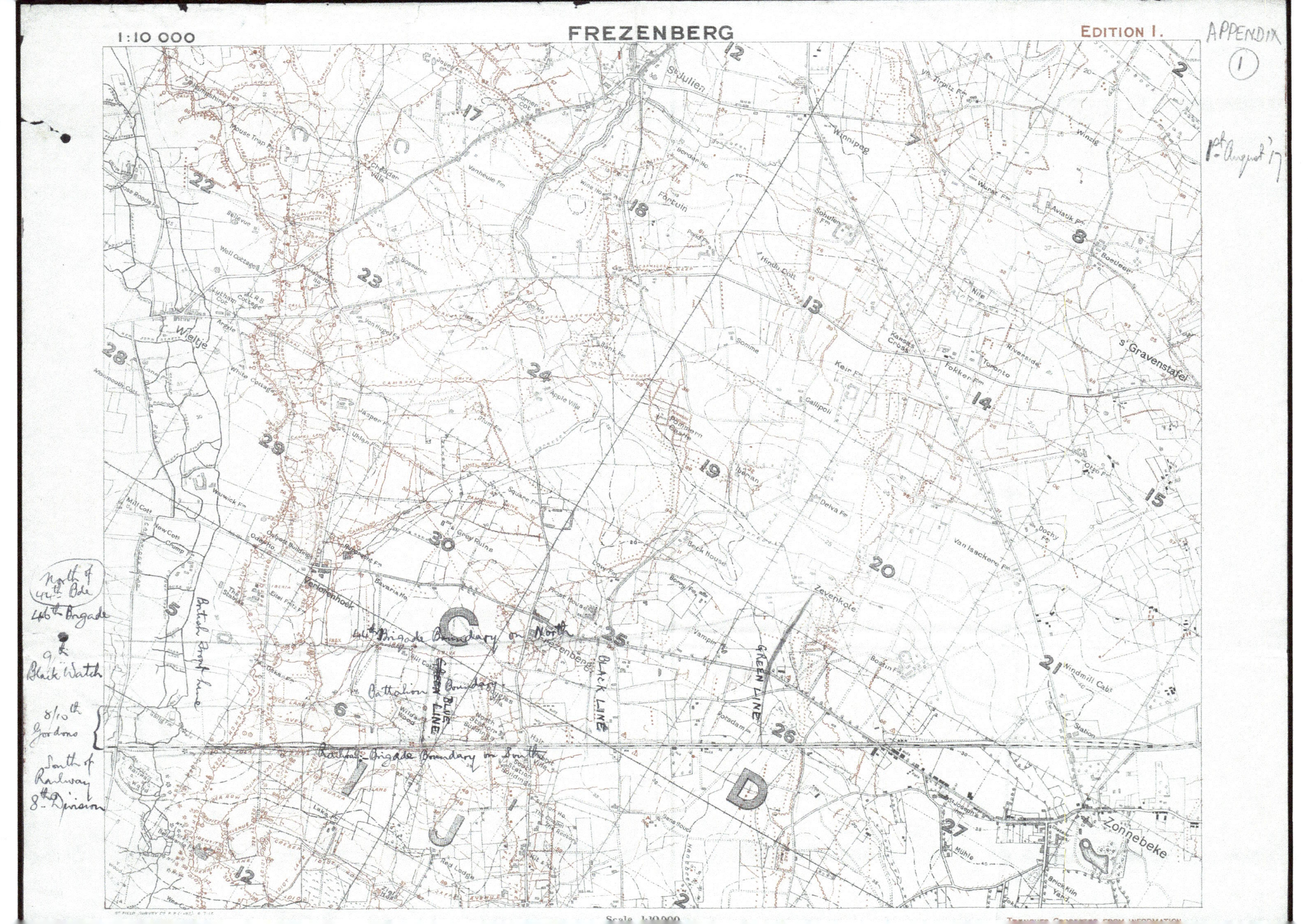

1:10 000
FREZENBERG
EDITION I.
APPENDIX
(1)
1st August '17
St Julien
Winnipeg
Winzig
Wurst Fm
Aviatik Fm
Boetleer
Fortuin
Hindu Cott
Nile
Kansas Cross
Toronto
Riverside
s' Gravenstafel
Fokker Fm
Keir Fm
Gallipoli
Somme
Wieltje
White Cottage
Apple Villa
Jasper Fm
Uhlan Fm
Iberian
Delva Fm
Oto Fm
Dochy Fm
Van Isackere Fm
Beck House
Zevenkote
Vampir
Frezenberg
Gray Ruins
Square Fm
Bavaria Ho
Verlorenhoek
Mill Cott
Warwick Fm
Potsdam
Windmill Cabt
Station
Zonnebeke
Mühle
Red Lodge
Lake
North of 44th Bde
46th Brigade
9th Black Watch
8/10th Gordons
South of Railway 8th Division
British Front Line
44th Brigade Boundary on North
Battalion Boundary
BLUE LINE
BLACK LINE
GREEN LINE
Railway Brigade Boundary on South
Scale 1:10,000

WAR DIARY

APPENDIX

(1)

1st July 1917

~~Secret~~ 8/10th (S) Bn. The Gordon Highrs.

Diary + File

OPERATION ORDER No. 106

By

Major J. G. Thom DSO MC, Comdg.

APP. No 2

Ref. Sheet 28 N.W. + 28 S.W. Trench Map

4th July 1917.

1. The Battalion less B Coy will be relieved tonight 4th/5th July by the 8th Seaforth Highrs.
The relieved platoons will march independently to Camp at H.16.a 3.8.
Movement will be in bodies not larger than 1 platoon. 200 yards distance to be maintained between platoons.

2. Guides: (1 per platoon + 2 for HQ) will rendezvous under 2/Lt A.W. Boyne at Battn HQ at 9.30 pm. They will proceed in small parties to REIGERSBURG Chateau where they will meet the relieving battalion. The Left/Right Front Coy will be brought in by PICCADILLY; Right Front Coy by No 2 Track.

3. Trench Stores will be handed over & receipts forwarded to Orderly Room by 2 pm 5th July.

4. Completion of relief will be reported by wire by code word "ZEBRA".

P.T.O.

5. B Coy. will be relieved on night of 5th/6th July by a company of Seaforth High^rs Guides will meet this Company at REIGERSBURG Chateau at 10.30 pm

6. ACKNOWLEDGE.

G.P. Geddes Lieut & Adj^t
5/7th Gordon High^rs

Copies 1 – 4 O.C. Coys
5 L.G.O.
6 R.Q.M.
7 5th Seaforth High^rs
8 War Diary
9. File.

Secret

ARRANGEMENTS for RELIEF
(In conjunction with O.O. No. 10[illegible])

1. An advanced party consisting of an N.C.O. from each Coy + 1 from H.Qrs will assemble at Battn H.Qrs at 8.30 pm tonight under an Officer to be detailed by O.C. D Coy. Party will proceed to the Camp & take over accommodation.

2. Transport Officer will detail the following transport to be at I.9.a.3.9. at 11 pm tonight
[illegible] Lewis Guns [illegible] will be loaded as Coys pass this point.
2 limbers for dixies, water tins, officers' mess kits. O.C. Coys will arrange to send parties down to load these on the limbers which must not be kept waiting on the road. These parties will accompany the limbers to Camp.
A limber for B Coys dixies, water tins & Officers' mess kits, and one for Lewis Guns S.A.A. etc. will be at I.9.a.3.9 at 11 pm 5th inst.

3. QM will arrange to send up rations & water for B Coy to be at above point at 11 pm tonight. O.C. B Coy will detail a party to meet them.

4. O.C. Coys will provide each guide with written instructions.

[illegible] G.P. Geddes Lieut + Adjt

Secret

APP. No. 3. Copy No. 9
War Diary

OPERATION ORDER No. 104

By

Major J. G. THOM D.S.O. Lt. Comdg.

REF. MAP 28 NW.

7th JULY 1917

1. The Battalion will be relieved tomorrow night, 8th inst., by the 11th A. & S. Highrs.
On relief, platoons will march independently to TORONTO CAMP.

2. Distances of 200 yards will be maintained between platoons.
Particular attention will be paid to march discipline during the march to Camp. Platoon Commanders will march in rear of their platoons.

3. Lieut. D. MACFARLANE (O.C. Details) will arrange for accommodation in Camp and detail guides to meet each platoon and headquarters as they arrive in Camp.

4. Transport Officer will detail Transport for Lewis Guns, S.A.A. &c., Officers valises & Mess Kits, and horses for cookers, medical & water carts, to be at Camp at 9-30 pm.
O.C. Coys will ensure that no time is wasted in loading the limbers.

P.T.O.

5. Completion of relief & arrival in TORONTO CAMP will be reported without delay to Battn H.Qrs.

6. ACKNOWLEDGE.

LIEUT & ADJT.
8/10th Gordon Highrs.

Copies. 1–4. O.C. Coys
5. R.S.M.
6. O.C. Details
7. T.O.
8. Q.M.
9. File.

APP. No. 4

8/10th (Service) Battalion, The Gordon Highlanders. Copy No. 10.

OPERATION ORDER No. 108.
By
Major J.G.Thom D.S.O., M.C., Comdg.

Ref. Sheet :
HAZEBROUCK 5A.
(Ed. 2.)

9th July 1917

1. The battalion will march to POPERINGHE STATION, and then proceed by rail to RUBROUCK Training Area to-morrow, 10th July.
2. Starting Point : Road Junction G.5.d.1.2.
Time : 7.30 a.m.
The Battalion will parade at 7 a.m. in the following order :-
H.Qrs., A, B, C, D Coys,
head of column to be at road junction G.18.a.3.7, facing N.W.

3. Distances will be maintained as follows :-
200 yards between platoons moving to entraining station.
200 yards between companies moving from detraining station.

4. Transport will move in accordance with instructions issued to the Transport Officer.

5. The usual halts will be observed.
Special attention is to be paid to the maintainence of the regulation pace and to march discipline.

6. Arrival in billets in the RUBROUCK Area will be reported to Bn.H.Qrs.
7. ACKNOWLEDGE.

(sgd) G.P.Geddes, Lieut & Adjt.

Copies 1 - 4 O.C. Coys. 5. R.S.M.
6 Quartermaster 7.T.O.
8 M.O. & L.G.O. 9. War Diary
10. File.

Index

44/115

SUBJECT.

8/10th Gordon Highlanders

No.	Contents.	Date.
	August 1917.	

(63,965). Wt.15,820—176. 2000. 9/21. Gp.164. A.&E.W.

CONFIDENTIAL Vol 27

WAR DIARY 44/15

OF

8/10th (Service) Battalion, The Gordon Highlanders.

FOR PERIOD

1st August 1917 To 31st August 1917

VOLUME 28.

Instructions regarding War Diaries and Intelligence Summaries are contained in F. S. Regs., Part II. and the Staff Manual respectively. Title pages will be prepared in manuscript.

WAR DIARY

~~or INTELLIGENCE SUMMARY.~~

(Erase heading not required.)

Sheet 406. Army Form C. 2118.

Place	Date	Hour	Summary of Events and Information	Remarks and references to Appendices
FRONT LINE	1917 AUGUST 1.		The line in which we relieved the 11th Argylls was a position about 400 yards beyond the Black Line, and the battalion was disposed as follows:- "C" and "D" Companies in the Front Line "B" Coy forming a defensive right flank along the Railway to join up with the 8th Division who were 400 yards behind us, and "A" Company in reserve in the Black Line. The morning of the 1st was quiet and observation difficult owing to heavy rain which had not ceased since 7 pm on the 31st July. At 3 pm the enemy launched a heavy counter attack on the 8th Division and on our battalion on a front of about 1000 yards. His advance was covered by an intense machine gun barrage which caused no heavy casualties. The 8th Division on our left began to retire which left our right flank exposed, and it finally became necessary for our two front Companies to retire for about 300 yards. In that position the battalion speedily reorganised, and with the assistance of a Company of the 7th Cameron Highlanders we counter attacked the enemy without delay under heavy machine gun fire.	Appendix I FREZENBERG MAP.

A5834 Wt. W4973/M687 750,000 8/16 D. D. & L. Ltd. Forms/C.2118/13.

Instructions regarding War Diaries and Intelligence Summaries are contained in F. S. Regs., Part II. and the Staff Manual respectively. Title pages will be prepared in manuscript.

WAR DIARY
or
INTELLIGENCE SUMMARY.
(Erase heading not required.)

Sheet 407.

Army Form C. 2118.

Place	Date	Hour	Summary of Events and Information	Remarks and references to Appendices
FRONT LINE	1917 AUGUST 1.		By 4 pm we had successfully driven back the enemy and regained our original front line. The success of the attack was wholly due to our superiority in rifle fire, and the spirit of the men, who fired from all positions as they advanced inflicting heavy casualties on the enemy who fled in disorder. Our artillery did not open fire until the fighting was finished but from 4 pm onwards kept up a heavy barrage on the enemy's positions and prevented him from retiring. Consequently many surrendered some of them waving white flags.	[initials]
	2nd		At 3.30 am the Battalion was relieved in the Front line by the 7th Cameron Highlanders, and withdrew to WILDE WOOD. At 6 am we were relieved in WILDE WOOD by the 7th LEINSTERS, and withdrew to the old British Front line.	[initials]
	3rd		On the afternoon of the 3rd after an uneventful period in O.B. 1 we marched out to the Forward Bivouac Camp one mile south of VLAMERTINGHE. It had rained almost incessantly for 3 days, and the men were very worn out.	
			Our casualties as far as ascertainable since going into the attack were Officers killed 2 wounded 14 ORs killed 36 missing 59 wounded 227	[initials]

A5834 Wt. W4973/M687 750,000 8/16 D. D. & L. Ltd. Forms/C.2118/13.

Instructions regarding War Diaries and Intelligence Summaries are contained in F. S. Regs., Part II. and the Staff Manual respectively. Title pages will be prepared in manuscript.

WAR DIARY

or

~~INTELLIGENCE SUMMARY.~~

(Erase heading not required.)

Sheet 408 Army Form C. 2118.

Place	Date	Hour	Summary of Events and Information	Remarks and references to Appendices
1917 BIVOUAC CAMP	August 4		The battalion was conveyed in buses from BIVOUAC CAMP to WINNIZEELE Training Area No 2. The battalion was in tents. A battalion mess for Officers was formed. Much rain during the day.	[illegible]
WINNIZEELE	5th		The day was devoted to inspections refitting and cleaning up.	[illegible]
"	6th		Companies were reorganised, and men had baths and a pay out.	[illegible]
"	7th		Reorganisation continued, and a short programme of training carried out.	
"			The Brigadier General presented the Silver Bugle won by the battalion in the Brigade Sports held at FILLIEVRES in May.	
			A draft of 89 ORs joined the battalion	[illegible]
"	8th		Specialist classes in Lewis Guns, Signalling, Bombing & Stretcher Bearing were formed, & general training continued.	[illegible]
"	9th		The Divisional Commander addressed the Battalion and spoke of the work done by the battalion in recent operations and its results	[illegible]
"	10th & 11th		Musketry drill programme and specialists training continued.	[illegible]
"	12th		Divine Services were held	[illegible]
"	13th		In a full days training programme, particular attention was paid to musketry.	[illegible]

T2134. Wt. W708—776. 500000. 4/15. Sir J. C. & S.

Instructions regarding War Diaries and Intelligence Summaries are contained in F. S. Regs., Part II. and the Staff Manual respectively. Title pages will be prepared in manuscript.

WAR DIARY

~~or INTELLIGENCE SUMMARY.~~

(*Erase heading not required.*)

Army Form C. 2118.

Sheet 409

Place	Date	Hour	Summary of Events and Information	Remarks and references to Appendices
1917	August			
WINNIZEELE	14		Training continued. A draft of 197 ORs joined, and proved to be a specially good draft, all having been in France previously. 2 Lt A.W. ROBERTSON joined the Battalion from RIPPON.	JB
	15		Usual Routine of training in Camp, ~~and~~ Commanding Officer's inspection of the draft in the forenoon, and tactical exercise on the Training Area in the afternoon.	JB
	16		General Marshall DSO saw the battalion practise attack schemes on the Training Area in the forenoon. Very successful sports were held during the afternoon. The Divisional Band, Brigade Massed Pipe Bands and the Pierrots contributed to the programme.	JB
	17		A light programme of training preparatory to move. At 2 pm the battalion marched 9 miles to BRANDHOEK Area No 3, and were billeted in tents. The day was very hot, and it was a trying march, owing to pavé roads and much traffic around POPERINGHE.	JB
	18		The battalion remained in Camp, + completed preparations for going into the line.	

T2134. Wt. W708—776. 500000. 4/15. Sir J. C. & S.

Instructions regarding War Diaries and Intelligence Summaries are contained in F. S. Regs., Part II. and the Staff Manual respectively. Title pages will be prepared in manuscript.

WAR DIARY

~~INTELLIGENCE SUMMARY.~~

(*Erase heading not required.*)

Sheet 410

Army Form C. 2118.

Place	Date	Hour	Summary of Events and Information	Remarks and references to Appendices
	1917			
BRANDHOEK AREA No. 3 (1 mile South of POPERINGHE)	August 18		Captain J. E. ADAMSON who had been taken on the strength on 10th inst, but had been detained for duty at the Corps Reinforcement Camp was detached permanently for duty at ~~that~~ Camp.	
"	19		The battalion marched 5 miles to a Forward Camp in H. 18 (Sheet 28 NW) about 1 mile West of YPRES, and was billeted in tents and bivouacs	
FORWARD CAMP	20	8.30 pm	After dark the battalion marched up to the line and occupied positions in the trench systems around VERLORENHOEK, being in Brigade support. There was comparatively little shelling, and the relief was accomplished without casualties.	
In the LINE	21		The day was quiet in the forward trench area. At 9.30 pm the battalion moved into position for the attack to be made on the morning of the 22nd for which the battalion was in support, with the 8th Seaforths in the front line on the right, the 7th Camerons on the left, and the 9th Black Watch in reserve. The movement was carried out without difficulty, all companies being in position by 2 am, 22nd inst.	

T2134. Wt. W708—776. 500000. 4/15. Sir J. C. & S.

Instructions regarding War Diaries and Intelligence Summaries are contained in F. S. Regs., Part II. and the Staff Manual respectively. Title pages will be prepared in manuscript.

WAR DIARY
~~or~~
~~INTELLIGENCE SUMMARY~~.

(Erase heading not required.)

Sheet 411.

Army Form C. 2118.

Place	Date	Hour	Summary of Events and Information	Remarks and references to Appendices
In the LINE	1917 August 22.		The attack was launched at 4.45 AM, and the battalion moved to POMMERN CASTLE from which the Camerons jumped off. Although our barrage was light, & not entirely continuous along the whole front of the attack, the advance went forward on the left for about 400 yards, when a check was met with, and 'B' Coy went forward to support the attack.	APPENDIX (2) O.O 103
			On the Brigade right the Seaforths had been held up by IBERIAN FARM, and 'A' Coy reinforced their front line. At this point very heavy fighting resulted in the attacking force on the right having to fall back on our original front line, with the exception of two strong posts which had been dug and garrisoned in positions midway between our front line and IBERIAN FARM. In these positions the left and right of the Brigade were forced to remain and consolidate.	APPENDIX (3) FREZENBERG MAP ED. 2
			On the left of our sector the 182nd Brigade advanced to GALLIPOLI, where they were held up, and on the right the 45th Brigade after advancing about 200 yards were obliged to fall back on their original front line. At 4 pm the enemy put down a heavy barrage on the line	

Instructions regarding War Diaries and Intelligence Summaries are contained in F. S. Regs., Part II. and the Staff Manual respectively. Title pages will be prepared in manuscript.

WAR DIARY

~~or~~

~~INTELLIGENCE SUMMARY.~~

(*Erase heading not required.*)

Sheet 412

Army Form C. 2118.

Place	Date	Hour	Summary of Events and Information	Remarks and references to Appendices
IN the LINE	1917 August 22nd		SQUARE FARM – STEENBECK, and were seen to be massing at ZEVENKOTE but the concentration was dispersed by our intense artillery barrage. The barrage continued until 9 pm. At 6.50 pm. orders were received to attack IBERIAN FARM in conjunction with the Seaforths and Black Watch at 12 midnight, but the enemy barrage prevented the preparations being completed in time and the attack was postponed until 1.30 AM. The Camerons had during the early hours of darkness been relieved in the front line by the Black Watch.	
	23rd	1-30 AM	Lieut FINDLAY and 20 men went forward to the NORTH of IBERIAN FARM and a similar party of the Seaforths went south of it, with the intention of surrounding the strong point. They reached the barbed wire defences of the FARM where they came under very heavy machine gun and rifle fire, which made it impossible to advance further and the parties retired. During the day there was a lull in the fighting, except for artillery fire, and the battalions reorganised.	

Instructions regarding War Diaries and Intelligence Summaries are contained in F. S. Regs., Part II. and the Staff Manual respectively. Title pages will be prepared in manuscript.

WAR DIARY

~~or~~

~~INTELLIGENCE SUMMARY.~~

(*Erase heading not required.*)

Sheet 413. Army Form C. 2118.

Place	Date	Hour	Summary of Events and Information	Remarks and references to Appendices
In the LINE	1917 August 23rd		During the day the line had been held by a mixed force of Seaforths Black Watch, 9th Gordons and ourselves, and at night the Seaforths and ourselves were relieved by the 10th Scottish Rifles. The relief was completed at 3 AM on the 24th and the battalion withdrew to support in VERLORENHOEK.	
	24th		We remained in support in the trench systems around VERLORENHOEK which were subjected to intermittent heavy shell fire, but we were fortunate in having few casualties.	
	25th		The same conditions prevailed during the day. After dark the Black Watch attempted to capture GALLIPOLI with our "C" Coy in support. Before they could advance far the Black Watch were held up and "C" Coy advanced through them and were able to drive on the attack some little distance before they too were held up by machine gun fire and had to dig in on a line which secured to us most of Hill 35	
	26th		At 2 am "A" Coy went forward in reserve ~~to the~~ Black Watch,	

T2134. Wt. W708—776. 500000. 4/15. Sir J. C. & S.

Sheet 414

Army Form C. 2118.

WAR DIARY

~~INTELLIGENCE SUMMARY~~

(Erase heading not required.)

Instructions regarding War Diaries and Intelligence Summaries are contained in F. S. Regs., Part II. and the Staff Manual respectively. Title pages will be prepared in manuscript.

Place	Date	Hour	Summary of Events and Information	Remarks and references to Appendices
In the LINE	1917 August 26		occupying POMMERN CASTLE. The day was again quiet, except for shelling. After dark the battalion was relieved, and marched back to Camp in H 18, and were in bivouacs. The total casualties for the tour were:- Offrs Killed 2 Wounded 3 Total 5. ORs Killed 22 Wounded 157 Missing 13 Total 192.	
			A draft of 15 ORs joined the battalion, and the following officers Lieut A KELLY, M.C. Lieut BEVERIDGE, 2 Lts J.M. ADAMS, J.W.K SMITH, T.E. FORSTER, S.M. HINTON.	
	27th		The morning was spent resting, and at 4.30 pm the Battalion marched back to TORONTO CAMP, & were billeted in huts	
	28th/29th		The weather was wet; the battalion cleaned up, refitted, and reorganised.	
	30th		Information was received of the award of decorations ~~awarded~~ to the battalion for operations 31st July to 2nd August as follows:- D.S.O. – A/Captain G.P. GEDDES. M.C. – Capt. J.A. SMITH, 2/Lt K.C. DAVIDSON, + CSM J. HINES, 3 DCMs & 12 Military Medals	
			The battalion marched to WATOU area No 2, and were	

Instructions regarding War Diaries and Intelligence Summaries are contained in F. S. Regs., Part II. and the Staff Manual respectively. Title pages will be prepared in manuscript.

WAR DIARY

or

~~INTELLIGENCE SUMMARY.~~

(*Erase heading not required.*)

Sheet 415

Army Form C. 2118.

Place	Date	Hour	Summary of Events and Information	Remarks and references to Appendices
WATOU AREA No 2	1917 Augt 30		billeted in tents and barns. On the way the battalion marched past the Army Commander	
			2 LTS LOVIE & J.F. MACGREGOR and 205 ORs joined the battalion. 72 of the men were from other regiments	JG
	31		The day was spent in inspections and a light programme of drill.	JG

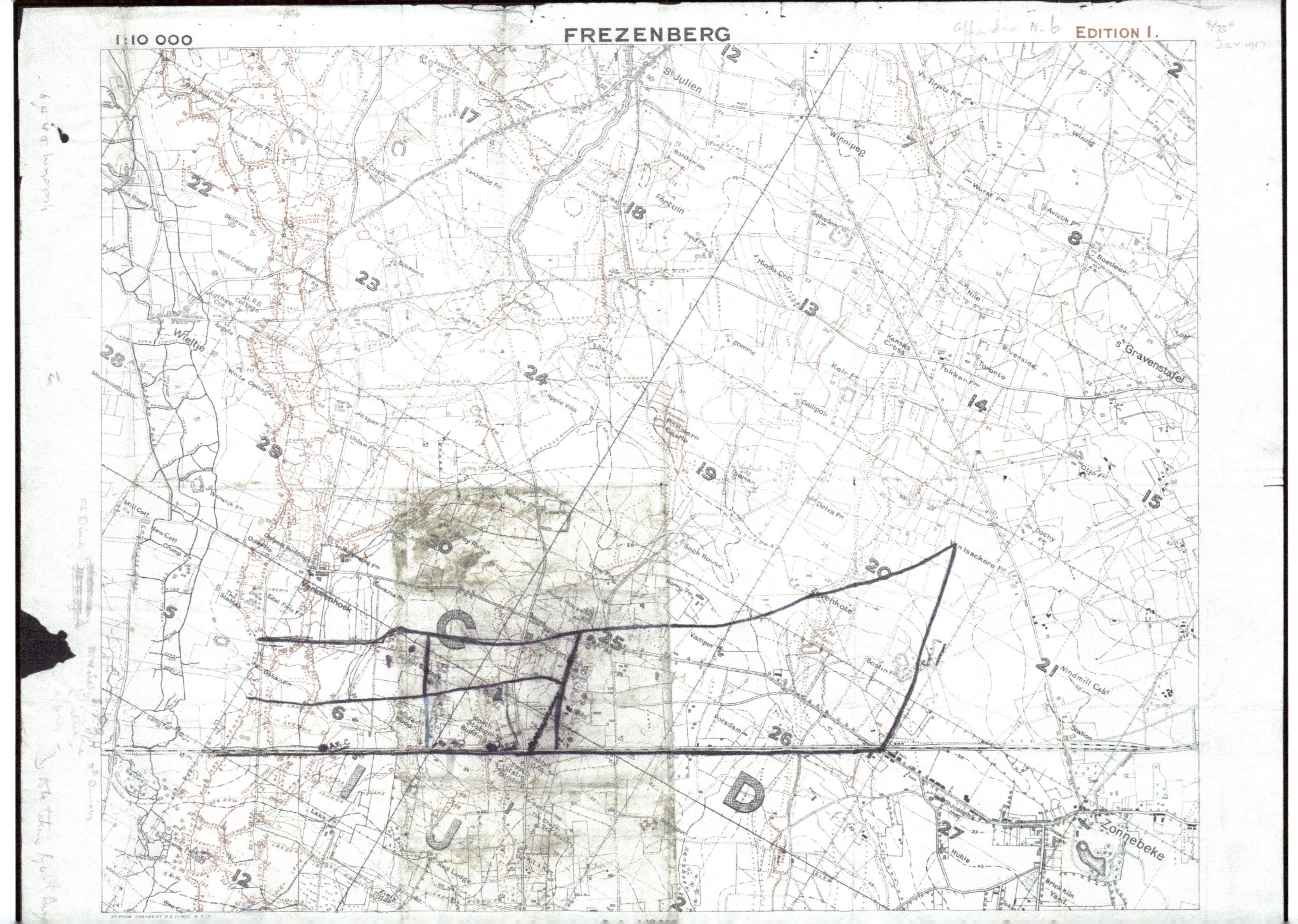

1:10 000
FREZENBERG
EDITION I.
St Julien
Winnipeg
Wurst Fm
Aviatik Fm
Boetleer
Winzig
Fortuin
Schuler Fm
Hindu Cott
Nile
Kansas Cross
Riverside
Toronto
Tokker Fm
St Gravenstafel
Keir Fm
Gallipoli
Somme
Apple Villa
Wieltje
Mouse Trap Fm
Cheddar Villa
Vanheule Fm
Bellevue
Well Cottage
White Cottage
Jasper Fm
Uhlan Fm
Pommern Castle
Iberian
Delva Fm
Otto Fm
Dochy Fm
Van Isackere Fm
Back House
Zevenkote
Vampir Fm
Bostin Fm
Windmill Cabt
Station
Potsdam
Frezenberg
Verlorenhoek
Mill Cott
New Cott
Zonnebeke
Mühle
Brick Kiln Vank
Red Lodge
Lake

SECRET

Operation Order No. 103
by
Lieut. Col. C. Reid, Comdg.
8/10 (S) Battn. The Gordon Hghrs

21-8-17

APPENDIX
No 2

Reference Map –
FREZENBERG, Edition No. 2

1. The 44th Infantry Brigade will attack in accordance with preliminary Instructions and Addenda I + II already issued. Units will move into positions shown on Map "C", already issued, on the night of the 21st./22nd. inst.

2. The 8/10 Gordon Hghrs will assemble 200 yards West of POMMERN REDOUBT as follows –:

A Coy. on right Front. B Coy. on left Front.
C Coy. in Support.
D Coy. in Reserve.
Bn. H.Q. in SQUARE FARM.
70 yards distance.

The positions are shown in Plan "A".

3. a. D Coy. will detail one platoon to follow the leading wave of the 8th. Seaforth Hghrs., and mop up and garrison IBERIAN FARM until relieved.

This platoon will report to Headquarters of the 8th. Seaforths (SQUARE FARM) by 1a.m. on Z Day.

b. C Coy. will detail one platoon to follow the leading wave of the 7th. Cameron Hghrs. and mop up and garrison GALLIPOLI FARM until relieved.

This platoon will report to Headquarters of the 7th Camerons (POMMERN REDOUBT) by 1a.m. on Z Day.

4. The 8/10 Gordon Hghrs – Support Battalion – will move up and occupy POMMERN REDOUBT and the vicinity as soon as it is vacated by the 7th. Cameron Hghrs. The Support Battn. is responsible for keeping touch with the leading battalions and for providing any necessary assistance. Leading companies will not move forward at a less distance than 500 yards from the attacking battalions.

When the objective is taken, the 8/10 Gordon Hghrs will dig themselves in on ~~the~~ a line of posts between DELVA FARM + GALLIPOLI COPSE. These posts will consist of short lengths of well traversed trenches or improvised shell holes.

In the event of any of the attacking battalions being counterattacked and driven back a counterattack will be delivered at once without waiting for orders.

Two Vickers Guns will be in assembly position

4 (Contd)

with D Coy. They will not move beyond POMMERN REDOUBT until the objective is taken. When the objective is taken, they will be posted about DELVA FARM, shooting S + S.E.

5. Battalion Dressing Station — SQUARE FARM.

6. Reports: See Appendix on "Communications."

7 Zero Hour and Hour for Synchronisation of Watches will be notified later.

8 Acknowledge.

G.P. Geddes.
Capt. + Adjutant.
8/10 Gordon Highrs.

Copies 1 - 4 : O.C. Companies
5 : M.O.
6 : L.G.O
7 : Signals
8 : 44 Brigade
9 : 8th Seaforth Highrs
10 : 7th Cameron Highrs.
11 : O.C. Sub-section 44 M.G. Coy
12 : War Diary + File

SECRET. Copy No.......

8/10th (Service) Battalion, The Gordon Highlanders.

PRELIMINARY INSTRUCTIONS No 1.

Ref - FREZENBERG
Sheet 1/10000

YPRES - AUGUST 1917.

1. The 15th Division has been ordered to continue the offensive on Z day.
The 61st Division is attacking on our Left.

45th Brigade will be on right of 15th Division, 44th Brigade on the left, and 46th Brigade in reserve.
184th Infantry Brigade will be on the left of 44th Infantry Brigade.

The 44th Infantry Brigade will attack with -
8th Seaforth Highrs. on Right,
7th Cameron Highrs. on Left,
8/10th Gordon Highrs. in Support,
9th Black Watch in reserve.

Assaulting battalions will attack on a front of 2 companies, each on a front of 2 platoons, 1 company in support, 1 company in reserve.
Two Vickers Guns will be attached to each of the assaulting and support battalions.

2. BOUNDARIES AND OBJECTIVES.
The Northern Boundary of the Brigade is from D.19.a.35.45 - North of the Northern House in GALLIPOLI, to D.14.c.45.60.

The Southern Boundary is from D.19.c.90.35. along the ZONNEBEKE stream.

The dividing line between battalions is D.19.a.7.1. to D.20.a.80.55.

The Objective runs from the Eastern edge of GALLIPOLI COPSE first to the West of BREMEN REDOUBT and then back to West of POTSDAM. It is essential that posts should secure the high ground immediately East of this line.

8th Seaforth Highlanders are responsible for the capture and mopping up of DELVA FM: and all buildings to the East of it.

7th Cameron Highlanders are responsible for the capture and mopping up of all buildings East of GALLIPOLI.

8/10th Gordon Highlanders will detail two special mopping up parties, each of one complete platoon, to mop up GALLIPOLI and IBERIAN FMS: They will follow the leading wave of assaulting battalions and will garrison the Farms until relieved.

All groups of buildings and other fortified localities must have mopping up parties and garrisons detailed for them

3. Prior to ZERO hour the assaulting battalions and moppers-up will be drawn up as close to the front line as practicable.
The remainder of the Support Battalion will be immediately West of POMMERN REDOUBT. They will occupy POMMERN REDOUBT as soon as vacated by 7th Cameron Highlanders.
The Reserve Battalion will be in O.G. system, as far East as a N. and S. line drawn through GREY RUINS.

The attack will be supported by the 15th, 16th and 5th Australian Divisional Artilleries.

The Creeping Barrage will probably move forward at the rate of 100 yards in 5 minutes.

Sheet 2. P.I. No.1.

The 9th Gordon Highlanders (Pioneers) will detail 6 platoons to consolidate and hold HILL 35 in D.19.b. These platoons will remain on HILL 35 till dusk when they will be relieved by the Brigade.

The attack of the Division will be covered by M.G. barrages from 32 guns found by 46th and 225th M.G. Companies under the orders of the Divisional M.G. Officer.

19th August 1917.

(Sgd) G.P.Geddes.
Captain & Adjutant.

Left 61 Divn.
184 Bde.
2/1 Bucks UHLAN FM.

Right 45 Bde.
11 Argylls 13 Royal Scots
6/7 R S F
6 Camerons

SECRET. Copy No. 11

ADDENDUM No.1.

TO Preliminary Instructions No.1.

20th Aug. 1917.

1. The Brigade Forward Dump (AR A.) is at C.30.c.6.5. AR B. will be established about D.19.b.7½.3½ during the night Z/Z plus 1. The Brigade Mobile Dump will function up to this point. Battalions are responsible for carrying from this point forward.

2. Prior to ZERO, Battalions will establish a small expense dump in their own trenches, for use during Z day. These dumps will each consist of 20 boxes S.A.A., 10 boxes Stokes, 10 boxes No. 23 Rifle Grenades. These stores will be dumped under Brigade arrangements at AR A. on X/Y night. O.C. D Coy will detail the necessary party to remove them, and will be responsible for carrying them to SQUARE FARM.

3. The Brigade Mobile Dump will be formed on the same lines as during the operations of 31-7-17, and will concentrate at the same location by 4 p.m. 20th inst.

The Brigade Transport Officer will arrange to draw the loads for the Explosive Section on the 20th inst. from H.18.c.4.1.

The Divisional Mobile Dump will be formed as before, and at same location.

4. Water. (a) 400 full petrol tins will be dumped at AR A. and will be sent forward by Mobile Dump when required.
(b) A reserve of 200 tins will be with the Brigade Mobile Dump.
(c) Forward Water Tanks are reported to be in position at C.30.d.5.5.

5. Rations. (a) Rations for Z day plus the (emergency) iron ration will be carried on the man at ZERO hour.
(b) Battalions moving forward from VLAMERTINGHE and YPRES areas on X/Y night will carry rations for Y and Z days plus the (emergency) iron ration.
(c) One additional iron ration (for consumption on Z plus 1 day) will be dumped at MILL COTTS.
(d) ½ ration of rum will be issued daily.
(e) The amount of solidified alcohol available will be notified later. It should only be used by advanced troops where cooking is impossible.

6. Details. Surplus personnel will be accommodated in the Detail Camp from the 20th inst. 44th Infantry Brigade at G.12.d.2.8.

7. Surplus Kit.
(a) A Divisional Store will not be formed.
(b) Surplus kits will be stored in Huts at H.7.a.2.1 under Unit arrangements with Camp Commandant there.
(c) Huts will be allotted to Battalions for Q.M.Stores in BRANDHOEK No.2 Area.

(signed) G.P.Geddes,
Captain & Adjutant.

Distribution :
Copy 1 - 4. O.C. Coys.
5. Q.M.
6. T.O.
7. L.G.O.
8. R.S.M.
9. M.O
10. Adjutant.
11.) Spare.
12.)

SECRET.

Copy No. 24

ADDENDUM No. 2.

To Preliminary Instructions No. 1.

20th Aug. 1917.

1. Maps "B" and "C" showing approximate positions of units of 44th Inf. Bde. on night 20/21st August and at ZERO are issued herewith. Amended objectives are also shown.

2.(i) On lifting from the line DELVA FM. - GALLIPOLI the creeping barrage will halt for 15 minutes.
(ii) The creeping barrage will contain a small percentage of 18-pdr. smoke shell.
(iii) If the weather is favourable gas and smoke will be used against enemy positions outside the zone of infantry attack.

3. Consolidation of positions - Machine Guns.
(i) 9th Gordon Highlanders will construct and man a chain of posts from the neighbourhood of IBERIAN East of Hill 35 to GALLIPOLI. They will also construct a line of posts across the spur between Hill 35 and the old battery position at D.19.b.1.8.
The detachment 9th Gordon Highlanders will move forward from O.B. lines at Zero and will commence work as soon as the hostile barrage permits.
44 M.G. Company will detail four guns to occupy this system, two to be about IBERIAN and two near GALLIPOLI. These two guns will join 9th Gordon Highlanders on Y/Z night and will move forward with them.

X (ii) When the objectives have been taken the assaulting battalions consolidate the ground won. The supporting battalion will construct a line of posts between DELVA FM and GALLIPOLI COPSE.

(iii) The garrisons of captured farms and strong posts are responsible for their immediate consolidation.

(iv) The Vickers guns attached to the three forward battalions will be posted as follows :-
(a) 8th Seaforth Highrs. - about D.20.a.9.5., shooting towards ZONNEBEKE.
(b) 7th Cameron Highrs. - about GALLIPOLI COPSE, shooting E. & N.E.
X (c) 8/10th Gordon Highrs - about DELVA FM. shooting S. & S.E.

(v) Posts should consist of short lengths of well traversed trench, or a group of improved shell- holes. Consolidation should not take the form of a continuous trench.

(vi) Strong Points are not intended to form rallying points on which units can fall back, but to break up an enemy's attack if he penetrates our line, and thus facilitate counter-attacks which must be made at once by Battalions and Companies, without waiting for orders.

4. Tanks. (i) No. 8 Company, "C" Battalion, Tank Corps, is co-operating in forthcoming operations.
(ii) Objectives of Tanks.
Left Section : GALLIPOLI, GALLIPOLI COPSE, HILL 35, IBERIAN FARM, DELVA FARM.

(signed) G.P. Geddes,
Captain & Adjutant.

Distribution :

Copy 1 - 4.	O.C. Coys.	8.	M.O.
5.	R.S.M.	9.	Q.M.
6.	L.G.O.	10.	T.O.
7.	Capt. Pearson.	11.	Adjutant.

APPENDIX No 3 21st AUGT 1917
St Julien
Winnipeg
s'Gravenstafel
Zonnebeke
Frezenberg
Wieltje
Zevenkote
Fortuin
Windmill Cabt
Van Isackere Fm
Scale 1:10,000

APPENDIX
No 3

22nd AUGUST 1917

[illegible]

[illegible]

Ct Geddes
Capt + Adjt

CONFIDENTIAL

Vol 28

WAR DIARY

OF

8/10th (Service) Battalion, The GORDON HIGHLANDERS.

FROM 1st September, 1917. to 30th September, 1917

(VOLUME 29.)

Instructions regarding War Diaries and Intelligence Summaries are contained in F. S. Regs., Part II. and the Staff Manual respectively. Title pages will be prepared in manuscript.

WAR DIARY
or
INTELLIGENCE SUMMARY.
(*Erase heading not required.*)

Sheet 416.

Army Form C. 2118.

Place	Date	Hour	Summary of Events and Information	Remarks and references to Appendices
WATOU AREA No. 2	1917 September 1		A full morning's training programme was carried out. The following awards for bravery during the fighting East of YPRES 31 July to 3rd August were granted to the Battalion	
			D.S.O. A/Captain G P GEDDES.	
			M.C. 2Lt. K C DAVIDSON	
			" Captain J.A SMITH RAMC attached this battalion	
			" S/10961 C.S.M. J. HINES	
			D.C.M. S/7972 Sergeant W. MARTIN	
			" S/4649 L/Cpl. W. GRAHAM	
			" S/8512 Pte. H GREIG	
			The battalion rested for the afternoon in view of the night's move.	J.6
	2.		At midnight on the night of the 1st/2nd the battalion marched to CAESTRE to entrain for ARRAS. The conditions were ideal for marching, a cool moonlight night, and the men did the 9 miles easily and well.	Appendix I.

Instructions regarding War Diaries and Intelligence Summaries are contained in F. S. Regs., Part II. and the Staff Manual respectively. Title pages will be prepared in manuscript.

WAR DIARY
or
INTELLIGENCE SUMMARY.
(Erase heading not required.)

Army Form C. 2118.

Sheet 417

Place	Date	Hour	Summary of Events and Information	Remarks and references to Appendices
	1917 SEPT			
CAESTRE	2	6 AM	The battalion reached CAESTRE at 4 am and the men had breakfasts before entraining. The train moved out at 6.30 am and after an uneventful journey ARRAS was reached at 2 pm Detrained & marched to MONTENESCOURT, 8 miles. The billets were poor and insufficient for three battalions and the Machine Gun Co. Officers accommodation in particular very poor	
	3		The day was devoted to inspections, cleaning up and resting. Weather dry and warm. The following message was received from the Army Commander Fifth Army with reference to the Divisions share in the YPRES fighting in July and August:- "The Commander of the Fifth Army bids good-bye to the "15th Division with great regret. Its reputation has been "earned on many battlefields and has never stood higher "than now. He wishes it all good fortune and many "further successes in the future. Will ye no come "back again?"	JC Appendix 2

T2134. Wt. W708—776. 500000. 4/15. Sir J. C. & S.

Instructions regarding War Diaries and Intelligence Summaries are contained in F. S. Regs., Part II. and the Staff Manual respectively. Title pages will be prepared in manuscript.

WAR DIARY
or
INTELLIGENCE SUMMARY.
(Erase heading not required.)

Sheet 418

Army Form C. 2118.

Place	Date	Hour	Summary of Events and Information	Remarks and references to Appendices
	1917 SEPT			
MONTENESCOURT.	4.		Training programme carried out in the forenoon and afternoon 41 ORs joined the battalion	
	5		Training continued. Nothing of importance to record	JG
	6		A general training programme, and a demonstration of the "Company in Attack" by B Coy filled the day. S/5674 PTE J CONDIE awarded the Military Medal The Divisional Pierrots and Cinema entertained the battalion in the evening	JG
	7		Battalion prepared for move to the Forward Area to be made in the afternoon. Battalion marched to RIFLE CAMP, (G 24 b. 7.4 Sheet 51B NW) a distance of 10 miles, and relieved the 7/8th KOSBs. The battalion was under canvas but accommodation was sufficient, and the site of the Camp a good one.	Appendix 3 JG
	8		Training under Company arrangements, with A Coy at Musketry on the Moat Range ARRAS.	JG

T2134. Wt. W708—776. 500000. 4/15. Sir J. C. & S.

Instructions regarding War Diaries and Intelligence Summaries are contained in F. S. Regs., Part II. and the Staff Manual respectively. Title pages will be prepared in manuscript.

WAR DIARY
or
INTELLIGENCE SUMMARY.
(Erase heading not required.)

Sheet 419

Army Form C. 2118.

Place	Date	Hour	Summary of Events and Information	Remarks and references to Appendices
	1917 SEPT			
RIFLE CAMP	9.		Divine services held jointly with other battalions of the Brigade.	JG
	10		Platoon training with special attention directed to "trench fighting"	JG
	11		Training continued with Specialists (Lewis Gunners, Scouts and Signallers) under their own instructors.	
			S/17162 PTE A CRAIK awarded the Military Medal.	JG
	12 + 13th		Working parties provided by Battalion for burying cable and training continued as far as possible.	JG
	14		The battalion relieved the 13th Royal Scots in the front line in the Sector immediately North of the River SCARPE (SECTOR LEFT Battalion of the LEFT BRIGADE, the Divisional front being four battalions)	
			The relief commenced immediately after dark, and was effected without incident or casualties. The front is roughly 1000 yards and was held by two Companies "C" on right D on left, with A and B in reserve in CRUMP TRENCH. The front line is held by posts, there being no trench for 300 yards immediately N of River	Appendix 4.

T2134. Wt. W708—776. 500000. 4/15. Sir J. C. & S.

Instructions regarding War Diaries and Intelligence Summaries are contained in F. S. Regs., Part II. and the Staff Manual respectively. Title pages will be prepared in manuscript.

WAR DIARY
or
INTELLIGENCE SUMMARY.
(Erase heading not required.)

Sheet 420

Army Form C. 2118.

Place	Date	Hour	Summary of Events and Information	Remarks and references to Appendices
	1917			
TRENCHES	SEPT 15		Trenches in this sector were found clean, and in good order, but much work remained to be done on revetting, duckboarding, dug outs and general preparation for wet weather. Working parties from A & B Companies worked on the communication trenches and the front companies cleared the front and support trenches and worked on shelters. On the night of 14/15th the enemy approached our No. 8 Post, and attempted to bomb it. It was decided to patrol "No Man's land" actively to prevent a recurrence of this and two parties went out on the night of the 15th but met with no enemy.	JB
	16th		Work on front and communication trenches continued. Enemy used trench mortar fire intermittently during the day. During the night patrols and wiring parties were also fired on by trench mortars and machine guns.	
			2nd Lt J SPENCE and 92 ORs joined the battalion, and were ordered up to trenches to increase numbers available for working parties.	JB

T2134. Wt. W708—776. 500000. 4/15. Sir J. C. & S.

Army Form C. 2118.

Instructions regarding War Diaries and Intelligence Summaries are contained in F. S. Regs., Part II. and the Staff Manual respectively. Title pages will be prepared in manuscript.

WAR DIARY
or
INTELLIGENCE SUMMARY.
(Erase heading not required.)

Sheet 421

Place	Date	Hour	Summary of Events and Information	Remarks and references to Appendices
IN trenches	1917 Sept 17		Work continued. Nothing of importance to record during the day. The following officers joined the battalion:- 2nd LTs J.B SIMPSON, J.L ROSEDALE, C.R McGECHAN. Rejoined 2nd LTs F.M.LEE, C.D GRAHAM. At 12 midnight the Brigade on our left (17th Division) carried out a raid. We co-operated with rifle grenade & Lewis Gun fire to hold the attention of the enemy on our front. The raid was very successful, prisoners being taken, & many of the enemy killed. The explosion of a Company bomb dump by an enemy grenade had unfortunate results Sgt F Macgregor D Coy being killed and three ORs wounded.	[initials]
	18		A & B Coys relieved C & D Coys in the front line during the day, outlying posts being relieved after dark. A new communication trench was commenced joining up CORONA SUPPORT SOUTH and CEYLON AVENUE. Other work on trenches continued	[initials]
	19		Revetting and construction of dug outs etc continued. At night all available men were employed on the widening and deepening of the new communication trench.	[initials]

T2134. Wt. W708—776. 500000. 4/15. Sir J. C. & S.

Instructions regarding War Diaries and Intelligence Summaries are contained in F. S. Regs., Part II. and the Staff Manual respectively. Title pages will be prepared in manuscript.

WAR DIARY
or
INTELLIGENCE SUMMARY.
(Erase heading not required.)

Sheet 422

Army Form C. 2118.

Place	Date	Hour	Summary of Events and Information	Remarks and references to Appendices
In trenches	1917 Sept 20.		Throughout the day heavy trench mortar fire inflicted a few casualties on us and on men of other units working in this sector. Work proceeded however, and wiring parties and patrols went out as usual. New communication trench almost completed.	[initials]
	21		Work as usual during the day. After dark the battalion was relieved by the 9th Black Watch, and went back to support two companies in dug outs and shelters at H 23 c, and Headquarters and the other two Companies (A + B) in shelters at STIRLING CAMP, H 13 d 8 8 (Sheet 51B N.W.) The relief was effected without incident or casualties.	
			The casualties for the 8 days in the line were 5 ORs killed and 23 wounded.	[initials]
In support (STIRLING CAMP)	22		The forward Companies C + D Coys provided working parties, and A + B Coys carried out inspections, gas drill and a light programme of training. Weather dry + warm, and all Companies comfortably billetted. 2nd LTS. H.A. AITKEN + G S P NOBLE joined the battn	[initials]

T2134. Wt. W708—776. 500000. 4/15. Sir J. C. & S.

Instructions regarding War Diaries and Intelligence Summaries are contained in F. S. Regs., Part II. and the Staff Manual respectively. Title pages will be prepared in manuscript.

WAR DIARY
or
INTELLIGENCE SUMMARY.
(Erase heading not required.)

Sheet 423

Army Form C. 2118.

Place	Date	Hour	Summary of Events and Information	Remarks and references to Appendices
In support (STIRLING CAMP)	1917 Sept 23 & 24th		Forward Companies on working parties, and STIRLING CAMP Coys training by platoons. 13 ORs joined the battalion on 23rd	JG
	25th		Working parties and training continued. Specialist classes (Lewis Gun Scouts & Signallers) began a short course under their own instructors. One platoon of B Coy proceeded to Divisional Musketry Camp at ETRUN for a 6 days course. LT A KELLY M.C. left to rejoin his old Battalion, the 5th, handing over command of D Coy to 2nd Lt J KEIR	JG
	26th		Training and working parties as usual.	JG
	27th		A & B Companies relieved C & D Companies in the forward Camp, & took over the working parties, C & D coming back to STIRLING CAMP for training.	
	28/29th		Nothing to record. Parties and training carried on	
	30th		Divine service for Headquarters and Companies in STIRLING CAMP in conjunction with 9th Gordons	

T2134. Wt. W708—776. 500000. 4/15. Sir J. C. & S.

Appendix I

Coy No.______

8/10th (Service) Battalion, The Gordon Highlanders.

OPERATION ORDER No.109.

| Ref. Sheet : 27. 1/40,000 |

By

Lieut-Colonel C.Reid, Comdg.

1st Sept. 1917.

1. The battalion will march to CAESTRE to-night, 1st / 2nd Sept. and entrain there for ARRAS. Approximate length of journey - 9 hours.

Route to CAESTRE : Via Cross Roads K.36.d.0.4 - GODWAERSVELDE - KEMELHOF - CAESTRE Railway Station.

The battalion will parade in close column, ready to move off at 12 midnight.

Order of March : Headquarters, C, B, A, D Coys.

2. Transport will move off at 10.30 p.m. and march by the above route. 2/Lieut.KEIR, Sgt.Millward and 10 other ranks to be detailed by Headquarters, will proceed with the Transport and report to the Brigade Major at the Station on arrival. This party will be required to control traffic, water-points, latrines etc.
Two guides will be allotted to the Transport. They will report to 2/Lieut.KEIR at Orderly Room at 10 p.m. to-night.
A party of 2 Officers and 100 other ranks has been detailed from the 8th Seaforth Highlanders to entrain the transport at the entraining station., and a similar party has been detailed from the 7th Cameron Highlanders to detrain the transport at the detraining station.

3. The train leaves CAESTRE at 6 a.m. to-morrow. 2nd inst. All troops to be entrained by 5.30 a.m.
(a) The train consists of 1 Officers' carriage; 17 flat trucks; 30 covered trucks.

(b) (i) Each flat truck will take an average of 4 axles.
(ii) Each covered truck will take :
6 H.D.Horses or 8 L.D.Horses
or
40 men.

(c) No personnel or stores will be allowed in the brake vans at each end of the train, or on the roofs of the trucks. No covered trucks shouldbe used for baggage, as it restricts space available for personnel.

(d) All doors of covered trucks and carriages on the right hand side of the train, when on the main line, must be kept closed.

4. O.C. A and D Coys will each detail a picket of 1 Sergeant, 1 L/Corpl. and 8 men for each end of the train to prevent troops leaving the train at each stop.

(signed) G.P.Geddes,
Captain & Adjutant.

Distribution :
Copy 1 - 4. O.C. Coys. 5. R.S.M.
6. 2/Lieut.KEIR 7. Quartermaster.
8. Transport Sgt. 9. L.G.O.
10 Medical Officer 11. War Diary.
12. File.
13. Adjutant's copy.

Appendix 2

N O T I C E S.

The following message has been received from the Army Commander Fifth Army, and is communicated for information of all ranks :-

"The Commander of the Fifth Army bids good-bye to the "15th Division with great regret. Its reputation has "been earned on many battlefields and has never stood "higher than now. He wishes it all good fortune and "many further successes in the future. Will ye no "come back again".

Appendix 3.

SECRET. Copy No 4/.

8/10th (Service) Battalion, The Gordon Highlanders.

OPERATION ORDER No.112

By

Lieut-Colonel C.Reid, Comdg.

Ref. Sheets :
51B NW, 1/20,000;
51C, 1/40,000;
LENS, 1/100,000.

6th Sept 1917.

1. The battalion will march to RIFLE CAMP (G.24.b.7.4) to-morrow, 7th Sept., relieving the 7/8th K.O.S.Bs.
Route : DUISANS - ST.POL-ARRAS ROAD - ROND POINT (G.21.b.5.½) - ST.NICHOLAS.

Starting Point : Road Junction L.2.c.2.4.
Time : 5 p.m.

The battalion will parade, ready to march off, at 3.20 p.m. Head of column to be at Cross Roads ~~K.21.a.4.6~~, facing N.W. K.21.b.30.
Order of March : H.Qrs., D,A,B,C Coys and Transport.
Pipers & Drummers will march with their Co[illegible]

2. Distances will be maintained on the march as follows :-

Between Companies .... 200 yards.
Between rear Coy and Transport ... 100 yards.
Between Units .... 400 yards.

3. Halts will be at 10 minutes to the clock hour.

4. Advance Party (Lieut.J.COLLIER, C.Q.M-Sgts and 1 N.C.O. from H.Q. will report at RIFLE CAMP at 5 p.m.
They will take over accommodation, and meet the battalion at the bridge, ST.NICHOLAS - G.16.c.4.5.

5. Completion of relief and falling-out states will be reported at once to Battalion Headquarters.

6. ACKNOWLEDGE.

(signed) G.P.Geddes,
Captain & Adjut.

Issued through signals at 1 p.m.

Distribution :

Copy			
1 - 4.	O.C. Coys.	5.	L.G.O.
6.	M.O.	7.	Lieut.COLLIER.
8.	R.S.M.	9.	Quartermaster.
10.	Transport Sgt.	11.	44th Inf.Bde.
12.	War Diary.	13.	File.

H(324)

APPENDIX 4

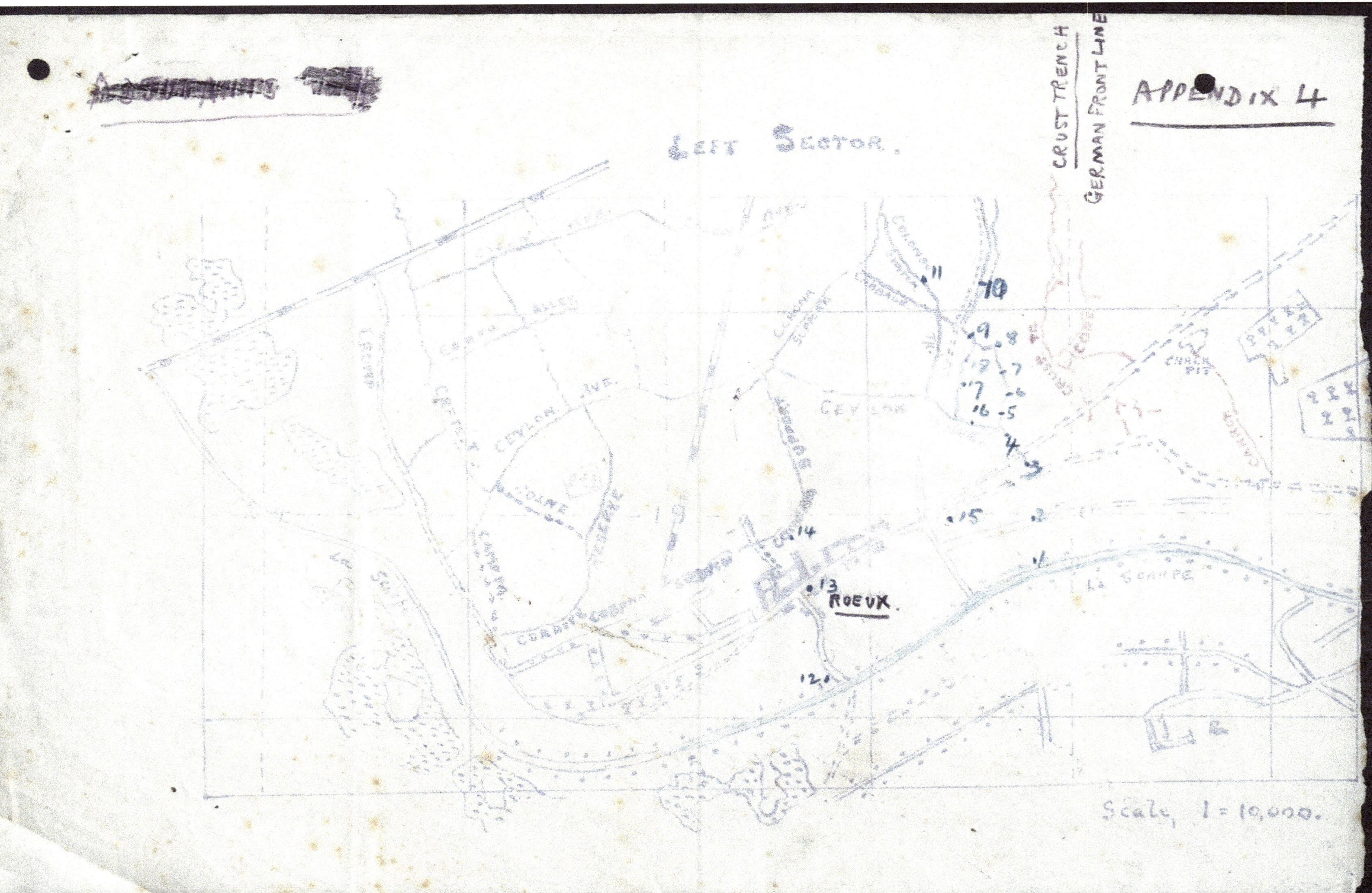
LEFT SECTOR.
CRUST TRENCH
GERMAN FRONT LINE
CHEMICAL WORKS
CHALK PIT
CEYLON
CEYLON AVE.
CORONA
SUPPORT
ROEUX
LA SCARPE
Scale, 1 = 10,000.

Index

SUBJECT.

8/10th London Highlanders

No.	Contents.	Date.
	October 1917.	

(63,965). Wt.15,820—176. 2000. 9/21. Gp.164. A.&E.W.

CONFIDENTIAL Vol 29

WAR DIARY

OF

8/10th (Service) Battalion, THE GORDON HIGHLANDERS.

For Period

1st October 1917 to 31st October, 1917

VOLUME 30

Instructions regarding War Diaries and Intelligence Summaries are contained in F. S. Regs., Part II. and the Staff Manual respectively. Title pages will be prepared in manuscript.

WAR DIARY
or
INTELLIGENCE SUMMARY.
(Erase heading not required.)

Sheet 424

Army Form C. 2118.

Place	Date	Hour	Summary of Events and Information	Remarks and references to Appendices
STIRLING CAMP.	1917 October 1		The Battalion was relieved as Support Battalion of the Left Brigade by the 12th H.L.I. and with the other Battalions of the Brigade moved into Divisional Reserve. The battalion took over the accommodation vacated by the 12th H.L.I. at BALMORAL CAMP (G.17.d.5.8.) Sheet 51B NW. Working parties of 200 ORs to be found for next four days, the remainder of the battalion to continue training.	Appendix I.
			2 LT. A WILSON rejoined battalion from No. 2 Training Camp ETAPLES where he had been on duty as an instructor for two months	
			LT W J P BEVERIDGE assumed temporary command of "C" Coy.	[illegible]
BALMORAL CAMP	2		The following decorations were awarded the battalion for bravery in operations EAST of YPRES on 22nd to 26th August 1917	
			Military Cross. A/Captain J. LYNN	
			2 LT R J WATSON	
			Distinguished Conduct Medal. S/6535 A/Sgt F. McGREGOR (since deceased) S/5712 Cpl T. SINCLAIR, S/13862 Cpl W. WHITEHEAD, S/1970 L/Cpl T. HENDRY S/7084 Cpl A. NEILSON (attached 44th Trench Mortar Battery)	[illegible]

T2134. Wt. W708—776. 500000. 4/15. Sir J. C. & S.

Instructions regarding War Diaries and Intelligence Summaries are contained in F. S. Regs., Part II. and the Staff Manual respectively. Title pages will be prepared in manuscript.

WAR DIARY
or
INTELLIGENCE SUMMARY.
(*Erase heading not required.*)

Sheet 425

Army Form C. 2118.

Place	Date	Hour	Summary of Events and Information	Remarks and references to Appendices
BALMORAL CAMP	1917 October 3		Captain N G PEARSON proceeded to England to the Senior Officers Course ALDERSHOT.	JB
	4		Captain J.B. WOOD MC returned from Senior Officers Course ALDERSHOT and assumed the duties of Second in Command.	JB
	5		Working parties were taken over by the 9th BLACK WATCH and the whole battalion was engaged in training.	
			2 Lt R. BUNTINE joined the battalion and posted to "C" Coy	JB
			A successful battalion concert was held	
	6		Training continued. Two Companies and LEWIS GUNNERS on MOAT RANGE, ARRAS	JB
	7		Very wet weather with high winds interfered with training. The following were awarded the Military Medal for bravery East of YPRES 22/26 August. S/10576 A/Cpl. H. HUNTER, 1511 Sgt H MORTON S/6425 L/Cpl A McDONALD, S/4762 A/Cpl J McCLUSKEY, 1454 Pte J HENRY	JB
	8		2nd Lts J.R BRUCE and 2 Lt A WILLIAMS joined the battalion from England	

T2134. Wt. W708—776. 500000. 4/15. Sir J. C. & S.

Instructions regarding War Diaries and Intelligence Summaries are contained in F. S. Regs., Part II. and the Staff Manual respectively. Title pages will be prepared in manuscript.

WAR DIARY
or
INTELLIGENCE SUMMARY.
(Erase heading not required.)

Sheet 426

Army Form C. 2118.

Place	Date	Hour	Summary of Events and Information	Remarks and references to Appendices
BALMORAL CAMP	1917 October 9		The battalion relieved the 11th Argyle & Sutherland Highlanders in the left section of the Right Brigade. Relief was by daylight, began at 8 am and was completed without incident or casualties at 11.30 am	Appendix 2
			The battalion was disposed with "A" Coy in right front, "B" Coy in left front, "C" Coy in support and "D" Coy in reserve. The front line in this section is held with the battalion front of 700 yards divided into 4 "islands", each island being garrisoned by one platoon with a platoon in close support. Enemy trenches were distant about 250 yards away. Our trenches were dry and well duckboarded, and with sufficient shelters in front line, and dugouts ~~and~~ in support and reserve trenches	MAP Appendix 3
			As the 11th Argyles reported enemy activity in No Man's Land an energetic policy of patrolling was arranged, at least two patrols to cover the whole of the front every night	
FRONT TRENCHES	10th		Mutual artillery activity, & some trench mortar fire on our front line, but sector generally quiet all day.	

T2134. Wt. W708–776. 500000. 4/15. Sir J. C. & S.

Instructions regarding War Diaries and Intelligence Summaries are contained in F. S. Regs., Part II. and the Staff Manual respectively. Title pages will be prepared in manuscript.

WAR DIARY
or
INTELLIGENCE SUMMARY.
(Erase heading not required.)

Sheet 427

Army Form C. 2118.

Place	Date	Hour	Summary of Events and Information	Remarks and references to Appendices
	1917 October			
TRENCHES	10		Patrols at night reported enemy wire strong. Long grass and many shell holes some filled with barbed wire in ground between trenches	JB
"	11		The day quiet, and patrols at night found no trace of the enemy outside his wire.	
			Captain W P HERBERT, MRC USA assumed medical charge of the Battalion vice Captain J A SMITH, MC RAMC who proceeded to England on completion of his contract.	JB
"	12		Nothing of importance to record	JB
"	13		An inter Company relief was made "C" Coy moving to right front "D" to left front "A" Coy to support "B" Coy to reserve. Otherwise quiet.	Appendix 4 JB
"	14		At 10 am. 2 Lt A S WILLIAMS was wounded & Sgt BELL killed by a trench mortar shell which fell between them in the front line trench	
			From 9 am our artillery heavily bombarded the enemy's trenches opposite the 12th Division on our right, and also along the enemy front opposite the 7th Camerons who were on our right and on the immediate left of the 12th Division. There was little retaliation	

T2134. Wt. W708—776. 500000. 4/15. Sir J. C. & S.

Instructions regarding War Diaries and Intelligence Summaries are contained in F. S. Regs., Part II. and the Staff Manual respectively. Title pages will be prepared in manuscript.

WAR DIARY
or
INTELLIGENCE SUMMARY.
(Erase heading not required.)

Sheet 428

Army Form C. 2118.

Place	Date	Hour	Summary of Events and Information	Remarks and references to Appendices
	1917 October			
TRENCHES	14		At 4.55 pm after a short thermite bombardment three battalions of the 12th Division made an attack on the enemy. Two patrols each of 1 Officer 1 NCO & 4 men left our lines to obtain identifications Lt G.S.M. MILNE killed & 2 Lt J.B. SIMPSON wounded. Full report on these patrols appended (No. 6.)	Appendix 5 Appendix 6
			The attack by the three battalions resulted in the capture of 64 prisoners. About 200 enemy dead seen in trenches.	
			The enemy shelled our communication trenches until midnight	J/o
	15th 16th		Both days passed without any unusual occurence	J/o
	17		The battalion was relieved by the 9th Black Watch, and moved into Brigade support in WILDERNESS CAMP (H.31.b.0.3 Sheet 51B NW)	Appendix 7 J/o
WILDERNESS CAMP	18		The day was spent in cleaning up and inspections	J/o
	19		The following Tempy Second Lieutenants to be Tempy Lieuts from 1st July A.W. BOYCE, A. WILSON, G.S.M. MILNE (since killed in action)	
			Working parties provided for work under Divisional arrangements, and a programme of training carried out	J/o

T2134. Wt. W708—776. 500000. 4/15. Sir J. C. & S.

Instructions regarding War Diaries and Intelligence Summaries are contained in F. S. Regs., Part II. and the Staff Manual respectively. Title pages will be prepared in manuscript.

WAR DIARY
or
INTELLIGENCE SUMMARY.
(*Erase heading not required.*)

Sheet 429

Army Form C. 2118.

Place	Date	Hour	Summary of Events and Information	Remarks and references to Appendices
	1917 October			
WILDERNESS CAMP	20		Training continued. Captain F J C MOFFAT awarded the DSO for bravery East of YPRES on 31st July	JC
"	21		Divine services were held. The battalion was relieved as support battalion of the Brigade by the 7th Camerons and became reserve Battn of the Brigade, but Camps were not changed	Appendix 8 JC
"	22 23rd & 24th		Working parties were provided, and the remainder of the battalion continued training	JC
"	25		The battalion was relieved in Brigade reserve, and with the other battalions of the Brigade moved into ARRAS as Divisional reserve. All companies were billeted in the GRANARY, accommodation being good	Appendix 9
ARRAS			LT. COL. D MACLEOD, DSO. reassumed command of the Battalion	JC
	26		2LT. C McGREGOR rejoined the battalion & was posted to B Coy. Working parties found. Baths and training for the remainder of the battalion. Captain J E ADAMSON rejoined the battalion.	JC

Instructions regarding War Diaries and Intelligence Summaries are contained in F. S. Regs., Part II. and the Staff Manual respectively. Title pages will be prepared in manuscript.

WAR DIARY
or
INTELLIGENCE SUMMARY.
(Erase heading not required.)

Sheet 430

Army Form C. 2118.

Place	Date	Hour	Summary of Events and Information	Remarks and references to Appendices
	1917 October			
ARRAS	27		Training continued.	FG
	28		Divine services were held The following Tempy Second Lieuts to be Tempy Lieuts from July 1st 1917:- F.M. LEE, S.M. HINTON.	FG
	29		Usual routine and training	FG
	30		Companies were practised in attack on strong points in conjunction with the 44th Trench Mortar Battery firing live shell	FG
	31		Training continued	FG

WAR DIARY.
APPENDIX I

SECRET.

Copy No. ________

8/10th (Service) Battalion, The Gordon Highlanders.

Ref. Map :
51B N.W.
Edition 7A.
1/20,000

OPERATION ORDER No. 115.

By

Lieut-Colonel Charles Reid, Comdg.

30th Sept 1917

1. The Battalion will be relieved as Support Battalion of the Left Brigade on 1st October by the 12th H.L.I., and with the other Battalions of the Brigade will come into Divisional Reserve.

2. The Battalion, after being relieved, will take over the accommodation vacated by 12th H.L.I., BALMORAL CAMP at G.17.d.5.8.

3. Working Parties will be taken over and relieved in accordance with attached Table.

4. Stores, Tools, anti-aircraft mountings, anti-gas appliances, aeroplane photographs, maps, defence schemes, work programmes will be handed over and receipts taken. Lists to be handed in to Orderly Room by 8 p.m. 1st October.

5. Coy Q.M.Sgts, and L/Cpl.Hendry for Battn.H.Qrs., together with 1 N.C.O. per Coy and 1 for H.Qrs., will report to 2/Lieut.A.W.BOYCE at STIRLING CAMP at 10 a.m. and proceed to BALMORAL CAMP to take over accommodation, stores etc.

6. O.C. D Coy will detail a Lewis Gun team of 1 N.C.O. and 5 men, with gun complete and anti-aircraft sights, to proceed to ST.POL on 2nd October for anti-aircraft work under orders to be issued later.

7. Relief of the Forward Companies will take place at 3 p.m. and of Battalion Headquarters and the Companies in STIRLING CAMP at 3.30 p.m.

8. O.C. Companies will obtain from O.C. Coys of the relieving unit a certificate that accommodation has been left thoroughly clean. These certificates to be handed in to Orderly Room by 8 p.m. 1st Oct.

9. 2 Guides for the detached platoon at H.28.a.6.8. will be at Cross Roads, East end of FEUCHY, H.21.d.8.3, at 2.30 p.m.

10. All movement will be by platoons at 10 minutes interval.

11. Strict attention to be paid to march discipline. Officer, or where there is no Officer, senior N.C.O., will march in rear of platoon.

12. Reports : O.C. Coys will report personally at Orderly Room completion of relief and Coys settled in new Camp.
Battalion Headquarters will close at STIRLING CAMP at 3.30 p.m. and open at BALMORAL CAMP at 4 p.m.

13. ACKNOWLEDGE.

(signed) J. Collier,
Lieut & A/Adjutant.

Distribution :-

Copy 1 - 4. O.C. Coys.
5. R.S.M.
6. Q.M.
7. T.O.
8. L.G.O.
9. M.O.
10. H.Q., 44th Inf.Bde.
11. 12th H.L.I.
12 & 13. War Diary & File.

WAR DIARY
APPENDIX 2

8/10th (Service) Battalion, The Gordon Highlanders.

SECRET

OPERATION ORDER No.116 Copy No. 12

1. The battalion will relieve the 11th Argyll & Sutherland Highrs. in the left section of the Brigade Front tomorrow, the 9th instant.

2. DISPOSITIONS :-

A Coy Gordons will relieve B Coy Argylls in the right front.
B " " " " A " " " " left "
C " " " " D " " " " support.
D " " " " C " " " " reserve.

On relief, the battalion will be disposed as follows :-

A Coy - H.Qrs. in CURB ALLEY (I.31.b.45.10)
1 platoon --- Island No.7.
1 platoon --- Island No.8.
2 platoons --- Support Line.

B Coy - H.Qrs. in SCABBARD SUPPORT (I.31.a.85.85)
1 platoon --- Island No.9.
1 platoon --- Island No.10.
2 Platoons --- Support Line.

C Coy - H.Qrs. in BAYONET TRENCH (I.36.b.90.30).
4 platoons --- BAYONET TRENCH.

D Coy - H.Qrs. in JOHNSTONE AVENUE. (near HAPPY VALLEY).
3 platoons --- JOHNSTONE AVENUE.
1 platoon --- "H" Post in LONE AVENUE.

Bn.H.Qrs in WELFORD RESERVE.

O.C. C Coy will detail one Lewis Gun and team to be attached to each of A and B Coys for anti-aircraft defence. These guns will report to their respective companies before marching off, and will be rationed by them while in the front line.

3. GUIDES -

Guides as under will be at Cross Roads near FEMPOUX LOCK - H.23.b.3.4. - at 9.30 a.m.-

A Coy) 1 for each Island, 1 for each support platoon, and
B ") 1 for each Coy H.Qrs.

C Coy)
D ") 1 for each platoon, and 1 each Coy H.Qrs.

Bn.H.Qrs. 2 guides.

The battalion will march off in the following order :-
A, B Coys, H.Qrs., C and D Coys.
The first platoon of A Coy will march off at 8 a.m.

All movement will be by platoons at 5 minutes interval. This must be rigidly adhered to in communication trenches.

4. Particular care is to be taken that no rifles, or loads carried on the shoulder project above the parapet, as it is essential that the unusual movement should not be observed by the enemy. In the event of an enemy aeroplane flying over our lines, troops must take cover at once and remain in perfectly still.

O. O. No.116 (contd)

4. (contd)
Each platoon will be preceded through the C.Ts. by a scout who will give warning of its approach, and secure a free passage.

Out-going troops will give way to in-coming troops.

5. Trench stores, tools, anti-aircraft mountings, anti-gas appliances, aeroplane photographs, trench maps, Defence Schemes, work Programmes, S.O.S. signals, will be taken over and receipts given. Lists of articles taken over will be forwarded to Bn.H.Q. by 7 p.m., 9th instant.

6. Administrative Instructions and work Tables will be issued separately.

7. Completion of Relief will be notified to Bn.H.Qrs. by the code word "SLEET", and also by runner.

8. ACKNOWLEDGE.

(Sgd) G.P.Geddes,
Captain & Adjutant.

Copies to - O.C. Coys.
L.G.O.
R.S.M.
T.O.
Q.M.
11th A & S H.
45th Inf.Bde.
War Diary
File.

Issued through signals - 5 p.m.

WAR DIARY

Appendix 3

MAP enlarged from 51B NW and 51B SW

Our trenches:- BLUE
Enemy " RED
SAPS lettered:- Y. X. W. V. etc.

45th INF. BDE. MAP No1

20th SEPT 17

RIFLE TR.
LONE AVE
LONG AVE
WESTERN RESERVE
LEMON AVENUE
ORANGE AVENUE
JOHN AVENUE
HARNESS LANE
CORD SWITCH NORTH
MONCHY TR.
DEVILS TRENCH
GUN TR.
LANE
CARTRIDGE TR.
SKYE TR.
KEELING COPSE
CIGAR COPSE
NARROW
SHAFFLE TR.
ARROW HEAD COPSE
TWIN COPSES
POODLE TR.
LOCK TR.
B. de SUREPINES
MONCHY-le PREUX
ORCHARD
CIRCLE TR.
EAST RES.
CHAIN
H I
N O
31
32
36
1
2
6
R
V
W
X
Y

SECRET

War Diary

Appendix 4

OPERATION ORDER No. 81

1. [illegible] 12 [illegible]

C [illegible] A [illegible]

D [illegible] B [illegible]

[illegible] A + B [illegible]

[illegible]

2. GUIDES

(a) [illegible] C Coy [illegible] LONE AVENUE [illegible] RIFLE SUPPORT [illegible]

(b) [illegible] D Coy [illegible] 11 C) [illegible]

3. ROUTE

C Coy – LONE AVENUE – RIFLE SUPPORT – HAMMERS

~~D Coy – LONE AVENUE – SEABOARD SUPPORT –~~ STRAND ALLEY

* A Coy – LONE ALLEY – CHIME SUPPORT – RIFLE SUPPORT – LONE AVENUE

B Coy – HAMMERS – RIFLE SUPPORT – LONE AVENUE

4. MOVEMENT

[illegible]

5. [illegible]

6. [illegible]

7. [illegible] completed [illegible] HQ [illegible] MAGGIE

8. Acknowledge

G. R. Geddes

Capt & Adjt

1st Gordon Highlanders

Issued through Signals at [illegible]

SECRET — 8/10 Gordon Highrs. — GH/119 13.10.17

WAR DIARY OR Appendix 5

OPERATION ORDER No 118

I. At zero hour on the 14th inst. the Division on our right is carrying out an enterprise against the German trenches on its front.

The action will be preceded by a bombardment lasting 6 hours. During the bombardment Lewis Gunners are to be prepared to take advantage of any movement.

From zero hour all men, as far as possible are to be kept under cover until the enemy retaliation ceases.

At zero hour DEVIL'S TRENCH will be bombarded with special shells. The bombardment will cease at zero + 10 minutes & will not be resumed.

II At zero + 12 minutes the 8/10th GORDON HIGHRS will send out two patrols to the German front line to secure identifications & obtain information.

The patrols will dash across to the enemy front line & seize any enemy they may see near their point of entry. If recently killed Germans are seen in the trench, some identification must be removed from them, if it is impossible to capture a prisoner.

At zero + 5 minutes 44th Trench Mortar Battery will fire 10 rounds rapid at each of the points of entry. This will be repeated at zero + 10 minutes.

III (1) Left Party will start from X sap & proceed in a N.E. direction through the gap in the enemy's wire at I.31.b.8.7. The point of entry into the enemy's trench will be about I 31 b 9.9

Lieut G S M Milne 1 NCO + 4 men of B Coy will form this party. Two of the men will not go through the gap in the wire but will remain at the gap + act as a covering party.

(2) OC D Coy will send out 1 NCO + 2 men with a Lewis Gun from "Y" sap at the same time to a point at the crest of the hill I 31 b 7½.7. to deal with any MG which may open on the raiding party.

(3) During the raid the Stokes will keep up a steady fire on the enemy's trench 100 yards on either side of the point to be entered.

(4) Two Very Lights fired from Y sap towards gap in enemy wire will be the signal to return at Zero + 27 minutes

IV. (1) No 2 Party will start from "V" Sap + proceed in a N E direction through the gap in the enemy's wire at I 32 c ½. 8. The point of entry into the enemy's trench will be about I 32 c 2.8

This party will consist of 1 Officer 1 NCO + 4 men from C Coy

(2) A Lewis Gun at W Sap will cover the rush + open on any machine gun seen firing

(3) Two Very Lights fired from "W" sap towards the gap in the enemy's wire will be the signal to return at Zero + 27 minutes.

V Equipment to be carried –

Rifle + Bayonet
1 Bandolier SAA
2 bombs
Wirecutters
Box Respirator

VI Prisoners to Battn HQ

VII Zero hour will be notified later

VIII Watches will be synchronised at Battn HQ at 12 noon 14th Oct. OC Coys will each send an Officer to attend

IX As a signal to wounded or missing men, the Division on our right is sending up a succession of three RED Very Lights at 4, 8 & 9 pm on the 14th

X ACKNOWLEDGE

C McGeddes CAPTAIN & ADJUTANT
8/10th Gordon Highlanders

Copies to OC Coys
LGO
44th Inf Bde
TM Bty
File

WAR DIARY

Army Form C. 2121.
(In pads of 100.)

"A" Form.
MESSAGES AND SIGNALS.

No. of Message

Prefix Code m. Words. Charge.

Office of Origin and Service Instructions.

Sent At m. To By

This message is on a/c of: [illegible] Service. Recd. at m.

(Sig. of "Franking Officer.")

Date From By

TO { Headquarters [illegible] Inf Brigade

Sender's Number	Day of Month	In reply to Number	AAA
G/138	17		

Report on Operations this afternoon

No 1 party consisting of Lieut G S M Milne, 1 NCO & 4 men started from X sap immediately after the second burst of Stokes at 2.0 + 10 minutes. They proceeded towards the gap at I 31 c 5 7 without being fired on but as soon as an attempt was made to enter the gap a M G opened fire from the left. The party took cover in shell holes preparatory to making

From
Place
Time

The above may be forwarded as now corrected. (Z)

Censor. Sig. of Addressor or person authorised to telegraph in his name.

* This line should be erased if not required.

(27964) Wt. W492/M1647. [E 1187]. 130,000 Pads—5/17. M.R.Co.,Ltd. Forms/C.2121.

"A" Form.

Army Form C. 2121.
(In pads of 100.)

MESSAGES AND SIGNALS. No. of Message..................

Prefix........ Code........m	Words.	Charge.	This message is on a/c of:	Recd. at........m.
Office of Origin and Service Instructions.	Sent		........Service.	Date
	At........m.			From
	To			
	By		(Sig. of "Franking Officer.")	By

TO 2

Sender's Number	Day of Month	In reply to Number	AAA
*			

a dash for the enemy's trench. But when they got up a volley of bombs was thrown and Lieut Milne was killed. The remainder of the party threw several bombs into the trench but evidently no Germans were hit. Three Germans were then seen running back from the front line over the open about 50 yards to the right of our patrol. The enemy had no rifles or equipment, and our patrol sniped one of them. On realising that they

From
Place
Time

The above may be forwarded as now corrected. .... Censor.

(Z) .... Sig. of Addressor or person authorised to telegraph in his name.

* This line should be erased if not required.

(27964) Wt. W492/M1647. [E 1187]. 130,000 Pads—5/17. M.R.Co.,Ltd. Forms/C.2121.

Army Form C. 2121.
(In pads of 100.)

"A" Form.

MESSAGES AND SIGNALS.

No. of Message..........

Prefix.......... Code..........m	Words.	Charge.	This message is on a/c of:	Recd. at..........m.
Office of Origin and Service Instructions.	Sent		..........Service.	Date
	At..........m.			From
	To			
	By		(Sig. of "Franking Officer.")	By

TO

Sender's Number	Day of Month	In reply to Number	AAA
*			

could not enter the trench on account of the bombing and machine gun fire, our party decided to retire. They attempted to pick up Lieut. Milne, but a shower of bombs was thrown at them, and another man wounded. The patrol then returned.

The enemy's wire was found to be very strong but the gap had been well cut. The enemy were very much on the alert.

Lieut. Milne's body will be brought in by our patrols tonight

From			
Place			
Time			

The above may be forwarded as now corrected. (Z)

Censor. Sig. of Addressor or person authorised to telegraph in his name.

* This line should be erased if not required.

(27964) Wt. W492/M1647. [E 1187]. 130,000 Pads—5/17. M.R.Co.,Ltd. Forms/C.2121.

"A" Form. Army Form C. 2121. (In pads of 100.)

MESSAGES AND SIGNALS. No. of Message ....

Prefix .... Code .... m	Words.	Charge.	This message is on a/c of:	Recd. at .... m.
Office of Origin and Service Instructions.	Sent		.... Service.	Date ....
	At .... m.			From ....
	To			
	By		(Sig. of "Franking Officer.")	By ....

TO

Sender's Number	Day of Month	In reply to Number	AAA
*			

No. 2 Party:—

Started from V. Sap. They had to get out several minutes before their time as the Thermite was falling in our own trenches. The Party consisted of 2/LT J.B. SIMPSON, 1 NCO + 11 men. They made a dash for the gap at I.32.C.4.8. But before they got within 30 yards of it Lieut Simpson and all his men had been wounded by M.G. fire. Even although wounded Lieut Simpson and 2 men made

From

Place

Time

The above may be forwarded as now corrected. (Z)

Censor. Sig. of Addressor or person authorised to telegraph in his name.

* This line should be erased if not required.

(27964) Wt. W492/M1647. [E 1187]. 130,000 Pads—5/17. M.R.Co.,Ltd. Forms/C.2121.

"A" Form.

Army Form C. 2121.
(In pads of 100.)

MESSAGES AND SIGNALS.

No. of Message

Prefix ... Code ... m	Words.	Charge.	This message is on a/c of:	Recd. at ... m.
Office of Origin and Service Instructions.	Sent		... Service.	Date
	At ... m.			From
	To			
	By		(Sig. of "Franking Officer.")	By

TO | | 4 | |

Sender's Number	Day of Month	In reply to Number	AAA

a determined effort to reach the enemy's flank the M G fire however was too heavy and the party withdrew. The wire at this point also was very strong.

Casualties for the two patrols amounted to:—

1 Officer and 1 O.R. killed
1 Officer and 4 O.Rs wounded

(SD) CHARLES REID
Lieut. Col.
Cmdg 5/10 Gordon Highrs

From
Place
Time

The above may be forwarded as now corrected. (Z)

Censor. Sig. of Addressor or person authorised to telegraph in his name.

* This line should be erased if not required.

(27964) Wt. W492/M1647. [E 1187]. 130,000 Pads—5/17. M.R.Co.,Ltd. Forms/C.2121.

SECRET 8/10TH (S) BN. THE GORDON HIGHLANDERS

W.D.

OPERATION ORDER No 119

BY

LIEUT-COLONEL CHARLES REID COMDG.

Appendix 7

TUESDAY 16-10-17

1. The battalion will be relieved in the front line tomorrow, 17th inst, by the 9th Black Watch.

On relief, H.Qrs, C & D Coys will proceed to WILDERNESS CAMP SOUTH, H.31.b.0.3. A Coy will proceed to dug-outs in H.28.c.4.6., where they will be accomodated until further notice. B Coy will take over the accomodation at present occupied by one company, 9th Black Watch, in JOHNSON AVENUE.

No out-going platoon to pass the junction of JOHNSTON and LANCER before 10 am.

ROUTE - LANCER AVENUE - FEUCHY.

A Coy 9th Black Watch will relieve C Coy 8/10th Gordons
C " " " " D
D " " " " A
B " " " " B

2. GUIDES (1 per platoon, 1 per Coy H.Qrs, 2 for Bn H.Qrs, & 2 from A Coy for the A.A. Lewis Gun positions in BAYONET TRENCH) will report to LIEUT A.W. BOYCE at the WATER POINT at 6 am. The party will then proceed to Road Junction, FAMPOUX (H.23.b.3.2) where they will meet the incoming battalion.

Guides from C & D Coy H.Qrs will guide in the A.A. Lewis Guns, which will be found by the Support Coy of the 9th Black Watch (i.e. for the Lewis Guns at C & D Coy H.Qrs respectively).

Guides from D Coy will be at junction of JOHNSON and LANCER at 7.15 am to meet C Coy 9th Black Watch which is at present in JOHNSON AVENUE.

3. MOVEMENT - All movement to be by platoons at 4 minutes interval. Exact timing must be rigidly adhered to. All parties must be preceded by a

Scout, who will secure a free passage for his party. As the relief is to be carried out in daylight, great care must be taken that the enemy does not observe the unusual movement. Lewis Guns, rifles, etc. must not be carried in such a way that they project above the parapet.

4. All trench stores, tools, defence schemes, aeroplane photographs, trench maps, anti-gas appliances, anti-aircraft mountings and sights complete, programmes for work, etc. will be handed over & receipts taken. Lists to be handed in to Orderly Room by 6 pm, 17th inst.

5. Completion of relief will be wired by the code word "RAIN", & also sent by runner.

6. ACKNOWLEDGE.

C A Geddes CAPT & ADJT
8/10TH GORDON HIGHLANDERS

Issued thro' Signals 4-30pm

Copies 1-4 - OC Coys
5 - LGO
6 - MO
7 - Signals
8 - QM & TO
9 - War Diary
10 - File
11 - 9th Black Watch

WAR DIARY
Appendix 8

S E C R E T. Copy No. 9

8/10th (Service) Battalion, The Gordon Highlanders.

O P E R A T I O N O R D E R No.120.

By

Major J.B.Wood, M.C., Comdg

20th Oct. 1917.

1. On 21st Oct. the 8/10th Gordon Highlanders (Support) will be relieved by the 7th Cameron Highlanders (Reserve).

2. Camps will not be changed.

3. B Coy 8/10th Gordons will be relieved by a Company of the 7th Cameron, and on relief will proceed to WILDERNESS CAMP.
Guides from B Coy (1 per platoon) and 1 for Coy H.Qrs.) will be at the junction of JOHNSON AVENUE and LANCER LANE at 3.30 p.m.
All movement to be by platoons at 200 yards interval.

4. Working Parties :
Parties R.E. 1,2,10 & 11 (B Coy), Party R.E.4 (C Coy) and Party "U" (D Coy) will be taken over by the 7th Cameron Highrs. from 4 p.m. to-morrow.

Transport for B Coy's Lewis Guns, dixies, officers' mess kits etc will be at the bottom of LANCER LANE at 4 p.m.

6. Guides for B Coy from WILDERNESS CAMP will be at the bottom of LANCER LANE at 4 p.m.

7. Acknowledge.

(signed) G.P.Geddes,
Captain & Adjutant.

Distribution :
Copy 1 - 4. O.C. Coys.
5. R.S.M.
6. T.O.
7. Q.M.
8. 7th Cameron Highrs.
9. War Diary
10. File.

WAR DIARY
appendix 9

S E C R E T.
8/10th (Service) Battalion, The Gordon Highlanders.

Copy No. WD

O P E R A T I O N   O R D E R   No.121.

Ref. Sheet :
ARRAS,
51B N.W.

By
Major J.B.Wood, M.C., Comdg.

24th Oct 1917.

1. The battalion will be relieved in Brigade Reserve to-morrow, 25th inst., as follows :-

(a) B,C (less 1 platoon) and D Coys and H.Qrs. by three Companies and Headquarters of the 12th H.L.I.
Coys will parade ready to march off at 2-15 p.m., and on relief will proceed by Coys at 5 mins.interval to the GRANARY, ARRAS (beside the Cathedral), taking over the billets vacated by the 10th Scottish Rifles.

(b) A Coy by a company of the 10th Scottish Rifles.

Guides : (1 per platoon and 1 for Coy.H.Qrs.) will meet the relieving company of the Scottish Rifles at Road Junction, FEUCHY, H.21.d.8.0. at 3 p.m.
On relief, A Coy will entrain at Station B.307 (H.27.b.6.9) at 3.45 p.m., and proceed by train to "Q" Dump (ARRAS), G.21.b.9.7. From this point, the company will march to their billets in The GRANARY.
O.C.A Coy will hand over all details of Working Party "A1" to the relieving Commander of the Scottish Rifles.

2. The strictest attention is to be paid to march discipline. Pipers and Drummers will march with their Coys.

3. (a) Training Stores, Bombs, S.A.A., Anti-aircraft Mountings (NOT including sights) and ~~anti-gas appliances~~ will be handed over and receipts obtained.
(B) O.C.A,B,C,D Coys and H.Qrs. will each detail one N.C.O. to report to Lieut.A.W.Boyce at 10.30 a.m. at Orderly Room, WILDERNESS CAMP. This party will take over billets, S.A.A., bomb & training stores in ARRAS from the 10th Scottish Rifles.
(c) Lists of articles handed over and taken over will be forwarded to Battn.H.Qrs. by 10 a.m. 26th inst., together with all Anti-Aircraft Lewis Gun sights on charge.

4. O.C.C Coy will detail one complete platoon (not less than 1 Sgt. and 30 ORs.) to be attached for work to the Inland Water Transport (Party "M").
This platoon will be accomodated by the I.W.T. and will report to them at FAMPOUX LOCK at 3 p.m., 25th inst. I.W.T. will ration this party from 26th Oct. inclusive.
A cook and cooking utensils to be taken.

5. Completion of relief & arrival in billets will be reported at once to Battn.H.Qrs. A Coy will wire relief complete by code word "JOHN".

(signed) G.P.Geddes,
Capt & Adjutant.

Issued through Signals at 5 p.m.
Copies 1 - 4. O.C. Coys, 5 . RSM., 6. L.G.O., 7. QM. 8. T.O.
9. M.O. 10. Signals, 11 & 12. W.D. and File.

CONFIDENTIAL

Vol 30

WAR DIARY

OF

8/10th (Service) Bn, The Gordon Highlanders

PERIOD

1st November 1917 1st December 1917

VOLUME - 31

Instructions regarding War Diaries and Intelligence Summaries are contained in F. S. Regs., Part II. and the Staff Manual respectively. Title pages will be prepared in manuscript.

WAR DIARY
or
INTELLIGENCE SUMMARY.
(Erase heading not required.)

Sheet 431

Army Form C. 2118.

Place	Date	Hour	Summary of Events and Information	Remarks and references to Appendices
ARRAS	1917 Nov. 1.		Training continued.	JBW
	2.		The Battn relieved the 13th Royal Scots in the Left Subsector of Left Sector. Relief carried out expeditiously & unmolested. Battn proceeded by train to Lamfoux.	
	3 & 4.		Both quiet days in the line, except for a little trench mortar & rifle grenading firing of left company, which caused extra work but no casualties.	
	5.		T/Lieut. D. Macfarlane to be T/Captain 15/6/17.	
			Two Patrols from B (left Co.) examined enemy wire opposite them where they found a gap. Both patrols were fired on. An attempt to ~~wire~~ improve our own wire was stopped by the enemy.	
	6		C & D. Cos relieved A & B. in the front line.	
	7		A heavy artillery & trench mortar bombardment of our front system lasting from 1 to 10 p.m. took place. Two posts were destroyed & much damage caused to our front & support lines & communication trenches. Several men were buried but all were rescued alive, & only one had	

Instructions regarding War Diaries and Intelligence Summaries are contained in F. S. Regs., Part II. and the Staff Manual respectively. Title pages will be prepared in manuscript.

WAR DIARY
or
INTELLIGENCE SUMMARY.
(Erase heading not required.)

Sheet No 432 Army Form C. 2118.

Place	Date	Hour	Summary of Events and Information	Remarks and references to Appendices
	1917 Nov 8		to go to Hospital. One man killed on No 10 (our extreme left) Post. Work concentrated on repairing the damage caused by bombardment. An officers Patrol bombed the enemy post at Roeux Bridge at 6·30 pm & again at 5 am on 9th result unknown.	JBW
	9		T/2 Lt K.C. Davidson MC to be T/Lieut. 11/2/17. A quiet day in the line. Some rain which made tracks fall in in parts.	
	10		The Battn was relieved in the front line by 9th Black Watch. During relief duck-board tracks, communication trenches & paths were heavily shelled, & caused about 20 casualties to the incoming Battn & hindered the relief. Battn on relief moved to Brigade Support. Hdqrs Railway Cutting H·23 c (Sheet 51B N.W.) C & D Cos close to Hdqrs B Co in Lancer Lane. A Co. in Stirling Camp (H·13 d).	JBW
	11		The whole Battn employed on working & carrying parties. B Co. greatly improved Lancer Lane which was falling in. Enemy shelled the neighbourhood of Bn Hdqrs & C & D Cos with gas shells	

T2134. Wt. W708–776. 500000. 4/15. Sir J. C. & S.

Instructions regarding War Diaries and Intelligence Summaries are contained in F. S. Regs., Part II. and the Staff Manual respectively. Title pages will be prepared in manuscript.

WAR DIARY
or
INTELLIGENCE SUMMARY.
(Erase heading not required.)

Sheet No 433

Army Form C. 2118.

Place	Date	Hour	Summary of Events and Information	Remarks and references to Appendices
Near Fampoux	1917 Nov 11.		from 2 am on 12th till 4 am. Alarm was quickly given & no casualties were suffered. Sore throats were however common next day.	JOW
	12 & 13.		Working parties continued throughout these days.	
	& 14.		Enemy again shelled our area with gas shells from 3 to 4 am on morning of 13th without however causing any casualties. The gas precautions proved equal to the occasion.	
	14.		The Battn was relieved in support by 7th Cameron Highrs & on relief proceeded to Rifle Camp in G.24.b.8.3 (Sheet 51B NW) Relief was complete by 3 pm & Battn arrived in Rifle Camp by 4 pm. Large working parties were found that night, chiefly carrying up Livens Projectors.	
	15, 16 & 17.		Large working parties were found by the Bn during these days, & those not thus employed were practised in wiring & revetting, the revetting consisting of work on the huts as protection from bombs.	

Instructions regarding War Diaries and Intelligence Summaries are contained in F. S. Regs., Part II. and the Staff Manual respectively. Title pages will be prepared in manuscript.

WAR DIARY
or
INTELLIGENCE SUMMARY.
(Erase heading not required.)

Sheet No 434

Army Form C. 2118.

Place	Date	Hour	Summary of Events and Information	Remarks and references to Appendices
	1917 Nov			
Rifle Camp	18.		The Battn was relieved in Brigade Reserve by 10th Scottish Rifles (46th Bde) & on relief proceeded to billets in the Granary Arras the Bde being now in Divl reserve. Battn arrived in Arras by 3.30pm	
ARRAS.	19.		The Battn being duty Battn of the Bde had to find working parties of over 200. Also a party of 125 proceeded to FEUCHY to work under the New Zea and Tunnellers for 4 days.	
	20, 21 & 22.		Training was carried out as per programme on the Butte de Tir ground, the rifle range & near railway triangle.	JBW
	23.		Training continued. In afternoon Association & Rugby football matches were played against the 9th Gordon Highrs (Pioneers) result Assn 9th Bn 1 goal 8/10th Bn 0. Rugby 9th Bn 14 points, 8/10th Bn 3 points.	
	24.		Training continued. Battn was duty Bn for the Brigade & furnished large working parties.	
	25.		Training continued. Brig. Genl inspected Coys on the rifle range.	

T2134. Wt. W708—776. 500000. 4/15. Sir J. C. & S.

Instructions regarding War Diaries and Intelligence Summaries are contained in F. S. Regs., Part II. and the Staff Manual respectively. Title pages will be prepared in manuscript.

WAR DIARY
or
INTELLIGENCE SUMMARY.
(Erase heading not required.)

Sheet 435

Army Form C. 2118.

Place	Date	Hour	Summary of Events and Information	Remarks and references to Appendices
Arras	1917 Nov 26.		The Bn relieved the 6th Cameron Highrs in Brigade Support & proceeded to Stirling Camp (Hdqrs B & D Coys) two Coys (A & C) in Happy Valley.	
Stirling Camp.	27.		Working Parties found by Bn was the sole amusement of the place, also a few high velocities came within respectable distance	
~~Arras~~	28.		The Bn returned to Arras, the 44th Bde being withdrawn to reserve. Nobody took over Stirling Camp. We returned to the usual billets in the Granary	
	29.		The Bn was allotted the Divl Range for the day, & all Coys proceeded there	JBM
	30		St Andrews Day. Bathing & cleaning up. Hdqrs Mess had as guests for ~~the~~ dinner the Brig Genl Bde Major & Staff Capt & Capt Herbert USA Att. MO. A rattling good night.	
	Decr 1		The Bn relieved the 6th Camerons in the left Sector of the Left Brigade	

T2134. Wt. W708—776. 500000. 4/15. Sir J. C. & S.

CONFIDENTIAL Vol 31

WAR DIARY

OF

8/10th (Service) Battalion, THE GORDON HIGHLANDERS

For Period

2nd December 1917 31st December 1917

VOLUME 32.

Instructions regarding War Diaries and Intelligence Summaries are contained in F. S. Regs., Part II. and the Staff Manual respectively. Title pages will be prepared in manuscript.

WAR DIARY
or
INTELLIGENCE SUMMARY.
(Erase heading not required.)

Sheet 436

Army Form C. 2118.

Place	Date	Hour	Summary of Events and Information	Remarks and references to Appendices
Trenches –	2nd to 4th		The Battalion held the front line trenches in the left sector of the left Brigade – much work was done on the trenches. The weather was fine. Casualties – On the 3rd 3 men wounded. " On the 4th 7 men wounded (6 gassed)	[illegible] Maj.
"	5th	5 pm.	B and D. Companies relieved A and C. Companies. The relief was carried out quietly and without casualties.	[illegible] Maj.
"	6th to 8th.		Work on trenches continued. The weather continued fine. Casualties. On the 6th 3 men killed and 4 wounded (3 gassed)	[illegible] Maj.
"	9th		On the night of the 9th the Battalion was relieved in the front line by the 8th Seaforth Highlanders, and withdrew to the support battalion area in NORTHUMBERLAND AVENUE and LEMON TRENCH. The relief was carried out quietly. Casualties – 1 man wounded.	O.O. 132 – [illegible] Maj.
"	10th to 13th		The Battalion remained in support: during this period an attack by the enemy was considered probable, and the Battalion "Stood to" for 3 hours every morning. On the 12th Lt Colonel D. McLEOD. DSO was admitted to Field Ambce suffering from pneumonia following on gas poisoning and Major C. REID assumed command.	[illegible] Maj.

T2134. Wt. W708–776. 500000. 4/15. Sir J. C. & S.

Sheet 437

Army Form C. 2118.

WAR DIARY
or
INTELLIGENCE SUMMARY.
(Erase heading not required.)

Instructions regarding War Diaries and Intelligence Summaries are contained in F. S. Regs., Part II. and the Staff Manual respectively. Title pages will be prepared in manuscript.

Place	Date	Hour	Summary of Events and Information	Remarks and references to Appendices
Trenches	13th		On the night of the 13th the Battalion relieved the 7th Cameron Highlanders in the right sector of the left Brigade.	O.O. 133. [illegible]
"	13th to 17th		The Battalion held the front line Trenches. Much work was completed during this period.	[illegible]
			Casualties. on the 14th 1 man wounded.	
			" on the 15th 6 men wounded.	
			" on the 17th 1 man killed.	
"	17th		On the 17th the Battalion was relieved by the 7th/8th K.O.S.B. and returned to billets in the GRANARY ARRAS.	O.O. 134 [illegible]
ARRAS.	18th		Battalion in rest.	
"	19th		" " " Lt. Colonel D. McLEOD DSO died of pneumonia following on gas poisoning in No 8 C.C.S.	
"	20th		" " " Battalion on Brigade Duty.	[illegible]
			Training, musketry and route-marching carried on.	
			A and B Coys held their Christmas dinners.	
"	21st		" " " Training continued. C and D Companies held Christmas dinners	

T2134. Wt. W708—776. 500000. 4/15. Sir J. C. & S.

Instructions regarding War Diaries and Intelligence Summaries are contained in F. S. Regs., Part II. and the Staff Manual respectively. Title pages will be prepared in manuscript.

WAR DIARY
or
INTELLIGENCE SUMMARY.
(Erase heading not required.)

Sheet 438.

Army Form C. 2118.

Place	Date	Hour	Summary of Events and Information	Remarks and references to Appendices
ARRAS	21st		Major Lord DUDLEY GORDON D.S.O. assumed Command of the Battalion.	
			Funeral of Lt Colonel D McLEOD D.S.O. at No 8 C.C.S. DUISANS.	[illegible]
			Lt. A.W. BOYCE appointed assistant Adjutant with effect from 2nd December.	
" "	22nd		Training continued.	
			Major C. REID assumed the duties of 2nd in command.	
			Capt. J.B. WOOD M.C. assumed Command of A Company vice Capt. J. LYNN. M.C.	
			The undermentioned officers are mentioned in Field Marshal Sir DOUGLAS HAIG'S despatches dated 21st December for gallant service and devotion to duty in the field.	
			Major Lord DUDLEY GORDON DSO.	[illegible]
			" J. G. THOM. DSO MC.	
			" C. REID.	
			Capt F.J.C. MOFFAT D.S.O.	
			Capt and Adjt. G.P. GEDDES DSO.	
			Lieut A.W. BOYCE	
			No S/1709 CQMS J F KEIR, S/6943 CQMS J HANNIGAN. and S/1869 Sgt J. BRYCE.	

Instructions regarding War Diaries and Intelligence Summaries are contained in F. S. Regs., Part II. and the Staff Manual respectively. Title pages will be prepared in manuscript.

WAR DIARY
or
INTELLIGENCE SUMMARY.
(Erase heading not required.)

Army Form C. 2118.

Sheet 439.

Place	Date	Hour	Summary of Events and Information	Remarks and references to Appendices
	Dec.			
ARRAS.	23rd		The Battalion relieved the 13th Royal Scots in the trenches as Support Battalion of the right section of the Divisional Front. The relief was carried out without incident.	O.O. 135 [illegible]
Trenches		6-40pm.	At 6.40 pm. the enemy put down a heavy barrage on the front and support lines of the right battalion. The S.O.S. signal was sent up and the Battalion "stood to". By 7.15 pm all was comparatively quiet.	
Trenches	24th		The Battalion took over F (Island) post from the 9th Black Watch. Wiring and work on trenches continued. Weather very cold. Snow and hard frost.	
Trenches.	25th and 26th		Work on trenches and wiring continued. Casualties. on 26th 1 man wounded. Enemys artillery broke the ice on lagoon south of Island post: he appeared to anticipate an attack across the ice.	[illegible]
Trenches	27th		The Battalion relieved the 9th Black Watch in the front trenches in the left section of the right subsector. after dusk. The relief was carried out without any casualties although there was a considerable amount of shelling at the time.	O.O. 136

Instructions regarding War Diaries and Intelligence Summaries are contained in F. S. Regs., Part II. and the Staff Manual respectively. Title pages will be prepared in manuscript.

WAR DIARY
or
INTELLIGENCE SUMMARY.
(Erase heading not required.)

Sheet. 440.

Army Form C. 2118.

Place	Date	Hour	Summary of Events and Information	Remarks and references to Appendices
Trenches	Dec. 27th		Dispositions. A. B. and D. Companies in front line C. Company in ROEUX Caves.	
"	28th		Wiring and work on trenches carried out. Enemy showed considerable activity with Trench Mortars and aerial darts: Casualties 1 man killed.	
"	29th		Work on trenches continued. Weather still very cold.	
"	30th		" " " " " "	
			Officers of 2nd Irish Guards came up to reconnoitre the line.	[illegible] Maj.
"	31st.		Work on trenches continued. The pipe band of the Battalion came up to ROEUX caves, where they played a programme of music from 11 pm. till 12-15 am on the 1st. Casualty on 31st 1 man wounded.	

T2134. Wt. W708—776. 500000. 4/15. Sir J. C. & S.

SECRET

Copy No......11...

8/10th (Service) Battalion, The Gordon Highlanders.

OPERATION ORDER No.132.

By

Lieut-Colonel D.Macleod, D.S.O., Comdg.

8th Decr. 1917.

1. The battalion will be relieved in the Left Sub-Sector on the 9th December by the 8th Seaforth Highlanders, commencing at 4.30 p.m.

A Coy 8th Seaforth Highrs relieving B Coy 8/10th Gordon Highrs.
B " " " " " D " " " "
C " " " " " A " " " "
D " " " " " C " " " "

2. The Right Front Coy will remain in position until all Posts of the relieving Coy are in position, then file out by platoons down CURSE and CALEDONIA AVENUE.

The Left Front Coy will act similarly, filing out by CIVIL AVENUE with its Left leading.

A and C Coys will go out by CIVIL and CALEDONIA AVENUE respectively, 200 yards being maintained between platoons.

3. All trench stores, tools, air photographs, trench maps and anti-gas appliances will be handed over to the relieving unit.

4. On relief, the battalion will move into Brigade Support, at N.11.c.7.8. to replace the 9th Black Watch.

5. An advance party of 1 N.C.O. and 1 man per Coy and Bn. H.Qrs. under Lieut. A.WILSON will rendezvous at junction of CIVIL AVENUE and HUMID TRENCH at 9 a.m., and will report at H.Qrs. 9th Black Watch, N.11.c.7.8. at 10 a.m. to take over stores and accomodation; and afterwards meet their respective Coys at the junction of HUDSON TRENCH and CLYDE AVENUE to act as guides.

6. O.C. C Coy will detail 2 Lewis Guns and teams complete, also 7 N.C.Os. and 38 men to relieve guards now furnished by the Black Watch. These will also march under Lieut. WILSON, reporting to him at the same place and at the same time as the advance party.

7. Receipts in duplicate for all stores taken over and handed over to reach Bn. H.Qrs. by 9 a.m. on 10th December.

8. Completion of relief will be reported to Bn. H.Qrs. by the code word "JOCK".

9. ACKNOWLEDGE.

(Sgd) A.T.Boyce.
Lieut. & Adjutant.

Distribution -
1 - 4 O.C. Coys.
5 Lieut. Wilson
6 Seaforth Highrs.
7 Black Watch.
8 T.O.
9 Q.M.
10 R.S.M.
11 War Diary
12 File
13 Signals
14 Spare.

SECRET Copy No......11....

8/10th (Service) Battalion, The Gordon Highlanders.
OPERATION ORDER No.133

By
Captain J.B. Wood, M.C., Comdg. 12th Decr.1917.

1. The 8/10th Gordon Highlanders will relieve the 7th Cameron Highlanders in the Right sub-sector of the Left Section of the Divisional Front tomorrow, 13th December 1917.

2. DISPOSITIONS -

A Coy Gordons will relieve	C Coy Camerons	in Right Front.
C "	"	"	D "	"	"	Left Front.
D "	"	"	B "	"	"	Support.
H.Qrs.	"	"	H.Qrs.	"		
B Coy	"	"	A Coy	"	"	Reserve.

The relief will be carried out in the above order.

Coys will move up in the following order of Posts, which must be organised beforehand :-

A Coy - 1A, 1B, 2, 2A, 2B, 3, 3A.
C Coy - 4, 4A, 4B, 4C, 4D, 5, 5A, 5B, 6.
D Coy - Strong Point "C" (garrison - 1 platoon), Strong Point "D" (garrison - 1 platoon and extra Lewis Gun) remainder of D Coy.
Headquarters.
B Coy.

3. GUIDES - 1 per platoon for each of the 2 Front Coys, and 1 for each Strong Point will be at the junction of CAMEL TRENCH and CADIZ TRENCH at 4.30 p.m.

ROUTE - NORTHUMBERLAND AVENUE and CAMEL TRENCH.
Starting time - 4.15 p.m.

4. Every Precaution will be taken to conceal movement during relief from hostile observation. Lewis Guns, rifles, etc., will not be carried in such a way that they project over the Parapet.

5. Trench Stores, defence schemes, tools, position calls, anti-aircraft poles and mountings with sights, and anti-gas appliances, will be taken over and receipts given. Lists to be forwarded to the Orderly Room by 9 a.m., 14th December.

6. 1 N.C.O. per Coy, 1 from H.Qrs., and 1 for each Strong Point, and the Nos. 1 of the Lewis Guns of each Front Coy and Strong Points will proceed at 1 p.m. to take over stores.

7. Completion of relief will be notified to Bn. H.Qrs. by the code word "JOE".

8. ACKNOWLEDGE.

(Sgd) A.W.Boyce,
Lieut. & Adjutant.

Distribution -
1 - 4 O.C. Coys.
5 L.G.O.
6 R.S.M.
7 Q.M.
8 T.O.
9 Signals
10 7th Camerons.
11 War Diary
12 File
13 Spare.

SECRET Copy No. 10

8/10th (Service) Battalion, The Gordon Highlanders.

OPERATION ORDER No.134.

By 16th Dec. 1917.

Major Charles Reid, Comdg.

1. The 8/10th Gordon Highlanders will be relieved by 7/8th K.O.S.Bs. in the Right sub-sector on the 17/18th December.

2. DISPOSITIONS:

A Coy 8/10th Gordons	will be relieved by	C Coy 7/8th K.O.S.Bs.
C " " "	" " "	D " " "
D " " "	" " "	B " " "
H.Q. " "	" " "	H.Q. " "
B Coy " "	" " "	A Coy " "

The relief will be carried out in the above order.

Relieving Coys will move up in the order of Posts, The garrisons of which must be organised beforehand.

3. GUIDES -
1 per platoon, 1 per Coy H.Qrs., and 3 from Bn.H.Qrs. will rendezvous at Bn.H.Qrs. at 4 p.m. under an N.C.O. to be detailed by O.C. B Coy. Party complete will then proceed to SIMPLE ARCH to guide the incoming units.

4. ROUTE -
Right Front Coy - CAMEL, CROOK, COLD, CORK.
Left Front Coy - CAMEL, COLD, CURLY, CRANK.
Support Coy - CADIZ, CAMEL.
Reserve Coy - COLT, CAMEL.

5. All trench stores, defence schemes, tools, position calls, anti-aircraft poles and mounting with sights, and anti-gas appliances will be handed over and receipts taken. Lists to be forwarded to Orderly Room by 9 a.m., 18th December.

6. On relief, the 8/10th Gordons will move into Brigade Reserve in the GRANARY, ARRAS.

7. ROUTE OUT -
A Coy - COLD ALLEY, CROOK ALLEY, CAMEL, } QUARRY, FAMPOUX LOCK, TOWING
C Coy - CASH ALLEY, CALICO, CAMEL. } PATH, ATHIES LOCK

8. Completion of relief will be notified to Bn.H.Qrs. by the code word "FRITZ".

9. Arrival in new area will be reported by Coys to Bn.H.Qrs.

10. ACKNOWLEDGE.

(Sgd) A.W. Boyce.
Lieut. & Adjutant.

Distribution -
1 - 4 O.C.Coys.
5 L.G.O.
6 R.S.M.
7 T.O.
8 Q.M.
9 K.O.S.Bs.
10 War Diary
11 File.
12 Signals.
13 Spare.

SECRET. Copy No. ______

8/10th (Service) Battalion, The Gordon Highlanders.

OPERATION ORDER No. 135.

By

Major the Lord Dudley Gordon, DSO. Comdg.

22nd Dec. 1917.

1. The 8/10th Gordon Highlanders will relieve the 13th Royal Scots as Support Battalion of the Right Section of the Divisional Front, to-morrow, 23rd Dec.
   "A" Coy 8/10th Gordons will relieve "A" Coy, 13th Royal Scots.
   "B" Coy " " " " "B" Coy, " " "
   "C" Coy " " " " "C" Coy, " " "
   "D" Coy " " " " "D" Coy, " " "

2. Dispositions :-

   A Coy to CORDITE RESERVE, astride CORFE AVENUE.
   C Coy to CRUMP TRENCH from H.24.b.8.1 to CORONA SWITCH.
   B Coy to "K","L","M" Posts in LANCER AVENUE, with 1 platoon South of PELVES LANE.
   D Coy to LANCER AVENUE between Road Junction H.29.b.7.5 and PELVES LANE.
   Bn.H.Q. to Railway Cutting at H.23 central.

   A Coy will also take over the anti-aircraft Lewis Gun positions at Left Battn.H.Qrs. in CRETE TRENCH and at I.13.c.95.22.

3. Guides :

   A Coy : 1 per platoon and 1 for each A.A.Lewis Gun position will be at TRIPLE ARCH at 9.40 a.m.

   B & D Coys : 1 per platoon will be at the foot of the Staircase at H.23.c.35.90 (on the FEUCHE Road) at 10.30 a.m.

   C Coy : 1 per platoon will be at TRIPLE ARCH at 4.15 p.m.

   Times above are to be rigidly adhered to. Companies will not arrive at the rendezvous before the specified hour, nor are they to be halted on the way up except for the usual hourly halts.

4. An advanced party of 2 N.C.Os. and of 2/Lieut.F.W.LOVIE and 1 N.C.O. from H.Qrs. will proceed with B Coy in the morning to take over stores etc. from C Coy and H.Qrs. of the Royal Scots.

5. Hours of parade and arrangements for trains will be notified later.

6. All movement East of the N.& S.Grid Line between map squares G & H. will be by platoons at 4 minutes' interval.
   Every precaution will be taken to conceal movement during the relief from hostile observation. Lewis Gun, rifles etc. will not be carried in such a way that they project over the parapet.
   Should enemy aircraft come over in daylight whilst relief is in progress all movement will cease at once, and will not be resumed until the aeroplane is out of view.

7. (i) Trench stores, Battn.Defence Schemes, air photographs, tools, position calls, anti-aircraft poles and mountings (but NOT sights) in position, and anti-gas appliances will be taken over and receipts given.
   (ii) Reserve S.A.A., grenades, billets and training stores will be handed over by Lieut.A.W.Boyce and receipts obtained.
   (iii) Lists of all articles taken over and handed over will be forwarded to Battn.H.Qrs. by 10 a.m., 24th inst.

8. Instructions for the relief of Working Parties will be issued separately.

9. Completion of relief will be notified to Battn.H.Qrs. by the Code Word "ARCHIE".

10. Acknowledge.

(signed) G.P.Geddes,
Captain & Adjutant.

Copies to O C'Coys, 2nd in Command, L.G.O.
Sniping Officer, M.O., Q.M., T.O.
R.S.M., Signals, W.D., File.

Copy No. ....

S E C R E T.

8/10th (Service) Battalion, The Gordon Highlanders.

O P E R A T I O N   O R D E R   No.136

By

Major the Lord Dudley Gordon, D.S.O., Comdg.

26th Dec. 1917.

1. The 8/10th Gordon Highrs. will relieve the 9th Black Watch in the Left Section of the Right Sub-Sector to-morrow, 27th Dec.

A Coy	8/10th	Gordon	Highrs.	will	relieve	A Coy,	9th	Black	Watch.
C Coy	"	"	"	"	"	C Coy,	"	"	"
Bn. H. Qrs.	"	"	"	"	"	Bn. H. Q.,	"	"	"
B Coy,	"	"	"	"	"	B Coy	"	"	"
D Coy	"	"	"	"	"	D Coy	"	"	"

The relief will be carried out in the above order.

2. Dispositions :

A Coy .... Left Front (Posts 42 - 48 inclusive).
B Coy .... Centre Front (Posts 36 - 41 inclusive).
D Coy .... Right Front (Posts 28 - 35 inclusive).
C Coy ... Support (BURMA CAVE and Posts S.3 & 4.).
Bn. H. Qrs.... CRETE TRENCH.

Each front line Post consists of 1 N.C.O. and 6 men.
Posts S.3 and 4 of 1 N.C.O. and 3 men.
There is a Lewis Gun in each of Posts 28, 30, 32, 35, 36, 40, 44, 46 and 48.
O.C.Coys will organise their Companies into the above Posts before moving o

3. Guides : (1 per platoon) will be provided as follows :-

A Coy : At A Coy's H.Q. in CORINTH RESERVE at 4 p.m.
C Coy : At C Coy's H.Q. in CRUMP at 4 p.m.
B & D Coys: At Junction of CEYLON and CORONA at 4.30 p.m.

4. Routes :

A Coy. ...... CORFU.
C Coy. ...... CORONA SWITCH and CORONA SUPPORT.
Bn.H.Qrs. ...... Railway - SINGLE ARCH.
B Coy. ...... LANCER - Railway - TRIPLE ARCH - CEYLON - CORONA SUPPORT - CORFU.
D Coy. ...... LANCER - Railway - TRIPLE ARCH - CEYLON - CORONA SUPPORT - CABBAGE.

5. "F" Post will be relieved by the 9th Black Watch before dawn to-morrow. O.C.C.Company will arrange for a guide to be at "C" Coy H.Q. in CRUMP at 6.15 a.m.

6. All Trench stores, tools, A.A.mountings and sights, air photos, Defence Schemes, will be taken over and receipts forwarded to Orderly Room by 9 p.m., 28th Dec.

7. O.C.Coys will each detail 1 Sergeant to proceed in advance to take over stores etc. They will report to 2/Lieut.F.W.LOVIE at the H.Q., 9th Black Watch at 1 p.m.
An Advanced Party of 1 N.C.O. and 1 man from each Coy, 9th Black Watch, will report at corresponding H.Qrs. 8/10th Gordon Highrs. and take over all stores etc.

8. Completion of relief will be wired to Bn. H.Qrs. by the Code word "WILLIE".

9. ACKNOWLEDGE.

(sgd) G.F.Geddes, Capt & Adjt.

Distribution : Copies 1 - 4. O.C.Coys, 5. 2nd in Command, 6. L.G.O.,
7. Intell.Offr., 8. R.S.M., 9. Signals, 10. Q.M.
11. T.O., 12. 9th Black Watch, 13 & 14. W.D. & File.

44 Inf Bde
15

CONFIDENTIAL

Vol 32

WAR-DIARY

OF

8/10th (Service) Battn., The Gordon Highlanders

For Period

2nd January, 1918 — 31st January, 1918.

VOLUME 33.

SECRET. No. 18

8/10th (Service) Battalion, The Gordon Highlanders.

OPERATION ORDER No.137.

By

Major the Lord Dudley Gordon, D.S.O., Comdg.

30th Dec.1917

1. The 8/10th Gordon Highlanders will be relieved in the Left Sub-Sector on the night of the 2nd January 1918, by the 2nd Irish Guards.
On relief, the battalion will proceed to the GRANARY, ARRAS.

Left Front - C Coy, 8/10th Gordons will be relieved by No.4 Coy, Irish Guards.
Centre " - B Coy, " " " " " " No.2 Coy, " "
Right Centre Front -
D Coy " " " " " " No.1 Coy, " "
Bn.H.Qrs. " " " " " " Bn.H.Q., " "
Support - A Coy " " " " " " No.3 Coy, " "
The relief will be carried out in the above order.

2. Guides : 1 per platoon and 1 for each Coy.H.Qrs., 2 for Battn.H.Qrs., and 1 for each anti-aircraft Lewis Gun position (In CORFU - I.13.c.25.32; and CORONA SUPPORT - I.19.b.51.48) will rendezvous at Battn.H.Qrs. under 2/Lieut.E.W.Lovie at 3.45 p.m. Guides will then proceed to A.10 station - H.22.b.0.3., where they will meet the incoming battalion at 4.30 p.m.
O.C.Coys must ensure that the most thoroughly reliable guides are selected, and that routes specified in Para 3 are reconnoitred by day and by night.

3. Routes :

(a) IN : No.4 Coy Irish Guards : via CANAL BANK to SINGLE ARCH - Road to CORFU AVENUE - CORONA SUPPORT - COCOA.
No.2 Coy : CANAL BANK to TRIPLE ARCH - CEYLON AVENUE - CORONA SUPPORT - CORFU AVENUE.
No.1 Coy : CANAL BANK to TRIPLE ARCH - CEYLON AVENUE - CORONA SUPPORT - CABBAGE.
Bn.H.Qrs : CANAL BANK TO SINGLE ARCH - CRETE TRENCH.
No.3 Coy : CANAL BANK to TRIPLE ARCH - CEYLON AVENUE - CORONA SUPPORT.

(b) OUT : C Coy, 8/10 G.H. : CORONA SUPPORT - CORFU - SINGLE ARCH - RED HOUSE.
B Coy : CORONA SUPPORT - CORFU - SINGLE ARCH - RED HOUSE.
D Coy : CEYLON - TRIPLE ARCH - RED HOUSE.
Bn.H.Q. : SINGLE ARCH - RED HOUSE.
A Coy : ST.PLEASANT CAVE - CORDITE - CEYLON - TRIPLE ARCH - RED HOUSE.
"B" Post : The garrison of "B" Post will come in and go out by CHEMICAL TRENCH.

4. All movement East of the N & S.Grid Line between map squares "G" and "H" will be by platoons at 4 minutes interval; West of this line - by companies at 200 yards interval.

5. All trench stores, tools, S.A.A. and explosive stores, anti-aircraft mountings (but NOT sights), anti-gas appliances, Battn.Defence Schemes, air photographs, trench maps, artillery programmes, position calls, will be handed over and receipts obtained.
Lists, in duplicate, of all stores taken over will reach Bn.H.Q. by 10 a.m., 3rd Jan.

6. Lieut.A.WILSON will proceed in advance to take over Reserve S.A.A., Grenades, billets and training stores in ARRAS.
Lists, in duplicate, of all stores taken over will reach Bn.H.Q. as per para 5.

7. Completion of relief will be wired to Bn.H.Q. by code word "TAM".

8. Acknowledge.

(sgd) G.P.Geddes, Capt & Adjt.

Distribution : Copies 1 - 4. O.C., A,B,C,D Coys. 5. 2nd in Command, 6. L.G.O., 7. Sniping Officer, 8. Q.M., 9. T.O. 10. M.O., 11. Signals, 12. R.S.M. 13. 2nd Irish Guards, 14. 1st Scots Guards, 15. 8th Black Watch, 16. 7th Camerons. "D" Coy, 7th Camerons, 17. War Diary, 18. File.

CONFIDENTIAL

WAR DIARY

OF

8/10th (Service) Battalion, The Gordon Highlanders

For PERIOD

1st February, 1918 - 28th February, 1918

VOLUME - 34.

Instructions regarding War Diaries and Intelligence Summaries are contained in F. S. Regs., Part II. and the Staff Manual respectively. Title pages will be prepared in manuscript.

WAR DIARY
or
INTELLIGENCE SUMMARY.
(*Erase heading not required.*)

Shet 444

Army Form C. 2118.

Place	Date	Hour	Summary of Events and Information	Remarks and references to Appendices
	1918			
ARRAS.	Feb 1st	11 am.	Inspection of Battalion Transport by B.G.C.	
"	" 2nd		An inter-platoon competition was held on the BUTTE DE TIR. Marks were given for drill, turnout, kit inspection etc. Winning platoon No 8 platoon commanded by 2/Lieut. A.J.F. DUNCAN.	[illegible]
"	" 3rd		Elimination competitions of Brigade inter-platoon rifle competitions on Divisional Range.	
"	4th		Finals of Brigade interplatoon rifle competitions.	
TRENCHES	5th		The Battalion relieved the 1st Bn KINGS OWN Regiment and one Company 2nd ESSEX regiment, becoming Support Battalion of the right Brigade 15th Division. The battalion furnished working parties during the night. The relief was carried out without incident.	O.O. 157 [illegible]
"	6th		Wiring and work on trenches continued. Enemy artillery showed considerable activity during the day. Lieut C.B McFARLANE and one man wounded.	[illegible]
"	7th		Wiring and work on trenches continued.	
"	8th		At dawn the German Artillery commenced a heavy bombardment of our support and reserve trenches which continued till 7 am when it	

Instructions regarding War Diaries and Intelligence Summaries are contained in F. S. Regs., Part II. and the Staff Manual respectively. Title pages will be prepared in manuscript.

WAR DIARY
or
INTELLIGENCE SUMMARY.
(Erase heading not required.)

Sheet 445.

Army Form C. 2118.

Place	Date	Hour	Summary of Events and Information	Remarks and references to Appendices
	1918 Feb-			
TRENCHES.	8th Cont.		gradually died away. By 7-15 am all was quiet.	
"	9th		Work on trenches continued: Battalion Headquarters was heavily shelled from 2.30 - 4 pm.	[illegible]
"	10th		Work on trenches continued.	
"	11th		Army Commander visited trenches held by the Battalion.	
			The Battalion relieved the 8th Seaforth Highlanders in the front line, after dark. The relief was completed without incident.	O.O. 138 [illegible]
"	12th		Hostile Artillery fired on our trenches intermittently during the day.	
"	13th		Work on trenches continued. Hostile Artillery fairly active. 1 man killed & 5 wounded by shell fire near PICK CAVE.	
"	14th		Hostile Artillery quieter. Lieut KEMP wounded while on patrol during the night.	
"	15th		Work on trenches continued. Our trench mortars were active and caused the enemy casualties.	[illegible]
"	16th		Work on trenches continued. Weather bright & clear. Artillery on both sides more active.	
"	17th		Weather continued bright. Hostile artillery active. A German who attempted	

T2134. Wt. W708—776. 500000. 4/15. Sir J. C. & S.

Instructions regarding War Diaries and Intelligence Summaries are contained in F. S. Regs., Part II. and the Staff Manual respectively. Title pages will be prepared in manuscript.

WAR DIARY
or
INTELLIGENCE SUMMARY.
(Erase heading not required.)

Sheet 446 -

Army Form C. 2118.

Place	Date	Hour	Summary of Events and Information	Remarks and references to Appendices
	Feb			
TRENCHES	17th	cont.	to cross over to our lines at dawn was shot.	
			The Battalion was relieved after dark by the 7th Cameron Highlanders, and withdrawn into reserve in the Bois des BOEUFS. The relief was carried out without incident.	OO 141.
BOIS DE BOEUFS CAMP.	18th to 22nd.		The Battalion remained in reserve. Working parties were furnished day & night for work in the line. Training was carried on: musketry, Lewis gun etc.	
TRENCHES	23rd	Feb.	The Battalion relieved the 8th Seaforth Highlanders on this date, taking up positions in Support. An enemy relief was discovered to be taking place the same night & our relief was held up to allow the Artillery to bombard enemy positions.	O.O. 142
"	25th	"	Companies in Brown Line were bombarded with 5.9s at two periods of the day.	
"	26th	"	Brown Line was again shelled, but no damage done.	
"	27th	"	Enemy Artillery was active all day shelling especially	

T2134. Wt. W708—776. 500000. 4/15. Sir J. C. & S.

WAR DIARY
or
INTELLIGENCE SUMMARY. Sheet 447.
(Erase heading not required.)

Army Form C. 2118.

Instructions regarding War Diaries and Intelligence Summaries are contained in F. S. Regs., Part II. and the Staff Manual respectively. Title pages will be prepared in manuscript.

Place	Date	Hour	Summary of Events and Information	Remarks and references to Appendices
Trenches	Feb 27	contd.	Support line from Pick to Cambrai Road. This was apparently retaliation for our shelling enemy T.M's as it took place several times during the day after we had finished firing.	E.W.L.
"	28th		A barrage was put down on our forward area during the afternoon. During the time we were in Support working parties were provided by day & night.	

T2134. Wt. W708—776. 500000. 4/15. Sir J. C. & S.

44th Brigade.

15th Division.

8th/10th BATTALION

THE GORDON HIGHLANDERS

M A R C H 1 9 1 8

Appendices attached:-

Report on Operations 21st-29th March.
Congratulatory Message.

Instructions regarding War Diaries and Intelligence Summaries are contained in F. S. Regs., Part II. and the Staff Manual respectively. Title pages will be prepared in manuscript.

WAR DIARY
or
INTELLIGENCE SUMMARY.
(Erase heading not required.)

44/15 ~~448~~ 8/10 Gordon Highlanders Army Form C. 2118.

Vol 34

Place	Date	Hour	Summary of Events and Information	Remarks and references to Appendices
Trenches	1918 MCH: 1	–	The Battalion remained in the Front Line until 7th March, during which period the enemy were exceedingly quiet + nothing of any importance took place. The enemy opposite our sector appeared as though the country was new to them + exposed themselves freely especially at Dawn. Our Snipers took advantage of every exposure + accounted for a good many.	44 B.L.
"	7th	–	On the night of 7th the Battalion was relieved in the Front Line by the 7th Cameron Highlanders. On completion of the relief, which was without incident, the Battalion moved in small parties to BOIS DES BOEUFS CAMP, then becoming the Reserve Battalion of the Right Brigade.	O.O. 146
Billets	9	–	The men were kept at constant training and with the exception of a few working parties the days were entirely devoted to training.	
TRENCHES	12		On the night of the 12th the Battalion relieved the 8th Seaforth Highlanders in Support, the relief was carried out across country in Artillery Formation, and with the exception of a couple of casualties was without incident.	O.O. 147
	15		The enemy sent over a small balloon containing Propaganda which was brought down	

T2134. Wt. W708—776. 500000. 4/15. Sir J. C. & S.

Instructions regarding War Diaries and Intelligence Summaries are contained in F. S. Regs., Part II. and the Staff Manual respectively. Title pages will be prepared in manuscript.

WAR DIARY
or
INTELLIGENCE SUMMARY.
(Erase heading not required.)

449

Army Form C. 2118.

Place	Date	Hour	Summary of Events and Information	Remarks and references to Appendices
	1918 MCH:			
Trenches	15	-	Just behind our Head Quarters.	
"	21st		The battalion was holding the line South of MONCHY. At about 3 AM the Germans opened a tremendous bombardment which lasted for 4 hours, no infantry attack followed.	[illegible]
"	22/23	Night	Orders were received from Brigade for the Brigade to evacuate the line and to withdraw to the BROWN LINE leaving one company to fight a rearguard action. The withdrawal took place quite orderly and without knowledge of the enemy.	
			On the morning of the 23rd the enemy opened a heavy bombardment assisted by many Trench Mortars which was followed by an Infantry attack. The Company left to fight rearguard action inflicted any casualties on the enemy and then withdrew joining the remainder of the battalion in a camp near TILLOY.	
			About midday on the 23rd orders were received for us to relieve the 7th Bn Cameron Highlanders in Reserve who were in the Army Line	

T2134. Wt. W708—776. 500000. 4/15. Sir J. C. & S.

Instructions regarding War Diaries and Intelligence Summaries are contained in F. S. Regs., Part II. and the Staff Manual respectively. Title pages will be prepared in manuscript.

WAR DIARY
or
INTELLIGENCE SUMMARY.
(Erase heading not required.)

450.

Army Form C. 2118.

Place	Date	Hour	Summary of Events and Information	Remarks and references to Appendices
	March			
Trenches	26		We relieved the 7th Cameron Highlanders again in Support	OO 153
"	28	3 AM	The enemy opened a terrific bombardment consisting of a large amount of gas & H.E. shells which lasted till 7 AM. Soon afterwards an attack was launched under a terrific barrage. The 7th Cameron Highlanders who were then holding the Front line were badly knocked about and we sent two Companies to assist them and who did fine work thus greatly checking the German advance. Fighting continued violently all day and at about 12.30 pm orders were received to withdraw to the Army Line as the enemy had turned the flanks of the Divisions on our Right and Left. This was carried out in good order, the men fighting a heroic rearguard action the whole way. As casualties were heavy the Battalion was relieved by the 8th Bn. Seaforth Highlanders and withdrew to trenches behind TELEGRAPH HILL	Jm. Lt [illegible] OO 154
	29th	4 AM	We were relieved by a Battalion of the CANADIANS, and	

T2134. Wt. W708–776. 500000. 4/15. Sir J. C. & S.

Instructions regarding War Diaries and Intelligence Summaries are contained in F. S. Regs., Part II. and the Staff Manual respectively. Title pages will be prepared in manuscript.

WAR DIARY
or
INTELLIGENCE SUMMARY.
(Erase heading not required.)

451

Army Form C. 2118.

Place	Date	Hour	Summary of Events and Information	Remarks and references to Appendices
Trenches	29th		we proceeded and occupied trenches West of BAILLEUL.	JM. [illegible]
			At night we were again relieved by a Battalion of CANADIANS	OO.155
			and returned to ARRAS where we were billeted in the	
			HOTEL DE VILLE	
	30th		The men rested all day.	
	31st		The Battalion again moved into the line to relieve a	
			Battalion of the 45th Infantry Brigade (6th Cameron Highrs.)	
			During operations the Battalion suffered the following	
			casualties: OFFICERS - 2/Lt G.R. McGECHAN - Killed; Wounded	
			Lieutenants: K.A. ROBERTSON - R BUNTINE - J.W.T. LEITH, MC.	
			A.J.F. DUNCAN - T.E. FORSTER.	
			OTHER RANKS. Killed 25	
			Wounded 193	
			Missing 79	
			The following letter was received by Major Charles REID who	
			was in command of the Battalion during the battle:	

T2134. Wt. W708—776. 500000. 4/15. Sir J. C. & S.

Instructions regarding War Diaries and Intelligence Summaries are contained in F. S. Regs., Part II. and the Staff Manual respectively. Title pages will be prepared in manuscript.

WAR DIARY
or
INTELLIGENCE SUMMARY.
(Erase heading not required.)

Army Form C. 2118.

452.

Place	Date	Hour	Summary of Events and Information	Remarks and references to Appendices
			" My dear Major, " I wish to send you my sincerest congratulations, and to thank " you and all ranks under your command for the grand work " during the whole of this last tour of two months, which " culminated in the gallant fight put up by your Battalion " on the 28th, and I consider that it was entirely due to this " fight that the 15th Division was practically saved from " destruction, or at any rate from retirement." " I should like to convey to all ranks in your battalion my " sincerest sympathies with them for their losses, and the " many friends they have left behind in the great struggle." " The Divisional Commander today, in expressing his thanks " for the work of the 44th Infantry Brigade, in all sincerity " told me that your work had saved ARRAS." " Yours very sincerely " (Sd) Edward HILLIAN."	[illegible]

T2134. Wt. W708—776. 500000. 4/15. Sir J. C. & S.

[illegible] 8/10 Gordon Hghrs

Operation Order No. 153
by Major Charles Reid Comdg.

25.3.18.

1. The 8/10 Gordon Hghrs will relieve the 7th Cameron Hghrs in Support [illegible] 25th March. Relief to [illegible] at dusk.

2. Dispositions.

A Coy will relieve A Coy Camerons [illegible] Front.
B " " " [illegible] " [illegible]
C " " " C " [illegible]
D " " " [illegible] " [illegible] Support.
H.Q. at N.8.a.5.3

3. Coys will move off in the order A, C, B & D. Leading Coy to move off at 8.15pm.
Movement to be by platoons at 100 yards interval.

4. S.A.A. & tools details of work will be handed over, ~~also tools~~ and taken over. Receipts to be forwarded to O.R. by 9am 26th.

5. Rations will arrive at Bn. H.Q. at 10 pm. Parties will be detailed from each Coy. to draw them.

6. [illegible] AIRY COTTAGE at 10.30 pm. [illegible] Coys will [illegible] their parties to be [illegible] water.

7. Relief complete to be sent to Bn. H.Q. by the code word [illegible].

8. Acknowledge.

G.P. Geddes
Capt. & Adjt.

5.15 pm   8/10 Gordon Highrs

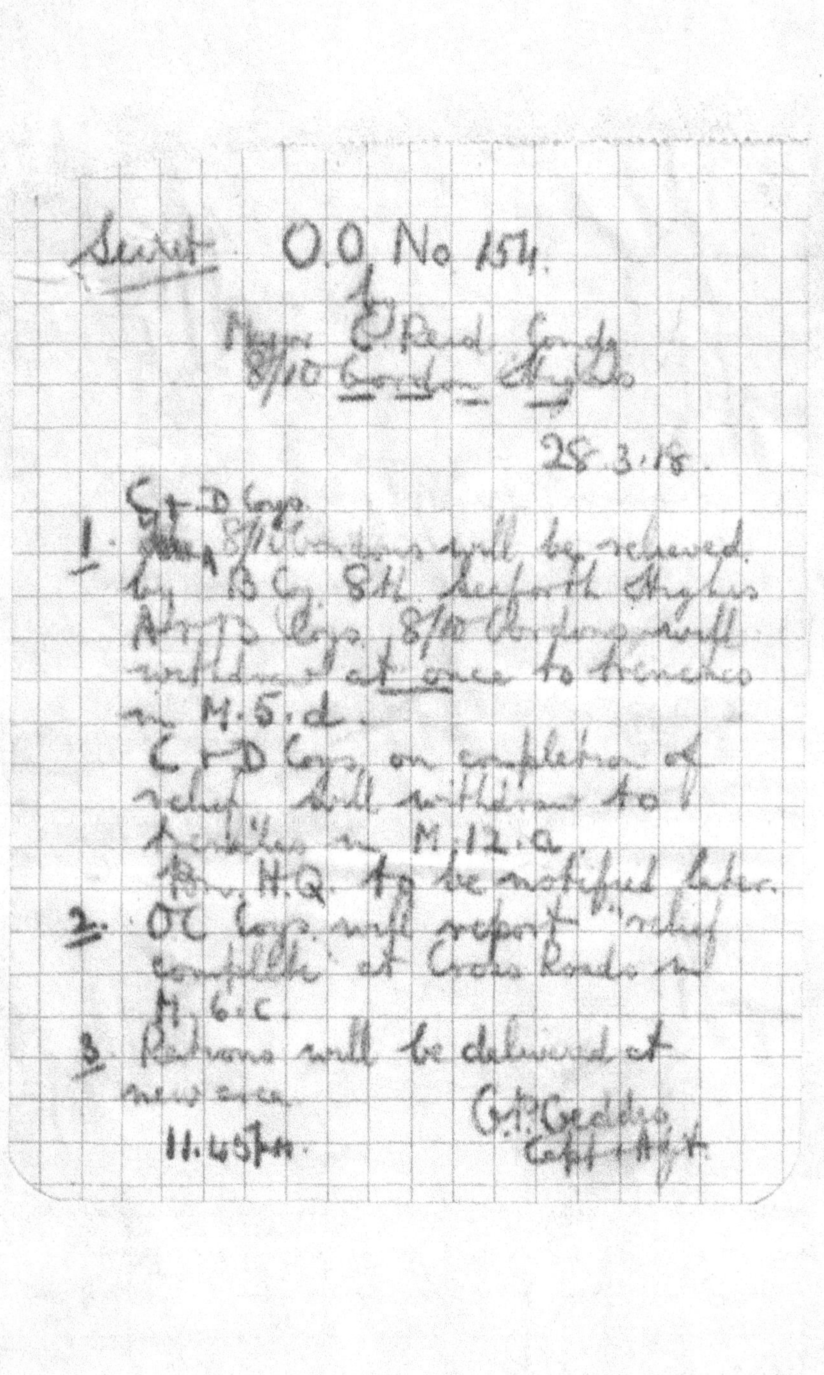

Secret O.O. No 154.

by

Major C. Reid Gordon
8/10 Gordon Highlrs

28.3.18.

1. C & D Coys 8/10 Gordons will be relieved by B Coy 8th Seaforth Highlrs. A & B Coys. 8/10 Gordons will withdraw at once to trenches in M.5.d.
C & D Coys on completion of relief will withdraw to trenches in M.12.a
Bn. H.Q. to be notified later.
2. OC Coys will report "relief complete" at Cross Roads in M.6.c
3. Rations will be delivered at new area.

11.45pm.

G.P. Geddes
Capt & Adjt.

Secret 8/10 Gordon Highlrs.

Operation Order No 150

by

Major Charles Reid Commdg.

29th March 1918

1. The 8/10 Gordon Highlrs will be relieved To-night 29th Inst. by The 2nd Canadian Battn. On relief the Battn. will be disposed in an area To be notified later.

2. Companies will be relieved by Corresponding Companies

3. Guides, 1 per Platoon + 2 for Batt H.Q. will parade under 2nd LOVIE at 7.30 P.M at Batt H.Q. Guides will then meet incoming Battalion at G.22.c.0.8. (Rly: Crossing) at 9.15 P.M.

4. Any Tools or Stores of any kind will be handed over + Receipts obtained.

5. Relief Complete To be reported at once by runner To Batt H.Q. This runner will also guide To H.Q. a runner from relieving Coy.

6. Acknowledge. Sd. G.P. Geddes
Capt. + Adjutant.

Copy of letter received by Major Reid from our Brigade Commander

"My dear Major,

I wish to send you my sincerest congratulations and to thank you and all ranks under your command for the grand work during the whole of this last tour of two months, which culminated in the gallant fight put up by your Battalion on the 28th, and I consider that it was entirely due to this fight that the 15th Division was practically saved from destruction, or at any rate from retirement.

I should like to convey to all ranks in your Battalion my sincerest sympathies with them for their losses, & the many friends they have left behind in the great struggle.

The Divisional Commander today, in expressing his thanks for the work of the 44th Bde., in all sincerity told me that your work had saved ARRAS.

30.3.18. Yrs. very sincerely, Edward Hilliam"

"A" Form.

Army Form C. 2121.
(In pads of 100.)

MESSAGES AND SIGNALS.

No. of Message..............

Prefix........ Code.............. m Office of Origin and Service Instructions.	Words.	Charge.	This message is on a/c of: .... Service. (Signature of "Franking Officer.")	Recd. at .... m. Date.......... From .... By..........
	Sent At.............. m. To.............. By..............			

TO Headquarters
44th Inf. Bde.

Sender's Number.	Day of Month.	In reply to Number.	AAA
* OH/143	8		

Herewith my narrative of operations from 21st.-29th March, inclusive.

Reference Para. 2-: the map issued to me is not suitable for showing our dispositions. Please send a map showing both the Army Line & the Brown Line for me to mark in the dispositions and send in at once.

[illegible]
Major
Comdg. 8/10 Gordon Hrs.

From
Place
Time

The above may be forwarded as now corrected. (Z)

Censor. Signature of Addressor or person authorised to telegraph in his name.

* This line should be erased if not required.

(3198.) Wt. W 12952/M1294. 375,000 Pads. 1/17. H. W. & V., Ld. (E. 818.)

8/10th (Ser.) Battalion, The Gordon Highlanders

I.

NARRATIVE – 21st/27th MARCH 1918

II.

OUR DISPOSITIONS ON MORNING OF 28th MARCH 1918 AS ON ATTACHED MAP MARKED 'A'.

III.

ACTION ON 28th MARCH 1918

IV.

NARRATIVE – 29th MARCH 1918

V.

APPENDIX – COMMUNICATIONS

I - NARRATIVE - 21st - 24th March 1918.

At 5-10 am on the morning of 21st March 1918, the battalion was "standing-to" in the front line East of MONCHY when the enemy opened a terrific bombardment consisting of gas and H.E shells. This bombardment lasted four hours, and was not followed by any infantry attack. The casualties on this occasion numbered 30, which was considered slight in view of the fierceness of the bombardment. The remainder of the day was quiet.

About 10 pm on the 22nd, the battalion received orders from Brigade to withdraw to ARTILLERY CAMP on TILLOY - BEAURAINS Road, leaving one company to hold front line & to fight a rearguard action, so as to inflict as many casualties as possible on the enemy in case of attack. The withdrawal of the other three companies took place quietly and in an orderly manner without knowledge of the enemy, and with no casualties.

At 6.30 am on the 23rd, the enemy opened a heavy bombardment assisted by a large number of T. Ms.

This bombardment was followed by an attack, and the company left behind retired fighting a rearguard action with slight losses. The enemy ceased attacking about 11 am and was then holding a line of shell holes in front of LES FOSSES FARM.

The night of 23rd was quiet, and on the 24th the battalion relieved the 7th Cameron Highlanders in Army Line, and then became the Support Battalion.

On the 25th, the battalion was ordered to occupy the NEUVILLE-VITASSE SWITCH, as an enemy attack was anticipated any moment.

The days of 26th and 27th were spent in these positions, and the enemy's artillery was comparatively quiet.

II.

Our disposition on morning of 28th, as on attached map

III. ACTION ON 28th March 1918

At 3 am on the 28th, the enemy started a terrific bombardment, consisting of Gas and HE, which lasted 3 hours. This bombardment was followed by an attack which penetrated the front line, which at that time was held by the 7th Cameron Highlanders. About 8 am, the enemy were seen advancing over the BROWN LINE in large numbers over a wide front. The 7th Cameron Highrs were forced back, and the survivors took up a position on our left in the VITASSE SWITCH. Our two forward companies manned the VITASSE SWITCH LINE, and were on the point of counter-attacking without an artillery barrage which could not be arranged in time, when the report came from the left of the line that the enemy were well down the CAMBRAI ROAD on our left flank. Our dispositions were then altered. 'B' Company continued to hold the VITASSE SWITCH Line, and 'C' Company held the 'Strong Post Line'. This move was carried out under cover of L.G. and Rifle fire with about 20 casualties. At this point I had a telephone message from the O.C. 4th Cameron Highrs that he was withdrawing his headquarters. Before moving, he informed me that parties of the Division on our right had been seen moving back slowly. 'B' Company were still on the telephone (buried cable) & they informed me that the 6th Cameron Highrs on their left were withdrawing, as the enemy by this time was at FEUCHY-CHAPEL Cross Roads. As by this time both flanks were in the air, I gave orders to withdraw gradually, fighting a rearguard action. 'B' Company then withdrew through 'C' Company who covered their withdrawal. A patrol was sent by 'C' Company to AIRY CORNER to find out the situation on the left flank, also a Lewis Gun section to cover the flank of the withdrawal. Finally 'C' Company withdrew by sections to Battalion Headquarters, where the battalion took up a position facing NORTH and EAST.

Three reserve M. G^s of 15th M. G Battalion were now brought into use to cover the withdrawal of 'A' and 'D' Companies to the old trenches in the vicinity of Battalion H.Q^rs. Splendid targets were obtained in this position, both by riflemen and Lewis Gunners, and the reserve S.A.A at Battalion H.Q^rs was found very useful. At dusk, companies were re-organised and patrols pushed forward as far as the VITASSE SWITCH, and on the flanks which were found to be in the air. Out-posts were then established; two companies occupying the Out-post line and two companies in support, protecting the flanks. The most advanced posts were on either side of Battalion H.Q^rs.

IV. NARRATIVE of 29th March 1918

At 2 am. the position held by the battalion was taken over by the 8th Seaforth Highlanders, and the battalion withdrew to the Western slopes of TELEGRAPH HILL.

About 1-30 am. 29th, orders were received that the

battalion would be relieved in these positions by a battalion of the 2nd Canadians, and on relief the battalion was to occupy old trenches West of BEAURAINS. The relief was completed by 10 a.m. About 4.30 p.m. on 29th, orders were again received that the battalion would be relieved in these positions by a battalion of 3rd Canadians, commencing about 8.30 p.m. The relief was completed about midnight, and the battalion returned to billets in Hotel-de-Ville, ARRAS.

V. APPENDIX - COMMUNICATIONS

Within a few moments of the opening of the bombardment all communications to the Rear were cut, and all messages during the whole of the battle were sent by runner. Communication was maintained by buried cable with the two forward companies and the forward battalion up to the moment the order was given to withdraw.

Walter Reid.
Major.

8/4/18

Comdg. 1st Gordon Highrs

"A" Form.

Army Form C. 2121.
(In pads of 100.)

MESSAGES AND SIGNALS.

No. of Message..............

Prefix........... Code.............. m	Words.	Charge.	This message is on a/c of:	Recd. at .... m.
Office of Origin and Service Instructions.	Sent		.... Service.	Date ....
	At............ m.			From ....
	To............			
	By............		(Signature of "Franking Officer.")	By............

TO H.Q. 46th Inf Bde

Sender's Number.	Day of Month.	In reply to Number.	AAA
* GH/145	8		

Reference my GH/143 of today:- Herewith sketch map shewing dispositions.

[signature]
Major
Comdg. 8/10 Gordon Hrs.

From
Place
Time

The above may be forwarded as now corrected. (Z)

Censor. Signature of Addressor or person authorised to telegraph in his name.

* This line should be erased if not required.

(3198.) Wt. W 12952/M1294. 375,000 Pads. 1/17. H. W. & V., Ld. (E. 818.)

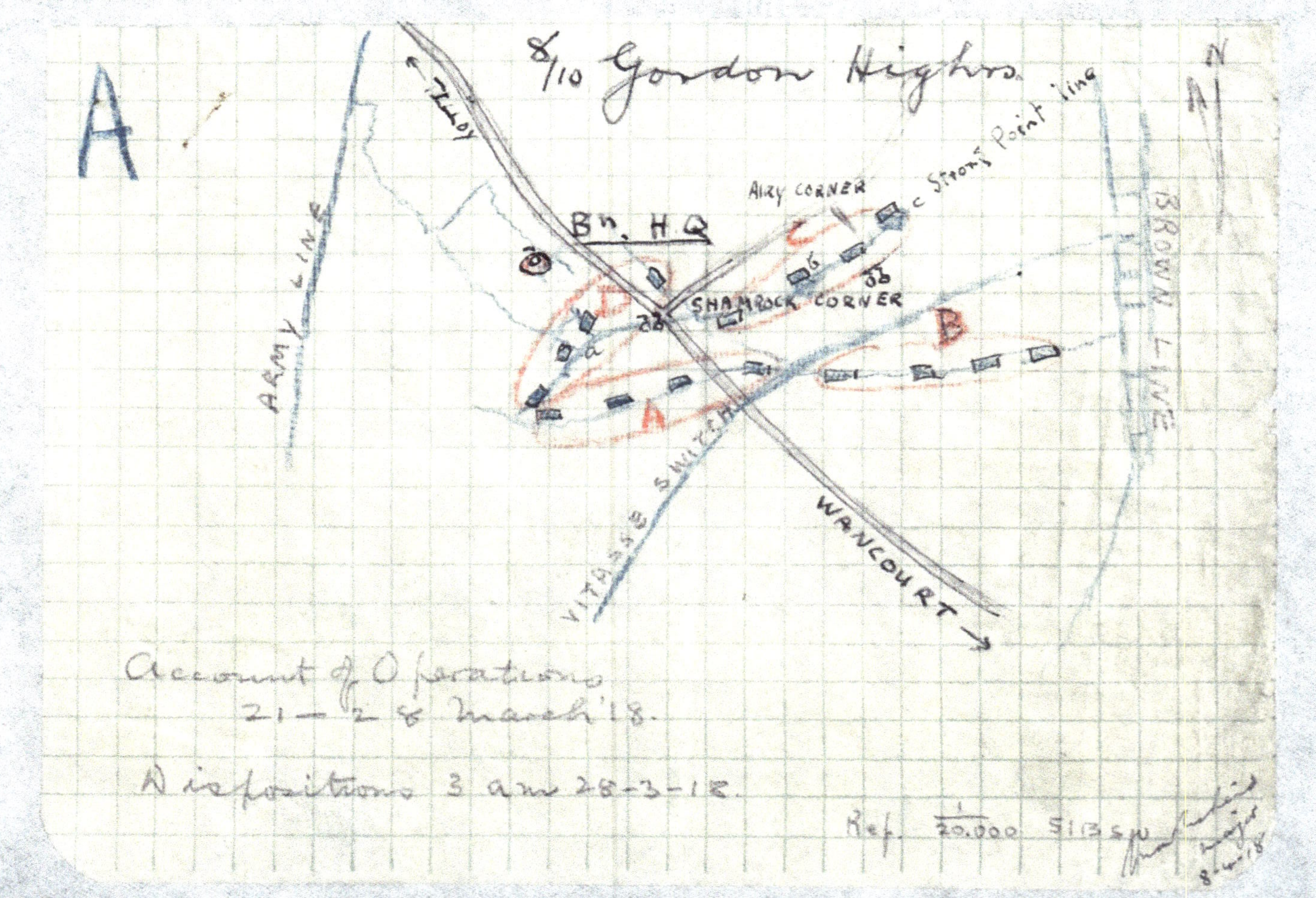
A
8/10 Gordon Highrs.
BROWN LINE
ARMY LINE
Bn. HQ
AIRY CORNER
SHAMROCK CORNER
Strong Point line
WANCOURT
VITASSE SWITCH
A
B
C
D
Account of Operations
21 — 28 March '18.
Dispositions 3 am 28-3-18.
Ref. 1/20,000 51B S.W.

15th Division.
44th Brigade.

8/10th BATTALION

THE GORDON HIGHLANDERS

APRIL 1 9 1 8

Appendices attacehed -

Battalion Operation Orders.

CONFIDENTIAL

Vol 35

WAR DIARY

OF

8/10th (Service) Battalion, The Gordon Highlanders

For Period

1st April, 1918. 27th April 1918

VOLUME 36.

Instructions regarding War Diaries and Intelligence Summaries are contained in F. S. Regs., Part II. and the Staff Manual respectively. Title pages will be prepared in manuscript.

WAR DIARY
or
INTELLIGENCE SUMMARY. 4S:3

(Erase heading not required.)

Army Form C. 2118.

Place	Date	Hour	Summary of Events and Information	Remarks and references to Appendices
Trenches	1918 Apl. 3rd.		The Battalion side stepped and took over portions of 45th Brigade in front line. The relief was carried out with no casualties but took a long time to complete as the night was very dark making it very difficult to find the way about.	OO 156
"	4th.		The Battalion was relieved in front line by portions of 45th Brigade and on relief returned to Billets in ARRAS	OO 157
ARRAS.	5/7th		Billets in ARRAS.	
	8th.		The Battalion relieved the 45th. Brigade in front line	
Trenches	9th.	9am	Through a thick mist enemy attempted to raid our left Company but was driven off with casualties without gaining a footing in our trenches. Our casualties - 2 wounded.	
"	11th.		Enemy shelled our front & support lines heavily from 8.45 am - 9.15 am but no Infantry attack followed.	
"	14th.		The Battalion was relieved by 13th Royal Scots. 45th Bde - and on relief returned to Billets in PETIT PLACE, ARRAS. The relief	OO 160

T2134. Wt. W708-776. 500000. 4/15. Sir J. C. & S.

Instructions regarding War Diaries and Intelligence Summaries are contained in F. S. Regs., Part II. and the Staff Manual respectively. Title pages will be prepared in manuscript.

WAR DIARY
or
INTELLIGENCE SUMMARY. 454
(Erase heading not required.)

Army Form C. 2118.

Place	Date	Hour	Summary of Events and Information	Remarks and references to Appendices
"	1918 Apl. 14th		was carried out quietly and without casualties.	
ARRAS	15th		The Battalion relieved Scottish Rifles of 46th Bde in St SAUVEUR CAVES and became support Battalion.	
"	18th		The Battalion was relieved in support by 7th Cameron Highrs and on relief returned to Billets in ARRAS.	OO 162
	20th		Battalion relieved 13th Royal Scots in front line and became the right Battalion of the right Brigade.	OO 163
Trenches	21st		A Prisoner captured down South belonging to the 6th Essex escaped from the Enemy lines. After being challenged he was allowed to enter our line. The prisoner (a Cpl.) gave very valuable information as to treatment of prisoners, their location &c.	
"	23rd		Two prisoners captured by Enemy on 25th March belonging to the 7th Cameron Highrs escaped from German Camp at 10 pm and reached our line at 3 am and gave valuable information.	
			The Battalion relieved in front line by 1st London Regt. – 56th Div. and marched to DAINVILLE. The relief was carried out without Casualties.	OO 164

T2134. Wt. W708–776. 500000. 4/15. Sir J. C. & S.

Secret.

8/10th Gordon Highrs

OPERATION ORDER No. 156

By

Major Charles Reid.

3rd April 1918

1. The Divisional boundaries are to be readjusted tonight 3/4th April.

2. The 8/10th Gordon Highrs will take over the Outpost Line from N-2-a-9-9 to H-33-a-5-6 & the Army Front Line from H-31-a-8-0 to H-32-a-7-7.

3. Dispositions:

D Coy - Right Outpost Line
B Coy - Left Outpost Line
C Coy - (Right) Army Front Line
A Coy - (Left) Army Front Line
Bn. H.Q. - Old artillery dugout at H-31-b 3-8.

4. (1) D Coy Gordons will relieve B Coy Scottish Rifles

Guides: 1 per post & 1 for Coy H.Q. to be at Junction of CAMBRAI and TILLOY - WANCOURT Roads - G-36-b 9-9 at 9 pm

(2) B Coy Gordons will relieve part of A Coy [illegible]

Guides: 1 per post & 1 for Coy HQ to be at H-35-d 2-2 at 9 pm

(3) A & C Coys will be relieved by a Company of 1st Canadian Battalion. All arrangements for relief & for guides &c to be made between O.C. A & C Coys & O.C. Coy of the Canadians.

PTO

4 contd.
On completion of above relief:-
(4) A Coy. Gordons will relieve A Coy. Scottish Rifles.
Guides: 1 per platoon & 1 for Coy. H.Q. to be at Junction of Army Line & WANCOURT Road – N.1.b.3.4 at 9 pm.
(5) C Coy. Gordons will relieve C Coy. K.O.S.B's.
Guides: as for B Coy.

5. It is essential that the relief should be carried out with the utmost rapidity, otherwise it will not be possible for the 46th Bde. to complete by 5 am.

6. Trench Stores, tools, SAA & explosive stores will be handed over & taken over & receipts forwarded to Orderly Room by 9 am 4th inst.
Tools of B & D Coys. will be collected & dumped at Bn. H.Q. before relief commences.
RED Very Lights (SOS) will be taken over from 46th Bde.

7. Points of junction in the Outpost line on completion of relief will be reported as early as possible to Bn. H.Q., also dispositions.

8. Relief complete to be reported at once to Bn. H.Q. by code word "SNOW" by runner.
An orange coloured lamp will be flashed from Bn. H.Q. to guide Coy. Runners.

9. Acknowledge

(PTO)

3

Capt & Adjt.
8/10th Gordon Highrs.

Copies to :-
OC Coys — 7/8th K.O.S.B's
Signals — 10th S. R.
Lt Millward — 8th Seaforths
W. D. — File.

Issued through Signals - 12-30pm

Secret.

8/10th Gordon Highrs

OPERATION ORDER No 154.

By

MAJOR CHARLES REID.

4th April 1918.

1. The 8/10th Gordon Highrs will be relieved in the Outpost Line & Army Line tonight as follows:–

(I) D Coy, Gordons, will be relieved by B Coy 11th A&SH in the Right of the Outpost Line.
Guides: 1 per platoon & 1 for Coy H.Q to be at Junction of PELVES LANE and Bn H.Q. Trench H.25.d.2.2 at 9 pm

(II) A Coy Gordons will be relieved by D Coy 11th Argylls in the Right of the Army Front Line
Guides: as for D Coy.

(III) B Coy Gordons will be relieved by 3 platoons No 2 Coy, 6th Camerons in the Left of the Outpost Line
Guides: 1 per platoon (ie 3) & 1 for Coy HQ to be at H.25.d.2.2 at 8.45 pm

IV. C Coy Gordons, will be relieved by 1 platoon No 2 Coy & 2 platoons No 1 Coy, 6th Camerons in the Left of the Army Front Line.
Guides: 1 per platoon (ie 3) to be at H.25.d.2.2 at 8.45 pm

V. Bn HQ, Gordons will be taken over by Bn H.Qrs 6th Cameron Highrs – H.31.b.3.8.
1 Guide will be at H.25.d.2.2 at 8.45 pm.
All guides will report to 2/Lieut. F.W. LOVIE at

PTO

0.0.15/4.

the above rendezvous. He will ensure that the guides are told off correctly.

An orange lamp will be flashed from this point to guide the incoming battalions and Company runners.

3. On relief, companies will proceed to their former billets in the PETIT PLACE, ARRAS. Lieut Boyce will proceed in advance to take over billets & stores etc.

Trench Stores, tools, munitions, S.O.S lights, hot food containers etc. will be carefully handed over & receipts forwarded to Orderly Room by 9 am. 5th inst.

Every effort will be made to collect as many stores as possible to hand over.

All petrol tins will be brought back with Coys.

Transport for Coy Mess kits, Lewis Guns etc. will be at St PATRICKS CORNER at 10-30 pm.

Relief complete to be wired to Bn HQ by the code word BEETLE. O.C. Coys will also report personally to Bn HQ on completion of relief.

ACKNOWLEDGE.

G.P. Geddes Capt & Adjt

Issued to:-

O.C. Coys.	6th Camerons
2/Lt Boyce	11th A & S H
Sgt Millward	War Diary & File

Secret

8/10th Gordon Highrs

OPERATION ORDER No. 154.

By

MAJOR CHARLES REID

4th April 1918

1. The 8/10th Gordon Highrs will be relieved in the Outpost Line & Army Line tonight as follows:—

(i) D Coy, Gordons will be relieved by B Coy 11th A & S H in the Right of the Outpost Line.
Guides: 1 per platoon & 1 for Coy H.Q. to be at Junction of PELVES LANE and Bn HQ Trench H.25.d.2.2 at 9 pm.

(ii) A Coy Gordons will be relieved by D Coy 11th Argylls in the Right of the Army Front Line
Guides: as for D Coy.

(iii) B Coy Gordons will be relieved by 3 platoons No. 2 Coy, 6th Camerons in the Left of the Outpost Line
Guides: 1 per platoon (i.e. 3) & 1 for Coy HQ to be at H.25.d.2.2 at 8-45 pm

IV. C Coy Gordons will be relieved by 1 platoon No. 2 Coy + 2 platoons No. 1 Coy, 6th Camerons in the Left of the Army Front Line.
Guides: 1 per platoon (i.e. 3) to be at H.25.d.2.2 at 8.45 pm

Bn HQ Gordons will be taken over by Bn HQrs 6th Cameron Highrs – H.31.b.3.8.
Guide will be at H.25.d.2.2 at 8.45 pm.
All guides will report to 2/Lieut F.W. Lovie at

(PTO)

to [illegible] rendezvous. He will ensure that the guides are told off correctly.

Any orange lamp will be flashed from this point to guide the incoming battalions and Company runners.

2. On relief, companies will proceed to their former billets in the PETIT PLACE, ARRAS. Lieut Boyce will proceed in advance to take over billets, stores etc.

3. Trench stores, tools, munitions, S.O.S. lights, hot food containers etc. will be carefully handed over & receipts forwarded to Orderly Room by 10 am 5th inst.

Every effort will be made to collect as many stores as possible to hand over.

All petrol tins will be brought back with Coys.

4. Transport for Coy mess kits, Lewis Guns, etc will be at St PATRICKS CORNER at 10-30 pm.

5. Relief complete to be wired to Bn HQ by the code word BEETLE. OC Coys will also report personally to Bn HQ on completion of relief.

7. ACKNOWLEDGE.

G.P. Geddes Capt & Adjt

Copies to :-

OC Coys.
2/Lt Lowrie
Sgt Millward

6th Camerons
11th A & S.H.
War Diary File.

Copy No [illegible]

SECRET. 8/10 Gordon Hghrs
Operation Order No. 160
by
Major Charles Reid, Comdg.

12th April 1918.

1 The 8/10 Gordon Hghrs will be relieved in the PILLOY OUTPOST and FIRING LINES by the 13th Royal Scots on the night 13/14th April.

2 (1) "C" Coy. Gordons will be relieved by "C" Coy. Royal Scots in the Left of the Outpost Line.
Guides: 1 per platoon and 1 for Coy. HQ will be at H.25.C.0,2 (on PELVES LANE, 200 yards West of ST. PATRICK'S CORNER) at 8.30pm.

(2) "A" Coy. Gordons will be relieved by "A" Coy Royal Scots in the right of the Outpost Line.
Guides: 1 per platoon and 1 for Coy. HQ. will be on the CAMBRAI ROAD, 200 yards East of its junction with PELVES LANE, (about G.30.C.3,2) at 8.30pm.

(3) Bn. H.Q. will be relieved by Bn. H.Q. Royal Scots.
Location: H.31.b.3.8.

2 (3) Contd.
Guides: 1 for C.O., 1 for Bn. H.Q., & 1 for the Cooks to be at same rendezvous as for 2(1) at 8.30 pm.

(4) "B" Coy. Gordons will be relieved by "D" Coy. Royal Scots in the Left of the TILLOY FIRING LINE.
Guides: 1 per platoon and 1 for Coy. H.Q to be as for 2(1).

(5) "D" Coy. Gordons will be relieved by "B" Coy. Royal Scots in the Right of the TILLOY FIRING LINE.
Guides: 1 per platoon and 1 for Coy. H.Q. to be as for 2(2).

(6) The relief will be carried out in the above order.

(7) All guides will rendezvous at Bn. H.Q at 5 a.m. tomorrow, 13th inst. R.S.M. will arrange for accomodation for the day. Rations for the day to be carried.
Lieut. BLACK will be in charge of guides.

3. On relief, the battalion will proceed to the usual billets in the PETIT PLACE.
Lieut. A.W. Boyce will proceed in advance to take over stores etc.

4. All trench stores, dumps, tools, a detailed plan of the dispositions, and programme of work in hand

3.

will be handed over and receipts obtained.

Lists of stores etc. handed over will be forwarded to Bn. H.Q. by 9am, 14th inst.

5. Relief complete to be reported at once to Bn. H.Q. by wire by the Code Word "BOOT." It will also be reported by runner who will guide to Bn. H.Q. runners from relieving companies.

6 Acknowledge.

G.P. Geddes.
Capt. & Adjutant.
8/10 Gordon Highlanders.

Distribution:

Copies 1 – 4. O.C. Coys.
5. Lieut. Black.
6. R.S.M.
7. Details.
8. 13th Royal Scots.
9. 8th Seaforth Hghrs.
10 War Diary.
11 File.
12. Spare.

Secret

8/10 Gordon Highrs

Operation Order No. 162
by
Major Charles Reid, Comdg.

17th April, 1918.

1. The 8/10 Gordon Highrs will be relieved by the 7th Cameron Highrs tomorrow 18th April. On relief the battalion will withdraw to the PETIT PLACE, & be disposed as follows:-

Bn. H.Q. -- 46, Rue des Trois Visages.
A + D Coys -- East side of PETIT PLACE.
B + C Coys -- North side of PETIT PLACE.

2. Companies will be relieved by sister companies. Relief to be carried out as follows:-

C Coy: to be clear of "B" Exit, G.29.d.6.4 by 8.45am.
Route: "B" Exit — IMPERIAL STREET — Road South of Brigade H.Q.

B Coy: to be clear of "B" Exit by 9.15am.
Route: Same as for C Coy.

D Coy: not to pass junction of O.B.2 and SCOTTISH AV. before 9.45am.
Route: O.B.2 — SCOTTISH AVENUE — Road South of Brigade H.Q.

A Coy: to move when relieved.
Route: down the Tunnel System.

Every precaution must be taken to avoid movement being observed by the enemy. All movement will be by ½ platoons at two minutes' interval. There must be connecting files between parties.

4. The 7th Cameron Hghrs will move up the Tunnel System.

R.S.M. will detail a picquet of police to be posted at the junctions at G.30.c.1,1 and G.30.c.2,0 to direct the companies of the Camerons to their different areas.

5. Trench stores, defense scheme etc. to be handed over and receipts forwarded to Orderly Room by 3pm.

O.C. Coys. will each detail an officer and 1 N.C.O. per platoon to remain and hand over accomodation etc. to the Camerons.

6. Two limbers for dixies, mess kits etc will be at Bn. H.Q. at 9am.

7. Relief complete will be wired to Bn H.Q. by Code Word "SUSAN". Arrival in billets will also be reported.

8. Acknowledge.

G.P. Geddes,
Capt. Adjt
8/10 Gordon Hghrs

Copies to —
O.C. Coys
Lt Black
R.S.M.
7th Camerons
W.D.
File.

SECRET.

The Gordon Highlanders. Copy No. [illegible]

OPERATION ORDER No.163.

By

Major Charles Reid, Comdg.

19th April'18

1. The 8/10th Gordon Highlanders will relieve the 13th Royal Scots in the Right Front System to-morrow night, 20/21st April.

2. The relief will be carried out in the following order :-

(a) B Coy Gordons will relieve C Coy Royal Scots in the Left of the Outpost Line.
Guides : 1 per platoon and 1 for Coy HQ. will be on PELVES LANE, 200 yards East of its junction with the CAMBRAI ROAD, at 9 p.m.

(b) D Coy Gordons will relieve A Coy Royal Scots in the Right of the Outpost line.
Guides : 1 per platoon and 1 for Coy HQ. will be on the CAMBRAI ROAD, 200 yards East of its junction with PELVES LANE, at 9 p.m.

(c) Battn.HQ. Gordons will relieve Battn.HQ. Royal Scots at H.31.b.4.8.
Two guides as for 2 (a) also 1 guide for Battn.Cooks.

(d) C Coy Gordons will relieve D Coy Royal Scots in the Left Support Line.
Guides : as for 2 (a).

(e) A Coy Gordons will relieve B Coy Royal Scots in the Right Support Line.
Guides : As for 2 (b).

3. Companies will march off in the order laid down in Para 2. The first platoon of B Coy will march off at 8.30 pm. and thereafter movement will be at 2 minutes' interval. Connecting files must be sent out. The last platoon of A Coy must be clear of O.B.1. by 9.45 p.m.
Lieut.R.A.M.Black will be at the junction of the CAMBRAI Road and PELVES LANE to control traffic and ensure schedule time being adhered to. He will also see that limbers are kept on the right side of the road - that there is no double banking or blocking of the traffic and no congestion on the road.

(P.T.O.

O.O.163.

4. 1 limber per Coy, 1 for Battn.HQ. and 1 for dixies and cooking utensils will be at the PETIT PLACE by 8 p.m. All Lewis Guns, S.A.A., Signalling gear, Mess kits & dixies will be loaded by 8.15 p.m.

Limbers will proceed in front of their companies and halt at their respective rendezvous for guides.

5. All trench stores, tools, aeroplane photographs, programm of work, dumps and explosive stores will be taken over. Lists of stores taken over will reach Battn.HQ. by 8 a.m., 21st April.

6. Completion of relief will be wired to Battn.HQ. by the code word "ROPE".

7. Acknowledge.

[signature]
Captain & Adjutant
8/10th Bn.,The Gordon Highrs.

Distribution:-

Copies 1 - 4. O.C.Coys.
5. Lieut.R.A.M.Black.
6. R.S.M.
7. Signals.
8. Details.
9. 13th Royal Scots
10. War Diary.
11. File.

Vol. 36

CONFIDENTIAL.

WAR DIARY

OF

8/10th (Service) Battalion, The Gordon Highlanders

For Period

From: 1st May, 1918 To: 31st May. 1918.

VOLUME 37.

Instructions regarding War Diaries and Intelligence Summaries are contained in F. S. Regs., Part II. and the Staff Manual respectively. Title pages will be prepared in manuscript.

WAR DIARY
or
~~INTELLIGENCE SUMMARY.~~
(Erase heading not required.) 8/10 Batt^n Gordon Highrs 456.

Army Form C. 2118.

Place	Date	Hour	Summary of Events and Information	Remarks and references to Appendices
	1918.			
CAMBLAIN-CHATELAIN.	May 1-3.		Hard training was carried out, of which musketry formed the principal part.	
	May 3.		Orders were received for move back to ARRAS on the 4th.	1. O.O. 165.a
ETRON Y huts. L.2.c.5.6. Ref map. 51.C.	May 4.	10 a.m.	The battalion entrained at PERNES.	
		12.30 P.m.	The battalion arrived at MAROEUIL and marched to Y huts ETRUN.	
WAKEFIELD CAMP A.22.c.2.1. Ref map 51.B. N.W.	May 6.	3 p.m.	The battalion left Y huts and marched to WAKEFIELD CAMP near ECURIE.	2. O.O. 165.b
	May 7-9.		Training was carried out daily, particular attention being paid to ~~rapid~~ loading and rapid fire.	
ROEUX Sector.	May 10.		The 44th Brigade moved into the front line, relieving the 46th brigade. The 45th Brigade on the left with the 51st Highland Division beyond them; on our right the 56th Division.	3. O.O. 167. 4. the 44 Bde O.O. 264. and Adminis. Instr. attached
			Dispositions of brigade:— 8th Seaforths right, 7th Camerons left, 8/10 Gordons reserve.	
			Brigade boundaries:— South – ARRAS – DOUAI railway; North – line running East and West 300 yards North of grid line through H.15., H.16., H.17 central.	FEUCHY TRENCH map 1/10,000.

T2134. Wt. W708–776. 500000. 4/15. Sir J. C. & S.

Instructions regarding War Diaries and Intelligence Summaries are contained in F. S. Regs., Part II. and the Staff Manual respectively. Title pages will be prepared in manuscript.

WAR DIARY
or
~~INTELLIGENCE SUMMARY~~.
(Erase heading not required.)

Army Form C. 2118.

457.

8/10 Bn Gordon Highrs

Place	Date	Hour	Summary of Events and Information	Remarks and references to Appendices
STIRLING CAMP.	May 10.		2 companies and Bn H.Q. at Stirling Camp, railway embankment H.13.b. 2 companies forward in ATHIES and CAM VALLEY (H.15.d.).	Ref. ORANGE HILL 1/20,000. UGP
	May 11-17.		Battalion in support. Working parties of over 300 per night.	UGP
Front Line.	May 17.		The battalion relieved the 7th Cameron Highrs in left subsection. North boundary as for 44th Bde. South boundary River SCARPE. Dispositions – see O.O. 168.	5. O.O. 168. UGP
	17-24.		Battalion in the line. Patrolling was actively carried out nightly, particular attention being paid to the Island, H.23. a. and b. Two platoons of the right support company were required to watch the river bank by night. Our front line ran through FAMPOUX, but the front post of the battalion on our right was only advanced to broken bridge at H.22.a.7.3., thus leaving a gap of over 1000 yards along the river on our right flank. A good deal of work was done deepening the front line, wiring front and support lines, and deepening C.T.'s.	UGP
	24.		The 45th Bde relieved the 44th Bde in the line.	UGP

T2134. Wt. W708—776. 500000. 4/15. Sir J. C. & S.

Instructions regarding War Diaries and Intelligence Summaries are contained in F. S. Regs., Part II. and the Staff Manual respectively. Title pages will be prepared in manuscript.

WAR DIARY
or
~~INTELLIGENCE SUMMARY.~~
(*Erase heading not required.*)

458.

Army Form C. 2118.

2/10 Bn Gordon Highrs

Place	Date	Hour	Summary of Events and Information	Remarks and references to Appendices
	May 22		We were relieved by the 11th Bn Argyll & Sutherland Highrs. Luckily the full moon, which caused the failure of one of our patrols the previous night, was somewhat obscured, and the relief was over at 12.15 a.m.	OO.169
WAKEFIELD CAMP.	May 25		The battalion were all back in WAKEFIELD CAMP by 2.30 a.m.	
			Total casualties for the tour May 10–24 —	
			Missing believed killed 2nd Lt A. CANTLAY.	
			Wounded A/Capt. W.J.P. BEVERIDGE, 2nd Lt. J.R. BRUCE, 2nd Lt. J.M. MACKENZIE. MM.	
			Other ranks missing 1; wounded 22.	
	25–31.		Fine weather and good observation. Enemy artillery paid some attention to back areas including some neighbouring camps.	
			Training was carried on daily, particularly that of the Lewis Gunners to meet the new issue of 8 guns per battalion.	
			The following awards were made for gallantry in the field.	
			The D.S.O. Major CHARLES REID.	
			M.C. Lieut. B.L. KEYES, M.O.R.C., U.S.R. (attached).	
			The following were mentioned in despatches April 7th 1918 — Major CHARLES REID. D.S.O. Capt N.G. PEARSON, Lieut A.W. BOYCE, A/Sgt. J. MARSHALL (Gazette 24/5/18)	

A5834 Wt. W4973/M687 750,000 8/16 D. D. & L. Ltd. Forms/C.2118/13.

A. B. C. D. R.S.M. T.O. Q.M. Lt Sibley

Appendix I. O.O. 165a.

1. The Battalion will entrain at PERNES STATION for Y Huts and will detrain at MAREUIL. Train departs 10 AM.
2. Lt SIBLEY will report to Lt MARTIN of Bgde HQ, at PERNES 8.45 AM. He will act as entraining & detraining officer. He will obtain numbers of entraining from orderly Room which he will hand to Lt MARTIN on arrival at PERNES.
3. The Battalion will parade on Battalion Parade ground in close column of Coys at 8.45 AM. 1 Marker for Coy Report to R.S.M. at 8.30 AM. The Battalion will then be told off in parties of 40 under an officer or N.C.O. & will entrain in these parties. There is to be no entrainment or detrainment except by word of command.
4. Billets will be clean & inspected by 8.15 AM.
5. Dress as ordered in G.H.55.

Administrative Instructions.

1. Valises, Mess kits etc., shoemakers & Tailors material to be stacked at orderly Room by 7.30 AM. Transport will arrange to collect & convey to new area. Transport now passes starting Point at 8.30 AM and not 11.30 as was previously ordered. Starting Point I.17.c.0.2

Ow Boyce Lt & a/adj

3.30 AM 4/5/18

SECRET.

Copy No. 4

44th Highland Brigade Operation Order No. 264.

3rd May, 1918.

1. The Brigade Group will move to "Y" Huts, ETRUN and ARRAS area, tomorrow, 4th May, 1918.

2. The dismounted personnel will proceed by train in accordance with the table on reverse.

3. The mounted portion, under command of Capt. J.B.WOOD, D.S.O., M.C., will proceed by march route in accordance with the March Table on the reverse.

4. Lieut. McCROSTIE, 7th Cameron Highlanders and 2/Lieut. MARTIN, 8/10th Gordon Highlanders will act as entraining and detraining officers at PERNES and CALONNE RICOUART respectively.

5. Units will each detail an entraining and detraining officer. These officers will report to the Brigade entraining officers at their respective stations of entrainment 1½ hours before the trains are due to depart.
They will hand in entraining states to this officer.

6. Units will not enter the station yards before being given permission to do so by their entraining officers.

7. All Officers will be warned that the strictest discipline to be maintained throughout the entrainment and detrainment .
There is to be no entrainment or detrainment except by word of command.

8. Tactical trains are being provided, each consisting of 44 3rd Class ~~compartments~~ trucks or "Covers", each to hold 40, 2 1st Class coaches, 2 vans for baggage, 2 brake vans, one at either end, which may not be entered.

9. Units will be told off into parties of 40, under an Officer and senior N.C.O. before leaving their parade grounds, and will entrain in these parties.

10. Blankets will be carried on the man. ~~On arrival at the station ..... they will be made up into bundles of 10 and placed in the baggage van.~~

11. ACKNOWLEDGE.

12. Bde. H.Q. will close at AUCHEL at 10 A.M., and open on arrival.

R.C. Tonley

Captain,
Brigade Major,
44th Infantry Brigade.

Issued thro' Signals - 11 P.M.

DISTRIBUTION.

Copy No.		Copy No.	
1.	War Diary.	11.	Staff Captain.
2.	File.	12.	44th Bde. Signals.
3.	8th Seaforth Highrs.	13.	Bde. Transport Officer.
4.	8/10th Gordon Highrs.	14.	15th Div. G.
5.	7th Cameron Highrs.	15.	15th Div. Q.
6.	44 T.M.Battery.	16.	15th Div. Train.
7.	9th Gordon Highrs. (P).	17.	No.2 Coy., Train.
8.	91st Field Coy., R.E.	18.	Town Major, AUCHEL.
9.	46th Field Ambulance.	19.	Bde. Intelligence Offcr.
10.	2 Coy., 15th Bn., M.G.C.	20.	Bde. Bombing Offcr.
		21.	A.P.M., 15th Division.

ENTRAINING AT PERNES STATION. I.13.a.0.6. **Train departs - 10 A.M.** **DETRAIN - MAROEUIL.**

UNIT.	Head of column to reach Cross Roads H.18.b.7.7. at -
8th Seaforth Highrs.	9. 0 A.M.
Brigade Headquarters.	9.10 A.M.
2 Coy.,15th Bn., M.G.C.	9.15 A.M.
8/10th Gordon Highrs.	9.25 A. M.

ENTRAINING AT CALONNE RICOUART STATION. I.10.d.5.1. **Train departs 10.30 A.M.** **DETRAIN ACQ.**

UNIT.	Head of column to reach I.11.c.0.9.	
44 T.M.Battery.	9.25 A.M.	
7th Cameron Highrs.	9.30 A.M.	To be clear of Cross Roads C.22.c.8.2. by 9.5 A.M.
9th Gordon Highrs.(P).	9.40 A.M.	Not to reach --- --- ----- before 9.10 A.M.
91st Field Co., R.E.	9.50 A.M.	--- --- --- --- ----- ---- 9.20 A.M.
46th Field Ambulance.	9.55 A.M.	

NOTES.

(a) Should it be necessary for any unit to halt, care will be taken to clear the road.

(b) All times will be most rigidly adhered to.

S E C R E T.

44th Brigade G.41.- 3.5.18.

8th Seaforth Highrs.
8/10th Gordon Highrs.
7th Cameron Highrs.
44 T.M.Battery.
44th Bde. Signals.

91st Field Coy., R.E.
9th Gordon Highrs.(P).
46th Field Ambulance.
Staff Captain.

Warning Order

Reference 44th Brigade G.41. dated 1.5.18. (sent to units of Brigade only).

The dismounted portion of the Brigade Group will entrain to-morrow - probably in two trains as follows :-

From PERNES about 10 A.M.
Brigade Headquarters.
7th Cameron Highrs.
9th Gordon Highrs. (P).
91st Field Coy., R.E.
44 T.M.Battery.

From CALONNE RICOURT 11.30 A.M.
8th Seaforth Highrs.
8/10th Gordon Highrs.
46th Field Ambulance.
Divl. Employment Company.

Numbers entraining to be wired or sent S.D.R. to Brigade Headquarters forthwith.

The transport, under command of Captain J.B.WOOD, D.S.O., M.C., 8/10th Gordon Highrs., will proceed by march route via DIVION - HOUDAIN ESTREE CAUCHEE - CAMBLIGNEUL - AUBIGNY - HAUTE AVESNES.
BRUAY will not be entered.
Starting point - Fosse de la CLARENCE, I.17.c.0.2.
Time - probably 11.30 A.M.
Order or march -

8th Seaforth Highrs	11.30 A.M.
8/10th Gordon Highrs	11.45 A.M.
Brigade Headquarters	12. 0 NOON.
7th Cameron Highrs	12. 5 P.M.
9th Gordon Highrs.(P)	12.20 P.M.
91st Field Co.,R.E.	12.35 P.M.
46th Field Ambulance	12.45 P.M.

500 yards interval to be observed between transport of each unit.

Blankets will be carried rolled in bandoliers - on the man.

Should trains start later or both from one Station, cookers will provide meals before entraining - otherwise haversack rations will have to be carried.

W Ashmin Henderson Capt
for Brigade Major,
44th Infantry Brigade.

Issued at 11 A.M.
thro' Signals.

Copies to :-
15th Div. 'G'.
15th Div. 'Q'.
Bde. Transport Officer.

Appendix 2.

SECRET. Copy No.

The Gordon Highlanders.

OPERATION ORDER No. 165.6.

By

Lieut-Colonel the Lord Dudley Gordon, D.S.O., Comdg.

6th May 1918.

1. The Battalion will move forward into WAKEFIELD CAMP, G.4.b.3.8, to-night 6th / 7th instant.

2. Route : Main ARRAS ROAD - ROND POINT - St. CATHERINES.

3. Companies will march off in their own time in the order - H.Qrs., D, C, B, A Coys.

H.Qrs.	to pass	Guard	Room	at	East-end	of	Camp at	3. 1 p.m.
D Coy	"	"	"	"	"	"	"	3. 4 p.m.
C Coy	"	"	"	"	"	"	"	3. 7 p.m.
B Coy	"	"	"	"	"	"	"	3. 10 p.m.
A Coy	"	"	"	"	"	"	"	3. 13 p.m.
Transport	"	"	"	"	"	"	"	3. 16 p.m.

4. 500 yards interval to be observed between units, and 300 yards between companies, as far as ST. CATHERINES. North of ST. CATHERINES, movement will be by platoons at 100 yards' interval.

5. Dress : Full marching order with blanket and waterproof sheet folded under supporting straps of pack. Tam-O-Shanters to be worn.

6. As Camps are for the most part under view, movement will be restricted in clear weather.

7. Lewis Guns, signalling gear, Orderly Room boxes and C Coy's cooking utensils to be loaded on limbers by 2.15 p.m.

Officers valises and mess kits for new area to be loaded on G.S. Wagons by 2 p.m.

Transport Officer will arrange to collect Tailors' and Shoemakers' material and officers' valises not for the line and convey to GOUVES.

8. Arrival in new area will be reported to Bttn. HQrs. by runner, stating number who fell out, if any.

9. Acknowledge.

(sgd) A.W. Boyce,
Lieut. & A/Adjutant.

Distribution :

Copies 1 - 4. O.C.Coys. 7. Q.M.
5. M.G.[illegible] 8. T.O.
6. 2/Lieut. Sibley. 9. War Diary, 10. File.

Appendix 3.

S E C R E T.

Copy No. 1

The Gordon Highlanders.

O P E R A T I O N   O R D E R   No. 167.

By

Lieut-Colonel the Lord Dudley Gordon, D.S.O., Comdg.

9th May 1918.

1. The 8/10th Gordon Highlanders will relieve the 9th Black Watch on night of 10th / 11th May 1918.
On relief the Battalion will become the Support Battalion of the Right Brigade.

2. Dispositions : Companies will relieve sister companies of the Black Watch :-

A Coy in trench astride the ATHIES - FAMPOUX Road in H.15.c.
B Coy in STIRLING CAMP NORTH.
C Coy in STIRLING CAMP SOUTH.
D Coy in trenches North of the Road in H.13.c.
Battn. H.Q. in STIRLING CAMP.

3. The relief will be carried out in the order indicated in para 2.

4. Guides : 1 per platoon, 1 for Coy HQrs. and 1 for Battn. HQrs., will be at BLANGY Cross Roads at G.18.c.5.4 at 9.15 p.m.

5. The battalion will parade on Battalion Parade Ground ready to march off at 8 p.m.

6. Route : Artillery Track "A" - ST. NICHOLAS-FAMPOUX Road.
All movement to be by platoons at 100 yards interval.

7. All trench stores, tools, S.A.A., explosive stores etc. will be taken ov[er] and receipts given. Lists of stores taken over to be forwarded to Orderly Room by 9 a.m. 11th May 1918.

8. Completion of relief to be reported by wire to Battn. H.Qrs. by the code word "BLIGHTY".

9. Acknowledge.

(sgd) G.P.Geddes,
Captain & Adjutant.

Distribution :
Copies Nos. 1 - 4. O.C. Coys.
5. 2/Lieut. E.A. Sibley.
6. Quartermaster,
7. Transport Officer.
8. R.S.M.
9. 9th Black Watch.
10. War Diary.
11. File.

Appendix 4

SECRET. [handwritten mark]   Copy No.

44th Highland Brigade Operation Order No. 266.

9th May, 1918.

1. The 44th Infantry Brigade will relieve the 46th Infantry Brigade in the Right Section, 15th Div. Front on night 10/11th May.

2. 8th Seaforth Highrs. relieve 7/8th K.O.S.B. Right.
7th Cameron Highrs. relieve 10th Scottish Rifles. Left.
8/10th Gordon Highrs. relieve 9th Black Watch. Reserve.
44 T.M. Battery relieve 46 T.M.Battery. 6 guns in line.

3. Present dispositions will be taken over.

4. All trench stores, explosive stores, defence schemes, trench maps, aeroplane photographs, tools, programmes of work, will be taken over and receipts given. Lists in duplicate will reach Brigade Headquarters by 12 NOON, 11th May.

5. All details of relief will be arranged between Commanding Officer concerned, subject to the conditions laid down in para.6.

6.(a). No movement East of Railway in H.10. and 13 before 8-45 P.M.
(b). 7th Cameron Highlanders will be clear of Bridge, H.14.a. 0.3. by 9-30 P.M.
(c). 8/10th Gordon Highlanders will not reach above Bridge before 9-35 P.M.
(d). All movement by platoons in file at 100 yards interval.

7. Usual advance parties will go into the line to-day.

8. 44 T.M. Battery will arrange with B.T.O. for limbers to carry up guns.

9. ~~9th Black Watch~~ 10th Sco Rifles will take over Demolition guards from 8/10th Gordon Highlanders at 6 P.M., 10th May.

10. Administrative instructions will be issued by the Staff Captain.

11. Brigade Headquarters will close at VICTORY CAMP at 9 P.M., 10th May, and open at G.18.b.3.3. the same hour.

12. Completion of relief will be reported to Brigade Headquarters by code word "F O S S E".

R C Money
Captain,
Brigade Major,
44th Infantry Brigade.

Issued thro'
Signals.

D I S T R I B U T I O N.

Copy No. 1. War Diary.
2. File.
3. 8th Seaforth Highrs.
4. 8/10th Gordon Highrs.
5. 7th Cameron Highrs.
6. 44th T.M. Battery.
7. Staff Captain.
8. 44th Bde. Signals.
9. 15th Division 'G'.
10. 15th Division 'Q'.
11. 45th Inf. Bde.
12. 46th Inf. Bde.
13. 169th Inf. Bde.
14. 15th Div. Artillery.
15. A.D.M.S., 15th Division.
16. C.R.E., 15th Division.
17. 2nd Div. Artillery.
18. 1st Can. Div. Artillery.
19. B.T.O., 44th Inf. Bde.
20. 15th Div. Train.
21. 2 Coy., 15th Div. Train.
22. Area Commandant.
23. A.P.M., 15th Division.
24. Bde. Bombing Officer.

SECRET.

44th Brigade S.C.14.

All Units, 44th Inf. Bde.
Quartermasters of Battalions.
Brigade Transport Officer.

RATION SUPPLY TO RIGHT SECTION, CENTRE SECTOR, XVII CORPS FRONT.

1. 3 trucks have been placed at the disposal of the 44th Inf.Bde. and will be ready daily at 2 P.M. at MAROEUL (Light Railway siding).

2. Quartermaster, Right front and reserve Battalions will arrange to have their rations ready at Siding to load at that hour. A guard will be left with rations until such time as the train starts.

Quartermaster Sergts. will be allowed to travel on the train. Rations will arrive as follows :-

UNIT.	STATION.	MAP LOCATION.	TIME.	REMARKS.
Bde. H.Q. & Sig.Section. 1 Coy. Reserve Bn.	A.4.	G.24.a.5.9. BLANGY LOCK.	9 P.M.	Ration parties to be at respective stations at times stated to meet Q.M. Sergts. and clear rations.
Right Bn.H.Q. Reserve Bn.H.Q. 2 Coys. Reserve Bn.	A.7.	H.13.d.8.4. BROKEN BRIDGE.	9-15 P.M.	
4 Coys. Right Bn., 1 Coy. Reserve Bn.	ATHIES MILL SIDING.	H.20.b.9.9. ATHIES MILL.	9-30 P.M.	

3. Rations of Left Front Battalion will be taken forward by road to CAM VALLEY.

W. Ashwin Henderson
Captain,
Staff Captain,
44th Infantry Brigade.

9-5-18.

Copy to -
30th Light Railway Coy.

4. (Contd.)
for specific jobs of work, and if these are not all used on that work they must be removed or used on other work. Stores will therefore be taken forward nightly by horse transport to cover requirements. Whilst the dumps still exist at ATHIES, one flat truck will be kept there at the disposal of the right Brigade for the purpose of pushing up R.E. material by tramway (old light Railway) to area about PERU and DINGWALL trenches, (H.22.b.1.3. to b.7.4.)

5. EXPLOSIVES.
Divisional dump is established at G.9.b.3.5.
Dumps on charge of Right Brigade are at -

ST. LAURENT DUMP - G.18.b.1.2.
TILLOY DUMP - H.14.a.35.30.
CAM VALLEY DUMP. - H.15.d.2.7.
GUN PIT DUMP. - H.19.b.8.3.
ATHIES DUMP. - H.15.c.5.4.

All dumps are well stocked with grenades, S.A.A. and T.M. ammunition. Units may draw on signed authority of an officer from the N.C.O. in charge, of the Brigade Dump.

6. COOKING.
No cooking is possible in the left Battalion area forward of CAM VALLEY, and the front Coy. of the Right Front Battalion in FEUCH Y. Solidified alchol is the only possible safe means at present.
Cooking for one company is possible in CAM VALLEY at H.15.b.4.2.
Cooking of Right Fro nt Battalion is carried out at -
Bn. H.Q. - H.19.b.4.5.
1 Coy. - H.20.c.6.9.
1 Coy. - RAILWAY TRIANGLE.
1 Coy. - H.21.c.6.7.
1 Coy. - H.19.b.5.3.

Reserve Battalion cook at -
Bn.H.Q. - H.15.d.9.9.
1 Coy. - H.13.d.85.70.
1 Coy. - H.13.b.9.2.
1 Coy. - H.13.d.65.70.
1 Coy. - G.18.b.5.0.

7. MEDICAL.
Regimental Aid Posts are at -
Right Front Battalion - Dug-out in Railway Embankment at H.19.b.3.4.
Left Front Battalion - Dug-out PUDDING TRENCH, H.16.b.8.6.
Reserve Battalion - H.15.d.8.6.

EVACUATION FROM FRONT NORTH OF RIVER. By stretcher to relay post at CAM VALLEY, H.15.b.3.0. thence to advance dressing station Stn.L'ARBAYETTE, whence they are conveyed by motor ambulance to Hospital ST.JEAN, ARRAS.
SOUTH OF RIVER. From regimental aid post by motor ambulance at RAILWAY TRIANGLE to Hopital ST. JEAN, ARRAS. Main dressing station is situated at ST. CATHERINE, G.15. a.3.5.
In the event of operations commencing a walking wounded dressing station will be opened at ST. NICHOLAS.

No.5a Sanitary Section administers the area and is located at HOPITAL ST. JEAN. They should be applied to on all matters dealing with Sanitation.

SECRET. *Py.* 44th Highland Brigade.

ADMINISTRATIVE INSTRUCTIONS ISSUED IN CONJUNCTION WITH OPERATION ORDER NO. 266.

9th May, 1918.

Ref.Maps
Sheet 51.B.2/20,000.
51.C.1/40,000.

1. LOCATIONS.
List has been issued separately.
Transport lines will remain at SOUVES.

2. COMMUNICATIONS IN BATTLE AREA.
(a). Road.- The main line of approach to the area is by the ST. NICHOLAS - ST. LAURENT BLANGY - ATHIES Road.
The South side of the area is reached by crossing the BLANGY LOCK BRIDGE, and proceeding via BLANGY - FEUCHY Road.
(b). Rail.-A Light Railway, following the course of the River SCARPE, and functioned by the 30th Company R.E. (O) Coy., works forward to ATHIES MILL and feeds the greater part of the area.
A branch line breaking off this line at H.14.c.5.3. runs over the POINT DU JOUR ridge to H.10.c central and feeds the Northern part of the area.

3. SUPPLIES.
(a). Rations.- For Left Front Battalion.- By road and are dumped in CAM VALLEY, H.15.d.2.7.
For Right Front Battalion, Reserve Battalion, T.M. Battery and Brigade Headquarters - By rail. Train stops at convenient points, according to how units are disposed. (See special instructions on Ration Supply).
(b). Water.- The water supply in the forward part of the Left Sub-Section (Left Battalion Front) is carried out entirely by water tins filled at Quartermasters Stores and brought up with the rations.
Remaining units have a sufficient supply in their area. Wells exist at :-

H.19.b.4.3. - Right Battalion.
H.21.c.7.7. - Right Battalion.
H.14.b. 80.15. - Reserve Battalion.

Water points exist and are in working order at :-

H.20.d.70.85. - Right Battalion.
GORDON CAMP, H.19.b.2.8.- Reserve Battalion.
RIFLE CAMP, G.24.b.8.8. - Reserve Battalion.
G.18.b.80.10. - Water cart refilling point.

A spring from which drinking water can be obtained exists at ATHIES near the MILL.
A Pipe line to supply the whole area exists, but is temporarily out of repair. This is being put into working order by the R.E.

4. R.E. MATERIAL.
Dumps exist at :-

ATHIES MILL - H.21.b.3.7.
CANTEEN DUMP - H.13.b.2.7.
MAIN DIVL.DUMP,)
BLANGY DUMP.)- G.23.b.5.3.

The two former dumps are being depleted and will not be kept up. Stores can be drawn on the signature of the O.C. Field Coy. who administrates the R.E. requirements of the area. No. R.E. dumps will be maintained in advance of BLANGY. Small dumps may be formed

8. BATHS.
(a). Divisional baths are established at ANZIN-ST.AUBIN, capacity 120 per hour. Another bath existsat ST.NICHOLAS (Candle Factory). It will be opened shortly.
There is also a bathhouse at STIRLING CAMP. Owing to an indifferent water supply,etc. it is only possible at present to bath one company per day there. Clean clothes are issued at the Divisional Baths.
(b). The Divisional Clothing Store and Foden Disinfector are established at No.36 billet, AGNEZ-les-DUISANS. Units can draw clean clothing from this store. A similar amount of soiled clothing will be handed in in exchange. Applications for allotment of FODEN Disinfector are to be made to Lieut. WILLIAMS,15th Divisional Claims Officer.

9. CEMETERIES.
15th Divisional Burial Officer's Staff man cemeteriesat -

ANZIN - G.1d.76.34.
ROCLINCOURT - A.29.c.1.5.

Cemeteries in the right Brigade area suitable for burials are at -

H.13.a.9.5. near R.E. dump.
H.14.b.9.2. L'ABBAYETTE.

All other cemeteries in the area are closed. If any burials are carried out other than in those cemeteries an explanation of the reason will accompany the burial report. Padres to officiate at internments should be applied for through Brigade Headquarters, stating denomination of Padre required.

10. BATTLE STRAGGLERS AND TRAFFIC CONTROL.
Posts consist of 1 N.C.O. and 3 Men.
Brigade post is located at -
G.18.c.5.4. (Found by reserve Battalion from Regimental Police).
Battalion Battle Straggler Posts will be established at -
H.14.a.0.3. (Found by Reserve Battalion from Regimental Police.)
H.16.d.?.4. (Found by Right Front Battalion from Regimental Police.
H.19.b.4.6. (Found by Right Front Battalion from Regimental Police).

11. CANTEENS.
A recreation hut and canteen is being established near Brigade Headquarters at G.18.b.4.1. This should be a going concern by 15th May.

W. Robinson Henderson
Captain,
Staff Captain,
44th Infantry Brigade.

Copies to - All Units, 44th Inf. Bde.
B.T.O.
B.S.O.
Bde. Major.
Quartermasters of Battalions.

Appendix 5.

1198

SECRET.

Copy No. 4.

44th Highland Brigade Operation Order No.267.

Thursday 16th May, 1918.

1. On night 17th/18th May 8/10th Gordon Highlanders will relieve 7th Cameron Highlanders in Left Sub-Section.
On completion or relief 7th Cameron Highlanders will withdraw into Reserve, taking over accommodation vacated by 8/10th Gordon Highlanders.

2. All details of relief will be arranged between Commanding Officers concerned.

3. All trench stores - tools - explosive dumps - aeroplane photographs - trench maps and defence schemes (other than Brigade) will be handed over and receipts obtained. Lists, in duplicate, of stores handed over will reach Staff Captain by 12 NOON 19th May.

4. Observers will go into the line at 8 A.M. on 17th May.

5. Programmes of work in progress will be handed over.- Copies to reach Brigade Headquarters 12 NOON 19th May.

6. Completion of relief will be notified to Brigade Headquarters by Code Word "S N I P I N G".

Issued through
Signals -
7-0 P.M.

R.C. Money
Captain,
Brigade Major,
44th Infantry Brigade.

DISTRIBUTION.

Copy No.
1. File.
2. War Diary.
3. 9th Seaforth Highrs.
4. 8/10th Gordon Highrs.
5. 7th Cameron Highrs.
6. 44 T.M.Battery.
7. Staff Captain.
8. Signals.
9. 91st Field Coy., R.E.
10. 15th Division 'G'.
11. 15th Division 'Q'.
12. 2nd. Div. Artillery.
13. 2nd Div. T.M.O.

Copy No.
14. 46th Inf. Bde.
15. 169th Inf. Bde.
16. 15th Div. Train.
17. No.2 Coy.,Train.
18. B.T.O., 44th Inf. Bde.
19. Bde. Bombing Officer.

Secret

The Gordon Highlanders — Appendix 6.

Operation Order No. 169

by

Captain R. G. Pearson.

Trenches
23 May 1918

1. The 6th Gordon Highlanders will be relieved in the Left Sector of the Brigade Front by the 11th A & S Highlanders tomorrow night, 24/25th May. On completion of relief the Battalion will proceed to WAKEFIELD CAMP.

All movement along roads to be by platoons at 100 yards interval.

2. Dispositions

B	Coy Gordons will be relieved by	C	Coy A&S H. in Right Front
D	" " " " "	A	" " " Left Front
C	" " " " "	D	" " " Right Support
B	" " " " "	A	" " " Left Support
Batt. H.Qrs	" " " " "	Bn. H.Qrs	" " " CAM VALLEY (H 15 d 2.3)

The relief will be carried out in the above order.

3. Guides: 1 per platoon, 1 per Coy H.Qrs, and 2 for Batt. H.Qrs will meet the incoming battalion at the SW corner of CAM VALLEY at 10.15 p.m.

Lieut R. A. M. Black will be in charge of the guides. Guides from B and C Coys will report to Bn. H.Qrs at 3.30 a.m. 24th.

Guides from A & D Coys and Batt. H.Qrs will report to Batt. H.Qrs at 9.30 p.m. 24th.

The training of specially selected guides will be taken in hand at once. Each platoon guide must have implicit instructions as to the route he is to follow

4 Routes -

Rt Front Coy -- via FAMPOUX ROAD (Rear Posts to go by track from H 15 d to 35 - track through H21 b & 22 C - Light Railway)

Left Front Coy -- -Do-

Rt Support Coy -- via FAMPOUX ROAD - DINGWALL TRENCH (Rear Posts as for Right Front Coy)

Left Support Coy - CAM VALLEY - CAM AVENUE

5 (a) Advanced party, consisting of 1 N.C.O per Coy and 1 for Bn. H Qrs will parade at Bn. H Q under 2/Lieut Bruce at 3.15 a.m. tomorrow. This Party will proceed to WAKEFIELD CAMP and take over Stores and Camp. Rations for the day to be carried.

There is to be no movement of advanced parties, cooks etc. in the forward area between the hours of 4 a.m. and 10 p.m. 24th May

(b) Advanced parties from the Argylls will report to Coy H Qrs tonight at 12.30 p.m.

6 (a) All trench stores, explosives, aeroplane photographs, Bn Defence Schemes, and anti aircraft mountings (but **NOT** sights) will be handed over and receipts obtained.

(b) Training stores, defence schemes & reserves of SAA in WAKEFIELD CAMP will be taken over and receipts given.

(c) Lists of stores handed over and taken over will reach Bn H. Qrs by 9 a.m. 25th May [illegible] 1 leader per Coy, 1 per Bn H Qrs and 1 per [illegible] will be at SW Corner of CAM VALLEY at 10 45 pm. Officers chargers to be at same place at 11 00 pm.

8 Completion of relief to be wired at once to Bn H Qrs by the Code Word "FISH". Arrival in Camp to be reported to Bn H Qrs

9 Acknowledge

(Sgd) G P Geddes,
Captain & Adjutant,
4th Bn The Gordon Highrs

Distribution
Copies 1-4 - O C Coys
5 - [illegible]
6 - Signals
7 - [illegible]
8 - [illegible]
9 - W D
10 - File
11 - Commanding Officer

Issued through
Signals - p.m.

S E C R E T. **Copy No. 4** 4/95

44th Highland Brigade Operation Order No.268.

25th May, 1918.

1. The Brigade will be relieved in the line by the 45th Inf. Bde. on night 24th/25th May, 1918, in accordance with the attached table of reliefs.

2. On completion of relief the Brigade will be withdrawn to Divisional Reserve and will be accommodated in camps in the ST. CATHERINE - ROCLINCOURT Area.
All movement along roads will be by platoons at 100 yards interval.

3. Advanced parties of units of the Brigade sent to take o ver camps and reserve stores of S.A.A. etc., will be West of the ARRAS - LENS Railway line by 4 A.M. 24th May.
There is to be no movement of advanced parties, cooks etc., in the forward area between the hours of 4 A.M. and 10 P.M. 24th May.

4. Advanced parties of incoming units will report at Battalion Headquarters concerned at 10 P.M. 23rd May.

5. All details of relief will be arranged between Commanding Officers concerned.

6. There is to be no delay in conducting units to their positions.
The training of specially selected guides will be taken in hand at once.
All stores etc., will be carefully arranged, to facilitate ease in handing over.

7. All trench stores - explosive stores - aeroplane photographs - Defence Schemes (other than Brigade) - Trench Maps - anti-aircraft mountings, but NOT sights - will be handed over.
Lists, in duplicate, will reach Brigade Headquarters by 12 NOON 25th May.

8 Training Stores, Defence Schemes and reserves of S.A.A. etc. in Camps will be taken over and receipts given.- Lists to be forwarded to Brigade Headquarters as above.

9. Completion of relief will be notified to Brigade Headquarters by Code Word " C H A L K".

10. Brigade Headquarters will close at G.18.b.4.3. on completion of relief, and open at VICTORY CAMP at the same ho ur.
A representative of Brigade Headquarters will be at VICTORY CAMP from 9 P.M. 24th May.

11. ACKNOWLEDGE.

R McMoray
Captain,
Brigade Major,
44th Infantry Brigade.

Issued through Signals - 6.0 P.M.

D I S T R I B U T I O N.

Copy No.
1. War Diary.
2. File.
3. 8th Seaforth Highrs.
4. 8/10th Gordon Highrs.
5. 7th Cameron Highrs.
6. 44 T.M.Battery.
7. 15th Division 'G'.
8. 15th Division 'Q'.
9. 45th Inf. Bde.
10. 46th Inf. Bde.
11. Staff Captain, 44th Inf.Bde.
12. 44th Bde. Signal Section.

Copy No.
13. 168th Inf. Bde.
14. 2nd. Div. Artillery.
15. 36th Bde. R.F.A.
16. 41st Bde. R.F.A.
17. B.T.O., 44th Inf. Bde.
18. 91st Field Co.,R.E.
19. 15th Div. Train.
20. No.2 Coy., Train.
21. Area Comdt.
22. A.P.M., 15th Division.
23. A.D.M.S., 15th Division.

Table of reliefs to accompany 44th Brigade Operation Order No. 268.

UNIT.	RELIEVED BY	DESTINATION.	REMARKS.
8th Seaforth Highrs.	6th Cameron Highrs.	VICTORY CAMP.	Incoming Unit reaches BRIDGE, H.1[illegible].b.4.7. 10-15 p.m. H.19.b.4.7
8/10th Gordon Highrs.	11th A. & S. Highrs.	WAKEFIELD CAMP.	Incoming Unit reaches BRIDGE, H.14.a.0.3. 10 p.m. Overland Routes to be used as far as possible. The trench system will be avoided by incoming and outgoing Units. Guides will know all gaps in wire and best route to follow. Transport will not be permitted to proceed further up the road than CAM VALLEY.
7th Cameron Highrs.	13th Royal Scots.	FORTSMOUTH CAMP.	Incoming Unit reaches STIRLING CAMP 10-30 p.m.
44th T.M.Battery.	45th T.M.Battery.	EDINBURGH CAMP.	Incoming Unit reaches line ARRAS- - LENS Railway 10 p.m.

ATTACHED

TRAINING CADRE
39TH DIVISION
118TH INFY BDE

8-10TH BN GORDON HDRS

JUN - AUG 1918

DISBANDED 17 8 18

CONFIDENTIAL

WAR DIARY

OF

8/10th BATTALION, THE GORDON HIGHLANDERS.

FOR PERIOD

From 1st June 1918 to 30th June 1918.

VOLUME. 38.

Instructions regarding War Diaries and Intelligence Summaries are contained in F. S. Regs., Part II. and the Staff Manual respectively. Title pages will be prepared in manuscript.

WAR DIARY
or
INTELLIGENCE SUMMARY.
(Erase heading not required.)

Sheet 1

Army Form C. 2118.

Place	Date	Hour	Summary of Events and Information	Remarks and references to Appendices
Trenches	1918 June 1–5		On the night of 1st June the Battalion moved from WAKEFIELD CAMP to the front line and occupied the sector immediately North of the RIVER SCARPE. The relief was carried out quietly and without any casualties. The Battalion remained in the front line until the 5th. Throughout the five days the enemy was extremely quiet and nothing of any importance took place.	00170.
	6.		On the night of 6th the Battalion was relieved in the front line by 8th Seaforth Highlanders and on relief withdrew TO STIRLING CAMP, remaining in support. On the night of 6/7th orders were received from H.Q. that the 8/10 Gordons would be absorbed by 1/5 Gordon Highlanders, and that the absorption would take place forthwith. At the same time orders were received that Lt. Col. The Lord Dudley Gordon, D.S.O. then commanding the 8/10 Gordon Highrs, would along with 9 other Officers + 50 Instructors, form a Training Staff for Training Americans, and were to proceed to GOUVES and await instructions.	00171. [illegible]
	7		On night of 7th the 1/5 Gordon Highrs arrived at STIRLING CAMP and throughout the night the absorption took place + was completed on 8th. All surplus N.C.Os + men were sent to "Y" hutments and afterwards dispatched to the Base.	[illegible]
GOUVES	9		Orders were received from 44th Brigade for the TRAINING STAFF TO entrain at MAROEUIL, for BARLIN. The journey was done on a Light Rail-	[illegible]

D. D. & L., London, E.C. (A8104) Wt W1771/M2031 750,000 5/17 Sch. 52 Forms/C2118/14

S E C R E T. Copy No. W.D.

The Gordon Highlanders.

O P E R A T I O N O R D E R No. 170.

By

Lieut-Colonel the Lord Dudley Gordon, D.S.O., Comdg.

31st May 1918.

1. The 8/10th Gordon Highlanders will relieve the 7/8th K.O.S.Bs. in the Right Sector of the Left Brigade Front to-morrow night, 1/2nd June.

2. Dispositions :

"A" Coy Gordons	will	relieve	"C" Coy	K.O.S.Bs.	in the	Left Front.
"C" Coy	"	"	"A" Coy	"	"	". RightFront
"B" Coy	"	"	"B" Coy	"	"	Support.
"D" Coy	"	"	"D" Coy	"	"	Reserve.
Battn. H.Qrs.	"	"	Bn. H.Qrs.	"	at H.10.c.7.4.	

The relief will be carried out in the above order.

3. Guides : 1 per platoon and 1 for Coy HQ. and 2 for Battn. H.Qrs. will be at S.W. corner of CAM VALLEY at 9.45 p.m.

4. Routes : ST. CATHERINE'S ROAD to Road Junction G.9.c.8.1 - Road through G.15.b. and 16.a. & c. - FEBRUARY CIRCUS - ST. LAURENT-BLANGY - CAM VALLEY.

A Coy : via EFFIE. EFFIE SWITCH, MISSOURI, CABLE.
C Coy : via CASTLE LANE, CAMEL AVENUE.
B Coy : via CASTLE LANE.
D Coy : via EFFIE SWITCH.
Battn. HQ. : Cross track from CAM VALLEY to Battn. H.Qrs.

5. The Battalion will parade ready to march off in above order at 8.10 pm.

6. (i) An advanced party consisting of 1 Officer & 4 N.C.Os. from each of A, B, & C Coys, 2 N.C.Os. from D Coy and 1 N.C.O. from Battn. H.Qrs. will parade at Orderly Room at 8.45 p.m. to-night. 1 guide per Coy will meet party at S.W. corner of CAM VALLEY at 9.45 p.m.
2/Lieut. E.A. SIBLEY will be in charge.
(ii) Battalion Observers for one O.P. will report at 46th Bde. H.Qrs. at 8.30 p.m. to-night.

7. All movement to be by platoons at 100 yards interval.

8. (a) All trench stores, explosives, tools, air photographs, Battalion Defence Schemes and programmes of work will be taken over and receipts given.
(b) Training & explosive stores in Camp will be handed over and receipts taken.
(c) Lists of all stores etc. taken over and handed over will reach Battn. H.Qrs. by 10 a.m. 2nd June.

9. Completion of relief will be wired to Battn. H.Qrs. by the code word - "JOLLY".

10. Acknowledge.

(sgd) G.P. Geddes,
Captain & Adjutant.

Distribution :
Copies 1 - 4. O.C. Coys.
5. C.O.
6. QM & T.O.
7. 2/Lieut. Sibley.
8. Signals.
9. R.S.M.
10. 7/8th K.O.S.Bs.
11. War Diary.
12. File.

Secret.

Copy No. 12

8/10th (S) Bn, The Gordon Highrs
Operation Order No. 171.
By
Lieut Colonel the Lord Dudley Gordon, D.S.O. Comdg
6th June 1918.

1. The 8/10th Gordon Highlanders will be relieved by the 8th Seaforth Highlanders in the Right Sub section of the Brigade front, tonight, 6/7th June.

On completion of relief the 8/10th Gordon Highlanders will become Reserve Battalion of the Brigade.

2. Dispositions:-

"B" Coy Gordons will be relieved by "A" Coy Seaforths in the Right Front.
"A" Coy " " " " "B" Coy " " Left. Front.
"C" Coy " " " " "D" Coy " " Support.
"D" Coy " " " " "C" Coy " " Reserve.
"Bn, H.Qrs " " " " "Bn, H.Qrs" " at H.10.C.7.4.

The Seaforths will come up in the order C, A. B, D. Coys & Bn, H.Q.

3. Guides:- 1 per platoon, 1 per Coy. H.Qrs. for each of A.B. & D Coys and Bn, H.Qrs of the Seaforths will meet the relieving Coys at junction of CASTLE LANE and EFFIE TRENCH at 10 p.m.

Guides will rendezvous at Battn H.Qrs. under 2/Lieut E.A. SIBLEY at 9-15 p.m.

No guides will be provided for "C" Coy Seaforths

O.C. Coys must ensure that guides thoroughly reconnoitre the routes to be used for the relief.

4. On relief, Companies will proceed to the following areas:-

"D" Coy. --- EFFIE SWITCH (between EFFIE TRENCH & CAM AVENUE)
At present occupied by "C" Coy Seaforths.

"B" Coy ... EFFIE TRENCH in H. 9. d. At present occupied by "D" Coy. Seaforths.

"C" Coy ... EFFIE TRENCH from "B" Coy. to GAVRELLE Road.
At present occupied by "A" Coy Seaforths.

"A" Coy ... In Railway Cutting near Bn., H.Qrs. At present occupied by "B" Coy Seaforths.

"Bn, H Qrs" ... Railway Cutting at H. 14. a. 0. 9.

5. O.C. Coys will send at once an Advanced Party of

2 N.C.Os to take over stores and accomodation in the new areas 1 Guide per platoon will also accompany this party. These guides will return to their Coys to guide them to their positions on relief.

All movement by Daylight to be by Trenches.

6. All tools, trench stores, A.P. and Tracer ammunition, explosive stores, maps and aeroplane photos will be handed over and taken over.

Receipts to be forwarded to Orderly Room by 9 a.m 7th June

7 Completion of relief to be notified by Code Word CHEST, arrival in new area by Code Word NUT.

8. Acknowledge

Distribution:-

(Sgd) G P Geddes,
Captain & Adjutant
8/10th Bn, The Gordon Highlanders

Copies 1-4 .. O.C Coys
5 .. I.O.
6 Signals
7 . RSM
8 . Details
9. . 8th Seaforths
10. . 1/5th Gordons
11 . . C.O
12 . W.D.
13 . File
14 . Spare

WAR DIARY
or
INTELLIGENCE SUMMARY.
(Erase heading not required.)

Sheet 2

Army Form C. 2118.

Instructions regarding War Diaries and Intelligence Summaries are contained in F. S. Regs., Part II. and the Staff Manual respectively. Title pages will be prepared in manuscript.

Place	Date	Hour	Summary of Events and Information	Remarks and references to Appendices
BARLIN	9th		On arrival at BARLIN the TRAINING STAFF entrained for NORTKERQUE via CALAIS, arriving at NORTKERQUE at 6.15 AM on 11th. The Training Staff then came under the orders of 118th Infantry Brigade 39th Division.	[illegible] Lt.
NORTKERQUE	11th		The "Training Staff" was billeted in the Village of NORTKERQUE for the 11th & night of 11/12th.	
	12		On the morning of 12th the Training Staff marched to the Village of CAMPAGNE where they were billeted in the CHATEAU until 17th. During the period 12–17th the Staff was paraded daily and put through a certain amount of training.	
	17th		Orders were received from Brigade Headquarters to proceed to LANDRETHUN and on arrival there to take over + continue of the training of 2nd Battalion 119th Infantry American Regiment from 9th Black Watch, who had received orders to embark for England.	
LANDRETHUN LES ARDRES	18th		The training of the 2nd Battalion, 119 Infantry American Regiment, was continued by the training staff of 8/10 Gordon Highlrs.	
	21		The following non-commissioned officers received the "Meritorious Service Medal" in recognition of valuable services rendered. S/17103 C.Q.M. Sgt. J. F. KEIR S/4913. Sergeant J. REOCH.	

D. D. & L., London, E.C.
(A8204) Wt W1771/M2031 750,000 5/18 Sch. 52 Forms/C2118/14

Instructions regarding War Diaries and Intelligence Summaries are contained in F. S. Regs., Part II. and the Staff Manual respectively. Title pages will be prepared in manuscript.

WAR DIARY
or
INTELLIGENCE SUMMARY.
(Erase heading not required.)

Sheet 3.

Army Form C. 2118.

Place	Date	Hour	Summary of Events and Information	Remarks and references to Appendices
MENTQUE	26		The 2nd Batt. 119 American Infantry Regiment received orders to proceed to MENTQUE for firing a 3 days musketry course. ~~[illegible]~~ 2 officers and 12 N.C.O.s from the TRAINING STAFF accompanied them.	CWB Lt.
LANDRETHUN LES ARDRES	30		The 2nd Batt. 119 American Infantry Regiment with Training staff returned to billets in LANDRETHUN where training was continued.	

K.C. Davidson
Lieutenant
For Lieut. Colonel,
[illegible] 8/10th BATTALION, THE GORDON HIGHLANDERS.

D. D. & L., London, E.C.
(A8004) Wt W1771/M2031 750,000 5/17 Sch. 52 Forms/C2118/14

15

WO 32 (To 1/5)

CONFIDENTIAL.

WAR DIARY

OF

8/10th (Service) Battalion, The Gordon Highlanders.

For Period

1st July 1918. To: 31st July, 1918.

VOLUME 39.

Vol: 39.

Instructions regarding War Diaries and Intelligence Summaries are contained in F. S. Regs., Part II. and the Staff Manual respectively. Title pages will be prepared in manuscript.

WAR DIARY
or
INTELLIGENCE SUMMARY.
(*Erase heading not required.*)

Army Form C. 2118.

Sheet 462.

Place	Date	Hour	Summary of Events and Information	Remarks and references to Appendices
LANDRETHUN LES ARDRES	1918 July 24	–	At 9 AM the 2nd Battalion of 119th American Infantry Regiment proceeded from their Billets in LANDRETHUN LES ARDRES, to the forward area by march Route. Lt. Col. The Lord DUDLEY GORDON D.S.O. + Capt. R. T. O. BRACKEN of the 8/10 Gordon Highrs proceeded with them so as to give any information or assistance that may be desired.	
			The march to the forward area occupied four days and at the end of each days march the Battalion either Billeted, camped or Bivouacked in the following places.	
			1st day march Bivouacked in Eastern end of EPERLECQUES [illegible]	
			2nd " " " at RUBROUCK	
			3rd " " Billeted in HERZEELE	
			4th " " Camp at St. JEAN-TER-BIEZEN	
			when the 2nd Battalion of 119th American Infantry Regiment was settled in St. JEAN-TER-BIEZEN and no further assistance was	

D. D. & L., London, E.C. (A8201) Wt W777/M2031 750,000 5/17 Sch. 58 Forms/C2118/14

Instructions regarding War Diaries and Intelligence Summaries are contained in F. S. Regs., Part II. and the Staff Manual respectively. Title pages will be prepared in manuscript.

WAR DIARY
or
INTELLIGENCE SUMMARY.
(Erase heading not required.)

Sheet 463

Army Form C. 2118.

Place	Date	Hour	Summary of Events and Information	Remarks and references to Appendices
LANDRETHUN LES ARDRES	July 1918	–	required, Lt Col LORD DUDLEY GORDON D.S.O + Capt R T O BRACKEN returned to LANDRETHUN LES ARDRES where they rejoined the 8/10 Gordon Highlanders on 6th July 1918. During the absence of Lt Col The Lord Dudley Gordon, Capt K C Davidson M.C. commanded the Training staff, and daily training was carried out.	
"	16 to 17	–	A Divisional Tactical scheme was carried out which lasted for two days. On 16th the 8/10 Gordons were detailed as Outposts to the Division and took up an outpost position on the line LA PANNE MENTQUE (inclusive). On the morning of 17th the 118th Brigade formed the advance guard, 8/10 Gordons forming the right battalion vanguard. Operations ceased at midday of 17th and the battalion returned to their billets in LANDRETHUN LES ARDRES.	
	18		The Training Staff was paraded at 10 AM and the [illegible]	

D. D. & L., London, E.C. (A8004) Wt W1771/M2031 750,000 5/17 Sch. 52 Forms/C2118/14

Army Form C. 2118.

Sheet 464

WAR DIARY
or
INTELLIGENCE SUMMARY.
(Erase heading not required.)

Instructions regarding War Diaries and Intelligence Summaries are contained in F. S. Regs., Part II. and the Staff Manual respectively. Title pages will be prepared in manuscript.

Place	Date	Hour	Summary of Events and Information	Remarks and references to Appendices
LANDRETHUN LES ARDRES	18		Service ribbon was presented to the following Non Commissioned Officer for excellent services rendered to the Battalion. S/1703. C.Q.M.S. J. F. KERR.	AWB Col
"	23		The Battalion carried out [illegible] under orders of the Commanding Officer.	B.O. 1
"	25		The Battalion received orders from Brigade H.Q. to march to Billets in ZUTKERQUE on 26th.	AWB Col B.O. 2
ZUTKERQUE	26		The Battalion marched to Billets in ZUTKERQUE arriving there about 12 noon.	
	27		The Battalion received orders to march to WATTEN and to wait and take command of about 1,000 Scotch Reinforcements	AWB

D. D. & L., London, E.C. (A8094) W1 W3771/M2031 750,000 5/15 Sch. 52 Forms/C2118/14

Instructions regarding War Diaries and Intelligence Summaries are contained in F. S. Regs., Part II. and the Staff Manual respectively. Title pages will be prepared in manuscript.

WAR DIARY
or
INTELLIGENCE SUMMARY.
(Erase heading not required.)

Sheet 465

Army Form C. 2118.

Place	Date	Hour	Summary of Events and Information	Remarks and references to Appendices
WATTEN	27		which would arrive at WATTEN on 30th. The Battalion were billeted in WATTEN up to 30th.	
	30		The Battalion entrained at WATTEN and proceeded to MENDINGHEM with reinforcements, where they were accommodated for the night.	
	31		The Battalion now being in the 2nd Corps area with reinforcements were ~~called~~ turned into & called 2nd Corps Reinforcement Battalion (Temporarily). The Reinforcement Battalion then proceeded to PENTON CAMP (Sheet 27 F8.A.4.9) and were accommodated in tents.	[illegible]

K. Davidson
For Captain
LIEUT. COLONEL
COMDG. 8/10TH BATTALION, THE GORDON HIGHLANDERS.

D. D. & L., London, E.C.
(A8004) Wt W1771/M2031 750,000 5/17 Sch. 52 Forms/C2118/14.

SECRET. Copy No. 9

Ref. Sheet :
CALAIS 13,
1/100,000.

BATTALION ORDER No.1

By

Lieut-Colonel the Lord Dudley Gordon, D.S.O., Comdg.

1. The Battalion will find the Advanced Guard for the Brigade to-morrow, 23rd, moving along the Road : PONT d'ARDRES - ARDRES - LANDRETHUN - LICQUES.
   Dress : Fighting Order.
   1 day's rations to be taken on the man.

2. The Outpost Line is to be passed through at 8. 0 a.m.; the Scouts to pass Cross Roads just North of 2nd R in ARDRES at 8. 0 a.m.

3. "D" Coy will form the Vanguard as far as LANDRETHUN. This village will be occupied before any further advance is made.

   From LANDRETHUN, "B" Coy will advance through ECOTTES.
   "C" Coy along main LANDRETHUN - LICQUES Road.
   "D" Coy through YEST YEUSE to the Outpost position running from Mt. BELBERT (incl) to Farm just N. of C in CLERQUES (incl.).
   Battn. HQ. and "A" Coy along main LANDRETHUN - LICQUES Road.

4. Disposition to be taken up at Outpost Line.

   "B" Coy : Summit of Mt. BELBERT (inclusive) to Road passing through B of B. de COURTEBOURNE (excl.).

   "C" Coy : Road as above (incl) to Farm 400 yards N. of I in LA SOLITUDE (incl).

   "D" Coy : Remainder of front.

   "A" Coy : In Support in BOIS de COURTEBOURNE.

   Battn. HQ. : on main road in centre of BOIS de COURTEBOURNE.

5. All reports during march will be sent to head of main guard. Report Centre will move by bounds along main road.

6. All traffic through Outpost Line, both ways, is to be stopped. Any deserters, prisoners or suspected persons will be blindfolded and brought to Battn. H.Qrs.

7. Company Commanders patrolling in front of the PICQUET Line will be careful not to take maps or any useful information on them.

8. Signalling Officer will arrange for telephone communication between Coys as quickly as possible, and will also pay special attention to LATERAL communication.

9. Outposts will be relieved 10 p.m. 23 / 24th inst.

10. Pass Word - "RUFUS".

11. Acknowledge.

22.7.1918 - 5p.m.

(signed) A.W. Boyce,
Captain & Adjutant.

Distribution :

Copies 1 - 4. O.C. Coys. 5. Signalling Officer.
6. Bde. H.Qrs. 7. Quartermaster.
8. Transport Officer. 9. War Diary.
10. File

The Gordon Highlanders.

BATTALION ORDERS

By

Lieut-Colonel the Lord Dudley Gordon, DSO., Comdg.

25th July 1918.

DUTIES. 137.

Orderly Officer to-morrow - Captain E.A.Sibley.

DETAIL FOR TO-MORROW. 138.

Reveille .... 6. 0 a.m. Breakfast .... 7. 0 a.m.
Dinners ..on arrival in new area. Lights Out ....10.15 p.m.

ARRANGEMENTS FOR MOVE. 139.

1. Officers' valises and mess kits to be stacked at Q.M.Stores by 8 a.m. R.S.M. will detail a party to load on G.S.Wagon.

2. Blankets will be securely rolled in bundles of ten and stacked at Q.M.Stores by 7.45 a.m. R.S.M. will detail a party to load on G.S.Wagon.

3. All tents not in use will be returned to-night to Billet Warden. Sgt.Riddler will arrange to collect same.
All other tents will be struck and rolled at 6.30 a.m. Sgt.Riddler will arrange to collect and return to billet warden. A receipt will be obtained by him for all tents returned and handed into Orderly Room.

4. All palliasses will be stacked at Q.M.Stores by 7.45 a.m.

5. All billets will be left thoroughly clean and ready for inspection by the Orderly Officer at 9 a.m.

(signed) A.W.Boyce,
Captain & Adjutant.

21

SECRET AND CONFIDENTIAL.

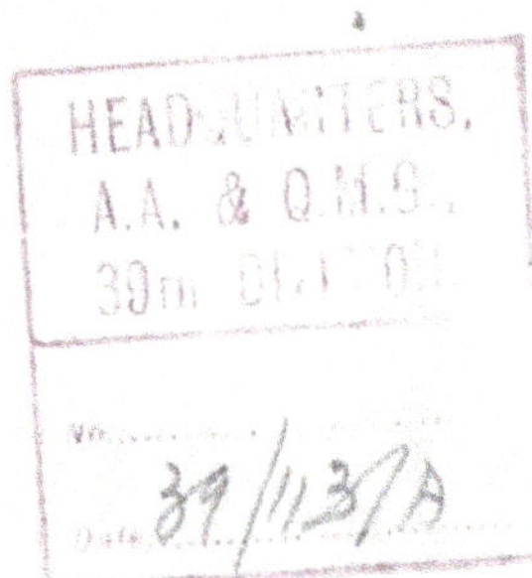

39/113/A.

D.A.G.,3rd Echelon,
G. H. Q.

Receipt sent

Herewith War Diary of 8/10th Bn.The Gordon Highlanders for the period 1st - 17th August, 1918, the Battalion having been disbanded from the latter date.

Kindly acknowledge receipt to this Office.

20th August, 1918.

Major-General,
Commanding 39th Division

Vol: 40.

8/10 Gordon Hrs

Army Form C. 2118.

Sheet 466.

Instructions regarding War Diaries and Intelligence Summaries are contained in F. S. Regs., Part II. and the Staff Manual respectively. Title pages will be prepared in manuscript.

WAR DIARY
or
INTELLIGENCE SUMMARY.
(Erase heading not required.)

Place	Date	Hour	Summary of Events and Information	Remarks and references to Appendices
PENTON CAMP 27/F8 a.4.9.	1918 Aug. 1		The Reinforcements were organised into Companies and as far as possible into Fighting Platoons.	
	2		The day was devoted to cleaning up of the camp and to increasing the accommodation	
	3-8		The majority of the men were utilised on working parties working on the EAST POPERINGHE LINE.	
	9		The following drafts were dispatched from the Battalion + entrained at MENDINGHEM STATION 6 AM. 29 O.R. To 3rd Division 29 O.R. To 9th do do 410 O.R. To 15th do do 160 O.R. To 51st do do	
	10		The following drafts were dispatched from the Battalion + entrained at MENDINGHEM STATION 6 AM. 410 O.R. 15th Division	

Instructions regarding War Diaries and Intelligence Summaries are contained in F. S. Regs., Part II. and the Staff Manual respectively. Title pages will be prepared in manuscript.

WAR DIARY
or
INTELLIGENCE SUMMARY.
(Erase heading not required.)

Sheet 467

Army Form C. 2118.

Place	Date	Hour	Summary of Events and Information	Remarks and references to Appendices
PENTON CAMP 27/F.8.a.4.9	Aug: 11th		The Battalion received a warning order to return to 39th Div as all reinforcements had been disposed of.	RWB
	14th		The Battalion rejoined 39th Division, leaving F.8.a.4.9 at 5.45 am + entrained at MENDINGHEM for AUDRICQ. On arrival at AUDRICQ the Battalion march to ZUTKERQUE where they were billeted.	O.O. 8 RWB
	17th		The Battalion received orders from 39th Division that the 8/10th Gordon Highrs were to be disbanded immediately and staff to proceed as reinforcements to 1/7 Gordon Highrs 51st Division. Authority 8/9084/320 dated 9.8.18 from D.A.G. 3rd Echelon G.H.Q. The Battalion entrained at AUDRICQ same day for 57th Division.	RWB

D. D. & L., London, E.C. (A8004) Wt W1771/M2031 750,000 5/17 Sch. 52 Forms/C2118/14

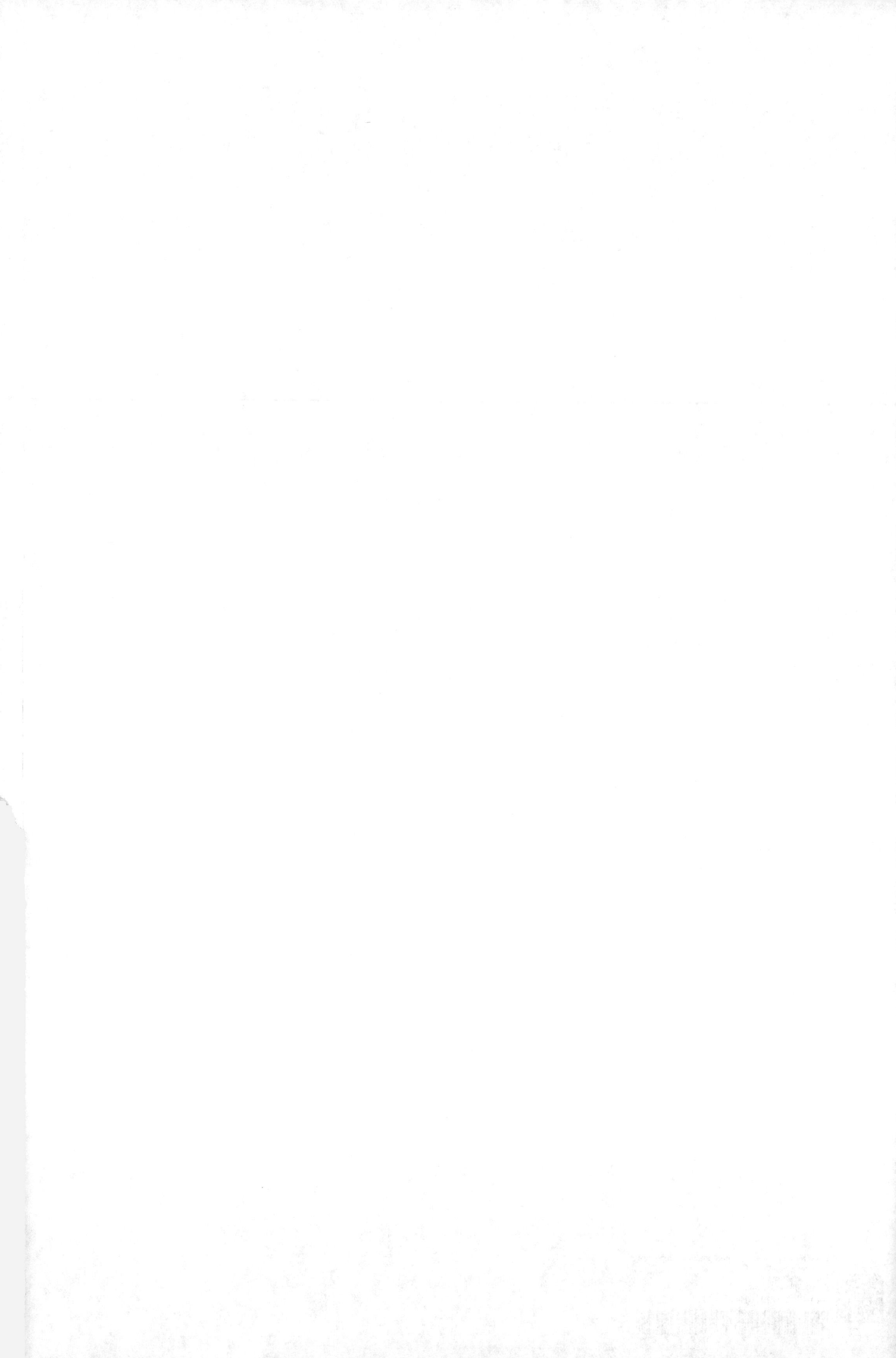

www.ingramcontent.com/pod-product-compliance
Lightning Source LLC
Chambersburg PA
CBHW081428300426
44108CB00016BA/2324

* 9 7 8 1 4 7 4 5 0 9 5 7 2 *